# Foodi Multi-Cooker

# Cookbook for Beginners

## 550 Quick, Easy and Delicious Foodi Multi-Cooker Recipes for Smart People on a Budget

### By: Jessica Nelson

# TABLE OF CONTENTS

# Introduction

The Foodi Multi-cooker is revolutionary! You can cook virtually anything - It is an all-in-one multi-functional kitchen appliance, which can be used as pressure cooker, slow cooker, rice cooker, air fryer, etc. That means you can almost make all your dishes from meats and main courses to rice, potatoes, vegetables of every description, dessert to even yogurt. Better yet, pressure cooking and air frying cooking allows you to prepare foods up to 70% faster, and 75% less fat, on average, than conventional cooking methods do, which means you save energy in addition to your precious time.

Foodi Multi-cooker is really very convenient and can save users too much time and money! Meantime, the recipes it provides are nutritious and delicious, even tender inside and crispy outside. It really can give people all kinds of flavors! It is very easy to use, usually all you need to do is just dump all ingredients into the pot, then close the cover and wait for few minutes, and finally you will get your favorite tasty dish!

The recipes are simple and easy to understand. By using this cookbook Anyone can make the delicious recipes with the Foodi Multi-cooker. You just need to know the right measurements, and you will have a great recipe ready for you. You do not have to deal with fire or flames on the stoves, Foodi Multi-cooker has made life easier for the people now.

This cookbook presents a carefully hank-picked easy and delicious recipes that you can cook in your Foodi. Just Pick the best recipes you like and start cooking with your Foodi Multi-cooker now. You will be amazed at how simple it is to use. The machine plays with you, but you need to make sure to handle it with care. It gives you healthy food with all the nutrients your body requires. Thus, you can feed your family with healthy meals without stressing yourself too much or spending long hours inside the kitchen.

The Foodi Multi-cooker is a real kitchen partner. And this amazing cookbook is the ultimate companion to your Foodi Multi-cooker.

In order to quickly master your Ninja Foodi, the first you must know is the works of the various function buttons of the gadget. Here are some of the function buttons you will see in the housing unit:

**Pressure:** This button allows you to cook food 70% faster than conventional cooking methods. You can also pressure release either quickly or naturally

**Slow Cook:** This button allows you to cook food at a lower temperature just like conventional slow cookers. This setting may be adjusted from 4 to 12 hours. Once the cooking time is complete, the KEEP WARM function will automatically activate once the food is cooked

**Steam:** This button allows you to utilize steam to gently cook delicate food at high temperature. Use at least a cup of liquid to steam your food. To use this function, install the pressure lid to cook your food through steam

**Broil:** Use this button to brown or caramelize the surface of your food. It cooks food at a higher temperature to create that brown surface. Use the crisping lid to broil food for even browning. There is no temperature adjustment for this function but you can adjust the temperature. Make sure to preheat the unit before putting in the ingredients

**Bake/Roast:** This method allows you to use your multi-cooker as an oven or roaster so that you can make roasted meats, baked treats, and many others. Let the unit preheat for at least 5 minutes before putting in the ingredients. Use the crisping lid to bake or roast your food

**Sear/Sauté:** This button allows you to use the Ninja Foodie as a browning meat. It is good for searing or browning meat and sautéing spices. It can also be used to simmer sauces. This setting does not come with a time adjustment. Once you are done browning, press the START/STOP button to stop the process. Use this function with the crisping lid or in the open position. You can also put on the pressure lid as long as the pressure valve release is on the VENT position. Always use non-stick utensils when stirring the contents inside the pan

**Dehydrate:** This dehydrates food between 1050F and 1950F. You can use this button to dehydrate meats, vegetables and fruits to make healthy snacks. For better results, it is best to get the dehydrating rack so that you can dehydrate more foods within a small area. This function is only available in certain models of Ninja Foodi

**Air Crisp:** This button allows you to use this multi-cooker as an air fryer so that it gives your food the crispiness and crunch with little or no oil. This setting cooks food between the temperature of 3000F and 4000F. It is important to preheat the unit before adding in the ingredients for better results. Use the crisping lid instead of the pressure lid when using this function.

**Power:** This button allows you to shut off the unit and also stop all cooking modes

**Preset Cooking Buttons:** There are about 8 in number and includes Pressure. Steam. Slow Cook, Sear/Sauté, Air Crisp, Bake/Roast, Broil and Dehydrate

**Time Arrow Buttons:** Use the up and down arrows to adjust the cooking time

**Temp. Arrow Buttons:** You can use the up and down arrows to increase or decrease the cooking temperature of the device respectively.

**Start/Stop Button:** After you have set the cooking temperature and time, to start cooking, press this button. Then when your food is done, pressing this same button will stop the cooking process

**Keep Warm Button:** The function of this button is to keep your food warm at a food-safe temperature

**Standby:** After 10 minutes of idleness, this mode will be activated automatically

## First Time Usage Tips

1. Unbox the gadget and discard all the packaging materials, tapes and even the promotional labels.
2. Remove all the accessories from the package
3. Carefully read the manual and pay special attention to instructions about how to operate the unit, usage warnings, as well as crucial safety tips to prevent damage and injury
4. Using hot, soapy water, wash the silicone ring, condensation collector, removable cooking pot, Reversible Rack, Cook & Crisp Basket and pressure lid. Rinse and dry these accessories thoroughly.
5. Check the pressure to make sure no debris is in the valves. Never place the pressure lid or the cooker base in the dishwasher
6. Place the silicone ring around the outer edge of the silicone ring rack under the lid. Make sure it is completely inserted and that it is lying flat under the silicone ring rack
7. Before each use, the silicone ring should be well seated in the silicone ring rack and the anti-clog cap must be mounted correctly on the pressure release valve
8. Install the condensation collector by sliding it into the slot found on the cooker base. If you want to remove it, just slide it out

## Maintenance and Safety Tips

Safety and maintenance are the 2 most important aspects you must consider in everything especially when using electrical gadgets. Pay special attention to these Ninja Foodi safety and maintenance tips

1. Before using the unit, check the voltage required and make sure the fittings in your kitchen are compatible. Always keep power cords away from heat sources
2. Always check the unit before use. Pay particular attention to the silicone ring to make sure it is not broken or deformed and that it is completely fastened.
3. Also, ensure that the unit is free from dried food particles
4. Place the unit on an even and stable surface to prevent leaks or falls
5. Keep children and pets away when the Ninja Foodi is in use because some parts of the unit's exterior heats up and may cause burns.
6. When releasing pressure, follow what is recommended by the Ninja Foodi cooking guide
7. Do not touch or place your hand over the release valve when releasing pressure.
8. Before cleaning the unit and accessories, ensure that it has cooled down properly
9. Always bring out time periodically to check the entire gadget and replace spoilt accessories

## Cleaning and Usage Tips

If you want this gadget to last for you, then you need to know these cleaning and usage tips:

1. Always unplug the unit from the electrical source before cleaning to avoid electric shocks
2. Do not put the multi-cooker base or housing in the dishwasher because it contains all the electronic parts.
3. Wipe the multi-cooker base or housing with a damp cloth before wiping it dry with a clean towel
4. Take out the cooking pot, silicone ring, reversible rack, basket, and diffuser are dishwasher friendly. You can also wash them on the kitchen sink if you don't have a dishwasher
5. The pressure lid, release valve, and anti-clog cap can also be washed with soap and water. Do not wash them in the dishwasher because they are small and can be lost in the process
6. Clean the crisping lid by wiping it down with wet cloth or towel
7. If there are food residues that adhered on the cooking basket, rack, and cooking pot, soak them in water first before putting in the dishwasher
8. Never use scouring pads to remove debris from the gadget
9. Air dry all parts before assembling together.

# Breakfasts

## Cheesy Meat Omelet

**(Ready in about:** 20 min | **Servings:** 2)

**Ingredients:**

- 1 beef sausage; chopped
- 4 slices prosciutto; chopped
- 1 cup grated mozzarella cheese
- 4 eggs
- 3 oz. salami; chopped
- 1 tablespoon chopped onion
- 1 tablespoon ketchup

**Directions:**

1. Preheat the Ninja Foodi to 350 degrees F on Air Crisp mode. Whisk the eggs with the ketchup, in a bowl. Stir in the onion. Spritz the inside of the Ninja Foodi basket with a cooking spray. Add and brown the sausage for about 2 minutes.
2. Meanwhile, combine the egg mixture, mozzarella cheese, salami and prosciutto. Pour the egg mixture over the sausage and stir it. Close the crisping lid and cook for 10 minutes. Once the timer beeps, ensure the omelet is just set. Serve immediately.

## Cheesy Bacon Grits

**(Ready in about:** 20 min | **Servings:** 4)

**Ingredients:**

- 3 slices smoked bacon; diced
- 1 cup ground Grits
- 1 ½ cups grated Cheddar cheese
- ½ cup water
- ½ cup milk
- 2 teaspoon butter
- Salt and black pepper

**Directions:**

1. To preheat the Ninja Foodi, select Sear/Sauté mode and set to HIGH pressure. Cook bacon until crispy, about 5 minutes. Set aside.
2. Add the grits, butter, milk, water, salt, and pepper to the pot and stir using a spoon. Close the pressure lid and secure the pressure valve.
3. Choose the Pressure mode and cook for 3 minutes on High. Press Start/Stop. Once the timer has ended, turn the vent handle and do a quick pressure release. Add in cheddar cheese and give the pudding a good stir with the same spoon.
4. Close crisping lid, press BAKE/ROAST button and cook for 8 minutes on 370 degrees F. Press Start key.
5. When ready, dish the cheesy grits into serving bowls and spoon over the crisped bacon. Serve right away with toasted bread.

## Prosciutto, Mozzarella Egg in a Cup

**(Ready in about:** 20 min | **Servings:** 2)

**Ingredients:**

- 2 slices bread
- 4 tomato slices
- 2 prosciutto slices; chopped
- 2 eggs
- 2 tablespoon mayonnaise
- 2 tablespoon grated mozzarella
- Salt and pepper, to taste
- Cooking spray

**Directions:**

1. Preheat the Ninja Foodi to 320 degrees F. Grease two large ramekins with cooking spray. Place one bread slice in the bottom of each ramekin.
2. Arrange 1 prosciutto slice and 2 tomato slices on top of each bread slice. Divide the mozzarella between the ramekins.
3. Crack the eggs over the mozzarella. Season with salt and pepper. Close the crisping lid and cook for 10 minutes on Air Crisp mode. Top with mayonnaise.

# BBQ Chicken Sandwiches

## (**Ready in about:** 45 min | **Servings:** 4)

**Ingredients:**

- 4 chicken thighs, boneless and skinless
- 1½ cups iceberg lettuce, shredded
- 2 cups barbecue sauce
- 1 onion, minced
- 2 garlic cloves, minced
- 4 burger buns
- 2 tablespoon minced fresh parsley
- 1 tablespoon lemon juice
- 1 tablespoon mayonnaise
- Salt to taste

**Directions:**

1. Season the chicken with salt, and transfer into the inner pot. Add in garlic, onion and barbeque sauce. Coat the chicken by turning in the sauce. Seal the pressure lid, choose Pressure, set to High, and set the timer to 15 minutes. Press Start.
2. When ready, do a natural pressure release for 10 minutes. Use two forks to shred the chicken and mix into the sauce. Press Sear/Sauté and let the mixture to simmer for 15 minutes to thicken the sauce, until desired consistency.
3. Meanwhile, using a large bowl, mix the lemon juice, mayonnaise, salt, and parsley; toss lettuce into the mixture to coat.
4. Separate the chicken in equal parts to match the sandwich buns; apply lettuce for topping and complete the sandwiches.

# Bacon and Sausage Cheesecake

## (**Ready in about:** 25 min | **Servings:** 6)

**Ingredients:**

- 8 eggs, cracked into a bowl
- 8 oz. breakfast sau sage; chopped
- 4 slices bread, cut into ½ -inch cubes
- 1 large green bell pepper; chopped
- 1 large red bell pepper; chopped
- 1 cup chopped green onion
- ½ cup milk
- 2 cups water
- 1 cup grated Cheddar cheese
- 3 bacon slices; chopped
- 1 teaspoon red chili flakes
- Salt and black pepper to taste

**Directions:**

1. Add the eggs, sausage chorizo, bacon slices, green and red bell peppers, green onion, chili flakes, cheddar cheese, salt, pepper, and milk to a bowl and use a whisk to beat them together.
2. Grease a bundt pan with cooking spray and pour the egg mixture into it. After, drop the bread slices in the egg mixture all around while using a spoon to push them into the mixture.
3. Open the Ninja Foodi, pour in water, and fit the rack at the center of the pot. Place bundt pan on the rack and seal the pressure lid. Select Pressure mode on High pressure for 6 minutes, and press Start/Stop.
4. Once the timer goes off, press Start/Stop, do a quick pressure release. Run a knife around the egg in the bundt pan, close the crisping lid and cook for another 4 minutes on Bake/Roast on 380 degrees F.
5. When ready, place a serving plate on the bundt pan, and then, turn the egg bundt over. Use a knife to cut the egg into slices. Serve with a sauce of your choice.

# Egg Crumpet Sandwich

## (**Ready in about:** 25 min | **Servings:** 2)

**Ingredients:**

- 2 eggs, large
- 2 crumpets, split
- 2 tablespoons chopped bacon
- 2 tablespoon Monterey Jack cheese, grated
- 2 tablespoons butter
- ¼ teaspoon salt
- Black pepper to taste

**Directions:**

1. Brush two cups with 1 tablespoon of butter. Share the bacon into the cups, crack an egg into each one, and prick the egg yolks with a toothpick in different places. Sprinkle the top with salt and black pepper and divide the cheese on top to cover the eggs. Cover the cups with aluminium foil and crimp the sides down.
2. Pour 1 cup of water into the pot, fix the reversible rack at the bottom the pot, and arrange the cups on top.
3. Seal the pressure lid, select Pressure; adjust the pressure to High, and the cook time to 1 minute; press Start.
4. When done cooking, perform a quick pressure release, and carefully open the lid. Remove the rack and cups without taking off the foil.
5. Empty the water from the inner pot and return the pot to the base. Use tongs to lift the cups into the bottom of the pot and fix the reversible rack in the upper position of the pot.
6. Cover the crisping lid, choose Broil and adjust the time to 2 minutes; press Start. While heating, spread the remaining butter over the crumpet halves.
7. Open the crisping lid, arrange the crumpet halves on the rack with the buttered-side up, and close the lid. Choose Broil again and adjust the cooking time to 4 minutes; press Start
8. When the crumpets are ready, transfer to a cutting board, and remove the cups with tongs. Run a butter knife in and around the cups and turn out each egg onto the lower half of each crumpet. Top with the other half and serve.

## Very Berry Puffs

**(Ready in about:** 20 min | **Servings:** 3)

**Ingredients:**

- 3 pastry dough sheets
- 2 cups cream cheese
- 1 tablespoon honey
- 2 tablespoon mashed raspberries
- 2 tablespoon mashed strawberries
- ¼ teaspoon vanilla extract

**Directions:**

1. Divide the cream cheese between the dough sheets and spread it evenly. In a small bowl, combine the berries, honey, and vanilla. Divide the mixture between the pastry sheets. Pinch the ends of the sheets, to form puff.
2. You can seal them by brushing some water onto the edges, or even better, use egg wash. Lay the puffs into a lined baking dish.
3. Place the dish into the Ninja Foodi, close the crisping lid and cook for 15 minutes on Air Crisp mode at 370 F. Once the timer beeps, check the puffs to ensure they're puffed and golden. Serve warm.

## Pancetta Hash with Baked Eggs

**(Ready in about:** 50 min | **Servings:** 4)

**Ingredients:**

- 6 slices pancetta; chopped
- 2 potatoes, peeled and diced
- 4 eggs
- 1 white onion; diced
- 1 teaspoon freshly ground black pepper
- 1 teaspoon garlic powder
- 1 teaspoon sweet paprika
- 1 teaspoon salt

**Directions:**

1. Choose Sear/Sauté, set to Medium High, and choose Start/Stop to preheat the pot for 5 minutes.
2. Once heated, lay the pancetta in the pot, and cook, stirring occasionally; for 5 minutes, or until the pancetta is crispy.
3. Stir in the onion, potatoes, sweet paprika, salt, black pepper, and garlic powder. Close the crisping lid; choose Bake/Roast, set the temperature to 350°F, and the time to 25 minutes. Cook until the turnips are soft and golden brown while stirring occasionally.
4. Crack the eggs on top of the hash, close the crisping lid, and choose Bake/Roast. Set the temperature to 350°F, and the time to 10 minutes.

5. Cook the eggs and check two or three times until your desired crispiness has been achieved. Serve immediately.

## Prosciutto Egg Bake

**(Ready in about:** 45 min | **Servings:** 4)

**Ingredients:**
- 8 ounces prosciutto; chopped
- 1 cup shredded Monterey Jack cheese
- 1 cup water
- 1 cup whole milk
- 1 orange bell pepper, seeded and chopped
- 4 eggs
- 1 teaspoon salt
- 1 teaspoon freshly ground black pepper

**Directions:**
1. Break the eggs into a bowl, pour in the milk, salt, and black pepper and whisk until combined. Stir in the Monterey Jack Cheese.
2. Put the bell pepper and prosciutto in the cake pan. Then, pour over the egg mixture, cover the pan with aluminum foil and put on the reversible rack.
3. Put the rack in the pot and pour in the water. Seal the pressure lid, choose pressure and set to High. Set the time to 20 minutes and choose Start/Stop.
4. When done cooking, do a quick pressure release and carefully remove the lid that is after the pressure has completely escaped.
5. When baking is complete, take the pan out of the pot and set it on a heatproof surface, and cool for 5 minutes.

## Raspberry and Vanilla Pancake

**(Ready in about:** 15 min | **Servings:** 4)

**Ingredients:**
- ½ cup frozen raspberries, thawed
- 3 eggs, beaten
- 1 cup brown sugar
- 2 cups all-purpose flour
- 1 cup milk
- 2 tablespoon maple syrup
- 1 teaspoon baking powder
- 1 ½ teaspoon vanilla extract
- Pinch of salt
- Cooking spray

**Directions:**
1. In a bowl, mix the sifted flour, baking powder, salt, milk, eggs, vanilla extract, sugar, and maple syrup, until smooth. Gently stir in the raspberries.
2. Grease the basket of your Ninja Foodi with cooking spray. Drop the batter into the basket. Close the crisping lid and cook for 10 minutes on Air Crisp mode at 390 F. Serve the pancake right away.

## Maple Giant Pancake

**(Ready in about:** 30 min | **Servings:** 6)

**Ingredients:**
- 3 cups flour
- ⅓ cup olive oil
- ⅓ cup sparkling water
- ¾ cup sugar
- 5 eggs
- 2 tablespoon maple syrup
- ⅓ teaspoon salt
- 1 ½ teaspoon baking soda
- A dollop of whipped cream to serve

**Directions:**
1. Start by pouring the flour, sugar, eggs, olive oil, sparkling water, salt, and baking soda into a food processor and blend until smooth. Pour the batter into the Ninja Foodi and let it sit in there for 15 minutes. Close the lid and secure the pressure valve.
2. Select the Pressure mode on Low pressure for 10 minutes. Press Start/Stop.
3. Once the timer goes off, press Start/Stop, quick-release the pressure valve to let out any steam and open the lid.

4. Gently run a spatula around the pancake to let loose any sticking. Once ready, slide the pancake onto a serving plate and drizzle with maple syrup. Top with the whipped cream to serve.

## Chai Latte Oatmeal

**(Ready in about:** 20 min | **Servings:** 4)

**Ingredients:**
- 1 cup steel-cut oats
- ¼ cup agave syrup
- 3 ½ cups milk
- ½ cup raw peanuts
- ¼ teaspoon ground allspice
- 1 teaspoon coffee
- ¼ teaspoon ground cardamom
- 1 teaspoon vanilla extract
- 1½ teaspoon ground ginger
- 1¼ teaspoon ground cinnamon
- ½ teaspoon salt

**Directions:**
1. Using an immersion blender, puree peanuts and milk to obtain smooth consistency; transfer into the cooker pot. To the peanuts-milk mixture, add agave syrup, oats, ginger, allspice, cinnamon, salt, cardamom, tea leaves, and cloves to mix well.
2. Seal the pressure lid, choose Pressure, set to High, and set the timer to 12 minutes. Press Start.
3. Let pressure to release naturally on completing the cooking cycle. Add vanilla extract to the oatmeal and stir well before serving.

## Pumpkin Steel Cut Oatmeal

**(Ready in about:** 25 min | **Servings:** 4)

**Ingredients:**
- ½ cup pumpkin seeds, toasted
- 1 cup pumpkin puree
- 2 cups steel cut oats
- 3 cups water
- 1 tablespoon butter
- 3 tablespoon maple syrup
- ¼ teaspoon cinnamon
- ½ teaspoon salt

**Directions:**
1. Melt butter on Sear/Sauté. Add in cinnamon, oats, salt, pumpkin puree and water. Seal the pressure lid, choose Pressure, set to High, and set the timer to 10 minutes; press Start. When cooking is complete, do a quick release.
2. Open the lid and stir in maple syrup and top with toasted pumpkin seeds to serve.

## Creamy Zucchini Muffins

**(Ready in about:** 20 min | **Servings:** 4)

**Ingredients:**
- 1 ½ cups flour
- 3 eggs
- 1 cup milk
- ½ cup shredded zucchini
- 2 tablespoon sugar
- 2 tablespoon butter, melted
- 1 tablespoon yogurt
- 2 tablespoon cream cheese
- 1 teaspoon cinnamon
- 2 teaspoon baking powder

**Directions:**
1. In a bowl, whisk the eggs along with the sugar, a pinch of salt, cinnamon, cream cheese, sifted flour, and baking powder.
2. In another bowl, combine all liquid Ingredients Gently mix the dry and liquid mixtures. Stir in zucchini. Line the muffin tins and pour in the batter. Close the crisping lid and cook for 12 minutes on Air Crisp mode at 350 F.
3. Once the timer beeps, check with a toothpick to ensure the muffins are set. If necessary, return them to the Ninja Foodi, and cook for 2-3 more minutes. Transfer to a cooling rack before serving. Serve with a scraping of butter.

# Soft-Boiled Eggs

**(Ready in about:** 15 min | **Servings:** 4)

**Ingredients:**
- 4 large eggs
- 1 cups water
- Salt and ground black pepper, to taste.

**Directions:**
1. To the pressure cooker pot, add water and place a reversible rack. Carefully place eggs on it. Seal the pressure lid, choose Pressure, set to High, and set the timer to 3 minutes. Press Start.
2. When cooking is complete, do a quick pressure release. Allow cooling completely in an ice bath. Peel the eggs and season with salt and pepper before serving.

# Kale-Egg Frittata

**(Ready in about:** 20 min | **Servings:** 6)

**Ingredients:**
- 1 ½ cups kale; chopped
- 6 large eggs
- ¼ cup grated Parmesan cheese
- 1 cup water
- 2 tablespoon heavy cream
- ½ teaspoon freshly grated nutmeg
- cooking spray
- Salt and black pepper to taste

**Directions:**
1. In a bowl, beat eggs, nutmeg, pepper, salt, and cream until smooth; stir in Parmesan cheese and kale. Apply a cooking spray to a cake pan. Wrap aluminum foil around outside of the pan to cover completely.
2. Place egg mixture into the prepared pan. Add water into the pot of your Foodi. Set your Foodi's reversible rack over the water. Gently lay the pan onto the reversible rack.
3. Seal the pressure lid, choose Pressure, set to High, and set the timer to 10 minutes. Press Start. When ready, release the pressure quickly.

# Cranberry-Raspberry Chia Oatmeal

**(Ready in about:** 30 min | **Servings:** 4))

**Ingredients:**
- 2 raspberries; sliced
- ½ cup dried cranberries, plus more for garnish
- 2 cups old fashioned oatmeal
- 3¾ cups water
- ¼ cup plain vinegar
- 1 tablespoon cinnamon powder
- ½ teaspoon nutmeg powder
- ½ teaspoon vanilla extract
- ⅛ teaspoon salt
- Honey; for topping

**Directions:**
1. Combine the oatmeal, water, vinegar, nutmeg, cinnamon, vanilla, cranberries, raspberries, and salt in the pot. Seal the pressure lid, hit Pressure, set to High, and set the timer to 11 minutes. Press Start/Stop to start cooking the oats.
2. When the timer has ended, perform a natural pressure release for 10 minutes, then a quick pressure release to let off any remaining pressure, and carefully open the lid. Stir the oatmeal, drizzle with honey and more dried cranberries, and serve immediately.

## Plum Breakfast Clafoutis

**(Ready in about:** 60 min | **Servings:** 4)

**Ingredients:**

- 2 large eggs
- ⅓ cup half and half
- ⅓ cup sugar
- ½ cup flour
- 1 cup plums; chopped
- ⅔ cup whole milk
- 2 tablespoons confectioners' sugar
- ¼ teaspoon cinnamon
- 2 teaspoons butter, softened
- ½ teaspoon vanilla extract
- A pinch of salt

**Directions:**

1. Grease four ramekins with the butter and divide the plums into each cup. Pour the milk, half and half, sugar, flour, eggs, cinnamon, vanilla, and salt in a bowl and use a hand mixer to whisk the Ingredients on medium speed until the batter is smooth, about 2 minutes. Pour the batter over the plums two-third way up.
2. Pour 1 cup of water into the inner pot. Fix the reversible rack at the bottom of the pot and put the ramekins on the rack. Lay a square of aluminium foil on the ramekins but don't crimp.
3. Put the pressure lid together and lock in Seal position. Choose Pressure, set to high, and set the time to 11 minutes; press Start.
4. When ready, perform a quick pressure release and carefully open the lid. Use tongs to remove the foil. Close the crisping lid and choose Bake/Roast. Adjust the temperature to 400°F and the time to 6 minutes. Press Start to brown the top of the clafoutis.
5. Check after about 4 minutes to ensure the clafoutis are lightly browned; otherwise bake for a few more minutes. Remove the ramekins onto a flat surface. Cool for 5 minutes, and then dust with the confectioners' sugar. Serve warm.

## Butternut Squash Cake Oatmeal

**(Ready in about:** 35 min | **Servings:** 4)

**Ingredients:**

- 1 cup steel-cut oats
- ⅓ cup honey
- 3 ½ cups coconut milk
- ¼ cup toasted walnuts; chopped
- 1 cup shredded Butternut Squash
- ½ cup sultanas
- ¼ teaspoon ground nutmeg
- 1 teaspoon ground cinnamon
- ½ teaspoon vanilla extract
- ½ teaspoon fresh orange zest
- ¾ teaspoon ground ginger
- ½ teaspoon salt

**Directions:**

1. In the pressure cooker, mix sultanas, orange zest, ginger, milk, honey, squash, salt, oats, and nutmeg.
2. Seal the pressure lid, choose Pressure, set to High, and set the timer to 12 minutes; press Start. When ready, do a natural pressure release for 10 minutes. Into the oatmeal, stir in the vanilla extract and sugar. Top with walnuts and serve.

## Sweet Bread Pudding

**(Ready in about:** 45 min | **Servings:** 3)

**Ingredients:**

- 8 slices of bread
- 2 eggs
- ¼ cup sugar
- ¼ cup honey
- 1 cup milk
- ½ cup buttermilk
- 4 tablespoon raisins
- 2 tablespoon chopped hazelnuts
- 2 tablespoon butter, softened
- ½ teaspoon vanilla extract
- Cinnamon for garnish

**Directions:**

1. Beat the eggs along with the buttermilk, honey, milk, vanilla, sugar, and butter. Stir in raisins and hazelnuts. Cut the bread into cubes and place it in a bowl.
2. Pour the milk mixture over the bread. Let soak for about 10 minutes. Close the crisping lid and cook the bread pudding for 25 minutes on Roast mode. Leave the dessert to cool for 5 minutes, then invert onto a plate and sprinkle with cinnamon to serve.

## Savory Custards with Ham and Cheese

**(Ready in about:** 40 min | **Servings:** 4)

**Ingredients:**

- 4 large eggs
- 1 ounce cottage cheese; at room temperature
- 2 serrano ham slices; halved widthwise
- ¼ cup caramelized white onions
- ¼ cup half and half
- ¼ cup grated Emmental cheese
- ¼ teaspoon salt
- Ground black pepper to taste

**Directions:**

1. Preheat the inner pot by choosing Sear/Sauté and adjust to Medium; press Start. Put the serrano ham in the pot and cook for 3 to 4 minutes or until browned, turning occasionally.
2. Remove the ham onto a paper towel-lined plate. Next, use a brush to coat the inside of four 1- cup ramekins with the ham fat. Set the cups aside, then, empty and wipe out the inner pot with a paper towel, and return the pot to the base.
3. Crack the eggs into a bowl and add the cottage cheese, half and half, salt, and several grinds of black pepper. Use a hand mixer to whisk the Ingredients until co cheese lumps remain.
4. Stir in the grated emmental cheese and mix again to incorporate the cheese. Lay a piece of ham in the bottom of each custard cup. Evenly share the onions among the cups as well as the egg mixture. Cover each cup with aluminum foil.
5. Pour 1 cup of water into the inner pot and fix the reversible rack in the pot. Arrange the ramekins on top. Lock the pressure lid in Seal position; choose Pressure, adjust to High, and set the timer to 7 minutes. Press Start.
6. After cooking, perform a quick pressure release. Use tongs to remove the custard cups from the pressure cooker. Cool for 1 to 2 minutes before serving.

## Cheesy Shakshuka

**(Ready in about:** 50 min | **Servings:** 4)

**Ingredients:**

- 1 small red onion; chopped
- 2 (14.5-ounce) cans diced tomatoes with their juice
- ½ red bell pepper, seeded and chopped
- 1 medium banana pepper, seeded and minced
- 4 eggs
- ⅓ cup crumbled goat cheese
- 2 garlic cloves; chopped
- 2 tablespoon fresh cilantro; chopped
- 3 tablespoons ghee
- ½ teaspoon smoked paprika
- ½ teaspoon red chili flakes
- ¼ teaspoon black pepper; freshly ground
- 1 teaspoon salt
- ½ teaspoon coriander, ground

**Directions:**

1. Choose Sear/Sauté on you Foodi and set on Medium to preheat the inner pot; press Start. Melt the ghee and sauté the onion, bell pepper, banana pepper, and garlic. Season lightly with salt and cook for 2 minutes until the vegetables are fragrant and beginning to soften.
2. Then, stir in the tomatoes, coriander, smoked paprika, red chili flakes, and black pepper. Seal the pressure lid, choose pressure and adjust the pressure to High and the timer to 4 minutes. Press Start to continue cooking.

3. When the timer has read to the end, perform a quick pressure release. Gently crack the eggs onto the tomato sauce in different areas. Seal the pressure lid again, but with the valve set to Vent. Choose Steam and adjust the cook time to 3 minutes. Press Start to cook the eggs.
4. When ready, carefully open the pressure lid. Sprinkle with the shakshuka with goat cheese and cilantro. Dish into a serving platter and serve.

## Crustless Quiche

**(Ready in about:** 40 min | **Servings:** 2)

**Ingredients:**
- 4 eggs
- ¼ cup chopped kalamata olives
- ¼ cup chopped onion
- ½ cup milk
- ½ cup chopped tomatoes
- 1 cup crumbled feta cheese
- 1 tablespoon chopped basil
- 1 tablespoon chopped oregano
- 2 tablespoon olive oil
- Salt and pepper to taste

**Directions:**
1. Brush a pie pan with the olive oil. Beat the eggs along with the milk, salt, and pepper. Stir in all of the remaining Ingredients.
2. Pour the egg mixture into the pan. Close the crisping lid and cook for 30 minutes on Air Crisp mode at 340 F. Leave to cool before serving.

## Poached Egg Heirloom Tomato

**(Ready in about:** 10 min | **Servings:** 4)

**Ingredients:**
- 4 large eggs
- 2 large Heirloom ripe tomatoes; halved crosswise
- 4 small slices feta cheese
- 1 cup water
- 2 tablespoon grated Parmesan cheese
- 1 teaspoon chopped fresh herbs, of your choice
- Salt and black pepper to taste
- Cooking spray

**Directions:**
1. Pour the water into the Ninja Foodi and fit the reversible rack. Grease the ramekins with the cooking spray and crack each egg into them.
2. Season with salt and pepper. Cover the ramekins with aluminum foil. Place the cups on the trivet. Seal the lid.
3. Select Steam mode for 3 minutes on High pressure. Press Start/Stop.Once the timer goes off, do a quick pressure release. Use a napkin to remove the ramekins onto a flat surface.
4. In serving plates, share the halved tomatoes, feta slices, and toss the eggs in the ramekin over on each tomato half. Sprinkle with salt and pepper, parmesan, and garnish with chopped herbs.

## French Dip Sandwiches

**(Ready in about:** 1 hr 35 min | **Servings:** 8)

**Ingredients:**
- 2 ½ pounds beef roast
- 2 tablespoon olive oil
- 1 onion; chopped
- 4 garlic cloves; sliced
- ½ cup dry red wine
- 2 cups beef broth stock
- 1 teaspoon dried oregano
- 16 slices Fontina cheese
- 8 split hoagie rolls

**Directions:**
1. Generously apply pepper and salt to the beef for seasoning. Warm oil on Sear/Sauté and brown the beef for 2 to 3 minutes per side. Set aside on a plate.
2. Add onions and cook for 3 minutes, until translucent. Mix in garlic and cook for one a minute until soft.

3. To the Foodi, add red wine to deglaze. Scrape the cooking surface to remove any browned sections of the food using a wooden spoon's flat edge; mix in beef broth and take back the juices and beef to your pressure cooker. Over the meat, scatter some oregano.
4. Seal the pressure lid, choose Pressure, set to High, and set the timer to 50 minutes; press Start. Release pressure naturally for around 10 minutes. Transfer the beef to a cutting board and slice.
5. Roll the sliced beef and add a topping of onions. Each sandwich should be topped with 2 slices fontina cheese.
6. Place the sandwiches in the pot, close the crisping lid and select Air Crisp. Adjust the temperature to 360°F and the time to 3 minutes. Press Start. When cooking is complete, the cheese should be cheese melt.

## Sausage Wrapped Scotch Eggs

**(Ready in about:** 55 min | **Servings:** 4)

**Ingredients:**
- 12 ounces Italian sausage patties
- 4 eggs
- 1 cup water
- 1 cup panko bread crumbs
- Nonstick cooking spray; for preparing the rack
- 2 tablespoons melted unsalted butter

**Directions:**
1. Pour 1 cup of water into the inner pot. Put the reversible rack in the pot at the bottom, and carefully place the eggs on top. Seal the pressure lid, choose Pressure, set the pressure to High, and the cook time to 3 minutes. Press Start.
2. While cooking the eggs, fill half a bowl with cold water and about a cup full of ice cubes to make an ice bath.
3. After cooking, perform a quick pressure release, and carefully open the lid. Use tongs to pick up the eggs into the ice bath. Allow cooling for 3 to 4 minutes; peel the eggs.
4. Pour the water out of the inner pot and return the pot to the base. Grease the reversible rack with cooking spray, fix the rack in the upper position, and place in the pot.
5. Cover the crisping lid; choose Air Crisp, set the temperature to 360°F and the timer to 4 minutes. Press Start to preheat.
6. While preheating the pot, place an egg on each sausage patty. Pull the sausage around the egg and seal the edges.
7. In a small bowl, mix the breadcrumbs with the melted butter. One at a time, dredge the sausage-covered eggs in the crumbs while pressing into the breadcrumbs for a thorough coat.
8. Open the crisping lid and place the eggs on the rack. Close the crisping lid; choose Air Crisp, adjust the temperature to 360°F, and the cook time to 15 minutes. Press Start.
9. When the timer has ended, the crumbs should be crisp and a deep golden brown color. Remove the eggs and allow cooling for several minutes. Slice the eggs in half and serve.

## Deviled Eggs

**(Ready in about:** 20 min | **Servings:** 6)

**Ingredients:**
- 10 large eggs
- ¼ cup cream cheese
- ¼ cup mayonnaise
- 1 cup water
- ¼ teaspoon chili powder
- salt and ground black pepper to taste

**Directions:**
1. Add water to the Foodi's pot. Insert the eggs into the steamer basket; place into the pot. Seal the pressure lid, choose Pressure, set to High, and set the timer to 5 minutes. Press Start.When ready, release the pressure quickly.
2. Drop eggs into an ice bath to cool for 5 minutes. Press Start. Peel eggs and halve them.
3. Transfer yolks to a bowl and use a fork to mash; stir in cream cheese, and mayonnaise. Add pepper and salt for seasoning. Ladle yolk mixture into egg white halves.

# Strawberry French Toast

**(Ready in about:** 45 min | **Servings:** 4)

**Ingredients:**

- 3 strawberries; sliced; divided
- 6 slices brioche; cubed
- 3 eggs
- ¼ cup milk
- ¼ cup ricotta cheese; at room temperature
- ¼ cup chopped almonds
- ½ cup water
- 2 tablespoons brown sugar; divided
- 2 tablespoons firm unsalted butter; sliced
- 2 tablespoons maple syrup
- 1 tablespoon sugar
- 1 teaspoon vanilla extract
- 1 teaspoon cinnamon powder
- Cooking spray

**Directions:**

1. Crack the eggs into a bowl and whisk with the milk, sugar, vanilla, and cinnamon. Set aside. Grease a baking dish with cooking spray and in a single layer, spread half of the brioche cubes in the pan. Layer half of the strawberry slices on the bread and dust with 1 tablespoon of brown sugar.
2. Spoon and spread the ricotta cheese on top of the strawberries. Then, make another layer of bread, strawberries, brown sugar, and ricotta cheese.
3. Pour the egg mixture all over the layered Ingredients ensuring to give the bread a good coat.
4. Next, pour the water into the pot. Fix the pan on the reversible rack, and put the rack with a pan in the pot. Seal the pressure lid, choose Pressure, set to High, set the timer to 20 minutes, and choose Start/Stop to begin toasting.
5. Once the timer has read to the end, perform a quick pressure release to let all the pressure out, and carefully open the lid.
6. Top the French toast with the sliced butter, almonds, and maple syrup. Close the crisping lid; choose Bake/Roast, set the temperature to 390°F, and set the time to 5 minutes.
7. Check the toast's doneness for your desired crispiness, otherwise, cook for a few more minutes. Serve immediately.

# Cheesy Ham Sandwich

**(Ready in about:** 10 min | **Servings:** 1)

**Ingredients:**

- 2 slices of American cheese
- 2 slices of bread
- 1 slice of ham
- 2 teaspoon butter

**Directions:**

1. Spread one teaspoon of butter on the outside of each of the bread slices. Place one cheese slice on the inside of one bread slice, top with ham slice and another cheese slice. Cover with the second bread slice to create the sandwich.
2. Place into the Ninja Foodi basket, close the crisping lid and cook for 4 minutes on Air Crisp mode at 370 F. Flip the sandwich and cook for an additional 4 minutes.
3. When the timer beeps, remove the sandwich, cut diagonally and serve immediately with ketchup or chutney.

# Paprika Shirred Eggs

**(Ready in about:** 20 min | **Servings:** 2)

**Ingredients:**

- 4 eggs; divided
- 4 slices of ham
- 2 tablespoon heavy cream
- 3 tablespoon Parmesan cheese
- ¼ teaspoon pepper
- 2 teaspoon butter; for greasing
- 2 teaspoon chopped chives
- ¼ teaspoon paprika

**Directions:**
1. Grease a pie pan with the butter. Arrange the ham slices on the bottom of the pan to cover it completely. Use more slices if needed.
2. Whisk one egg along with the heavy cream, salt, and pepper, in a small bowl. Pour the mixture over the ham slices. Crack the other eggs over the ham.
3. Scatter Parmesan cheese over, close the crisping lid and cook for 14 minutes on Air Crisp mode at 320 F. Sprinkle with paprika and garnish with chives.

## Pepper and Artichoke Frittata

**(Ready in about:** 60 min | **Servings:** 4)

**Ingredients:**
- ¼ large orange bell pepper; chopped
- ½ small red onion; chopped
- 1 cup coarsely chopped artichoke hearts
- ¼ cup full cream milk
- ¾ cup shredded Colby cheese; divided
- ¼ cup grated Pecorino Romano or similar cheese
- 8 large eggs
- 2 tablespoons unsalted butter
- ½ teaspoon salt
- ¼ teaspoon freshly ground black pepper

**Directions:**
1. On your Foodi, press Sear/Sauté and adjust to Medium-High; press Start. Melt the butter and sauté the onion, bell pepper, and artichoke hearts in the butter. Cook for 5 minutes or until the onion and pepper are soft.
2. While the vegetables soften, whisk the eggs with salt and allow sitting for 1 minute. Pour the milk into the eggs and whisk again then stir ½ cup of colby cheese into the mixture.
3. When the vegetables are cooked, pour the egg mixture into the pot. Gently stir to distribute the vegetables evenly. Reduce the heat to Medium and cook the eggs, undisturbed, until the edges are set about 7 to 9 minutes.
4. Press Stop to cancel the Sear/Sauté function. Then, run a silicone spatula around the edges of the frittata to loosen from the side of the pot. Close the crisping lid; choose Bake/Roast and set the temperature to 370 F, and the cook time to 3 minutes. Press Start to begin baking.
5. After 1 minute, open the lid and sprinkle the remaining ¼ cup of Colby and the Pecorino Romano cheese over the frittata. Close the lid and cook for the remaining 2 minutes.
6. Open the lid by which time the cheese should have melted and the top not browned, but set. Sprinkle the frittata with black pepper, let rest for 2 minutes, and slice into wedges, to serve.

## Toasted Bagel

**(Ready in about:** 6 min | **Servings:** 1)

**Ingredients:**
- 1 bagel
- 2 tablespoon butter, softened
- 1 tablespoon Parmesan cheese
- 1 teaspoon dried basil
- 1 teaspoon dried parsley
- 1 teaspoon garlic powder
- Salt and pepper, to taste

**Directions:**
1. Cut the bagel in half. Place in the Ninja Foodi, close the crisping lid and cook for 3 minutes on Air Crisp mode at 370 F.
2. Combine the butter, Parmesan, garlic, basil, and parsley, in a small bowl. Season with salt and pepper, to taste. Spread the mixture onto the toasted bagel.
3. Return the bagel to the Ninja Foodi, and cook for an additional 3 minutes on Roast mode. Serve with tangy tomato relish on the side.

## Cheesy Onion Omelet

**(Ready in about:** 10 min | **Servings:** 1)

**Ingredients:**
- 2 eggs
- ½ onion; sliced
- 1 tablespoon olive oil
- 2 tablespoon grated cheddar cheese
- 1 teaspoon soy sauce
- ¼ teaspoon pepper

**Directions:**
1. Whisk the eggs along with the pepper, onion, and soy sauce, in a bowl, until well-combined. Grease a baking tray with olive oil and pour in the egg mixture.
2. Close the crisping lid and cook for 5-6 minutes on Air Crisp mode at 350 F. Once the timer beeps, check to ensure the eggs have set.
3. Top with the grated cheddar cheese. Fold the omelet in half and serve with a green salad.

## Veggie Salmon Balls

**(Ready in about:** 40 min | **Servings:** 4)

**Ingredients:**
- 2 (5 oz) packs steamed salmon flakes
- 3 large potatoes, cut into chips
- 1 Red onion; chopped
- 3 eggs, cracked into a bowl
- 1 cup breadcrumbs
- ¼ cup chopped parsley
- 4 tablespoon butter; divided
- 4 tablespoon mayonnaise
- 2 tablespoons olive oil
- 1 red bell pepper, seeded and chopped
- 1 teaspoon garlic powder
- 2 teaspoon Worcestershire sauce
- Salt and black pepper to taste

**Directions:**
1. Turn on the Ninja Foodi and select Sear/Sauté mode on High pressure. Heat the oil and add half of the butter. Once it has melted, add the onions and the chopped red bell peppers. Cook for 6 minutes while stirring occasionally. Press Start/Stop.
2. In a mixing bowl, add salmon flakes, sautéed red bell pepper and onion, breadcrumbs, eggs, mayonnaise, Worcestershire sauce, garlic powder, salt, pepper, and parsley.
3. Use a spoon to mix well while breaking the salmon into the tiny pieces. Use your hands to mold 4 patties out of the mixture. Add the remaining butter to melt, and when melted, add the patties. Fry for 4 minutes, flipping once.
4. Then, close the crisping lid, select Bake/Roast mode and bake for 4 minutes on 320 degrees F. Remove them onto a wire rack to rest. Serve the cakes with a side of lettuce and potato salad with a mild drizzle of herb vinaigrette.

## Paprika Hard-Boiled Eggs

**(Ready in about:** 25 min | **Servings:** 3)

**Ingredients:**
- 6 eggs
- 1 cup water
- 1 teaspoon sweet paprika
- Salt and ground black pepper, to taste

**Directions:**
1. In the Foodi, add water and place a reversible rack on top. Lay your eggs on the rack. Seal the pressure lid, choose Pressure, set to High, and set the timer to 5 minutes. Press Start.
2. Once ready, do a natural release for 10 minutes. Transfer the eggs to ice cold water to cool completely. When cooled, peel and slice. Season with salt and pepper. Sprinkle with sweet paprika before serving.

# Lunch Recipes

## Pumpkin Chipotle Soup

**(Ready in about:** 25 min | **Servings:** 4)

**Ingredients:**

- 1 large butternut pumpkin, cut into small pieces
- 1 onion; chopped
- 2 chipotle peppers, seeded and finely minced
- 1 pinch ground cinnamon
- 1 cup half-and-half
- 4 cups vegetable broth
- 1 tablespoon olive oil
- ¼ teaspoon grated nutmeg
- ¼ teaspoon ground cloves
- 1 teaspoon ground black pepper
- 1 teaspoon salt

**Directions:**

1. Warm oil on Sear/Sauté and sauté nutmeg, pepper, clove, cinnamon, and onion for 3 to 5 minutes until translucent. Add pumpkin and cook for 5 minutes as you stir infrequently. Pour in the broth and add chipotle peppers and any remaining pumpkin.
2. Seal the pressure lid, choose Pressure, set to High, and set the timer to 10 minutes; press Start. When ready, release pressure quickly.
3. Stir in half-and-half and transfer to a blender to purée until you obtain a smooth consistency.

## Chicken Wings Broth

**(Ready in about:** 1 hr 30 min | **Servings:** 8)

**Ingredients:**

- 2 pounds chicken wings
- 2 large carrots; diced
- 1 small handful fresh parsley
- 1 small handful fresh thyme
- 4 cloves garlic
- 4 spring onions; diced
- 1 bay leaf
- 6 cups water

**Directions:**

1. In the Foodi, add chicken, carrots, parsley, thyme, onions, garlic, and bay leaf. Pour in water. Seal the pressure lid, choose Pressure, set to High, and set the timer to 45 minutes. Press Start.
2. Release pressure naturally for about 10 minutes. Use a fine-mesh strainer to strain the broth and Allow cooling to room temperature. Transfer the broth to containers and seal. Place in the refrigerator for a maximum of one week.

## Roasted Tomato and Chorizo Soup

**(Ready in about:** 30 min | **Servings:** 6)

**Ingredients:**

- 3 chorizo sausage; chopped
- 28 ounces fire-roasted diced tomatoes
- 2 shallots; sliced
- 3 cloves garlic, minced
- ½ cup fresh ripe tomatoes
- ½ cup raw cashews
- ½ cup thinly sliced fresh basil
- 4 cups beef broth
- 1 tablespoon olive oil
- 1 tablespoon red wine vinegar
- 1 teaspoon salt
- ½ teaspoon ground black pepper

**Directions:**

1. Warn oil on Sear/Sauté and cook chorizo until crispy. Remove to a to a plate lined with paper towel. To the pot, add in garlic and onion and cook for 5 minutes until soft. Season with salt.
2. Stir in red wine vinegar, broth; diced tomatoes, cashews, tomatoes, and black pepper. Seal the pressure lid, choose Pressure, set to High, and set the timer to 8 minutes. Press Start. When ready, release pressure quickly.

3. Pour the soup into an immersion blender and process to obtain a smooth consistency. Divide into deep bowls, top with crispy chorizo and decorate with basil. Serve and enjoy!

## Cheesy Ham Eggplant Boats

**(Ready in about: 17 min | Servings: 2)**

**Ingredients:**
- 6 ham slices; chopped
- 1 cup mozzarella cheese, shredded
- 2 eggplants
- 1 teaspoon dried parsley
- Cooking spray
- Salt and pepper, to taste

**Directions:**
1. Grease the Ninja Foodi basket with cooking spray; set aside. Cut the eggplants lengthwise in half and scoop some of the flesh out, leaving the skin intact. Season with salt and pepper.
2. Chop the scooped flesh and mix with mozzarella cheese, salt, and pepper. Divide the cheese mixture between the eggplant halves. Cover with ham slices, and sprinkle with parsley.
3. Put the eggplant in the greased basket, close the crisping lid and cook for 12 minutes on Air Crisp mode at 350 F. Serve with a fresh salad.

## Chicken on Green Bed

**(Ready in about: 20 min | Servings: 1)**

**Ingredients:**
- 4 oz. chicken breasts; cubed
- 1 garlic clove, minced
- 3 large kale leaves; chopped
- ½ cup shredded romaine lettuce
- ½ cup baby spinach leaves
- 3 tablespoon olive oil; divided
- 1 teaspoon balsamic vinegar
- Salt and pepper, to taste

**Directions:**
1. Place the chicken in a bowl along with 1 tablespoon olive oil and garlic. Season with salt and pepper; toss to combine. Place on a lined baking dish and cook for 14 minutes on Roast mode in your Ninja Foodi at 390 F.
2. Add the greens in a large bowl. Pour the remaining olive oil, balsamic vinegar, salt, and pepper, and toss to combine.
3. When the timer rings out, remove the chicken from the Ninja Foodi. Arrange the greens on a serving platter and top with the chicken, to serve.

## Hawaiian Pizza

**(Ready in about: 15 min | Servings: 2)**

**Ingredients:**
- 2 tortillas
- 8 thin pineapple slices
- 8 ham slices
- 8 mozzarella slices
- 2 tablespoon tomato sauce
- Fresh basil leaves; chopped

**Directions:**
1. Spread each tortilla with tomato sauce. Scatter over the ham, pineapple, and mozzarella. Place the pizza into your Ninja Foodi basket, close the crisping lid and cook for 10 minutes on Air Crisp mode.
2. When the timer beeps, remove and allow to sit for 2 minutes before slicing. Sprinkle the basil over and serve with napkins.

## Homemade Vegetables Soup

**(Ready in about:** 40 min | **Servings:** 5)

**Ingredients:**

- 1 leek; sliced
- 2 carrots; diced
- 1 celery stalk; chopped
- 4 potatoes, quartered
- 1 ½ cups vegetable stock
- 1 red bell pepper; diced
- 2 cloves garlic, minced
- 2 tablespoon parsley
- 2 tablespoon olive oil
- 1/4 teaspoon red pepper flakes
- Salt and pepper to taste

**Directions:**

1. Heat olive oil on Sear/Sauté. Add garlic and leek and cook for 5 minutes. Add in red bell pepper, carrots, salt, potatoes, red pepper flakes, and pepper. Mix in vegetable stock.
2. Seal the pressure lid, choose Pressure, set to High, and set the timer to 15 minutes. Press Start. When ready, allow the pressure to release naturally for 10 minutes. Add cilantro and coconut milk to the soup. Use an immersion blender to blend the soup until smooth.

## Chicken Noodle Soup

**(Ready in about:** 40 min | **Servings:** 6)

**Ingredients:**

- 1 pound chicken breasts, bone-in, skin-on
- 8 ounces extra-wide dry egg noodles
- 1 onion, minced
- 1 turnip; chopped
- 1 bay leaf
- 3 cloves garlic, minced
- 6 cups chicken broth
- 1 cup celery rib; chopped
- 1 tablespoon olive oil
- 1 tablespoon dry basil
- Salt and ground black pepper to taste

**Directions:**

1. Set your Foodi to Sear/Sauté, set to Medium High, and choose Start/Stop to preheat the pot. Warm olive oil; stir in garlic and onion and cook for 3 minutes until soft. Mix in celery, bay leaf, basil, and turnip.
2. Add 3 cups chicken broth to the pot and deglaze. Scrape any brown bits from the pan's bottom and add chicken. Seal the pressure lid, choose Pressure, set to High, and set the timer to 10 minutes; press Start. When ready, naturally release the pressure for about 7 minutes.
3. Transfer chicken breasts to another bowl. Do away with the skin and bones. Using two forks, shred the meat.
4. Set the cooker to Sear/Sauté. Transfer the chicken back to the pot; add the noodles and the remaining chicken stock. Simmer the stock and cook for 10 minutes until noodles are done. Add pepper and salt for seasoning.

## Chicken Soup

**(Ready in about:** 1 hr 10 min | **Servings:** 8)

**Ingredients:**

- 1 ½ pounds chicken drumsticks, boneless
- 4 celery stalks 1 cup fennel bulb; chopped
- 2 eggs, beaten
- 2 garlic cloves
- 3 parsley; chopped
- 2 onions; diced
- 2 carrots; diced
- 2 bay leaves
- ½ cup matzo meal
- 2 tablespoon canola oil
- 1 teaspoon baking powder
- Salt and ground black pepper to taste

**Directions:**

1. In your pressure cooker, add chicken drumsticks, bay leaves, onion, carrots, pepper, garlic, parsley, salt, and fennel. Add enough water such that Ingredients are covered by 2 inches.

2. Seal the pressure lid, choose Pressure, set to High, and set the timer to 30 minutes; press Start. Release pressure naturally; for about 10 minutes.
3. Meanwhile, mix baking powder, eggs, oil, pepper, salt and matzo meal in a small bowl. Use a plastic wrap to close the bowl and place in a refrigerator for 10 minutes.
4. Get rid of celery stalks from the pressure cooker. Transfer chicken to a cutting board and strip and shred it from the bones. Take back to the pot. Select Sear/Sauté and boil the soup. Roll matzo mixture into 1-inch balls and place in the boiling soup. Cook for 3 mins to heat through as you gently stir.

## Italian Style Sausage Patties

**(Ready in about:** 20 min | **Servings:** 4)

**Ingredients:**

- 1 lb. ground Italian sausage
- 1 egg, beaten
- ¼ cup breadcrumbs
- ¼ teaspoon garlic powder
- 1 teaspoon dried parsley
- 1 teaspoon red pepper Flakes
- ½ teaspoon salt
- ¼ teaspoon black pepper

**Directions:**

1. Line the basket with parchment paper; set aside. Combine all Ingredients in a large bowl. Use your hands (clean!) to combine the mixture thoroughly. Make patties out of the sausage mixture and arrange them on the basket.
2. Close the crisping lid and cook for 14 minutes on Air Crisp at 350 F. After 7 minutes, flip each patty. Once ready, remove and serve with tzatziki sauce.

## Sweet Potato Egg Salad

**(Ready in about:** 20 min | **Servings:** 8)

**Ingredients:**

- 6 sweet potatoes, peeled and diced
- 4 large eggs
- ½ cup Arugula
- ¼ cup dill; chopped
- ⅓ cup Greek yogurt
- 2 ½ cups mayonnaise
- 1 ½ cups water
- Salt and ground black pepper to taste

**Directions:**

1. In your Foodi, add water. Place eggs and potatoes into the reversible rack; transfer to the pot and seal the pressure lid. Choose Pressure, and set timer to 4 minutes; press Start. After cooking has completed, release pressure quickly. Open the lid.
2. Take out the eggs and place in a bowl of ice-cold water for purposes of cooling. In a large bowl, combine yogurt, mayonnaise, and dill.
3. In a separate bowl, mash potatoes using a potato masher; mix with mayonnaise mixture to coat. Skin and dice the eggs; transfer to the potato salad and mix. Add pepper and salt to the salad before serving.

## Beef Broth

**(Ready in about:** 1 hr 10 min | **Servings:** 8)

**Ingredients:**

- 2 pounds beef stew meat
- 2 red chilies, deseeded and chopped
- 2 carrots; chopped
- 4 garlic cloves
- 2 leeks; chopped
- 1 onion; chopped
- 2 cups celery; chopped
- 8 cups water
- 1 teaspoon cider vinegar
- 1 teaspoon fresh ginger, grated
- salt to taste

**Directions:**

1. In the Foodi, mix meat, celery, garlic carrots, leeks, onion, red chilies, and ginger. Top with vinegar and water. Seal the pressure lid, choose Pressure, set to High, and set the timer to 45 minutes. Press Start. Release pressure naturally for 10 minutes, then release the remaining pressure quickly.

2. Use a fine-mesh strainer to strain the broth into a bowl; add salt for seasoning. Serve or refrigerate using sealable containers.

## Hearty Vegetable Soup

**(Ready in about:** 30 min | **Servings:** 5)

**Ingredients:**

- 28 ounces canned tomatoes
- 15 ounces canned garbanzo beans, rinsed and drained
- 1 cup frozen green peas
- 5 cups chicken broth
- 1 cup celery; chopped
- ¼ cup parmesan cheese, grated
- 1 onion; chopped
- 2 carrots, peeled and chopped
- 2 bay leaves
- 2 cloves garlic, minced
- 2 turnips, peeled and chopped
- 1 sprig fresh sage
- 2 tablespoon olive oil
- salt and ground black pepper to taste

**Directions:**

1. Set your Foodi to Sear/Sauté, set to Medium High, and choose Start/Stop to preheat the pot. Warm oil; stir in celery, carrots, and onion and cook for 4 minutes until soft. Add in garlic and cook for 30 seconds until crispy.
2. Into the Foodi, add vegetable broth, parsnip, garbanzo beans, bay leaves, tomatoes, pepper, salt, peas, and sage. Seal the pressure lid, press Pressure, set to High, and set the timer to 12 minutes; press Start.
3. Once done, release remaining pressure quickly. Serve topped with parmesan cheese.

## Curry Egg Salad

**(Ready in about:** 10 min | **Servings:** 6)

**Ingredients:**

- 6 eggs
- 2 spring onions, minced
- ¼ cup crème fraîche
- 2 cups water
- 1 tablespoon dill, minced
- 1 tablespoon curry paste
- 2 teaspoon mustard
- Cooking spray
- Salt and black pepper to taste

**Directions:**

1. Grease a cake pan with cooking spray. Carefully crack in the eggs. To the inner pot, add water. Set the pan with the eggs on a reversible rack.
2. Seal the pressure lid, choose Pressure, set to High, and the timer to 5 minutes; press Start. Once ready, do a quick release. Drain any water from the eggs in the pan. Loosen the eggs on the edges with a knife. Transfer to a cutting board and chop into smaller sizes.
3. Transfer the chopped eggs to a bowl. Add in onion, mustard, salt, dill, crème fraîche, curry powder, and black pepper.

# Borscht Soup

**(Ready in about:** 30 min | **Servings:** 4)

**Ingredients:**

- 2 beets, peeled and diced
- 1 dried habanero pepper, crushed
- 4 cups beef stock
- 3 cups white cabbage, shredded
- 1 cup leeks; chopped
- 2 tablespoon olive oil
- 1 tablespoon cayenne pepper, finely minced
- 2 teaspoon red wine apple cider vinegar
- 1 teaspoon garlic, smashed
- 1 teaspoon salt
- ¼ teaspoon paprika
- Greek yogurt for garnish

**Directions:**

1. Set your Foodi to Sear/Sauté, set to Medium High, and choose Start/Stop to preheat the pot. Warm the oil; stir in garlic and leeks and cook for 5 minutes until soft.
2. Mix in, stock, paprika, salt, peppers, vinegar, beets, white cabbage, cayenne pepper, and crushed red pepper.
3. Seal the pressure lid, choose Pressure, set to High, and set the timer to 20 minutes; press Start. When ready, do a quick pressure release. Place in serving bowls and apply a topping of Greek yogurt before serving.

# Broccoli and Potato Soup

**(Ready in about:** 35 min| **Servings:** 4)

**Ingredients:**

- 2 ½ pounds potatoes, peeled and chopped
- Cheddar cheese, grated for garnish
- ½ cup fresh chopped scallions; for garnish
- 4 cups vegetable broth
- ½ cup heavy cream
- ⅓ cup butter
- 2 cloves garlic, minced
- 1 onion; chopped
- 1 head broccoli, cut into florets
- Salt and black pepper to taste

**Directions:**

1. Melt the butter on Sear/Sauté. Add onion and garlic and cook for 5 minutes. Add in broth, potatoes, and broccoli, and mix well. Press the Start/Stop button.
2. Seal the pressure lid, choose Pressure, set to High, and set the timer to 5 minutes. Press Start. When ready, allow the pressure to release naturally for 10 minutes. Transfer the potato mixture in an immersion blender and puree until smooth.
3. Add in heavy cream and season with pepper and salt as desired. Divide among bowls and top with cheese and scallions.

# Beef Neck Bone Stock

**(Ready in about:** 2 hr 10 min | **Servings:** 8)

**Ingredients:**

- 2 pounds Beef Neck Bones
- 2 onions; chopped
- 1 carrot; chopped
- 2 bay leaves
- 10 peppercorns
- 2 cups celery; chopped
- 12 cups water, or more
- 1 teaspoon cider vinegar
- Salt to taste

**Directions:**

1. In the pot, add carrot, ginger, vinegar, onion, and beef bones. Add enough water to cover Ingredients. Seal the pressure lid, press Pressure, set to High, and set the timer to 120 minutes; press Start. Release pressure naturally for about 20 minutes. Remove the bones and bay leaves, and discard.
2. Use a fine-mesh strainer to strain the liquid. Allow the broth to cool. From the surface, skim fat and throw away. Refrigerate for a maximum of 7 days.

## Vegetable Soup

**Ingredients:**

- ½ red bell pepper; diced
- 1/4 head green cabbage; chopped
- 2 garlic cloves, minced
- 1 carrot; diced
- 1 parsnip; diced
- 1 celery stalk; diced
- 4 cups vegetable stock
- 1 cup leeks; chopped
- 1 cup sliced mushrooms
- 1 cup broccoli florets
- 1 cup cauliflower florets
- ½ cup fresh parsley; chopped
- ½ cup green beans
- 2 tablespoon olive oil
- 2 tablespoon nutritional yeast
- ½ teaspoon dried thyme
- ½ teaspoon ground black pepper
- ½ salt, or more to taste

**Directions:**

1. Heat oil on Sear/Sauté on Medium High. Add in garlic and onion and cook for 6 minutes until slightly browned. Add in vegetable stock, carrot, celery, broccoli, bell pepper, green beans, salt, nutritional yeast, cabbage, cauliflower, mushrooms, potato, thyme, and pepper.
2. Seal the pressure lid, choose Pressure, set to High, and set the timer to 25 minutes; press Start. When ready, release pressure naturally; for about 5 minutes. Stir in parsley and serve.

## Acorn Squash Soup

(**Ready in about:** 25 min | **Servings:** 4)

**Ingredients:**

- 1 (2 pounds) acorn squash, peeled, seeded; chopped
- 2 carrots, peeled and diced
- 1 onion; diced
- 4 cups vegetable broth
- 1/3 cup sour cream
- ½ cup coconut milk
- 2 tablespoon butter
- ½ teaspoon ground cinnamon
- ¼ teaspoon chili pepper
- A pinch of salt

**Directions:**

1. Set Foodi to Sear/Sauté, set to Medium High, and choose Start/Stop to preheat. Melt butter; add onion and cook for 3 minutes until soft. Add in carrots, cinnamon, squash, salt, and chili pepper and stir-fry for 2 minutes until fragrant.
2. Add the stock to the vegetable mixture. Seal the pressure lid, choose Pressure, set to High, and set the timer to 12 minutes; press Start. Quick-release the pressure.
3. Add soup to a food processor and puree to obtain a smooth consistency. Take the soup back To the Foodi, stir in coconut milk until you get a consistent color. Divide into serving bowls. Serve hot with a dollop of sour cream.

## Bacon Potato Salad

(**Ready in about:** 19 min | **Servings:** 6)

**Ingredients:**

- 6 red potatoes, peeled and quartered
- 6 slices smoked bacon; chopped
- 2 red onions; sliced
- ½ cup water
- ½ cup apple cider vinegar
- 3 tablespoon honey
- 1 teaspoon fresh flat-leaf parsley; chopped
- 2 teaspoon mustard
- 1 teaspoon salt
- 1/3 teaspoon black pepper

**Directions:**

1. On Sear/Sauté, set to Medium High, and choose Start/Stop to preheat the pot. Brown the bacon for 2 minutes per side. Set aside.

2. In a bowl, mix honey, salt, mustard, vinegar, water, and black pepper. In the inner pot, add potatoes; chopped bacon, and onions and top with vinegar mixture.
3. Seal the pressure lid, choose Pressure, set to High, and set the timer to 6 minutes. Press Start. When ready, allow the pressure to release naturally for 10 minutes. Place on serving plate and add fresh parsley for garnishing.

## Chicken Broth

**(Ready in about:** 50 min | **Servings:** 16)

**Ingredients:**

- 2 pounds chicken carcasses
- 2 large garlic cloves
- 1 onion, quartered
- 1 sprig fresh thyme
- 1 bunch fresh parsley
- 10 peppercorns
- 2 bay leaves
- 4 carrots, cut into chunks
- 1 cup leeks; chopped
- 1 cup celery; chopped
- Salt to taste

**Directions:**

1. To your Foodi, add chicken carcasses, onion, pepper, thyme, celery, carrots, garlic, parsley, and bay leaves; top with enough water. Seal the pressure lid, press Pressure, set to High, and set the timer to 30 minutes; press Start.
2. When ready, release the pressure quickly. Use a colander to drain the broth and do away with solids. Allow the broth to cool for about 1 hour.

## Applesauce with Cinnamon

**(Ready in about:** 45 min | **Servings:** 4)

**Ingredients:**

- 4 apples, cored; sliced
- ½ cup water
- 1 teaspoon honey
- 1 teaspoon ground cinnamon

**Directions:**

1. Add apples, cinnamon, water, and honey to your Foodi. Seal the pressure lid, choose Pressure, set to High, and set the timer to 4 minutes; press Start. Once ready, release pressure naturally for 10 minutes.
2. If you desire a chunky blend, stir vigorously. For smooth applesauce, puree the mixture in a blender. Allow cooling before transferring in containers for storage.

## Double Bean Zucchini Soup

**(Ready in about:** 35 min | **Servings:** 5)

**Ingredients:**

- 16 oz. zucchini noodles
- 1 onion; chopped
- 2 cloves garlic, minced
- 3 carrots; chopped
- 1 large celery stalk; chopped
- 5 cups vegetable broth
- 1 cup dried chickpeas
- ½ cup dried pinto beans, soaked overnight
- ½ cup dried navy beans, soaked overnight
- 1 tablespoon olive oil
- 1 teaspoon dried thyme
- Sea salt and ground black pepper, to taste

**Directions:**

1. Set your Foogi to Sear/Sauté, set to Medium High, and choose Start/Stop to preheat the pot. Warm oil; stir in garlic and onion and cook for 5 minutes until golden brown.
2. Mix in pepper, vegetable broth, carrots, salt, celery, beans, and thyme.Seal the pressure lid, choose Pressure, set to High, and set the timer to 15 minutes; press Start. Once ready, naturally pressure release for about 10 minutes.
3. Mix zucchini noodles into the soup and stir until wilted. Taste and adjust the seasoning.

## Leek and Potato Soup

**(Ready in about:** 30 min | **Servings:** 5)

**Ingredients:**

- 3 potatoes, peeled and cubed
- 3 leeks, white part only, thinly sliced
- 2 bay leaves
- 2 cloves garlic, minced
- ½ cup sour cream
- 4 cups vegetable broth
- 2 tablespoon butter
- 2 tablespoon rosemary
- 2 tablespoon fresh chives, to garnish
- salt and ground black pepper to taste

**Directions:**

1. Melt the butter on Sear/Sauté. Stir in garlic and leeks and cook for 3 to 4 minutes until soft. Stir in bay leaves, potatoes, and broth. Seal the pressure lid, press Pressure, set to High, and set the timer to 15 minutes; press Start.
2. When ready, release pressure quickly. Remove the bay leaves and cobs and discard.
3. Transfer soup to immersion blender and puree soup to obtain a smooth consistency. Add pepper and salt for seasoning. Apply a topping of and freshly diced chives. Serve with sour cream.

## Chicken Noodle Soup

**(Ready in about:** 15 min | **Servings:** 6)

**Ingredients:**

- 2 chicken breasts, boneless, skinless, cut into bite-size chunks
- 8 ounces dry egg noodles
- 2 garlic cloves, finely diced
- 1 carrot; chopped
- 2 celery stalks; chopped finely
- 6 spring onions; chopped
- 6 cups chicken broth
- 1 tablespoon canola oil
- 2 tablespoon chopped fresh parsley leaves
- Salt and ground black pepper, to taste

**Directions:**

1. Heat oil on Sear/Sauté. Add in celery, spring onion, garlic, and carrots. Cook for 5 minutes until tender. Add in chicken, egg noodles, 1 teaspoon salt, chicken broth, and black pepper.
2. Seal the pressure lid, choose Pressure, set to High, and set the timer to 15 minutes. Press Start. When ready, do a quick release, open the lid and add in parsley. Taste and adjust the seasoning before serving.

## Creamy Mushroom and Quinoa Pilaf

**(Ready in about:** 20 min | **Servings:** 4)

**Ingredients:**

- 1 onion; chopped
- 2 garlic cloves, smashed
- 1 carrot, peeled and chopped
- 1 stalk celery; diced
- ½ cup heavy cream
- 1 cup mushrooms; sliced
- 4 cups vegetable broth
- 2 cups quinoa, rinsed
- 3 tablespoon butter
- 1 teaspoon salt
- ½ teaspoon dried thyme

**Directions:**

1. Melt the butter on Sear/Sauté. Add onion, garlic, celery, and carrot, and cook for 8 minutes until tender. Mix in broth, thyme, quinoa, mushrooms, and salt.
2. Seal the pressure lid, choose Pressure, set to High, and set the timer to 10 minutes; press Start. When ready, release pressure quickly. Carefully open the lid and stir in heavy cream. Cook for 2 minutes to obtain a creamy consistency. Serve warm.

# Egg Rolls

**(Ready in about:** 18 min **| Servings:** 3)

**Ingredients:**
- 1 package egg roll wrappers (12 wrappers)
- 1 large grated carrot
- 1 cup grated mozzarella cheese
- 2 garlic cloves, minced
- ½ onion; chopped
- 1 cup ground beef
- 2 teaspoon olive oil
- ¼ teaspoon salt
- ¼ teaspoon pepper

**Directions:**
1. Place the onion, garlic, carrot, and beef in a saucepan over medium heat, and cook for 6-7 minutes. Take the pan off the heat.
2. Leave to cool for a few minutes, then mix in the mozzarella. Season to taste with salt, and pepper.
3. Grease the Ninja Foodi cooking basket with 1 teaspoon of the olive oil and set aside.
4. Lay the egg roll sheets onto a dry and clean surface; divide the mixture between them. Roll the egg rolls and tuck the corners and edges in to create secure rolls.
5. Lower the rolls into the Ninja Foodi cooking basket and brush them with the remaining olive oil. Close the crisping lid and cook for 13 minutes on Air Crisp mode at 370 F. Once ready, check if the rolls are golden and crispy. Serve with green salad.

# Vegetarian Black Bean Soup

**(Ready in about:** 30 min **| Servings:** 6)

**Ingredients:**
- 30 ounces canned diced tomatoes
- 1 (14 ounces) can black beans, rinsed and drained
- 2 serrano peppers, deseeded and chopped
- 1 onion; chopped
- 2 celery stalks; chopped
- 3 carrots; chopped
- 5 cups vegetable broth
- ¼ cup chopped fresh cilantro
- 1 teaspoon olive oil
- 2 teaspoon ground cumin
- 1 teaspoon fine sea salt
- Black pepper to taste

**Directions:**
1. Set your Foodi to Sear/Sauté, set to Medium High, and choose Start/Stop to preheat the pot.
2. Warm oil; add in carrots, onion, jalapeño peppers and celery and cook for 6 to 7 minutes until soft. Mix in broth, sea salt, black beans, cumin, tomatoes, and cilantro.
3. Seal the pressure lid, press Pressure, set to High, and set the timer to 8 minutes; press Start. Once ready, release pressure naturally for 10 minutes. Season with pepper before serving.

# Lentils Soup with Tortilla Topping

**(Ready in about:** 50 min **| Servings:** 6)

**Ingredients:**
- 1 onion; chopped
- 2 garlic cloves, minced
- 1 cup dry red lentils
- ½ cup prepared salsa verde
- 2 ½ cups vegetable broth
- 1 ½ cups tomato sauce
- 1 tablespoon smoked paprika
- 2 teaspoon ground cumin
- 1 teaspoon chili powder
- ¼ teaspoon cayenne pepper
- Salt and ground black pepper to taste
- Crushed tortilla chips for garnish

**Directions:**
1. To the Foodi, add in tomato sauce and vegetable broth. Stir in onion, salsa verde, cumin, cayenne pepper, chili powder, garlic, red lentils, and paprika. Season with salt and pepper.

2. Seal the pressure lid, press Pressure, set to High, and set the timer to 20 minutes; press Start. Once ready, release pressure naturally for 10 minutes. Divide into serving bowls and add crushed tortilla topping.

## Cauliflower Cheese Soup

**(Ready in about:** 20 min | **Servings:** 5)

**Ingredients:**

- 1 large head cauliflower, cut into florets
- 4 ounces blue cheese
- 1 potato, peeled and finely diced
- 1 bay leaf
- 1 onion; chopped
- 2 stalks celery; chopped
- 3 cups vegetable broth
- 2 cups milk
- 2 tablespoon butter
- ½ tablespoon olive oil

**Directions:**

1. Set your Foodi to Sear/Sauté, set to Medium High, and choose Start/Stop to preheat the pot. Warm oil and butter.
2. Add celery and onion and sauté for 3 to 5 minutes until onion becomes fragrant; stir in half the cauliflower and cook for 5 minutes until golden brown. Add in stock, bay leaf and the remaining cauliflower.
3. Seal the pressure lid, choose Pressure, set to High, and set the timer to 5 minutes; press Start. When ready, release the pressure quickly. Remove the bay leaf and discard.
4. Place the soup in an immersion blender, add in the milk and puree until smooth. Spoon the soup into serving bowls and top with blue cheese before serving.

## Chicken Farro Soup

**(Ready in about:** 1 hr | **Servings:** 6)

**Ingredients:**

- 4 boneless, skinless chicken thighs
- 1 large onion; sliced
- 2 celery stalks, cut into squares
- 1 bay leaf
- 3 large carrots; sliced
- 6 cups chicken broth
- ¼ cup white wine
- 1 cup farro
- 1 tablespoon olive oil
- 1 teaspoon garlic powder
- 1 teaspoon ground cumin
- 2 teaspoon fresh parsley leaves to garnish

**Directions:**

1. Warm oil on Sear/Sauté. Brown the chicken on all sides, approximately 6 minutes. Transfer the chicken to a bowl.
2. Into the pot, add wine to deglaze, scraping any brown bits present at the bottom of the cooker. Mix the wine with farro, cumin, stock, onion, carrots, celery, garlic powder, and bay leaf.
3. Close the lid and turn steam vent to sealing. Seal the pressure lid, choose Pressure, set to High, and set the timer to 20 minutes; press Start.
4. When cooking is done, naturally release the pressure for about 10 minutes. Divide between serving bowls and add parsley for garnish.

## Cream of Spinach and Mushroom Soup

**(Ready in about:** 25 min | **Servings:** 4)

**Ingredients:**

- 8 Button Mushrooms; sliced
- 2 sweet potatoes, peeled and chopped
- 1 red onion; chopped
- 1 cup creme fraiche
- 4 cups vegetable stock
- 1 cup spinach; chopped
- 2 tablespoon white wine
- 1 tablespoon olive oil
- 1 tablespoon dry Porcini mushrooms, soaked and drained
- ½ teaspoon sea salt
- ½ teaspoon black pepper

**Directions:**

1. Set your Foodi to Sear/Sauté, set to Medium High, and choose Start/Stop to preheat the pot. Press Start. Add in olive oil and sliced mushrooms and cook for 3 to 5 minutes until browning on both sides; set aside.
2. Add onion and spinach, and cook for 3 to 5 minutes until onion is translucent. Stir in chopped mushrooms, and cook for a further 5 minutes as you stir occasionally until golden brown.
3. Pour in wine to deglaze the bottom of the pot, scrape the bottom to remove browned bits. Cook for 5 minutes until all the wine evaporates.
4. Mix in the remaining chopped fresh mushrooms, potatoes, soaked mushrooms, wine, vegetable stock, and salt.
5. Seal the pressure lid, choose Pressure, set to High, and set the timer to 5 minutes. Press Start. Once cooking is complete, do a quick release.
6. Add in pepper and creme fraiche to mix. Using an immersion blender, whizz the mixture until smooth. Stir in the sautéed mushrooms. Add reserved mushrooms for garnish before serving.

## Minestrone Soup

**(Ready in about:** 25 min | **Servings:** 6)

**Ingredients:**

- 1 yellow onion; diced
- 1 (14 ounces) can Navy beans, rinsed and drained
- 1 (28 ounces) can diced tomatoes
- 1 (6 ounces) can tomato paste
- 2 cloves garlic, minced
- 1 carrot, peeled and diced
- 2 bay leaves
- 1 green bell pepper; chopped
- 3 cups chicken broth
- 1 cup celery; chopped
- 2 cups kale
- ½ cup white rice
- ¼ cup Parmesan cheese
- 2 tablespoon olive oil
- ½ teaspoon dried oregano
- ½ teaspoon dried parsley
- ½ teaspoon dried thyme
- ½ teaspoon salt
- ¼ teaspoon ground black pepper

**Directions:**

1. Warm olive oil on Sear/Sauté. Stir in carrot, celery and onion and cook for 5 to 6 minutes until soft. Add garlic and bell pepper and cook for 2 minutes as you stir until aromatic.
2. Stir in pepper, thyme, stock, salt, parsley, oregano, tomatoes, bay leaves, and tomato paste to dissolve; mix in rice. Seal the pressure lid, choose Pressure, set to High, and set the timer to 15 minutes; press Start. Once ready, do a quick pressure release.
3. Add kale to the liquid and stir. Use residual heat in slightly wilting the greens. Get rid of bay leaves. Stir in navy beans. Serve topped with parmesan cheese.

## Mexican Chicken Soup

**(Ready in about:** 35 min | **Servings:** 5)

**Ingredients:**

- 5 boneless, skinless chicken thighs
- 14 ounces canned whole tomatoes; chopped
- 1 (14.5 ounces) can black beans, rinsed and drained
- 5 cups chicken broth
- 2 cups frozen corn kernels, thawed
- ¼ cup Cheddar cheese, shredded for garnish
- 2 jalapeno peppers, stemmed, cored, and chopped
- 3 cloves garlic, minced
- 2 tablespoon tomato puree
- 1 tablespoon chili powder
- 1 tablespoon ground cumin
- ½ teaspoon dried oregano
- Crushed tortilla chips for garnish
- Fresh cilantro; chopped for garnish

**Directions:**
1. Place the chicken in your pressure cooker; add oregano, garlic, tomato puree, chicken stock, cumin, tomatoes, chili powder, and jalapeno peppers.
2. Seal the pressure lid, choose Pressure, set to High, and set the timer to 10 minutes; press Start. When ready, release pressure quickly. Transfer the chicken to a large plate.
3. On Sear/Sauté cook corn and black beans. Shred the chicken with a pair of forks, and return to the pot, stirring well. Simmer the soup for 5 minutes until heated through. Divide in serving plates; add a topping of cilantro, shredded cheese and crushed tortilla chips.

## French Onion Soup

(**Ready in about:** 45 min | **Servings:** 8)

**Ingredients:**
- 8 cups thinly sliced onions
- ½ cup dry white wine
- 4 cups beef stock
- 1 cup Swiss cheese, shredded
- ½ cup water
- 4 baguette slices
- 2 sprigs fresh thyme
- 2 bay leaves
- 2 tablespoon butter
- 2 teaspoon sugar
- 1 teaspoon salt
- ½ teaspoon ground black pepper

**Directions:**
1. Melt butter on Sear/Sauté. Add in onions and cook for 3 to 5 minutes until soft. To the onions, add water, pepper, sugar, and salt, and pepper as you stir.
2. Seal the pressure lid, press Pressure, set to High, and set the timer to 15 minutes; press Start. Once ready, do a quick release. Add beef stock, bay leaves and thyme sprigs into the pot.
3. Seal the pressure lid again, choose Pressure, set to High, and set the timer to 4 minutes; press Start. Quick-release pressure. Remove the bay leaves and thyme and discard. Preheat the oven's broiler.
4. Divide into four soup bowls. Top with ¼ cup swiss cheese and 1 baguette slice. Transfer the bowls to a baking sheet and cook for 2 to 4 minutes under the broiler until golden brown.

## Vegetable Stock

(**Ready in about:** 55 min | **Servings:** 10)

**Ingredients:**
- 2 onions; chopped
- 2 carrots; chopped
- 4 garlic cloves
- 10 peppercorns
- 2 bay leaves
- 8 cups cold water, filtered
- 1 cup bell pepper; chopped
- 2 cups celery; chopped
- 1 cup kale
- A handful of rosemary
- A handful of parsley
- Salt to taste

**Directions:**
1. In the pot, add onions, carrots, parsley, bay leaves, garlic, kale, celery, rosemary, and peppercorns; top with cold water. Seal the pressure lid, press Pressure, set to High, and set the timer to 15 minutes; press Start.
2. Release pressure naturally for 15 minutes, then release the remaining pressure quickly. Use a wide and shallow bowl to hold the stock you strain through a fine-mesh strainer.
3. Allow cool to room temperature. Seal into jars and place in the refrigerator for a maximum of 2 weeks.

## Ragu Bolognese

**(Ready in about:** 45 min | **Servings:** 10)

**Ingredients:**

- 2 pounds ground beef
- 4 ounces bacon; chopped
- 2 (28 ounces) cans crushed tomatoes
- 3 bay leaves
- 1 large onion, minced
- 2 celery stalks, minced
- 2 large carrots, minced
- ½ cup yogurt
- 1/4 cup chopped fresh basil
- 1 tablespoon butter
- 3 tablespoon dry white wine
- 1 teaspoon salt
- ½ teaspoon black pepper

**Directions:**

1. Set your Foodi on Sear/Sauté, set to Medium High, and choose Start/Stop to preheat the pot. Place in bacon and cook until crispy for 4 to 5 minutes.
2. Mix in celery, butter, carrots, and onion, and continue cooking for about 5 minutes until vegetables are softened. Mix in ¼ teaspoon pepper, ½ teaspoon salt, and beef, and cook for 4 minutes until golden brown.
3. Stir in the wine and allow to soak, approximately 4 more minutes. Add in bay leaves, tomatoes, and remaining pepper and salt.
4. Seal the pressure lid, choose Pressure, set to High, and set the timer to 15 minutes. Press Start. Once ready, release pressure naturally for 10 minutes. Add yogurt and stir. Serve alongside noodles and use basil to garnish.

## Tomato Soup

**(Ready in about:** 1 hr | **Servings:** 6)

**Ingredients:**

- 28 ounces canned tomatoes
- 1 onion; chopped
- 1 carrot, peeled and chopped
- 1 garlic clove, minced
- 4 Monterey Jack cheese; sliced
- 4 slices of bread
- 2 Gouda cheese; sliced
- 1 cup vegetable stock
- 1 cup heavy cream
- 4 tablespoon butter; at room temperature
- 2 tablespoon olive oil
- 2 tablespoon parsley, finely chopped
- Salt and ground black pepper to taste

**Directions:**

1. Warm oil on Sear/Sauté. Add in garlic, onion, carrot, pepper and salt and sauté for 6 minutes until soft. In the pot, add vegetable stock to deglaze. Scrape any brown bits from the pot.
2. Mix the stock with tomatoes. Seal the pressure lid, choose Pressure, set to High, and set the timer to 30 minutes; press Start. When the cooking is over, let naturally release pressure; for about 10 minutes.
3. Transfer soup to immersion blender and process to get a smooth consistency. Add in heavy cream and stir; add pepper and salt for seasoning.
4. Place 2 slices Monterey Jack cheese onto 1 bread slice and cover with 1 Gouda cheese slice, and the second slice of bread. Spread a tablespoon of butter and parsley over the top. Do the same with the rest of the cheese, bread, parsley, and butter.
5. Place the sandwiches on the crisping basket. Spread 1 tablespoon butter on top of each sandwich. Close the crisping lid, choose Air Crisp, set the temperature to 390°F, and set the time to 5 minutes. After 3 minutes, flip the sandwiches and cook for 2 more minutes.
6. When cooking ended, the sandwiches should be browned and all the cheese melt. Transfer sandwiches to a cutting board and chop into bite-sized cubes. Divide the soup into serving plates and apply a topping of parsley cheese croutons before serving.

## Spicy Soup with Collard Greens

**(Ready in about:** 20 min | **Servings:** 4)

**Ingredients:**

- 1 (1-pound) package fresh collard greens, trimmed
- 1 red chilli; sliced to serve
- 10 ounces ramen noodles
- 6 cups chicken broth stock
- 1 cup mushrooms; sliced
- A bunch of fresh cilantro; chopped to serve
- 2 tablespoon soy sauce
- 1 tablespoon olive oil
- 2 tablespoon garlic, minced
- 1 tablespoon chili powder
- ½ teaspoon ground ginger

**Directions:**

1. Set your Foodi to Sear/Sauté, set to Medium High, and choose Start/Stop to preheat the pot. Warm oil; stir in garlic and ginger and cook for 2 minutes until soft.
2. Add vegetable stock to the pot. Mix in chili powder, ramen noodles and soy sauce. Seal the pressure lid, press Pressure, set to High, and set the timer to 10 minutes; press Start.
3. When ready, release pressure quickly. Stir in collard greens until wilted. Ladle the soup into serving bowls and add red chili and cilantro to serve.

## Butternut Squash Curry

**(Ready in about:** 30 min| **Servings:** 5)

**Ingredients:**

- 1½ pounds butternut squash, roughly chopped
- 4 spring onions; chopped into lengths
- 4 cups chicken stock
- ½ cup buttermilk
- 1½ teaspoon ground cumin
- ¼ teaspoon cayenne pepper, or more to taste
- 1½ teaspoon ground turmeric
- 2 tablespoon curry powder
- 2 bay leaves
- A bunch of cilantro leaves; chopped
- salt and ground black pepper, to taste

**Directions:**

1. In your pressure cooker's pot, stir in squash, buttermilk, curry powder, turmeric, spring onions, stock, cumin, and cayenne pepper. Apply pepper and salt for seasoning. Add bay leaves to the liquid and ensure they are submerged.
2. Seal the pressure lid, choose Pressure, set to High, and set the timer to 10 minutes. When ready, naturally release the pressure for 10 minutes. Discard bay leaves.
3. Transfer the soup to a blender and process until smooth. Use a fine-mesh strainer to strain the soup. Divide into plates and garnish with cilantro before serving.

# Poultry Recipes

## Dumplings and Italian Season Chicken

**(Ready in about:** 40 min | **Servings:** 4)

**Ingredients:**
**For the Dumplings**

- 6 ounces self-rising flour
- ¾ cup heavy cream
- 1 large egg
- 1 teaspoon dried mixed herbs

**For the Chicken**

- 1¼ lb. skinless, boneless chicken thighs; cubed
- 2 large celery stalks; chopped
- 3 large carrots; cut into coins
- 3 cups chicken stock
- ⅔ cup peas, frozen
- 1 cup frozen pearl onions
- 3 tablespoon butter
- 3 tablespoon flour
- 1 teaspoon Italian seasoning mix
- 1 bay leaf

**Directions:**

1. To make the dumplings, whisk the egg and cream in a medium bowl until evenly combined and stir in the flour and mixed herbs until a stiff but soft dough forms. Refrigerate the dough while you make the chicken.
2. Select Sear/Sauté and adjust to Medium and press Start to preheat the pot for 5 minutes. Melt the butter, stir in the flour and Italian seasoning. Cook for 3 to 4 minutes, stirring occasionally, until the roux is golden brown. Pour in stock, whisking until combined.
3. Cook until the sauce has slightly thickened. Add the chicken, bay leaf, celery, and carrots to the inner pot. Seal the pressure lid, choose Pressure; adjust the pressure to High and the cook time to 6 minutes; press Start.
4. Once ready, perform a quick pressure release and carefully open the lid. Remove and discard the bay leaf. Stir in the peas and onion.
5. Take out the dumpling from the fridge and drop in small spoonfuls into the chicken and vegetables. Seal the pressure lid, choose Pressure; adjust the pressure to High and the cook time to 2 minutes; press Start.
6. After cooking, perform a quick pressure release and carefully open the lid. The dumplings will have cooked through and be pale in color.
7. Close the crisping lid and Choose Broil. Adjust the cook time to 7 minutes; press Start. When done cooking, the dumplings should be golden brown on top. Ladle into bowls and serve.

## Chicken with Tomato Salsa.

**(Ready in about:** 30 min | **Servings:** 4)

**Ingredients:**

- 4 chicken thighs; skinless but with bone
- 1 large red bell pepper, seeded and diced
- 1 large green bell pepper, seeded and diced
- 1 Red onion; diced
- 1 bay leaf
- ½ cup chicken broth
- 1 cup crushed tomatoes
- 1 tablespoon chopped basil
- 4 tablespoon olive oil
- ½ teaspoon dried oregano
- Salt and black pepper to taste

**Directions:**

1. Place the chicken on a clean flat surface and season with salt and pepper. Select Sear/Sauté mode on High, and heat the oil.
2. Once heated add the chicken to brown on both sides for 6 minutes. Then, add the onions and peppers. Cook for 5 minutes until nice and soft.

3. Add bay leaf, salt, broth, pepper, and oregano. Stir using a spoon. Close the pressure lid, secure the pressure valve, and select Pressure mode on High for 15 minutes. Press Start/Stop.
4. Once the timer has ended, do a natural pressure release for 5 minutes. Discard the bay leaf. Stir in tomatoes, close the crisping lid, select Broil mode and cook for 25 minutes.
5. Dish the chicken with the sauce into a serving bowl and garnish with the chopped basil. Serve over a bed of steamed squash spaghetti.

## Tandoori Chicken Thighs

**(Ready in about:** 45 min | **Servings:** 4)

**Ingredients:**

- 1½ pounds chicken thighs, boneless skinless
- 1 cup long grain white rice, rinsed and drained
- ½ cup cooked lima beans
- 1 cup plain Greek yogurt
- ¾ cup coconut milk
- ¼ cup water
- 1 tablespoon chopped fresh parsley
- 1 tablespoon ginger puree
- ½ teaspoon ground cumin
- 1 teaspoon turmeric powder
- 1 teaspoon sweet paprika
- ½ teaspoon chili pepper
- 1½ teaspoon garlic puree
- ½ teaspoon garam masala
- ⅛ teaspoon freshly ground black pepper
- 2½ teaspoon salt
- Cooking spray

**Directions:**

1. Season the chicken on both sides with salt and place the meat in a plastic zipper bag. Set aside and make the marinade.
2. In a medium bowl, mix the yogurt, salt, garlic, ginger, paprika, chili pepper, garam masala, cumin, turmeric, and black pepper. Pour the marinade over the chicken. Zip the bag and rub the marinade on the chicken to coat properly. Set aside.
3. Pour the rice into the Foodi's inner pot and mix in the coconut milk, water, and some salt to taste. Seal the pressure lid, choose Pressure; adjust the pressure to High and the cook time to 3 minutes. Press Start to commence cooking the rice.
4. After cooking, perform a natural pressure release for 6 minutes and then a quick pressure release to let out the remaining pressure. Carefully open the lid.
5. Stir in the lima beans and cover the rice with aluminum foil to prevent the rice from drying out. Oil the reversible rack with cooking spray. Place in the pot and slide the legs of the rack under the foil.
6. Remove the chicken from the marinade, hold for a while to allow the excess liquid drip back into the bag. Arrange the chicken on the greased rack in a single layer.
7. Close the crisping lid and choose Broil. Adjust the cook time to 16 minutes. Press Start/Stop. After 8 minutes, open the lid and flip the chicken and close the lid. Cook until the second side is crisp and browned on the edges. Serve the chicken with rice and garnish with the parsley.

## Chicken with Crunchy Coconut Dumplings.

**(Ready in about:** 70 min | **Servings:** 6)

**Ingredients:**

- 1 pound skinless, boneless chicken breasts; cubed
- 1 package refrigerated biscuits, at room temperature
- ½ cup heavy cream
- 2 cups chicken stock
- 1 white onion; chopped
- 2 carrots; diced
- 2 celery stalks; diced
- 1 tablespoon ghee
- 1 teaspoon fresh rosemary
- ½ teaspoon salt

**Directions:**

1. Choose Sear/Sauté on the pot and set to Medium High. Choose Start/Stop to preheat the pot. Melt the ghee and sauté the onion until softened, about 3 minutes.
2. Pour the carrots, celery, chicken, and stock into the pot. Season with the rosemary and salt.
3. Put the pressure lid together and lock in the Seal position. Choose Pressure, set to High, and set the time to 2 minutes. Choose Start/Stop to begin
4. When done cooking, perform a quick pressure release, and carefully open the lid.
5. Stir the heavy cream into the soup. Place the reversible rack in the higher position inside the pot, which will be over the soup and arrange the biscuits in a single layer in the rack.
6. Close the crisping lid. Choose Broil and set the time to 15 minutes. Choose Start/Stop to begin crisping. When ready, allow the biscuit and soup to rest for a few minutes and then serve.

## Herbed Chicken and Biscuit Chili.

**(Ready in about:** 90 min | **Servings:** 6)

**Ingredients:**

- 1½ pounds ground chicken
- 1 package refrigerated biscuits, at room temperature
- 1 onion; chopped
- 2 garlic cloves; minced
- 4 cups chicken broth
- 1 tablespoon olive oil
- 1 tablespoon ground cilantro
- 1 tablespoon dried oregano
- ⅛ teaspoon salt
- ⅛ teaspoon black pepper

**Directions:**

1. Choose Sear/Sauté on the Foodi and set to Medium-High; press Start/Stop to preheat the pot. Pour the oil, chicken, onion, and garlic into the inner pot and sauté until the onion is softened, about 3 minutes. Add the cilantro, oregano, broth, salt, and black pepper to the pot.
2. Put the pressure lid together and lock in the Seal position. Choose Pressure and set to High. Set the time to 10 minutes, then Choose Start/Stop to begin cooking.
3. When the time is over, perform a quick pressure release, and carefully open the lid. Spread the biscuits in a single layer over the chili. Close the crisping lid. Choose Broil and set the time to 15 minutes. Choose Start/Stop to commence browning.
4. When ready, remove the pot from the Foodi and place on a heat-resistant surface. Let the chili and biscuits rest for 10 to 15 minutes before serving.

## Barbeque Chicken and Kale Quesadillas

**(Ready in about:** 40 min | **Servings:** 4)

**Ingredients:**

- 4 medium flour tortillas
- 1 (10-to 12-ounce) bag fresh baby kale
- 1 jalapeño pepper; minced
- 6 ounces shredded Cheddar cheese
- 3 ounces cottage cheese, at room temperature
- ¼ cup minced onion
- 1 cup shredded cooked chicken
- ⅓ cup grated Pecorino Romano cheese
- ¼ cup butter; divided
- 2 teaspoon Mexican seasoning mix
- Cooking spray

**Directions:**

1. On your Foodi, choose Sear/Sauté and adjust to Medium. Press Start to preheat the inner pot. Drop in 1 tablespoon of butter and melt until foaming. Add the kale and cook for 1 to 2 minutes or until wilted while stirring occasionally.
2. Mix in the jalapeño and onion, continue cooking for 3 to 4 minutes, stirring occasionally, until the vegetables have softened and most of the liquid from the kale has evaporated.
3. Mix in the cottage cheese to melt and add the Mexican seasoning and the chicken. Stir to combine. Spoon the filling into a large bowl and stir in the shredded cheddar cheese. Set aside.

4. Use a paper towel to wipe out the inner pot and return the pot to the base. Oil the reversible rack with cooking spray and fix in the upper position of the pot.
5. Close the crisping lid and Choose Air Crisp; adjust the temperature to 375°F and the time to 5 minutes. Press Start to preheat.
6. To assemble the quesadillas, place a tortilla on a clean flat surface. Brush the top with olive oil and sprinkle 1 teaspoon of Pecorino Romano cheese on top. Press the cheese down with the palm of your hand to stick to the tortilla.
7. Spread about a ⅓ cup of filling over half the tortilla, leaving a ¼-inch border. Fold the other half over the filling and press gently. Repeat the process with the remaining tortillas, filling, and Pecorino Romano cheese.
8. Carefully transfer two quesadillas to the prepared rack. Close the crisping lid and Choose Air Crisp; adjust the temperature to 375°F and the cook time to 6 minutes. Press Start.
9. After 3 minutes, or when they are browned on top, use a spatula to flip the quesadillas. Continue cooking until browned on both sides.
10. Once ready, carefully remove the rack from the pot and use the spatula to transfer the quesadillas to the bottom of the pot to keep warm while you work on the other quesadillas.
11. Return the empty rack to the upper position of the pot and place the two remaining uncooked quesadillas on the rack. Repeat the cooking process. Serve the quesadillas with guacamole.

## Turkey Enchilada Casserole

### (**Ready in about:** 70 min | **Servings:** 6)

### Ingredients:
- 1 pound boneless; skinless turkey breasts
- 2 cups shredded Monterey Jack cheese; divided
- 2 cups enchilada sauce
- 1 yellow onion; diced
- 2 garlic cloves; minced
- 1 (15-ounce) can pinto beans, drained and rinsed
- 1 (16-ounce) bag frozen corn
- 8 tortillas, each cut into 8 pieces
- 1 tablespoon butter
- ¼ teaspoon salt
- ¼ teaspoon freshly ground black pepper

### Directions:
1. Choose Sear/Sauté on the pot and set to Medium High. Choose Start/Stop to preheat the pot. Melt the butter and cook the onion for 3 minutes, stirring occasionally. Stir in the garlic and cook until fragrant, about 1 minute more.
2. Put the turkey and enchilada sauce in the pot, and season with salt and black pepper. Stir to combine. Seal the pressure lid, choose Pressure, set to High, and set the time to 15 minutes. Choose Start/Stop.
3. When done cooking, perform a quick pressure release and carefully open the lid. Shred the turkey with two long forks while being careful not to burn your hands. Mix in the pinto beans, tortilla pieces, corn, and half of the cheese to the pot. Sprinkle the remaining cheese evenly on top of the casserole.
4. Close the crisping lid. Choose Broil and set the time to 5 minutes. Press Start/Stop to begin broiling. When ready, allow the casserole to sit for 5 minutes before serving.

## Chicken Tenders with Broccoli

### (**Ready in about:** 70 min | **Servings:** 2)

### Ingredients:
- 4 boneless; skinless chicken tenders
- 1 head broccoli; cut into florets
- ¼ cup barbecue sauce
- ¼ cup lemon marmalade
- 1 cup basmati rice
- 1 cup + 2 tablespoon water
- ½ tablespoon soy sauce
- 1 tablespoon sesame seeds, for garnish
- 2 tablespoon sliced green onions, for garnish
- 2 tablespoon melted butter; divided
- ¼ teaspoon salt
- ¼ teaspoon freshly ground black pepper
- Cooking spray

**Directions:**

1. Pour the rice and water in the pot and stir to combine. Seal the pressure lid, choose Pressure, set to High, and the timer to 2 minutes. Press Start/Stop to boil the rice.
2. Meanwhile, in a medium bowl, toss the broccoli with 1 tablespoon of melted butter, and season with the salt and black pepper. When done cooking, perform a quick pressure release, and carefully open the lid.
3. Place the reversible rack in the higher position inside the pot, which will be over the rice. Then, spray the rack with cooking spray. Lay the chicken tenders on the rack and brush with the remaining 1 tablespoon of melted butter. Arrange the broccoli around the chicken tenders.
4. Close the crisping lid. Choose Air Crisp, set the temperature to 400°F, and set the time to 10 minutes. Press Start/Stop to begin. In a bowl, mix the barbecue sauce, lemon marmalade, and soy sauce until well combined. When done crisping, coat the chicken with the lemon sauce.
5. Use tongs to turn the chicken over and apply the lemon sauce in the other side. Close the crisping lid, select Broil and set the time to 5 minutes; press Start/Stop.
6. After cooking is complete, check for your desired crispiness and remove the rack from the pot. Spoon the rice into serving plates with the chicken and broccoli. Garnish with the sesame seeds and green onions and serve.

## Chicken with Cilantro Rice

**Ready in about:** 70 min | **Servings:** 4)

**Ingredients:**

- 1 pound bone-in, skin-on chicken thighs
- 1 cup basmati rice
- ¾ cup chicken broth
- ½ cup tomato sauce
- 1 red onion; diced
- 1 yellow bell pepper; diced
- 2 tablespoon ghee divided
- 1 tablespoon cayenne powder
- 1 teaspoon ground cumin
- 1 teaspoon Italian herb mix
- ½ teaspoon salt
- Chopped fresh cilantro, for garnish
- Lime wedges; for serving

**Directions:**

1. Choose Sear/Sauté on the pot and set to Medium High. Choose Start/Stop to preheat the pot. Melt half of the ghee in the pot, and cook the onion for 3 minutes, stirring occasionally, until softened.
2. Include the yellow bell pepper, cayenne pepper, cumin, herb mix, and salt, and cook for 2 minutes more with frequent stirring.
3. Pour the rice, broth, and tomato sauce into the pot. Place the reversible rack in the higher position of the pot, which is over the rice. Put the chicken on the rack.
4. Seal the pressure lid, choose pressure, set to High, and set the time to 30 minutes. Choose Start/Stop to begin cooking the rice. When the time is over, perform a quick pressure release and carefully open the lid.
5. Brush the chicken thighs with the remaining 1 tablespoon of ghee. Close the crisping lid. Choose Broil and set the time to 5 minutes. Press Start/Stop.
6. When ready, check for your desired crispiness and remove the rack from the pot. Plate the chicken, garnish with cilantro, and serve with lime wedges.

## Saucy Shredded Chicken

**(Ready in about:** 35 min | **Servings:** 4)

**Ingredients:**

- 4 chicken breasts, skinless
- 2 cloves garlic; minced
- ½ cup chicken broth
- ¼ cup Sriracha sauce
- ½ cup honey
- 2 tablespoon butter
- ½ teaspoon red chili flakes
- 1 teaspoon grated ginger
- ½ teaspoon Cayenne pepper
- Salt and black pepper to taste
- Chopped scallion to garnish

**Directions:**

1. In a bowl, pour the chicken broth. Mix in honey, ginger, sriracha sauce, red pepper flakes, cayenne pepper, and garlic. Set aside. Put the chicken on a plate and season with salt and pepper. Set aside too. Select Sear/Sauté mode on High on your Foodi.
2. Melt the butter, and add the chicken in 2 batches to brown on both sides for about 3 minutes. Add the chicken back, and pour the pepper sauce over.
3. Close the pressure lid, secure the pressure valve, and select Pressure mode on High for 20 minutes. Press Start/Stop.
4. When ready, do a natural pressure release for 5 minutes and open the lid. Remove the chicken onto a cutting board and shred using two forks.
5. Return the shredded chicken to the pot, close the crisping lid and Select Air Crisp mode. Adjust the time to 4 minutes at 385 degrees F.
6. When ready, transfer the chicken to a serving bowl, pour the sauce over, and garnish with the scallions. Serve with a side of sautéed mushrooms.

## Spinach and Mushroom Chicken Stew

**(Ready in about:** 56 min | **Servings:** 4)

**Ingredients:**

- 4 chicken breasts; diced
- 1 ¼ lb. white Button mushrooms, halved
- 1 large onion; sliced
- 5 cloves garlic; minced
- 1 ½ cup sour cream
- 1 ½ cups chicken stock
- ½ cup spinach; chopped
- 1 bay leaf
- 3 tablespoon olive oil
- 3 tablespoon chopped parsley
- 1 teaspoon Dijon mustard
- 1 ¼ teaspoon cornstarch
- Salt and black pepper to taste

**Directions:**

1. Select Sear/Sauté mode and set to medium High to preheat. Once the pot is ready, heat the olive oil then include the onion and sauté for 3 minutes until soft. Add the mushrooms, chicken, garlic, bay leaf, salt, pepper, Dijon mustard, and chicken broth. Stir well.
2. Close the lid, secure the pressure valve, and press Pressure mode on High pressure for 15 minutes. Press Start/Stop.
3. Once the timer has ended, do a natural pressure release for 5 minutes and carefully open the lid. Stir the stew, remove the bay leaf, and scoop some of the liquid into a bowl. Add the cornstarch to the liquid and mix them until completely lump free.
4. Pour the liquid into the sauce, stir it, and let the sauce thicken to your desired consistency. Top it with the sour cream, close the crisping lid and select Broil mode. Cook for 2 minutes. Garnish with the chopped parsley and serve with steamed green peas.

## Mexican Style Green Chili Chicken

**(Ready in about:** 40 min | **Servings:** 4)

### Ingredients:

- 1½ pounds boneless skinless chicken breasts
- 12 ounces, baby plum tomatoes, halved
- 2 jalapeño peppers, seeded and chopped
- 2 large serrano pepper seeded and cut into chunks
- 2 large garlic cloves; minced
- ½ lime, juiced
- Tortilla chips
- 1 small onion; sliced
- ¼ cup minced fresh cilantro
- ¾ cup chicken stock
- ½ cup shredded Cheddar Cheese
- 1 tablespoon olive oil
- ½ teaspoon salt
- ½ teaspoon ground cumin
- 1 teaspoon Mexican seasoning mix
- Cooking spray

### Directions:

1. Choose Sear/Sauté on your Foodi and adjust to High. Press Start to preheat the inner pot. Heat the olive oil add the plum tomatoes; cook without turning, for 3 to 4 minutes.
2. Add the chicken stock while scraping the bottom of the pot to dissolve any browned bits. Stir in the cumin, Mexican seasoning, and salt. Add the chicken, jalapeños, serrano pepper, garlic, onion, and half the cilantro.
3. Seal the pressure lid, choose pressure; adjust the pressure to High and the cook time to 10 minutes. Press Start.
4. Meanwhile, grease the reversible rack with cooking spray and fix the rack in the upper position of the pot. Cut out a circle of aluminum foil to fit the rack and place on the rack.
5. Lay on a single layer of tortilla chips, sprinkle with half of the Cheddar cheese and repeat with another layer of chips and cheese. Set aside.
6. After cooking, perform a natural pressure release for 5 minutes. Take out the chicken from the pot and set aside. Then, with an immersion blender, purée the vegetables into the sauce.
7. Shred the chicken with two forks and return the pieces to the sauce. Add the remaining cilantro and the lime juice. Taste and adjust the seasoning and carefully transfer the rack of chips to the pot.
8. Close the crisping lid and Choose Air Crisp; adjust the temperature to 375°F and the time to 5 minutes; press Start. When done cooking, open the lid. Carefully take out the rack and pour the chips into a platter. Serve the chili in bowls with the chips on the side.

## Chicken Fried Rice

**(Ready in about:** 60 min | **Servings:** 4)

### Ingredients:

- 1 pound boneless; skinless chicken breasts; diced
- 1 (16-ounce) bag frozen mixed vegetables
- 1 onion; diced
- 4 garlic cloves; minced
- 2 cups chicken broth
- ¼ cup coconut aminos
- 1 cup long grain rice
- 1 tablespoon ghee
- ⅛ teaspoon salt
- ⅛ teaspoon freshly ground black pepper

### Directions:

1. Press Sear/Sauté on the pot and set to Medium High. Choose Start/Stop to preheat the pot. Melt the ghee and sauté the onion for 3 minutes. Add and sauté the garlic until fragrant, about 1 minute. Put the chicken in the pot and season with the salt and black pepper. Cook for 5 minutes to brown the chicken.
2. Pour the chicken broth, coconut aminos, and rice into the pot. Put the pressure lid together and lock the pressure release valve in the Seal position. Choose Pressure, set to High, and set the time to 3 minutes. Choose Start/Stop to begin cooking.
3. When the timer is done, perform a quick pressure and carefully open the lid.

4. Pour the frozen vegetables into the pot. Choose Sear/Sauté and set to Medium High. Choose Start/Stop to begin heating the vegetables through. Cook for 5 minutes while stirring occasionally. When ready, dish the fried rice with chicken and serve.

## Chicken Potato Pot Pie

**(Ready in about:** 70 min | **Servings:** 6)

**Ingredients:**

- 2 pounds boneless chicken breasts; cubed
- 2 potatoes; diced
- 8 oz. frozen sweetcorn
- 1 piecrust, at room temperature
- 4 tablespoon butter
- 1 onion; diced
- 2 garlic cloves; minced
- 1 cup chicken broth
- ½ cup whipping cream
- ½ teaspoon salt
- ½ teaspoon freshly ground black pepper

**Directions:**

1. Choose Sear/Sauté on the pot and set to Medium High. Choose Start/Stop to preheat the inner pot. Melt the ghee and sauté garlic and onion until softened, about 3 minutes.
2. Add the chicken, potatoes, and broth to the pot. Season with the salt and black pepper. Put the pressure lid together and lock in the Seal position. Choose Pressure, set to High, and the time to 10 minutes; press Start/Stop. When done cooking, do a quick pressure release.
3. Select Sear/Sauté and set to Medium High. Choose Start/Stop keep the pot in a simmering mode. Pour the frozen sweetcorn and whipping cream into the pot. Stir until the sauce thickens, about 3 minutes.
4. Place the piecrust on top of vegetables and cream mixture, folding over the edges if necessary. Cut out a small dent in the center of the pie to allow steam to escape when baking.
5. Close the crisping lid. Choose Broil and set the time to 10 minutes; press Start/Stop. When ready, remove the inner pot from the Foodi and place on a heat-resistant surface. Let the potpie rest for 10 to 15 minutes before serving.

## Juicy Orange Chicken

**(Ready in about:** 50 min | **Servings:** 6)

**Ingredients:**

- 6 chicken breasts, boneless, skinless; cubed
- 1 cup orange juice
- 2 cups cooked gnocchi
- ⅓ cup chicken stock
- ¼ cup soy sauce
- 2 tablespoon brown sugar
- 1 tablespoon garlic powder
- 2 tablespoon olive oil
- 1 tablespoon lemon juice
- 1 teaspoon chili sauce
- salt and black pepper to taste

**Directions:**

1. Warm oil on Sear/Sauté. In batches, sear chicken in the oil for 5 minutes until browned. Set aside in a bowl. In your pot, mix orange juice, water, sugar, chili sauce, garlic powder, vinegar, and soy sauce; stir in chicken to coat.
2. Seal the pressure lid, choose Pressure, set to High, and set the timer to 7 minutes; press Start. When ready, release the pressure quickly.
3. Take ¼ cup liquid from the pot to a bowl; stir in cornstarch to dissolve; mix into sauce in the pot until the color is consistent. Press Sear/Sauté. Cook sauce for 5 minutes until thickened; season with pepper and salt. Serve the chicken with gnocchi.

## Sesame Chicken Wings

**(Ready in about:** 65 min | **Servings:** 4)

**Ingredients:**

- 24 chicken wings
- 2 garlic cloves; minced
- 2 tablespoon honey
- 1 tablespoon toasted sesame seeds
- 2 tablespoon sesame oil
- 2 tablespoon hot garlic sauce

**Directions:**

1. Pour 1 cup of water into the Foodi's inner pot and place the reversible rack in the lower position of the pot. Place the chicken wings on the rack.
2. Seal the pressure lid, choose Pressure; adjust the pressure to High and the cook time to 10 minutes. Press Start to begin cooking the chicken.
3. While the wings cook, prepare the glaze. In a large bowl, whisk the sesame oil, hot garlic sauce, honey, and garlic.
4. After cooking, perform a quick pressure release, and carefully open the lid. Remove the rack from the pot and empty the water in the pot. Return the pot to the base.
5. Close the crisping lid and Choose Air Crisp; adjust the temperature to 375°F and the time to 3 minutes to preheat the inner pot. Press Start.
6. Toss the wings in the sauce to properly coat. Put the wings in the Crisping Basket, leaving any excess sauce in the bowl.
7. Place the basket in the Foodi and close the crisping lid. Choose Air Crisp and adjust the cook time to 15 minutes. Press Start to commence crisping.
8. After 8 minutes, open the lid and use tongs to turn the wings. Close the lid to resume browning until the wings are crisp and the glaze set. Before serving, drizzle with any remaining sauce and sprinkle with the sesame seeds.

## Chicken Thighs with Thyme Carrot Roast

**(Ready in about:** 50 min | **Servings:** 4)

**Ingredients:**

- 4 bone-in, skin-on chicken thighs
- 1 ½ cups chicken broth
- 1 cup basmati rice
- 2 carrots; chopped
- 2 tablespoon melted butter
- 2 teaspoon chopped fresh thyme
- 2 teaspoon chicken seasoning
- 1 teaspoon salt; divided

**Directions:**

1. Pour the chicken broth and rice in the pot. Then, put the reversible rack in the pot. Arrange the chicken thighs on the rack, skin side up, and arrange the carrots around the chicken.
2. Put the pressure lid together and lock in the Seal position. Choose Pressure, set to High, and the time to 2 minutes. Choose Start/Stop to begin cooking the chicken.
3. When done cooking, perform a quick pressure release, and carefully open the lid. Brush the carrots and chicken with the melted butter. Season the chicken with the chicken seasoning and half of the salt. Also, season the carrots with the thyme and remaining salt.
4. Close the crisping lid; choose Broil and set the time to 10 minutes. Choose Start/Stop to begin crisping. When done cooking, check for your desired crispiness, and the turn the Foodi off. Spoon the rice into serving plates, and serve the chicken and carrots over the rice.

## Herb Roasted Chicken

(**Ready in about:** 70 min | **Servings:** 4)

**Ingredients:**

- 1 (3½-pound) whole chicken
- ¼ cup coconut aminos
- ½ cup white wine
- 2 limes, juiced
- 6 cloves garlic, grated
- Juice of 1 lemon
- 2 tablespoon Italian herb mix
- 1½ tablespoon ground cumin
- 3 tablespoon olive oil
- 1 tablespoon salt

**Directions:**

1. Remove the neck from inside the chicken's cavity, trim off the excess fat and any remaining feathers. Rinse the chicken thoroughly with water and tie the legs with butcher's twine.
2. Pour the wine and lemon juice into the pot. Place the chicken in the crisping basket and fix the basket in the higher position of the pot.
3. Put the pressure lid together and lock in the Seal position. Choose Pressure and set to High. Set the time to 20 minutes, then Choose Start/Stop to begin cooking the chicken.
4. When the timer is done, perform a quick pressure release, and carefully open the pressure lid. In a bowl, combine the lime juice, the olive oil, coconut aminos, Italian herb mix, cumin, garlic and salt; mix until thoroughly combined. Brush the mixture over the chicken.
5. Close the crisping lid. Choose Air Crisp, set the temperature to 400°F, and set the time to 15 minutes. Choose Start/Stop to begin. If you prefer a crispier chicken, cook further for 5 to 10 minutes.
6. After about 10 minutes, lift the crisping lid and sprinkle the chicken with the fresh rosemary. Close the crisping lid and continue cooking.
7. Carefully open the lid and transfer the chicken to a plate. Let the chicken rest for 10 minutes before cutting and serving.

## Braised Chicken with Mushrooms and Brussel Sprouts

(**Ready in about:** 40 min | **Servings:** 4)

**Ingredients:**

- 4 chicken thighs, bone-in skin-on
- ½ small onion; sliced
- ¼ cup heavy cream
- 1 cup frozen halved Brussel sprouts; thawed
- ½ cup dry white wine
- ⅓ cup chicken stock
- 1 cup sautéed Mushrooms
- 1 bay leaf
- 1 tablespoon olive oil
- 1 teaspoon salt or to taste; divided
- ¼ teaspoon dried rosemary
- Freshly ground black pepper

**Directions:**

1. Season the chicken on both sides with half of the salt. On your pot, Choose Sear/Sauté and adjust to Medium-High. Press Start to preheat the inner pot.
2. Heat olive oil and add the chicken thighs. Fry for 4 to 5 minutes or until browned. Turn and lightly sear the other side, about 1 minute. Use tongs to remove the chicken into a plate and spoon out any thick coating of oil in the pot.
3. Sauté the onion in the pot and season with the remaining salt. Cook for about 2 minutes to soften and just beginning to brown for 2 minutes. Stir in the white wine and bring to a boil for 2 to 3 minutes or until reduced by about half.
4. Mix in the chicken stock, brussel sprouts, bay leaf, rosemary, and several grinds of black pepper. Arrange the chicken thighs on top with skin-side up.
5. Seal the pressure lid, choose Pressure; adjust the pressure to High and the cook time to 5 minutes. Press Start to begin cooking.
6. When the timer is over, perform a quick pressure release and carefully open the lid. Remove the bay leaf. Remove the chicken onto the reversible rack, and stir the mushrooms into the sauce. Carefully set the rack in the upper position of the pot.

7. Close the crisping lid and Choose Bake/Roast; adjust the temperature to 375°F and the cook time to 12 minutes. Press Start to commence browning.
8. When ready, open the lid and transfer the chicken to a platter. Stir the heavy cream into the sauce and adjust the taste with salt and pepper. Spoon the sauce and vegetables around the chicken and serve.

## Lemon and Paprika Chicken Thighs

(**Ready in about:** 26 min | **Servings:** 4)

**Ingredients:**

- 4 chicken thighs
- 1 lemon, zested and juiced
- 1 small onion; chopped
- 2 cloves garlic; sliced
- ½ cup chicken broth
- 1 ½ tablespoon heavy cream
- 1 ½ tablespoon olive oil
- ½ teaspoon garlic powder
- ½ teaspoon red pepper flakes
- ½ teaspoon smoked paprika
- 1 teaspoon Italian Seasoning
- Salt and black pepper to taste
- Lemon slices to garnish
- Chopped parsley to garnish

**Directions:**

1. Preheat the Foodi by selecting Sear/Sauté mode on Medium. Warm the olive oil and add the chicken thighs; cook to brown on each side for about 3 minutes. Remove the browned chicken onto a plate.
2. Melt the butter in the pot, then, add garlic, onions, and lemon juice. Deglaze the bottom of the pot and cook for 1 minute. Add the Italian seasoning, chicken broth, lemon zest, and the chicken.
3. Close the pressure lid, secure the pressure valve, select Pressure on High for 10 minutes. Press Start/Stop.
4. When ready, do a quick pressure release. Open the lid. Stir in the heavy cream. Close the crisping lid and select Broil mode. Set the time to 5 minutes. Serve with the steamed kale and spinach mix. Garnish with the lemons slices and parsley.

## Whole Chicken with Lemon and Onion Stuffing

(**Ready in about:** 55 min | **Servings:** 6)

**Ingredients:**

- 4 lb. whole chicken
- 1 yellow onion, peeled and quartered
- 1 lemon, quartered
- 2 cloves garlic, peeled
- 1 ¼ cups chicken broth
- 1 tablespoon herbes de Provence Seasoning
- 1 tablespoon olive oil
- 1 teaspoon garlic powder
- Salt and black pepper to season

**Directions:**

1. Put the chicken on a clean flat surface and pat dry using paper towels. Sprinkle the top and cavity of the chicken with salt, black pepper, Herbes de Provence, and garlic powder.
2. Stuff the onion, lemon quarters, and garlic cloves into the cavity. In the Foodi, fit the reversible rack. Pour the broth in and place the chicken on the rack. Seal the lid, and select Pressure mode on High for 25 minutes.
3. Press Start/Stop to start cooking. Once ready, do a natural pressure release for about 10 minutes, then a quick pressure release to let the remaining steam out, and press Stop.
4. Close the crisping lid and broil the chicken for 5 minutes on Broil mode, to ensure that it attains a golden brown color on each side.
5. Dish the chicken on a bed of steamed mixed veggies. Right here, the choice is yours to whip up some good veggies together as your appetite tells you.

## Chicken Cassoulet with Frijoles

(**Ready in about:** 60 min | **Servings:** 4)

**Ingredients:**

- 4 small chicken thighs, bone-in skin-on
- 2 pancetta slices; cut into thirds
- 1 medium carrot; diced
- ½ small onion; diced
- Olive oil, as needed
- ½ cup dry red wine
- 1 cup Pinto Beans Frijoles; soaked
- 3 cups chicken stock
- 1 cup panko breadcrumbs
- 1½ teaspoon salt
- ¼ teaspoon black pepper

**Directions:**

1. Season the chicken on both sides with salt and black pepper and set aside on a wire rack. On your Foodi, choose Sear/Sauté and adjust to Medium. Press Start to preheat the inner pot.
2. Add the pancetta slices in a single layer and cook for 3 to 4 minutes or until browned on one side. Turn and brown the other side. Remove the pancetta to a paper towel-lined plate.
3. Put the chicken thighs in the pot, and fry for about 6-7 minutes or until is golden brown on both sides. Use tongs to pick the chicken into a plate.
4. Carefully pour out all the fat in the pot leaving about 1 tablespoon to coat the bottom of the pot. Reserve the remaining fat in a small bowl.
5. Sauté the carrots and onion in the pot for 3 minutes with frequent stirring, until the onion begins to brown. Stir in the wine while scraping off the brown bits at the bottom. Allow boiling until the wine reduces by one-third and stir in the beans and chicken stock.
6. Seal the pressure lid, choose pressure; adjust the pressure to High and the cook time to 25 minutes. Press Start to commence cooking.
7. When done cooking, perform a quick pressure release and carefully open the lid. Return the chicken to the pot and cook for 10 minutes.
8. Combine the breadcrumbs with the reserved fat until evenly mixed. When done cooking, perform a natural pressure release for 5 minutes, then a quick pressure release to let out any remaining steam, and carefully open the lid.
9. Crumble the pancetta over the cassoulet. Spoon the breadcrumbs mixture on top of the beans while avoiding the chicken as much as possible.
10. Close the crisping lid; choose Broil, adjust the cook time to 7 minutes, and press Start/Stop. When the cassoulet is ready, allow resting for a few minutes before serving.

## Refried Black Beans and Chicken Fajitas

(**Ready in about:** 40 min | **Servings:** 4)

**Ingredients:**

- 1 pound chicken breasts; sliced
- 1 large (27-ounce) can black beans
- 1 yellow bell pepper; sliced
- 1 garlic clove, crushed
- 1 bacon slice, halved widthwise
- 1 red bell pepper; sliced
- 1 small onion; cut into 8 wedges
- 1 jalapeño pepper; sliced
- ¼ cup water
- 1 tablespoon Mexican seasoning mix
- 4 tablespoon olive oil; divided
- 1 teaspoon salt
- Corn tortillas to serve
- Avocado slices to serve
- Salsa to serve

**Directions:**

1. Pour the beans with liquid into the Foodi's inner pot. Stir in the garlic, bacon, water, and 2 tablespoons of olive oil. Seal the pressure lid, choose Pressure; adjust to High and the cook time to 5 minutes. Press Start.
2. In a large bowl, mix the chicken, yellow and red bell peppers, jalapeño, and onion. Drizzle with the remaining oil, sprinkle with the salt and Mexican seasoning and toss to coat. Set aside.

3. When the beans are ready, do a quick pressure release, and carefully open the lid. Pour out the beans with liquid into a large bowl and cover with aluminum foil to keep warm; set aside.
4. Place the Crisping Basket into the inner pot. Close the crisping lid and select Air Crisp. Adjust the temperature to 375°F and the time to 4 minutes. Press Start to preheat.
5. Uncover the beans. Remove and discard the bacon pieces and garlic clove. Fetch out about ¼ cup of the liquid and reserve it. Then, use a potato masher to break the beans into the remaining liquid until smooth while adding more liquid if needed. Cover the bowl again with aluminum foil.
6. When the pot has preheated, open the lid and add the vegetables and chicken to the basket. Close the crisping lid. Choose Air Crisp; adjust the temperature to 375°F and the cook time to 10 minutes. Press Start to begin browning.
7. After 5 minutes, open the lid and use tongs to turn the vegetables and chicken. Continue cooking until the vegetables are slightly browned and the chicken tender. Wrap the chicken and beans in warm tortillas and garnish with the avocado and salsa to serve.

## Chicken and Green Bean Coconut Curry

(**Ready in about:** 32 min | **Servings:** 8)

**Ingredients:**
- 4 chicken breasts
- ½ cup chicken broth
- 2 cup green beans; cut in half
- 2 cups coconut milk
- 2 red bell pepper, seeded and cut in 2-inch sliced
- 2 yellow bell pepper, seeded and cut in 2-inch slices
- 4 tablespoon red curry paste
- 2 tablespoon lime juice
- 4 tablespoon sugar
- Salt and black pepper to taste

**Directions:**
1. Add the chicken, red curry paste, salt, pepper, coconut milk, broth, and sugar, in the Foodi inner pot. Close the pressure lid, secure the pressure valve, and select Pressure mode on High for 15 minutes. Press Start/Stop.
2. Once the timer has ended, do a quick pressure release, and open the lid. Remove the chicken onto a cutting board and close the crisping lid. Select Broil mode. Add the bell peppers, green beans, and lime juice.
3. Stir the sauce with a spoon and cook for 4 minutes. Slice the chicken with a knife, pour the sauce and vegetables over and serve warm.

## Cheesy Buffalo Chicken.

Ready in about: 37 min | **Servings:** 4)

**Ingredients:**
- 4 chicken breasts, boneless and skinless
- 2 large white onions, finely chopped
- 4 oz. cream cheese; cubed in small pieces
- 3 cups chicken broth
- ½ cup crumbled Blue cheese + extra for serving
- ½ cup Hot sauce
- 2 cups finely chopped celery
- 1 tablespoon olive oil
- 1 teaspoon garlic powder
- 1 teaspoon dried thyme
- Salt and pepper, to taste

**Directions:**
1. Put the chicken on a clean flat surface and season with pepper and salt. Set aside. Select Sear/Sauté mode on High. Heat in olive oil, add onion and celery. Sauté them, constant stirring, until they are nice and soft, for about 5 minutes.
2. Then, add garlic powder and thyme. Stir and cook for about a minute, and add the chicken, hot sauce, and chicken broth. Season with salt and pepper. Close the pressure lid, secure the pressure valve, and select Pressure mode on High for 15 minutes. Press Start/Stop.
3. Meanwhile, put the blue cheese and cream cheese in a bowl, and use a fork to smash them together. Set the resulting mixture aside.

4. Once the timer has ended, do a natural pressure release for 5 minutes. Take out the chicken on to a flat surface with a slotted spoon and use two forks to shred them. Return shredded chicken to the pot, close the crisping lid, select Broil mode and cook for 5 minutes.
5. Add the cheese to the pot and stir until is slightly incorporated into the sauce. Dish the buffalo chicken soup into bowls. Sprinkle the remaining cheese over the soup and serve with sliced baguette.

## Chicken Caesar Salad

(**Ready in about:** 45 min | **Servings:** 4)

**Ingredients:**

- 2 chicken breasts; skinless boneless
- 1 oz. coarsely grated Parmigiano Reggiano cheese
- 1 garlic clove; minced
- ½ small Italian bread loaf; cubed
- ⅓ cup Caesar dressing; divided
- 1 romaine lettuce heart, torn into bite-size pieces
- 1 tablespoon unsalted butter
- 1½ tablespoon olive oil
- ¾ teaspoon salt plus more for sprinkling the croutons
- Grated Parmigiano Reggiano cheese; for serving
- Freshly ground black pepper

**Directions:**

1. Season the chicken with salt on both sides. Pour 1 cup of water into the inner pot. Put the reversible rack in the pot and place the chicken on the rack. Seal the pressure lid, choose Pressure; adjust the pressure to Low and the cook time to 5 minutes. Press Start.
2. Once done cooking, perform a natural pressure release for 8 minutes, and then a quick pressure release to let out any remaining pressure. Carefully open the lid. Set aside.
3. In a heatproof bowl, combine garlic, butter, and olive oil. Put the bowl in the Crisping Basket and place the basket in the pot.
4. Close the crisping lid and Choose Air Crisp; adjust the temperature to 375°F and the cook time to 2 minutes. Press Start to preheat the pot and melt the butter.
5. When done preheating, take out the basket from the pot and the bowl from the basket.
6. Pour the bread cubes into the bowl and toss to be well-coated in the butter and oil. Transfer the bread to the Crisping Basket and the basket into the pot.
7. Close the crisping lid and Choose Air Crisp; adjust the temperature to 375°F and the cook time to 10 minutes; press Start.
8. After 5 minutes, open the lid and toss the bread. Close the lid and continue cooking until the croutons are golden brown. Remove the basket from the pot and lightly season the croutons with salt. Allow cooling.
9. Cut the chicken into bite-size chunks. In a small bowl, toss the chicken with 3 tablespoons of Caesar dressing and set aside.
10. Place the lettuce on a salad bowl, pour the remaining dressing over nad toss to coat well. Mix with chesse and black pepper. Share the salad into four bowls, top with chicken, then croutons, and sprinkle with extra cheese.

## Chicken Breasts

(**Ready in about:** 15 min | **Servings:** 4)

**Ingredients:**

- 4 boneless; skinless chicken breasts
- 1/4 cup dry white wine
- 1 cup water
- ½ teaspoon marjoram
- ½ teaspoon sage
- ½ teaspoon rosemary
- ½ teaspoon mint
- ½ teaspoon salt

**Directions:**

1. Sprinkle salt over the chicken and set in the pot of the Foodi. Mix in mint, rosemary, marjoram, and sage. Pour wine and water around the chicken.
2. Seal the pressure lid, choose Pressure, set to High, and set the timer to 6 minutes. Press Start. Release the pressure naturally for 10 minutes.

## Chicken Chickpea Chili

**(Ready in about:** 25 min | **Servings:** 4)

**Ingredients:**

- 1 pound boneless; skinless chicken breast; cubed
- 2 (14.5 ounces) cans chickpeas, drained and rinsed
- 1 jalapeño pepper; diced
- 1 lime; cut into six wedges
- 3 large serrano peppers; diced
- 1 onion; diced
- ½ cup chopped fresh cilantro
- ½ cup shredded Monterey Jack cheese
- 2 ½ cups water; divided
- 1 tablespoon olive oil
- 2 tablespoon chili powder
- 1 teaspoon ground cumin
- 1 teaspoon minced fresh garlic
- 1 teaspoon salt

**Directions:**

1. Warm oil on Sear/Sauté. Add in onion, serrano peppers, and jalapeno pepper and cook for 5 minutes until tender; add salt, cumin and garlic for seasoning.
2. Stir chicken with vegetable mixture; cook for 3 to 6 minutes until no longer pink; add 2 cups water and chickpeas.
3. Seal the pressure lid, choose Pressure, set to High, and set the timer to 5 minutes. Press Start. Release pressure naturally for 5 minutes. Press Start. Stir chili powder with remaining ½ cup water; mix in chili.
4. Press Sear/Sauté. Boil the chili as you stir and cook until slightly thickened. Divide chili into plates; garnish with cheese and cilantro. Over the chili, squeeze a lime wedge.

## Sticky Orange Chicken

**(Ready in about:** 30 min | **Servings:** 4)

**Ingredients:**

- 2 chicken breasts; cubed
- 1 cup diced orange
- ⅓ cup soy sauce
- ⅓ cup chicken stock
- ⅓ cup hoisin sauce
- 3 cups hot cooked quinoa
- ½ cup honey
- ½ cup orange juice
- 1 garlic clove; minced
- 2 teaspoon cornstarch
- 2 teaspoon water

**Directions:**

1. Arrange the chicken to the bottom of the Foodi's pot. In a bowl, mix honey, soy sauce, garlic, hoisin sauce, chicken stock, and orange juice, until the honey is dissolved; pour the mixture over the chicken.
2. Seal the pressure lid, choose Pressure, set to High, and set the timer to 7 minutes. Press Start. When ready, release the pressure quickly. Take the chicken from the pot and set to a bowl. Press Sear/Sauté.
3. In a small bowl, mix water with cornstarch; pour into the liquid within the pot and cook for 3 minutes until thick. Stir diced orange and chicken into the sauce until well coated. Serve with quinoa.

# Thyme Chicken with Veggies

**(Ready in about:** 40 min | **Servings:** 4)

## Ingredients:

- 4 skin-on, bone-in chicken legs
- ½ cup dry white wine
- 1¼ cups chicken stock
- 1 cup carrots, thinly sliced
- 1 cup parsnip, thinly sliced
- 4 slices lemon
- 4 cloves garlic; minced
- 3 tomatoes, thinly sliced
- 2 tablespoon olive oil
- 1 tablespoon honey
- 1 teaspoon fresh chopped thyme
- salt and freshly ground black pepper to taste
- Fresh thyme; chopped for garnish

## Directions:

1. Season the chicken with pepper and salt. Warm oil on Sear/Sauté. Arrange chicken legs into the hot oil; cook for 3 to 5 minutes each side until browned. Place in a bowl and set aside. Cook thyme and garlic in the chicken fat for 1 minute until soft and lightly golden.
2. Add wine into the pot to deglaze, scrape the pot's bottom to get rid of any brown bits of food. Simmer the wine for 2 to 3 minutes until slightly reduced in volume.
3. Add stock, carrots, parsnips, tomatoes, pepper and salt into the pot.
4. Lay reversible rack onto veggies. Into the Foodi's steamer basket, arrange chicken legs. Set the steamer basket onto the reversible rack. Drizzle the chicken with honey then top with lemon slices.
5. Seal the pressure lid, choose Pressure, set to High, and set the timer to 12 minutes. Press Start. Release pressure naturally for 10 minutes. Place the chicken onto a bowl. Drain the veggies and place them around the chicken. Garnish with fresh thyme leaves before serving.

# Crispy Chicken with Carrots and Potatoes

**(Ready in about:** 35 min | **Servings:** 4)

## Ingredients:

- 4 bone-in skin-on chicken thighs
- 1 pound potatoes, quartered
- 2 carrots; sliced into rounds
- 2 dashes hot sauce
- ¼ cup chicken stock
- 2 tablespoon melted butter
- 1 tablespoon olive oil
- 1 teaspoon dried oregano
- ½ teaspoon dry mustard
- ½ teaspoon garlic powder
- ¼ teaspoon sweet paprika
- ½ teaspoon salt
- 2 teaspoon Worcestershire sauce
- 2 teaspoon turmeric powder

## Directions:

1. Season the chicken on both sides with salt. In a small bowl, mix the melted butter, Worcestershire sauce, turmeric, oregano, dry mustard, garlic powder, sweet paprika, and hot sauce to be properly combined and stir in the chicken stock.
2. On your Foodi, choose Sear/Sauté and adjust to Medium-High. Press Start to preheat the inner pot. Heat olive oil and add the chicken thighs and fry for 4 to 5 minutes or until browned. Turn and briefly sear the other side, about 1 minute. Remove from the pot.
3. Add the potatoes and carrots to the pot and stir to coat with the fat. Pour in about half of the spicy sauce and mix to coat. Put the chicken thighs on top and drizzle with the remaining sauce.
4. Seal the pressure lid, choose pressure; adjust the pressure to High and the cook time to 3 minutes; press Start. After cooking, do a quick pressure release, and carefully open the lid.
5. Transfer the chicken to the reversible rack. Use a spoon to gently move the potatoes and carrots aside and fetch some of the sauce over the chicken. Mix the potatoes and carrots back into the sauce and carefully set the rack in the pot.
6. Close the crisping lid and Choose Bake/Roast; adjust the temperature to 375°F and the cook time to 16 minutes. Press Start to begin crisping the chicken. When done cooking, open the lid and transfer the potatoes, carrots and chicken to a serving platter, drizzling with any remaining sauce.

## Chicken Meatballs Primavera

**(Ready in about:** 30 min | **Servings:** 4)

**Ingredients:**

- 1 lb. ground chicken
- ½ lb. chopped asparagus
- 1 cup chopped tomatoes
- 1 cup chicken broth
- 1 red bell pepper, seeded and sliced
- 2 cups chopped green beans
- 1 egg, cracked into a bowl
- 2 tablespoon chopped basil + extra to garnish
- 1 tablespoon olive oil + ½ tablespoon olive oil
- 6 teaspoon flour
- 1 ½ teaspoon Italian Seasoning
- Salt and black pepper to taste

**Directions:**

1. In a mixing bowl, add the chicken, egg, flour, salt, pepper, 2 tablespoons of basil, 1 tablespoon of olive oil, and Italian seasoning. Mix them well with hands and make 16 large balls out of the mixture. Set the meatballs aside.
2. Select Sear/Sauté mode. Heat half teaspoon of olive oil, and add peppers, green beans, and asparagus. Cook for 3 minutes, stirring frequently.
3. After 3 minutes, use a spoon the veggies onto a plate and set aside. Pour the remaining oil in the pot to heat and then fry the meatballs in it in batches. Fry them for 2 minutes on each side to brown them lightly.
4. After, put all the meatballs back into the pot as well as the vegetables. Also, pour the chicken broth over it.
5. Close the lid, secure the pressure valve, and select Pressure mode on High pressure for 10 minutes. Press Start/Stop. Do a quick pressure release. Close the crisping lid and select Air Crisp. Cook for 5 minutes at 400 degrees F, until nice and crispy.
6. Dish the meatballs with sauce into a serving bowl and garnish it with basil. Serve with over cooked pasta.

## Chicken Cordon Bleu

**(Ready in about:** 35 min | **Servings:** 4)

**Ingredients:**

- 2 large boneless skinless chicken breasts
- 12 ounces broccoli; cut into florets
- 4 thin ham slices
- 4 thin slices Emmental cheese
- ⅔ cup panko bread crumbs
- ¼ cup grated Pecorino Romano cheese
- Cooking spray
- 3 tablespoon melted butter
- 4 teaspoon Dijon mustard
- ¾ teaspoon salt

**Directions:**

1. Put the chicken breasts on a cutting board and slice through the breasts to form two thinner pieces from each breast to make 4 pieces in total. Season the chicken on both sides with ½ teaspoon of salt. Pour a cup of water into the inner pot. Put the reversible rack in the lower position of the pot and lay the broccoli florets on the rack. After, put the chicken on the broccoli.
2. Seal the pressure lid, choose Pressure; adjust the pressure to High and the cook time to 1 minute. Press Start to begin cooking the broccoli and chicken.
3. After cooking, perform a quick pressure release and carefully open the pressure lid. Take out the rack and set aside. Pour the water out of the pot and put the pot back on the base.
4. Place the chicken on the cutting board and the broccoli into the pot. Put 1 tablespoon of melted butter on the broccoli florets and sprinkle with the remaining salt. Stir to coat the broccoli with the butter.
5. Grease the reversible rack with cooking spray and fix in the upper position of the pot. Close the crisping lid and Choose Air Crisp; adjust the temperature to 360°F and the time to 4 minutes. Press Start to preheat.
6. Smear 1 teaspoon of mustard on each chicken piece. Lay each ham slice on each chicken and each Emmental cheese slice on each ham.

7. In a small bowl, combine the breadcrumbs, remaining butter, and the Pecorino Romano cheese. Sprinkle the breadcrumb mixture equally over the chicken.
8. Open the crisping lid and carefully transfer the chicken pieces to the rack. Close the crisping lid and choose Air Crisp; adjust the temperature to 360°F and the cook time to 10 minutes; press Start.
9. When done cooking, the crumbs should be crisp and have obtained a deep golden brown. Transfer the chicken pieces to a platter and serve with the broccoli.

## Honey Garlic Chicken

**(Ready in about:** 30 min | **Servings:** 4)

**Ingredients:**
- 4 boneless; skinless chicken breast; cut into chunks
- 4 garlic cloves, smashed
- 1 onion; diced
- ½ cup honey
- 1 tablespoon cornstarch
- 1 tablespoon water
- 2 tablespoon lime juice
- 3 tablespoon soy sauce
- 2 teaspoon sesame oil
- 1 teaspoon rice vinegar
- Salt and black pepper to taste

**Directions:**
1. Mix garlic, onion and chicken in your Foodi. In a bowl, combine honey, sesame oil, lime juice, soy sauce, and rice vinegar; pour over the chicken mixture.
2. Seal the pressure lid, choose Pressure, set to High, and set the timer to 15 minutes. Press Start. When ready, release the pressure quickly.
3. Mix water and cornstarch until well dissolved; stir into the sauce. Press Sear/Sauté. Simmer the sauce and cook for 2 to 3 minutes as you stir until thickened.

## White Wine Chicken

**(Ready in about:** 9 hrs | **Servings:** 4)

**Ingredients:**
- 3 chicken legs; cut into drumsticks and thighs
- 8 oz. Shiitake mushrooms, stems removed and cut into 4 pieces
- ½ bunch thyme; divided
- 3 Shallots, peeled
- 3 skinny carrots; cut into 4 crosswise pieces each
- 2 cloves garlic, crushed
- 2 bacon slices; chopped
- 1 ½ cups dry white wine
- 3 tablespoon butter; divided
- 1 tablespoon flour
- 3 tablespoon chopped parsley for garnishing
- Salt and black pepper to taste

**Directions:**
1. Put the chicken on a clean flat surface and season on both sides with salt and pepper. In a plastic zipper bag, pour the wine.
2. Add half of the thyme and chicken. Zip the bag and shake to coat the chicken well with the wine. Place it in the refrigerator for 6 to 8 hours.
3. After 8 hours, turn on the Foodi on High and fry the bacon on Sear/Sauté mode for about 8 minutes. Remove the bacon without the fat onto a plate using a slotted spoon. Set aside.
4. Pour the mushroom into the pot, season with salt and cook for 5 minutes. Then, remove at the side of the bacon.
5. Remove the chicken from the refrigerator onto a clean flat surface. Take out and discard the thyme but reserve the marinade. Pat the chicken dry with paper towels.
6. Melt half of the butter in the pot on Sauté. Place the chicken in the butter in batches and fry until dark golden brown on each side, about 12 minutes.
7. Add bacon, mushrooms, shallots, garlic, carrots, and a bit of salt. Cook the ingredients for 4 minutes and top with the wine and remaining thyme.

8. Close the pressure lid, secure the pressure valve, and select Pressure mode on High for 15 minutes. Press Start/Stop.
9. Meanwhile, add the flour and the remaining butter in a bowl, and smash them together with a fork. Set aside. Once the timer has ended, do a natural pressure release for 10 minutes.
10. Discard the thyme. Add the flour mixture to the sauce in the pot, stir until well incorporated. Adjust the seasoning with salt and black pepper.
11. Close the crisping lid and select Broil mode. Cook for 4 minutes. Press Start. Garnish with parsley and serve with steamed asparagus.

## Coq au Vin

**(Ready in about:** 60 min | **Servings:** 4)

**Ingredients:**

- 4 chicken leg quarters, skin on
- 4 serrano ham slices; cut into thirds
- 1¼ cups dry red wine
- ⅓ cup chicken stock
- ½ cup sautéed mushrooms
- ¾ cup shallots; sliced

- ¼ cup brown onion slices
- 1 tablespoon olive oil
- 1½ teaspoon tomato puree
- ½ teaspoon brown sugar
- 1½ teaspoon salt
- Black pepper to taste

**Directions:**

1. Season the chicken on both sides with 1 teaspoon of salt and set aside on a wire rack. On the Foodi, choose Sear/Sauté and adjust to Medium. Press Start to preheat the inner pot.
2. Heat the olive oil and place the ham in the pot in a single layer and cook for 3 to 4 minutes or until browned. Remove the ham to a plate and set aside.
3. Add the chicken quarters to the pot. Cook for 5 minutes or until the skin is golden brown. Turn the chicken over and cook further for 2 minutes; remove to a plate.
4. Carefully pour out almost all the fat leaving about a tablespoon to cover the bottom of the pot. Then, stir in the sliced onion and cook until the onion begins to brown.
5. Add ½ cup of red wine, stir, and scrape the bottom of the pan to let off any browned bits. Then, boil the mixture until the wine reduces by about 1/3, about 2 minutes.
6. Pour the remaining red wine, chicken stock, tomato puree, brown sugar, and a few grinds of black pepper into the pot. Boil the sauce for 1 minute, stirring to make sure the tomato paste is properly mixed. Add the chicken pieces with skin- side up, to the pot.
7. Put the pressure lid in place and lock to seal. Choose Pressure; adjust the pressure to High and the cook time to 12 minutes. Press Start to continue cooking.
8. After cooking, perform a natural pressure release for 10 minutes. Remove the chicken from the pot. Pour the sauce into a bowl and allow sitting until the fat rises to the top and starts firming up. Use a spoon to fetch off the fat on top of the sauce.
9. Pour the sauce back into the pot and stir in the mushrooms and pearl onions. Place the chicken on the sauce with skin side up. Close the crisping lid and select Broil. Adjust the cook time to 7 minutes; press Start.
10. When done cooking, open the lid and transfer the chicken to a serving platter. Spoon the sauce with mushrooms and pearl onions all around the chicken and crumble the reserved ham on top.

## Chicken with Roasted Red Pepper Sauce

**(Ready in about:** 23 min | **Servings:** 4)

**Ingredients:**

- 4 chicken breasts; skinless and boneless
- ¼ cup roasted red peppers; chopped
- ½ cup chicken broth
- ½ cup heavy cream
- 1 tablespoon basil pesto
- 1 tablespoon cornstarch
- ⅓ teaspoon Italian Seasoning
- ⅓ teaspoon minced garlic
- Salt and black pepper to taste

**Directions:**

1. In the inner pot of the Foodi, add the chicken at the bottom. Pour the chicken broth and add Italian seasoning, garlic, salt, and pepper.
2. Close the pressure lid, secure the pressure valve, and select Pressure mode on High for 15 minutes. Press Start/Stop.
3. Once the timer has ended, do a natural pressure release for 5 minutes and open the lid. Use a spoon to remove the chicken onto a plate. Scoop out any fat or unwanted chunks from the sauce.
4. In a small bowl, add the cream, cornstarch, red peppers, and pesto. Mix them with a spoon. Pour the creamy mixture into the pot and close the crisping lid.
5. Select Broil mode and cook for 4 minutes. Serve the chicken with sauce over on a bed of cooked quinoa.

## Roasted Chicken with Potato Mash

**(Ready in about:** 70 min | **Servings:** 4)

**Ingredients:**

- 2 bone-in chicken breasts
- ¾ cup chicken stock
- 3 medium Yukon Gold potatoes; scrubbed
- 3 tablespoon melted butter
- 2 tablespoon warm heavy cream
- 2½ teaspoon salt
- 4 teaspoon Cajun seasoning

**Directions:**

1. Pat the chicken dry with a paper towel and carefully slide your hands underneath the skin to slightly separate the meat from the skin.
2. Then in a small bowl, combine the salt and Cajun seasoning, and rub half of the mixture under the skin and cavity of the chicken.
3. Pour the chicken stock into the inner pot of the Foodi. Fix the reversible rack in a lower position of the pot and lay the chicken, on the side in the center of the rack. Also, arrange the potatoes around the chicken.
4. Seal the pressure lid, choose pressure; adjust the pressure to High and the cook time to 13 minutes. Press Start to begin cooking the chicken. Mix the remaining spice mixture with 2 tablespoons of the melted butter, and set aside.
5. When done pressure cooking, perform a natural pressure release for 10 minutes. Remove the potatoes and chicken onto a cutting board. Pour the cooking juices into a bowl and return the rack with chicken only to the pot. Baste the outer side of the chicken with half of the spice- butter mixture.
6. Close the crisping lid and choose Air Crisp; adjust the temperature to 360°F and the cook time to 16 minutes. Press Start. After 8 minutes, open the lid and flip the chicken over. Baste this side with the remaining butter mixture and close the lid to continue cooking.
7. With a potato masher, smoothly puree the potatoes, and add the remaining salt, melted butter, heavy cream, and 2 tablespoons of the reserved cooking juice; stir to combine. Taste and adjust the seasoning with salt and pepper and cover the bowl with aluminum foil to keep warm.
8. After cooking, transfer the chicken to a cutting board, leaving the rack in the pot.
9. Pour the remaining cooking sauce into the pot, choose Sear/Sauté and adjust to Medium-High. Place the bowl of potatoes on the rack to keep warm as the sauce reduces. Press Start and boil the sauce for 2 to 3 minutes or until reduced by about half.

10. Meanwhile, slice the chicken and lay the pieces on a platter. Remove the mashed potato from the pot and remove the rack. Spoon the sauce over the chicken slices and serve with the creamy potatoes.

## Chicken Noodle Soup with Crispy Bacon.

**(Ready in about:** 33 min | **Servings:** 8)

### Ingredients:

- 4 chicken breasts; skinless and boneless
- 1 large white onion; chopped
- 4 cloves garlic; minced
- 2 medium carrots; sliced
- 8 bacon slices; chopped
- 5 oz. dry egg noodles
- 2 cups sliced celery
- ½ cup chopped parsley
- 8 cups chicken broth
- 1 ½ teaspoon dried thyme
- Salt and black pepper to taste

### Directions:

1. Turn on the Foodi, and select Sear/Sauté mode on High. Press Start. Add the chopped bacon and fry for 5 minutes until nicely brown and crispy. Remove to a paper towel to soak up excess oil and set aside.
2. Add the onion and garlic to the pot and cook for 3 minutes until tender. Add the chicken breasts, noodles, carrots, celery, chicken broth, thyme, salt, and pepper. Close the pressure lid, secure the valve to seal, and select Pressure mode on High pressure. Adjust the time to 5 minutes and press Start/Stop.
3. Once the timer has ended, do a quick pressure release, and open the lid. Use a wooden spoon to remove the chicken onto a plate. Shred the chicken with two forks and add it back to the soup.
4. Stir in the bacon. Adjust the seasoning as desired. Close the crisping lid and cook on Broil mode for 5 minutes. Adjust the seasoning. Ladle the soup into serving bowls and serve with a side of bread.

## Mediterranean Chicken Breasts

**(Ready in about:** 30 min | **Servings:** 4)

### Ingredients:

- 4 chicken breasts, skinless
- 1 cup baby spinach, frozen
- ½ cup crumbled Feta cheese
- 1 cup water
- 2 tablespoon olive oil
- ½ teaspoon dried oregano
- ½ teaspoon garlic powder
- 2 teaspoon dried parsley
- Salt and black pepper to taste

### Directions:

1. Wrap the chicken in plastic and put on a cutting board. Use a rolling pin to pound flat to a quarter inch thickness. Remove the plastic wrap.
2. In a bowl, mix spinach, salt, and feta cheese and scoop the mixture onto the chicken breasts. Wrap the chicken to secure the spinach filling in it.
3. Use toothpicks to secure the wrap firmly from opening. Gently season the chicken pieces with oregano, parsley, garlic powder, and pepper.
4. Select Sear/Sauté mode on Foodi Ninja. Heat the oil, add the chicken, and sear to golden brown on each side. Work in 2 batches. Remove the chicken onto a plate and set aside.
5. Pour the water into the pot and use a spoon to scrape the bottom of the pot to let loose any chicken pieces or seasoning that is stuck to the bottom of the pot. Fit the reversible rack into the pot with care as the pot will still be hot.
6. Transfer the chicken onto the rack. Seal the lid and select Pressure mode on High pressure for 10 minutes. Press Start/Stop.
7. Once the timer has ended, do a quick pressure release. Close the crisping lid and cook on Bake/Roast mode for 5 minutes at 370 F. Plate the chicken and serve with a side of sautéed asparagus, and some slices of tomatoes.

# Chicken Florentine

(**Ready in about:** 30 min | **Servings:** 4)

**Ingredients:**

- 4 chicken thighs; cut into 1-inch pieces
- 6 oz. softened cream cheese; cut into small cubes
- 1 cup shredded Pecorino cheese
- 1 cup chopped sun dried tomatoes with herbs
- 2 cups baby spinach
- 1 ½ cups chicken broth
- 2 tablespoon Italian Seasoning
- 1 tablespoon olive oil
- ¼ teaspoon red pepper flakes
- Salt to taste

**Directions:**

1. Pour the chicken broth into the pressure cooker, and add the Italian seasoning, chicken, tomatoes, salt, and red pepper flakes.
2. Stir them with a spoon. Close the lid, secure the pressure valve, and select Pressure mode on High for 12 minutes. Press Start/Stop.
3. Once the timer has ended, do a quick pressure release, and open the lid. Add and stir in the spinach, parmesan cheese, and cream cheese until the cheese melts and is fully incorporated.
4. Close the crisping lid and cook on Broil mode for 5 minutes. Dish the chicken over a bed of zoodles or a side of steamed asparagus.

# Chicken in Masala Sauce

(**Ready in about:** 40 min | **Servings:** 4)

**Ingredients:**

- 2 pounds boneless; skinless chicken thighs,
- 29 ounces canned tomato sauce
- 4 lemon wedges
- 1 lemon, juiced
- 3 tomatoes; chopped
- ½ onion; chopped
- 2 garlic cloves; minced
- ½ cup natural yogurt
- 3 cups cooked basmati rice
- ¼ cup fresh chopped cilantro leaves
- 1½ tablespoon olive oil
- 3 tablespoon tomato puree
- 1 tablespoon garam masala
- 2 teaspoon curry powder
- 1 teaspoon ground coriander
- 1 teaspoon fresh ginger; minced
- ½ teaspoon ground cumin
- ⅛ teaspoon jalapeño pepper, seeded and chopped
- 1 teaspoon salt
- ¼ teaspoon freshly ground black pepper

**Directions:**

1. Apply black pepper and ½ teaspoon salt to the chicken. Set your Foodi to Sear/Sauté, set to Medium High, and choose Start/Stop to preheat the pot. Warm oil.
2. Add garlic and onion and cook for 3 minutes until soft. Stir in tomato puree, garam masala, cumin, curry powder, ginger, coriander, and jalapeño pepper; cook for 30 seconds until fragrant.
3. Stir in remaining ½ teaspoon salt, tomato sauce, and tomatoes. Simmer the mixture as you scrape the bottom to get rid of any browned bits; stir in chicken to coat.
4. Seal the pressure lid, choose Pressure, set to High, and set the timer to 10 minutes. Press Start. When ready, release the pressure quickly. Press Sear/Sauté and simmer the sauce and cook for 3 to 5 minutes until thickened.
5. Stir lemon juice and yogurt through the sauce. Serve garnished with lemon wedges and cilantro.

## Sage Chicken Thighs

**(Ready in about:** 35 min | **Servings:** 4)

**Ingredients:**

- 2 lb. chicken thighs, bone in and skin on
- 1 ½ cups diced tomatoes
- ½ cup balsamic vinegar
- 1 cup chicken broth
- ¾ cup yellow onion
- 2 tablespoon olive oil
- 2 tablespoon chopped parsley
- 2 teaspoon minced garlic
- 3 teaspoon chopped fresh sage
- Salt and pepper, to taste

**Directions:**

1. With paper towels, pat dry the chicken and season with salt and pepper. Select Sear/Sauté mode. Warm the olive and add the chicken with skin side down. Cook to golden brown on each side, for about 9 minutes. Remove onto a clean plate.
2. Then, add onions and tomatoes to the pot and sauté for 3 minutes, stirring occasionally with a spoon. Add in garlic and cook for 30 seconds, until fragrant.
3. Pour the chicken broth, and add some salt, sage, and balsamic vinegar. Stir them using a spoon. Add the chicken back to the pot.
4. Close the lid, secure the pressure valve, and select Pressure mode on High pressure for 15 minutes. Press Start/Stop to start cooking. When ready, do a quick pressure release.
5. Close the crisping lid and cook on Air Crisp mode for 5 minutes at 400 F. Garnish with parsley and serve with roasted tomatoes, carrots, and potatoes.

## Mexican Chicken and Wild Rice Bowls

**(Ready in about:** 30 min | **Servings:** 4)

**Ingredients:**

- 4 chicken breasts
- 1 cup sour cream
- 1 cup wild rice, rinsed
- 1 cup salsa
- 2 cups chicken broth
- 1 green bell pepper, seeded and diced
- 1 red bell pepper, seeded and diced
- 2 ¼ packets Taco Seasoning
- Salt and black pepper to taste

**To Serve:**

- Avocado slices
- Grated cheese, of your choice
- Chopped cilantro

**Directions:**

1. Pour the chicken broth into the inner pot, add the chicken. Pour the taco seasoning over. Add the salsa and stir lightly with a spoon. Close the pressure lid, secure the pressure valve, and select Pressure on High for 15 minutes. Press Start/Stop.
2. Once the timer has ended, do a quick pressure release, and open the lid.
3. Add the wild rice and peppers, and use a spoon to push them into the sauce. Close the pressure lid, secure the pressure valve, and select Pressure mode on High for 8 minutes. Press Start/Stop.
4. Once the timer has ended, do a quick pressure release, and open the lid. Gently stir the mixture, adjust the taste with salt and pepper.
5. Stir in sour cream, close the crisping lid and select Broil mode; cook for 2 minutes. Spoon the chicken dish into serving bowls. Top it with avocado slices, sprinkle with chopped cilantro and some cheese. Serve.

## Chicken Chili with Cannellini Beans

**(Ready in about:** 40 min | **Servings:** 4)

**Ingredients:**

- 3 chicken breasts; cubed
- 2 (14.5 ounces) cans Cannellini beans, drained
- 1 white onion; chopped
- ½ cup heavy whipping cream
- 1 cup sour cream
- 3 cups chicken broth
- 1 tablespoon butter
- 1 teaspoon cumin powder
- 1 teaspoon dried oregano
- Salt and black pepper

**Directions:**

1. Select Sear/Sauté mode and set to Medium. Melt the butter, and add onion and chicken. Stir and let cook the chicken for 6 minutes. Stir in the cannellini beans, cumin powder, oregano, salt, and pepper.
2. Pour in the broth, stir, close the pressure lid, and secure the pressure valve. Select Pressure mode on High for 10 minutes. Press Start/Stop.
3. Once the timer has ended, let the pot sit uncovered for 10 minutes, then do a quick pressure release. Stir in the whipping and sour cream.
4. Close the crisping lid and select Broil mode. Cook for 2 minutes. Serve warm with a mix of steamed bell peppers and broccoli.

## Chicken and Sweet Potato Corn Chowder

**(Ready in about:** 40 min | **Servings:** 8)

**Ingredients:**

- 4 boneless; skinless chicken breast; diced
- 19 ounces corn kernels, frozen
- 1 sweet potato, peeled and cubed
- 4 ounces canned diced green chiles, drained
- 3 garlic cloves; minced
- 2 cups cheddar cheese, shredded
- 2 cups creme fraiche
- 1 cup chicken stock
- Cilantro leaves; chopped
- 2 teaspoon chili powder
- 1 teaspoon ground cumin
- Salt and black pepper to taste

**Directions:**

1. Mix chicken, corn, chili powder, cumin, chicken stock, sweet potato, green chiles, and garlic in the pot of the Foodi. Seal the pressure lid, choose Pressure, set to High, and set the timer to 10 minutes. Press Start.
2. When ready, release the pressure quickly. Set the chicken to a cutting board and use two forks to shred it. Return to pot and stir well into the liquid.
3. Stir in cheese and creme fraiche; season with pepper and salt. Cook for 2 to 3 minutes until cheese is melted. Place chowder into plates and top with cilantro.

## Barbeque Chicken Drumettes

**(Ready in about:** 30 min | **Servings:** 4)

**Ingredients:**

- 2 lb. chicken drumettes, bone in and skin in
- 1 stick butter; sliced in 5 pieces
- ½ cup chicken broth
- BBQ sauce to taste
- ½ tablespoon cumin powder
- ½ teaspoon onion powder
- ¼ teaspoon Cayenne powder
- ½ teaspoon dry mustard
- ½ teaspoon sweet paprika
- Salt and pepper, to taste
- Cooking spray

**Directions:**

1. Pour the chicken broth into the inner pot of Foodi P and insert the reversible rack. In a zipper bag, pour in dry mustard, cumin powder, onion powder, cayenne powder, salt, and pepper.
2. Add the chicken, close the bag and shake to coat the chicken well with the spices. You can toss the chicken in the spices in batches too.
3. Then, remove the chicken from the bag and place on the rack. Spread the butter slices on the drumsticks. Close the lid, secure the pressure valve, and select Pressure mode on High pressure for 10 minutes. Press Start/Stop.
4. Once the timer has ended, do a quick pressure release, and open the lid. Remove the chicken onto a clean flat surface like a cutting board and brush them with the barbecue sauce using the brush. Return to the rack and close the crisping lid. Cook for 10 minutes at 400 F on Air Crisp mode.

## Crunchy Chicken Schnitzels

### (**Ready in about:** 25 min | **Servings:** 4)

**Ingredients:**

- 4 chicken breasts, boneless
- 2 eggs, beaten
- 4 slices cold butter
- 4 slices lemon
- 1 cup flour
- 1 cup breadcrumbs
- 2 tablespoon fresh parsley; chopped
- Cooking spray
- Salt and pepper to taste

**Directions:**

1. Combine the breadcrumbs with the parsley in a dish and set aside. Season the chicken with salt and pepper. Coat in flour; shake off any excess. Dip the coated chicken into the beaten egg followed by breadcrumbs. Spray the schnitzels with cooking spray.
2. Put them into the Foodi basket, close the crisping lid and cook for 10 minutes at 380 F. After 5 minutes, turn the schnitzels over. Arrange the schnitzels on a serving platter and place the butter and lemon slices over to serve.

## Chicken and Quinoa Soup

### (**Ready in about:** 30 min | **Servings:** 6)

**Ingredients:**

- 2 large boneless; skinless chicken breasts; cubed
- 6 ounces quinoa, rinsed
- 4 ounces mascarpone cheese, at room temperature
- 1 cup milk
- 1 cup heavy cream
- 1 cup red onion; chopped
- 1 cup carrots; chopped
- 1 cup celery; chopped
- 4 cups chicken broth
- 2 tablespoon butter
- 1 tablespoon fresh parsley; chopped
- Salt and freshly ground black pepper to taste

**Directions:**

1. Melt butter on Sear/Sauté. Add carrot, onion, and celery and cook for 5 minutes until tender. Add chicken broth to the pot; mix in parsley, quinoa and chicken. Add pepper and salt for seasoning.
2. Seal the pressure lid, choose Pressure, set to High, and set the timer to 5 minutes. Press Start. When ready, release the pressure quickly. Press Sear/Sauté.
3. Add mascarpone cheese to the soup and stir well to melt completely; mix in heavy cream and milk. Simmer the soup for 3 to 4 minutes until thickened and creamy.

# Chicken Wings with Lemon

(**Ready in about:** 40 min | **Servings:** 4)

**Ingredients:**

- 8 chicken wings
- ½ cup chicken broth
- 2 lemons, juiced
- ½ dried oregano
- 2 tablespoon olive oil
- ½ teaspoon cayenne pepper
- ½ teaspoon chili powder
- ½ teaspoon garlic powder
- ½ teaspoon onion powder
- Sea salt and ground black pepper to taste

**Directions:**

1. Coat the chicken wings with olive oil; season with chili powder, onion powder, salt, oregano, garlic powder, cayenne, and pepper.
2. In the steel pot of the Foodi, add your wings and chicken broth. Seal the pressure lid, choose Pressure, set to High, and set the timer to 4 minutes. Press Start. When ready, do a quick pressure release. Preheat an oven to high.
3. Onto a greased baking sheet, place the wings in a single layer and drizzle over the lemon juice. Bake for 5 minutes until skin is crispy.

# Paprika Buttered Chicken

(**Ready in about:** 45 min | **Servings:** 6)

**Ingredients:**

- 3.5-pound whole chicken
- ½ onion, thinly sliced
- 2 cloves garlic; minced
- 1 cup chicken stock
- ½ cup white wine
- 3 tablespoon butter, melted
- ½ teaspoon paprika
- ½ teaspoon ground black pepper
- ½ teaspoon dried thyme
- 1 teaspoon salt

**Directions:**

1. Into the Foodi, add onion, chicken stock, white wine, and garlic. Over the mixture, place the reversible rack. Apply pepper, salt, and thyme to the chicken; lay onto reversible rack breast-side up.
2. Seal the pressure lid, choose Pressure, set to High, and set the timer to 26 minutes. Press Start. When ready, release the pressure quickly.
3. While pressure releases, preheat oven broiler. In a bowl, mix paprika and butter.
4. Remove the reversible rack with chicken from your pot. Get rid of onion and stock.
5. Onto the chicken, brush butter mixture and take the reversible rack back to the pot. Cook under the broiler for 5 minutes until chicken skin is crispy and browned.
6. Set chicken to a cutting board to cool for about 5 minutes, then carve and transfer to a serving platter.

# Chicken Burgers with Avocado

(**Ready in about:** 15 min | **Servings:** 8)

**Ingredients:**

- 1 lb. ground chicken
- 1 tomato; sliced
- 1 red onion; chopped
- 1 Avocado; sliced
- ½ cup mayonnaise
- 1 egg, beaten
- 4 buns, halved
- 1 small red potato, shredded
- A pinch of ground chili
- A pinch of ground cumin
- Fresh cilantro; chopped
- Salt and pepper to taste
- Cooking spray

**Directions:**

1. Mix the chicken, onion, egg, potato, cumin, chili, cilantro, salt, and pepper in a large bowl with your hands until you have an even burger mixture.
2. Shape the mixture into 8 patties. Grease your Foodi basket with cooking spray.

3. Arrange the burgers onto the basket. Close the crisping lid and cook for 10 minutes, at 360 F. After 5 minutes, shake the patties.
4. To assemble your burgers, spread mayonnaise on the bottom of each half of the buns, top with a chicken patty, then put over a tomato slice. Cover with the other half of the buns and arrange on a serving platter to serve.

## Pesto Stuffed Chicken with Green Beans.

**(Ready in about:** 20 min | **Servings:** 4)

**Ingredients:**
- 4 chicken breasts
- ¼ cup dry white wine
- 1 cup green beans, trimmed and cut into 1-inch pieces

**For pesto:**
- ¼ cup Parmesan cheese
- ¼ cup extra virgin olive oil
- 1 cup fresh basil

- ¾ cup chicken stock
- 1 tablespoon butter
- 1 tablespoon olive oil
- 1 teaspoon salt

- 1 garlic clove, smashed
- 2 tablespoon pine nuts

**Directions:**
1. First make the pesto: in a bowl, mix fresh basil, pine nuts, garlic, salt, pepper and Parmesan and place in food processor. Add in oil and process until the desired consistency is attained. Adjust seasoning.
2. Apply a thin layer of pesto to one side of each chicken breast; tightly roll into a cylinder and fasten closed with small skewers. Press Sear/Sauté. Add oil and butter. Cook chicken rolls for 1 to 2 minutes per side until browned.
3. Add in wine cook until the wine has evaporated, about 3-4 minutes. Add stock and salt into the pot. Top the chicken with green beans.
4. Seal the pressure lid, choose Pressure, set to High, and set the timer to 5 minutes. Press Start. When ready, release the pressure quickly. Serve chicken rolls with cooking liquid and green beans.

## Lettuce Carnitas Wraps

**(Ready in about:** 50 min | **Servings:** 6)

**Ingredients:**
- 2 pounds chicken thighs, boneless; skinless
- 12 large lettuce leaves
- 2 cups canned pinto beans, rinsed and drained
- 1 cup pineapple juice
- ⅓ cup water
- ¼ cup soy sauce

- 3 tablespoon cornstarch
- 2 tablespoon maple syrup
- 2 tablespoon canola oil
- 1 tablespoon rice vinegar
- 1 teaspoon chili-garlic sauce
- salt and freshly ground black pepper to taste

**Directions:**
1. Warm oil on Sear/Sauté. In batches, sear chicken in the oil for 5 minutes until browned. Set aside in a bowl. Into your pot, mix chili-garlic sauce, pineapple juice, soy sauce, vinegar, maple syrup, and water; stir in chicken to coat.
2. Seal the pressure lid, choose Pressure, set to High, and set the timer to 7 minutes. Press Start. Release pressure naturally for 10 minutes. Shred the chicken with two forks. Take ¼ cup liquid from the pot to a bowl; stir in cornstarch to dissolve.
3. Mix the cornstarch mixture with the mixture in the pot and return the chicken.
4. Select Sear/Sauté and cook for 5 minutes until the sauce thickens; add pepper and salt for seasoning. Transfer beans into lettuce leaves; apply a topping of chicken carnitas and serve.

## Salsa Chicken with Feta

**(Ready in about:** 30 min | **Servings:** 6

**Ingredients:**
- 2 pounds boneless skinless chicken drumsticks
- 1 cup feta cheese, crumbled
- 1 ½ cups hot tomato salsa
- 1 onion; chopped
- ¼ teaspoon salt

**Directions:**
1. Sprinkle salt over the chicken; set in the inner steel pot of Foodi. Stir in salsa to coat the chicken. Seal the pressure lid, choose Pressure, set to High, and set the timer to 15 minutes. Press Start. When ready, do a quick pressure release.
2. Press Sear/Sauté and cook for 5 to 10 minutes as you stir until excess liquid has evaporated. Top with feta cheese and serve.

## Chicken Fajitas with Avocado

**(Ready in about:** 30 min | **Servings:** 4)

**Ingredients:**
- 4 chicken breasts, boneless and skinless
- 1 (24 ounces) can diced tomatoes
- 3 bell peppers, julienned
- 1 shallot; chopped
- 4 garlic cloves; minced
- 4 flour tortillas
- 1 avocado; sliced
- 1 taco seasoning
- 2 tablespoon cilantro; chopped
- 1 tablespoon olive oil
- Juice of 1 lemon
- salt and pepper to taste

**Directions:**
1. In a bowl, mix taco seasoning and chicken until evenly coated. Warm oil on Sear/Sauté. Sear chicken for 2 minutes per side until browned. To the chicken, add tomatoes, shallot, lemon juice, garlic, and bell peppers; season with pepper and salt.
2. Seal the pressure lid, choose Pressure, set to High, and set the timer to 4 minutes. Press Start. When ready, release the pressure quickly.
3. Move the bell peppers and chicken to tortillas. Add avocado slices and serve.

## Turkey Lettuce Cups

**(Ready in about:** 45 min | **Servings:** 4)

**Ingredients:**
- 1 pound boneless; skinless turkey breasts; cut into strips
- 1 romaine lettuce, leaves separated
- 1 cup coconut milk
- ⅓ cup chopped peanuts
- ¼ cup chopped fresh cilantro leaves
- ¾ cup olive oil
- 4 cloves garlic; minced
- 3 tablespoon rice wine vinegar
- 1 tablespoon Thai-style chili paste
- 3 tablespoon maple syrup
- 2 tablespoon pineapple juice
- 3 tablespoon soy sauce

**Directions:**
1. In the Foodi's pressure, mix peanut butter, garlic, rice wine vinegar, soy sauce, pineapple juice, honey, coconut milk, and chili paste until smooth; add turkey strips and ensure they are submerged in the sauce.
2. Seal the pressure lid, choose Pressure, set to High, and set the timer to 12 minutes. Press Start. When ready, release the pressure quickly. Place the turkey at the center of each lettuce leaf; top with cilantro and chopped peanuts.

## Chicken Cacciatore

**(Ready in about:** 40 min | **Servings:** 4)

**Ingredients:**
- 1 pound chicken drumsticks, boneless, skinless
- ½ cup dry red wine
- ¾ cup chicken stock
- 1 cup black olives, pitted and sliced
- 2 bay leaves
- 1 pinch red pepper flakes
- 1 (28 ounces) can diced tomatoes
- 1 carrot; chopped
- 1 red bell pepper; chopped
- 1 yellow bell pepper; chopped
- 1 onion; chopped
- 4 garlic cloves, thinly sliced
- 2 teaspoon olive oil
- 1 teaspoon dried basil
- 1 teaspoon dried parsley
- 2 teaspoon dried oregano
- 1½ teaspoon freshly ground black pepper
- 2 teaspoon salt

**Directions:**
1. Warm oil on Sear/Sauté. Add pepper and salt to the chicken drumsticks. In batches, sear the chicken for 5-6 minutes until golden-brown. Set aside on a plate. Drain the cooker and remain with 1 tablespoon of fat.
2. In the hot oil, sauté onion, garlic, and bell peppers for 4 minutes until softened; add red pepper flakes, basil, parsley, and oregano, and cook for 30 more seconds. Season with salt and pepper.
3. Stir in tomatoes, olives, chicken stock, red wine and bay leaves.
4. Return chicken to the pot. Seal the pressure lid, choose Pressure, set to High, and set the timer to 15 minutes. Press Start.
5. When ready, release the pressure quickly. Divide chicken between four serving bowls; top with tomato mixture before serving.

## Chicken Wings

**(Ready in about:** 25 min | **Servings:** 4)

**Ingredients:**
- 8 chicken wings
- 1 tablespoon onion powder
- 1 tablespoon garlic powder
- 1 tablespoon ranch salad mix
- 1 tablespoon cayenne pepper
- ½ teaspoon paprika
- Cooking spray

**Directions:**
1. Combine the paprika, ranch salad mix, onion powder, garlic powder, and cayenne pepper in a bowl. Pour the seasoning all over the chicken and oil with cooking spray.
2. Place in the Foodi basket, close the crisping lid and cook for 15 minutes at 380 F. After half of the cooking time, shake the wings. Oil the chicken again with cooking spray and continue cooking until the wings are crispy. Serve hot.

## Buffalo Chicken and Navy Bean Chili

**(Ready in about:** 45 min | **Servings:** 6)

**Ingredients:**
- 1 ½ pounds chicken sausage; sliced
- 1 (14 ounces) can diced tomatoes with green chilies
- 2 (14 ounces) cans navy beans, drained and rinsed
- 1 (28 ounces) can crushed tomatoes
- ¾ cup Buffalo wing sauce
- 1 shallot; diced
- ½ cup fennel; chopped
- ¼ cup minced garlic
- 1 tablespoon olive oil
- 1 tablespoon smoked paprika
- 2 teaspoon chili powder
- 2 teaspoon ground cumin
- ½ teaspoon salt
- ½ teaspoon ground white pepper

**Directions:**

1. Warm oil on Sear/Sauté. Add the sausages and brown for 5 minutes, turning frequently. Set aside on a plate.
2. In the same fat, sauté onion, roasted red peppers, fennel, and garlic for 4 minutes until soft; season with paprika, cumin, pepper, salt, and chili powder.
3. Stir in crushed tomatoes; diced tomatoes with green chilies, buffalo sauce, and navy beans. Return the sausages to the pot.
4. Seal the pressure lid, choose Pressure, set to High, and set the timer to 30 minutes. Press Start. When ready, do a quick pressure release. Spoon chili into bowls and serve warm.

## Butter Chicken

**(Ready in about:** 30 min | **Servings:** 6)

**Ingredients:**

- 2 pounds boneless; skinless chicken legs
- 3 Roma tomatoes, pureed in a blender
- 1 (14.5 ounces) can coconut milk, refrigerated overnight
- 1 large onion; minced
- ½ cup chopped fresh cilantro; divided
- 2 tablespoon Indian curry paste
- 2 tablespoon dried fenugreek
- 1 tablespoon Kashmiri red chili powder
- 2 tablespoon butter
- 1 tablespoon grated fresh ginger
- 1 tablespoon minced fresh garlic
- 1 teaspoon salt
- 2 teaspoon sugar
- ½ teaspoon ground turmeric
- 1 teaspoon garam masala
- Salt to taste

**Directions:**

1. Set your Foodi to Sear/Sauté, set to Medium High, and choose Start/Stop to preheat the pot and melt butter. Add in 1 teaspoon salt and onion. Cook for 2 to 3 minutes until fragrant. Stir in ginger, turmeric, garlic, and red chili powder to coat; cook for 2 more minutes.
2. Place water and coconut cream into separate bowls. Stir the water from the coconut milk can, pureed tomatoes, and chicken with the onion mixture. Seal the pressure lid, choose Pressure, set to High, and set the timer to 8 minutes. Press Start. When ready, release the pressure quickly.
3. Stir sugar, coconut cream, fenugreek, curry paste, half the cilantro, and garam masala through the chicken mixture; apply salt for seasoning. Simmer the mixture and cook for 10 minutes until the sauce thickens, on Sear/Sauté. Garnish with the rest of the cilantro before serving.

## Chicken in Pineapple Gravy

**(Ready in about:** 25 min | **Servings:** 4)

**Ingredients:**

- 4 boneless; skinless chicken thighs,
- ¼ cup pineapple juice
- 1 garlic clove; minced
- 2 tablespoon ketchup
- 1 tablespoon olive oil
- 2 tablespoon Worcestershire sauce
- 1 teaspoon cornstarch
- 2 teaspoon water
- A handful of fresh cilantro; chopped

**Directions:**

1. Warm oil on Sear/Sauté. In batches, sear chicken in oil for 3 minutes until golden brown; set aside on a plate. Mix, pineapple juice, Worcestershire sauce, garlic, and ketchup; add to the pot to deglaze, scrape the bottom to get rid of any browned bits of food. Place the chicken into the sauce and stir well to coat.
2. Seal the pressure lid, choose Pressure, set to High, and set the timer to cook for 5 minutes. Press Start. When ready, release the pressure quickly.
3. In a small bowl, mix water and cornstarch until well dissolved. Press Start/Stop and set to Sear/Sauté. Stir the cornstarch slurry into the sauce; cook for 2 minutes until the sauce is well thickened. Set in serving bowls and cilantro to serve.

## Honey Glazed Chicken Kabobs

**(Ready in about:** 20 min | **Servings:** 4)

**Ingredients:**

- 4 chicken breasts; skinless and cubed
- Juice from 1 Lime
- 4 tablespoon honey.
- ½ teaspoon ground paprika
- Salt and pepper to taste

**Directions:**

1. In a large bowl, combine the honey, soy sauce, lime juice, paprika, salt, and pepper. Add in the chicken cubes and toss to coat.
2. Load 8 small skewers with honey-glazed chicken. Lay the kabobs into the Foodi basket, close the crisping lid and cook for 15 minutes at 360 F. After 8 minutes, turn the kabobs over. Drizzle the remaining honey sauce and serve with sautéed veggies.

## Chicken with Bacon and Beans

**(Ready in about:** 45 min | **Servings:** 4)

**Ingredients:**

- 4 boneless; skinless chicken thighs
- 4 garlic cloves; minced
- 15 ounces red kidney beans, drained and rinsed
- 4 slices bacon, crumbled
- 1 (14.5 ounces) can whole tomatoes
- 1 red bell pepper; chopped
- 1 onion; diced
- 1 cup shredded Monterey Jack cheese
- 1 cup sliced red onion
- ¼ cup chopped cilantro
- 1 cup chicken broth
- 1 tablespoon tomato paste
- 1 tablespoon olive oil
- 1 tablespoon oregano
- 1 tablespoon ground cumin
- 1 teaspoon chili powder
- ½ teaspoon cayenne pepper
- 1 teaspoon salt
- 1 cup cooked corn

**Directions:**

1. Warm oil on Sear/Sauté. Sear the chicken for 3 minutes for each side until browned. Set the chicken on a plate. In the same oil, fry bacon until crispy, about 5 minutes and set aside.
2. Add in onions and cook for 2 to 3 minutes until fragrant. Stir in garlic, oregano, cayenne pepper, cumin, tomato paste, bell pepper, and chili powder and cook for 30 more seconds. Pour the chicken broth, salt, and tomatoes and bring to a boil. Press Start/Stop.
3. Take back the chicken and bacon to the pot and ensure it is submerged in the braising liquid. Seal the pressure lid, choose Pressure, set to High, and set the timer to 15 minutes. Press Start. When ready, release the pressure quickly.
4. Pour the kidney beans in the cooker, press Sear/Sauté and bring the liquid to a boil; cook for 10 minutes. Serve topped with shredded cheese and chopped cilantro.

## Chicken Pasta with Pesto Sauce

**(Ready in about:** 30 min | **Servings:** 8)

**Ingredients:**

- 4 chicken breast, boneless, skinless; cubed
- 8 oz. macaroni pasta
- 1 garlic clove; minced
- 1/4 cup Asiago cheese, grated
- 2 cups fresh collard greens, trimmed
- ¼ cup cream cheese, at room temperature
- 1 cup cherry tomatoes, halved
- ½ cup basil pesto sauce
- 3½ cups water
- 1 tablespoon butter
- 1 tablespoon salt; divided
- 1 teaspoon freshly ground black pepper to taste
- Freshly chopped basil for garnish

**Directions:**

1. To the inner steel pot of the Foodi, add water, chicken, 2 teaspoon salt, butter, and macaroni, and stir well to mix and be submerged in water.
2. Seal the pressure lid, choose Pressure, set to High, and set the timer to 2 minutes. Press Start. When ready, release the pressure quickly. Press Start/Stop, open the lid, get rid of ¼ cup water from the pot.
3. Set on Sear/Sauté. Into the pot, mix in collard greens, pesto sauce, garlic, remaining 1 teaspoon salt, cream cheese, tomatoes, and black pepper. Cook, for 1 to 2 minutes as you stir, until sauce is creamy.
4. Place the pasta into serving plates; top with asiago cheese and basil before serving.

## Chicken with Lemony Couscous

**(Ready in about:** 40 min | **Servings:** 4)

**Ingredients:**

- 4 chicken thighs
- 1 onion, thinly sliced
- 1 garlic clove; minced
- 1½ cups couscous
- 2 ½ cups chicken stock; divided
- Juice from 1 lemon

- 2 tablespoon za'atar mix
- 1 tablespoon ground sumac
- 2 tablespoon butter
- sea salt and freshly ground black pepper to taste
- Fresh parsley; chopped

**Directions:**

1. Season the chicken with salt, sumac, za'atar, and pepper. Melt butter on Sear/Sauté and sear the chicken in batches for 5 minutes per batch until lightly browned; set aside.
2. In the Foodi, add ¼ cup chicken stock to deglaze the pan, scrape the bottom to get rid of any browned bits of food. Add garlic and onion to the stock; cook for 3 minutes until soft.
3. Add the remaining chicken stock into the pan; add lemon juice and couscous. Add in chicken.
4. Seal the pressure lid, choose Pressure, set to High, and set the timer to 5 minutes. Press Start. Naturally release the pressure for 5 minutes. Transfer the couscous and chicken to a serving plate; add parsley to garnish.

## Ground Turkey and Potato Chili

**(Ready in about:** 55 min | **Servings:** 6)

**Ingredients:**

- 1 pound ground turkey
- 2 bell peppers; chopped
- 6 potatoes, peeled and sliced
- 1 small onion; diced
- 2 garlic cloves; minced
- 1 cups tomato puree
- 1 cups diced tomatoes
- 1 cup chicken broth

- 1 cup carrots; chopped
- 1 cups fresh or frozen corn kernels, roasted
- 1 tablespoon olive oil
- 1 tablespoon ground cumin
- 1 tablespoon chili powder
- salt and fresh ground black pepper

**Directions:**

1. Warm the olive on Sear/Sauté and stir-fry onions and garlic until soft, for about 3 minutes. Press Start. Stir in turkey and cook until thoroughly browned, about 5-6 minutes. Add the remaining ingredients, and stir to combine.
2. Seal the pressure lid, choose Pressure, set to High, and set the timer to 25 minutes; press Start. Once ready, do a quick release. Set on Sear/Sauté. Cook uncovered for 15 more minutes. Serve warm.

# Shredded Chicken and Wild Rice

**(Ready in about:** 45 min | **Servings:** 6)

**Ingredients:**

- 6 chicken thighs, skinless
- 3 cups chicken broth; divided
- 1 ½ cups wild rice
- 1 cup pumpkin, peeled and cubed
- 2 celery stalks; diced
- 2 onions; diced
- 2 garlic cloves, crushed
- 2 tablespoon olive oil
- 1/8 teaspoon smoked paprika
- ½ teaspoon ground white pepper
- ½ teaspoon onion powder
- 1 teaspoon Cajun seasoning
- 1 teaspoon salt
- ½ teaspoon ground red pepper

**Directions:**

1. Season the chicken with salt, onion powder, Cajun seasoning, ground white pepper, ground red pepper, and smoked paprika. Warm oil on Sear/Sauté.
2. Stir in celery and pumpkin and cook for 5 minutes until tender; set the vegetables on a plate. In batches, sear chicken in oil for 3 minutes each side until golden brown; set on a plate.
3. In the Foodi, add 1/4 cup chicken stock to deglaze the pan, scrape away any browned bits from the bottom; add garlic and onion and cook for 2 minutes until fragrant.
4. Take back the celery and pumpkin to Foodi; add the wild rice and remaining chicken stock. Place the chicken over the rice mixture.
5. Seal the pressure lid, choose Pressure, set to High, and set the timer to 10 minutes. Press Start. When ready, release the pressure quickly. Place rice and chicken pieces in serving plates and serve.

# Lemon Turkey Risotto

**(Ready in about:** 40 min | **Servings:** 4)

**Ingredients:**

- 2 boneless turkey breasts; cut into strips
- 2 cups chicken broth
- 1 cup Arborio rice, rinsed
- ¼ cup chopped fresh parsley, or to taste
- 2 lemons, zested and juiced
- 1 onion; diced
- 8 lemon slices
- 2 garlic cloves; minced
- 1 tablespoon dried oregano
- 1½ tablespoon olive oil
- ½ teaspoon sea salt
- salt and freshly ground black pepper to taste

**Directions:**

1. In a ziplock back, mix turkey, oregano, sea salt, garlic, juice and zest of two lemons. Marinate for 10 minutes.
2. Warm oil on Sear/Sauté. Add onion and cook for 3 minutes until fragrant; add rice and chicken broth and season with pepper and salt.
3. Empty the ziplock having the chicken and marinade into the pot. Seal the pressure lid, choose Pressure, set to High, and set the timer to 12 minutes. Press Start. When ready, release the pressure quickly.
4. Divide the rice and turkey between 4 serving bowls; garnish with lemon slices and parsley.

# Chicken and Zucchini Pilaf

**(Ready in about:** 40 min | **Servings:** 4)

**Ingredients:**

- 1 pound boneless and skinless chicken legs
- 1 zucchini; chopped
- 2 cups chicken stock
- 1 cup leeks; chopped
- 1 cup rice, rinsed
- 2 garlic cloves; minced
- 1 tablespoon chopped fresh rosemary
- 2 teaspoon chopped fresh thyme leaves
- 2 teaspoon olive oil
- salt and ground black pepper to taste

**Directions:**

1. Set your Foodi to Sear/Sauté, set to Medium High, and choose Start/Stop to preheat the pot. Warm oil. Add in zucchini and cook for 5 minutes until tender.
2. Stir in thyme, leeks, rosemary, pepper, salt and garlic. Cook the mixture for 3-4 minutes. Add ½ cup chicken stock into the pot to deglaze, scrape the bottom to get rid of any browned bits of food.
3. When liquid stops simmering, add in the remaining stock, rice, and chicken with more pepper and salt.
4. Seal the pressure lid, choose Pressure, set to High, and set the timer to 5 minutes. Press Start. Once ready, do a quick release.

## Chicken with Rice and Peas

(**Ready in about:** 30 min | **Servings:** 4)

**Ingredients:**

- 4 boneless; skinless chicken breasts; sliced
- 1 onion; chopped
- 1 celery stalk; diced
- 1 garlic clove; minced
- 2 cups chicken broth; divided
- 1 cup long grain rice
- 1 cup frozen green peas
- 1 tablespoon oil olive

- 1 tablespoon tomato puree
- ½ teaspoon paprika
- ¼ teaspoon dried oregano
- ¼ teaspoon dried thyme
- ⅛ teaspoon cayenne pepper
- ⅛ teaspoon ground white pepper
- Salt to taste

**Directions:**

1. Season chicken with garlic powder, oregano, white pepper, thyme, paprika, cayenne pepper, and salt. Warm the oil on Sear/Sauté. Add in onion and cook for 4 minutes until fragrant. Mix in tomato puree to coat.
2. Add ¼ cup chicken stock into the Foodi to deglaze the pan, scrape the pan's bottom to get rid of browned bits of food. Mix in celery, rice, and the seasoned chicken. Add in the remaining broth to the chicken mixture.
3. Seal the pressure lid, choose Pressure, set to High, and set the timer to 8 minutes. Press Start. Once ready, do a quick release. Mix in green peas, cover with the lid and let sit for 5 minutes. Serve warm.

## Shredded Chicken with Lentils and Rice

(**Ready in about:** 45 min | **Servings:** 4)

**Ingredients:**

- 4 boneless; skinless chicken thighs
- 1 garlic clove; minced
- 1 small yellow onion; chopped
- 1 cup white rice
- ½ cup dried lentils

- 3 cups chicken broth; divided
- 1 teaspoon olive oil
- Chopped fresh parsley for garnish
- Salt and ground black pepper to taste

**Directions:**

1. Set your Foodi to Sear/Sauté, set to Medium High, and choose Start/Stop to preheat the pot. Warm oil. Add in onion and garlic and cook for 3 minutes until soft; add in broth, rice, lentils, and chicken.
2. Season with pepper and salt. Seal the pressure lid, choose Pressure, set to High, and set the timer to 15 minutes. Press Start.
3. Once ready, do a quick release. Remove and shred the chicken in a large bowl. Set the lentils and rice into serving plates, top with shredded chicken and parsley and serve.

## Chicken Meatballs in Tomato Sauce

**(Ready in about:** 35 min **| Servings:** 5)

### Ingredients:

- 1 pound ground chicken
- 1 egg
- 15 ounces canned tomato sauce
- ¼ cup bread crumbs
- ¼ cup Pecorino cheese
- 1 cup chicken broth
- ⅓ cup crumbled blue cheese
- 3 tablespoon red hot sauce
- 1 tablespoon ranch dressing
- 2 tablespoon olive oil
- 1 teaspoon dried basil
- A handful of parsley; chopped
- salt and ground black pepper to taste

### Directions:

1. In a bowl, mix ground chicken, egg, pecorino, basil, pepper, salt, ranch dressing, blue cheese, 3 tablespoon hot sauce, and bread crumbs; shape the mixture into meatballs.
2. Warm oil on Sear/Sauté. Add in the meatballs and cook for 2 to 3 minutes until browned on all sides. Add in tomato sauce and broth. Seal the pressure lid, choose Pressure, set to High, and set the timer to 7 minutes. Press Start.
3. When ready, release the pressure quickly. Remove meatballs carefully and place to a serving plate; top with parsley and serve.

## Pork Soup

**(Ready in about:** 40 min **| Servings:** 4)

### Ingredients:

- 1 pound pork tenderloin; cut into thin strips
- 8 ounces rice noodles
- 1 lime; cut into wedges
- 2 yellow onions, halved
- 1 large piece fresh ginger, halved lengthwise
- 2-star anise
- 8 cups water
- 10 black peppercorns
- 2 tablespoon olive oil
- 2 teaspoon fennel seeds
- 1 teaspoon red pepper flakes
- ½ teaspoon coriander seeds
- 2 teaspoon salt
- A handful of fresh cilantro leaves

### Directions:

1. Set your Foodi to Sear/Sauté, set to Medium High, and choose Start/Stop to preheat the pot. Warm oil on Normal. Add ginger and onions and cook for 4 minutes; add in red pepper flakes, fennel seeds, star anise, peppercorns, and coriander seeds; cook for 1 minute as you stir. Add water, salt and pork into the pot.
2. Seal the pressure lid, choose Pressure, set to High, and set the timer to 60 minutes. Press Start. Release the pressure naturally for 10 minutes.
3. As the pho continues to cook, soak rice noodles in hot water for 8 minutes until softened and pliable; stop the cooking process by draining and rinsing with cold water. Separate the noodles into four soup plates.
4. Remove the pork from the cooker and ladle among bowls. Strain the broth to get rid of solids. Pour it over the pork and noodles; season with red pepper flakes. Garnish with lime wedges and cilantro leaves.

## Pulled Chicken and Peach Salsa

**(Ready in about:** 40 min | **Servings:** 4)

**Ingredients:**

- 4 boneless; skinless chicken thighs
- 15 ounces canned peach chunks
- 2 cloves garlic; minced
- 14 ounces canned diced tomatoes
- ½ teaspoon cumin
- ½ teaspoon salt
- Cheddar shredded cheese
- Fresh chopped mint leaves

**Directions:**

1. Strain canned peach chunks. Reserve the juice and set aside. In your Foodi, add chicken, tomatoes, cumin, garlic, peach juice (about 1 cup), and salt.
2. Seal the pressure lid, choose Pressure, set to High, and set the timer to 15 minutes. Press Start. When ready, do a quick pressure release.
3. Shred chicken with the use of two forks. Transfer to a serving plate. Add peach chunks to the cooking juices and mix until well combined.
4. Pour the peach salsa over the chicken, top with chopped mint leaves and shredded cheese. Serve immediately.

## Turkey and Brown Rice Salad with Peanuts

**(Ready in about:** 60 min | **Servings:** 4)

**Ingredients:**

- 1 pound turkey tenderloins
- 3 celery stalks, thinly sliced
- 1 apple, cored and cubed
- 1 cup brown rice
- ½ cup peanuts, toasted
- 4 cups water
- A pinch of sugar
- 3 tablespoon apple cider vinegar
- ⅛ teaspoon freshly ground black pepper
- ¼ teaspoon celery seeds
- 2¼ teaspoon salt
- 3 teaspoon peanut oil; divided

**Directions:**

1. Pour the water into the inner pot. Stir in the brown rice and 1 teaspoon of salt. Lock the pressure lid into the Seal position. Choose Pressure; adjust the pressure to High and the cook time to 10 minutes. Press Start.
2. Season the turkey on both sides with salt; set aside. After cooking the brown rice, perform a natural pressure release for 10 minutes. Carefully open the lid and spoon the rice into a large bowl to cool completely.
3. Put the turkey in the Crisping Basket and brush with 2 teaspoons of peanut oil. Fix in the basket. Close the crisping lid and Choose Bake/Roast; adjust the temperature to 375°F and the cook time to 12 minutes; press Start.
4. Pour the remaining peanut oil and the vinegar into a jar with a tight-fitting lid. Add the black pepper, celery seeds, salt, and sugar.
5. Close the jar and shake until the ingredients properly combined. When the turkey is ready, transfer to a plate to cool for several minutes. Cut it into bite-size chunks and add to the rice along with the peanuts, celery, and apple.
6. Pour half the dressing over the salad and toss gently to coat, adding more dressing as desired. Proceed to serve the salad.

## Chicken with BBQ Sauce

(**Ready in about:** 20 min | **Servings:** 6)

**Ingredients:**
- 2 pounds boneless skinless chicken breasts
- 1 small onion; minced
- 4 garlic cloves
- 1 cup carrots, thinly sliced
- 1½ cups barbecue sauce
- 1 teaspoon salt

**Directions:**
1. Apply a seasoning of salt to the chicken and place in the inner pot of the Foodi; add onion, carrots, garlic and barbeque sauce. Toss the chicken to coat.
2. Seal the pressure lid, choose Pressure, set to High, and set the timer to 15 minutes. Press Start. Once ready, do a quick release. Use two forks to shred chicken and stir into the sauce.

## Salsa Verde Chicken with Salsa Verde

(**Ready in about:** 50 min | **Servings:** 4)

**Ingredients:**
**Salsa Verde:**
- 1 jalapeño pepper, deveined and sliced
- ¼ cup extra virgin olive oil
- ¼ cup parsley
- ½ cup capers
- 1 lime, juiced
- 1 teaspoon salt

**Chicken:**
- 4 boneless skinless chicken breasts
- 1 cup quinoa, rinsed
- 2 cups water

**Directions:**
1. In a blender, mix olive oil, salt, lime juice, jalapeño pepper, capers, and parsley and blend until smooth. Arrange chicken breasts in the bottom of the Foodi pot. Over the chicken, add salsa verde mixture.
2. In a bowl that can fit in the cooker, mix quinoa and water. Set a reversible rack onto chicken and sauce. Set the bowl onto the reversible rack. Seal the pressure lid, choose Pressure, set to High, and set the timer to 20 minutes. Press Start.
3. When ready, release the pressure quickly. Remove the quinoa bowl and reversible rack. Using two forks, shred chicken into the sauce; stir to coat. Divide the quinoa, between plates. Top with chicken and salsa verde before serving.

## Saucy Chicken Breasts

(**Ready in about:** 45 min | **Servings:** 4)

**Ingredients:**
- 4 chicken breasts, boneless and skinless
- ½ cup chicken broth
- ½ cup chives; sliced
- 1 tablespoon cornstarch
- 1 tablespoon water
- 2 tablespoon olive oil
- 2 tablespoon soy sauce
- 2 tablespoon tomato paste
- 2 tablespoon honey
- 2 tablespoon minced garlic
- salt and ground black pepper to taste

**Directions:**
1. Season the chicken with pepper and salt. Warm oil on Sear/Sauté. Add in chicken and cook for 5 minutes until lightly browned.
2. In a small bowl, mix garlic, soy sauce, honey, and tomato paste; pour the mixture over the chicken. Stir in ½ cup broth. Seal the pressure lid, choose Pressure, set to High, and set the timer to 12 minutes. Press Start.

3. When ready, release the pressure quickly. Set the chicken to a bowl. Mix water and cornstarch to create a slurry; briskly stir the mixture into the sauce that is remaining in the pan for 2 minutes until thickened. Serve the chicken with the sauce and chives.

## Honey Garlic Chicken and Okra

**(Ready in about:** 25 min | **Servings:** 4)

**Ingredients:**
- 4 boneless; skinless chicken breasts; sliced
- 4 spring onions, thinly sliced
- 6 garlic cloves, grated
- ⅓ cup honey
- 1 cup rice, rinsed
- ¼ cup tomato puree
- ½ cup soy sauce
- 2 cups water
- 2 cups frozen okra
- 1 tablespoon cornstarch
- 2 tablespoon rice vinegar
- 1 tablespoon olive oil
- 1 tablespoon water
- 2 teaspoon toasted sesame seeds
- ½ teaspoon salt

**Directions:**
1. In the inner pot of the Foodi, mix garlic, tomato puree, vinegar, soy sauce, ginger, honey, and oil; toss in chicken to coat. In an ovenproof bowl, mix water, salt and rice. Set the reversible rack on top of chicken. Lower the bowl onto the reversible rack.
2. Seal the pressure lid, choose Pressure, set to High, and set the timer to 10 minutes; press Start. Release pressure naturally for 5 minutes, release the remaining pressure quickly.
3. Use a fork to fluff the rice. Lay okra onto the rice. Allow the okra steam in the residual heat for 3 minutes. Take the trivet and bowl from the pot. Set the chicken to a plate.
4. Press Sear/Sauté. In a small bowl, mix 1 tablespoon of water and cornstarch until smooth; stir into the sauce and cook for 3 to 4 minutes until thickened.
5. Divide the rice, chicken, and okra between 4 bowls. Drizzle sauce over each portion; garnish with spring onions and sesame seeds.

## Sticky Drumsticks

**(Ready in about:** 50 min | **Servings:** 4)

**Ingredients:**
- 1 lb. drumsticks
- 2 tablespoon honey
- 2 teaspoon dijon mustard
- Cooking spray
- Salt and pepper to taste

**Directions:**
1. Combine the honey, mustard, salt, and pepper in a large bowl. Add in the chicken and toss to coat. Cover and put in the fridge for 30 minutes.
2. Preheat your Foodi to 380 degrees F. Grease the Foodi basket with cooking spray. Arrange the drumsticks on the basket. Cook for 20 minutes on Air Crisp mode. After 10 minutes, shake the drumsticks.

## Basil Cheddar Stuffed Chicken

**(Ready in about:** 25 min | **Servings:** 4)

**Ingredients:**
- 2 large chicken breasts, skinless
- 4 cherry tomatoes, halved
- 4 slices cheddar cheese
- A handful of fresh basil leaves
- 2 tablespoon olive oil
- Salt and pepper to taste

**Directions:**
1. With a sharp knife; cut a slit into the side of each chicken breast. Put 2 slices of cheese, 3-4 basil leaves, and 4 cherry tomato halves into each slit. Use toothpicks to keep the chicken breasts closed.

2. Season the meat with salt and pepper, and brush with some olive oil. Grease the Foodi basket with the remaining olive oil and place the chicken breasts in the basket; close the crisping lid and cook for 12 minutes at 370 F.
3. After 6 minutes, turn the breasts over. Once ready, leave to sit the chicken breasts, then slice each one in half and serve with salad.

## Tuscany Turkey Soup

**(Ready in about:** 40 min | **Servings:** 4)

**Ingredients:**
- 1 pound hot turkey sausage
- 4 Italian bread slices
- 3 celery stalks; chopped
- 3 garlic cloves; chopped
- 1 (15-oz) can cannellini beans, rinsed
- 9 ounces refrigerated tortellini
- 1 Parmesan cheese rind
- 1 red onion; chopped
- ½ cup dry white wine
- 4 cups chicken broth
- 2 cups chopped spinach
- ½ cup grated Parmesan cheese
- 2 tablespoon melted butter
- 2 tablespoon olive oil
- ½ teaspoon fennel seeds
- 1 teaspoon salt
- Cooking spray

**Directions:**
1. On the Foodi, choose Sear/Sauté and adjust to Medium. Press Start to preheat the inner pot. Heat olive oil and cook the sausage for 4 minutes, while stirring occasionally until golden brown.
2. Stir in the celery, garlic, and onion, season with the salt and cook for 2 to 3 minutes, stirring occasionally. Pour in the wine and bring the mixture to a boil until the wine reduces by half. Scrape the bottom of the pot to let off any browned bits. Add the chicken stock, fennel seeds, tortellini, Parmesan rind, cannellini beans, and spinach.
3. Lock the pressure lid into place and to seal. Select Pressure; adjust the pressure to High and the cook time to 5 minutes; press Start. Brush the butter on the bread slices, and sprinkle with half of the cheese. Once the timer is over, perform a natural pressure release for 5 minutes.
4. Grease the reversible rack with cooking spray and fix in the upper position of the pot. Lay the bread slices on the rack.
5. Close the crisping lid and Choose Broil. Adjust the cook time to 5 minutes; press Start.
6. When the bread has browned and crisp, transfer from the rack to a cutting board and let cool for a couple of minutes. Cut the slices into cubes.
7. Ladle the soup into bowls and sprinkle with the remaining cheese. Share the croutons among the bowls and serve.

## Cordon Bleu Chicken

**(Ready in about:** 40 min | **Servings:** 4)

**Ingredients:**
- 4 skinless and boneless chicken breasts
- 4 slices Swiss cheese
- 4 slices ham
- 1 cup heavy whipping cream
- ½ cup dry white wine
- 3 tablespoon all-purpose flour
- 4 tablespoon butter
- 1 teaspoon chicken bouillon granules
- 1 teaspoon paprika

**Directions:**
1. Pound the chicken breasts and put a slice of ham and then a slice of swiss cheese on each of the breasts. Fold the edges over the filling and secure the sides with toothpicks.
2. In a medium bowl, combine the paprika and the flour and coat the chicken pieces. Close the crisping lid and fry the chicken for 20 minutes on Air Crisp mode at 380 F.
3. Meanwhile, in a large skillet over medium heat, melt the butter and add the bouillon and the wine. Reduce the heat to low.

4. Add in the heavy cream and let simmer for 20-25 minutes. When the chicken is done, remove to a serving platter and drizzle with the sauce; serve hot.

## Turkey Casserole

**(Ready in about:** 45 min | **Servings:** 5)

**Ingredients:**

- 1 pound turkey breast; cubed
- 2 (14 ounces) cans fire-roasted tomatoes
- ½ sweet onion; diced
- 3 cloves garlic; minced
- 1 jalapeno pepper; minced
- 2 bell peppers; cut into thick strips
- 1½ cups water
- 1 cup salsa
- 1 tablespoon olive oil
- 5 tablespoon fresh oregano; chopped
- 2 teaspoon ancho chili powder
- 2 teaspoon chili powder
- 1 teaspoon ground cumin
- Sea salt to taste

**Directions:**

1. Warm the oil on Sear/Sauté. Add in garlic, onion and jalapeño and cook for 5 minutes until fragrant. Stir turkey into the pot; cook for 5-6 minutes until browned.
2. Add in salsa, tomatoes, bell peppers, and water; apply a seasoning of sea salt, ancho chili powder, cumin, and chili powder. Seal the pressure lid, choose Pressure, set to High, and set the timer to 10 minutes on High. When ready, release the pressure quickly. Top with oregano and serve.

## Chicken with Prunes

**(Ready in about:** 55 min | **Servings:** 6)

**Ingredients:**

- 1 whole chicken, 3 lb
- ¼ cup packed brown sugar
- ½ cup pitted prunes
- 2 bay leaves
- 3 minced cloves of garlic
- 2 tablespoon olive oil
- 2 tablespoon capers
- 1 tablespoon dried oregano
- 1 tablespoon chopped fresh parsley
- 2 tablespoon red wine vinegar
- Salt and black pepper to taste

**Directions:**

1. In a big and deep bowl, mix the prunes, olives, capers, garlic, olive oil, bay leaves, oregano, vinegar, salt, and pepper.
2. Spread the mixture on the bottom of a baking tray, and place the chicken.
3. Preheat the Foodi to 360° F. Sprinkle a little bit of brown sugar on top of the chicken, close the crisping lid and cook for 45-55 minutes on Air Crisp mode. When ready, garnish with fresh parsley.

## Tom Yum Wings

**(Ready in about:** 4 hours 20 min | **Servings:** 2)

**Ingredients:**

- 8 chicken wings
- 2 tablespoon cornstarch
- 2 tablespoon tom yum paste
- 1 tablespoon water
- 2 tablespoon potato starch
- ½ teaspoon baking powder

**Directions:**

1. Combine the tom yum paste and water, in a small bowl. Place the wings in a large bowl, add the tom yum mixture and coat well.
2. Cover the bowl and refrigerate for 4 hours. Preheat the Foodi to 370 degrees F.
3. Combine the baking powder, cornstarch, and potato starch. Dip each wing in the starch mixture.
4. Place on a lined baking dish in the Foodi and cook for 7 minutes on Air Crisp mode. Flip over and cook for 5 to 7 minutes more.

## Chicken Stroganoff with Fetucini

**(Ready in about:** 35 min | **Servings:** 4)

**Ingredients:**

- 2 large boneless skinless chicken breasts
- 8 ounces fettucini
- ½ cup sliced onion
- ½ cup dry white wine
- 1 cup sautéed mushrooms
- ¼ cup heavy cream
- 1 ½ cups water
- 2 cups chicken stock
- 2 tablespoon butter
- 1 tablespoon flour
- 2 tablespoon chopped fresh dill to garnish
- ½ teaspoon Worcestershire sauce
- 1½ teaspoon salt

**Directions:**

1. Season the chicken on both sides with salt and set aside. Choose Sear/Sauté and adjust to Medium. Press Start to preheat the pot. Melt the butter and sauté the onion until brown, about 3 minutes.
2. Mix in the flour to make a roux, about 2 minutes and gradually pour in the dry white wine while stirring and scraping the bottom of the pot to release any browned bits. Allow the white wine to simmer and to reduce by two-thirds.
3. Pour in the water, chicken stock, 1 tablespoon of salt, and fettucini. Mix and arrange the chicken on top of the fettucini.
4. Lock the pressure lid to Seal. Choose Pressure; adjust the pressure to High and the cook time to 5 minutes; press Start. When done pressure-cooking, perform a quick pressure release.
5. Transfer the chicken breasts to a cutting board to cool slightly, and then cut into bite-size chunks. Return the chicken to the pot and stir in the Worcestershire sauce and mushrooms. Add the heavy cream and cook until the mixture stops simmering. Ladle the stroganoff into bowls and garnish with dill.

## Chicken Thighs with Cabbage

**(Ready in about:** 35 min | **Servings:** 4)

**Ingredients:**

- 1 pound green cabbage, shredded
- 4 slices pancetta; diced
- 4 chicken thighs, boneless skinless
- 1 cup chicken broth
- 1 tablespoon Dijon mustard
- 1 tablespoon lard
- Fresh parsley; chopped
- salt and ground black pepper to taste

**Directions:**

1. Warm lard on Sear/Sauté. Fry pancetta for 5 minutes until crisp. Set aside. Season chicken with pepper and salt. Sear in Foodi for 2 minutes each side until browned. In a bowl, mix mustard and chicken broth.
2. In your Foodi, add pancetta and chicken broth mixture. Seal the pressure lid, choose Pressure, set to High, and set the timer to 6 minutes. Press Start. When ready, release the pressure quickly.
3. Open the lid, mix in green cabbage, seal again, and cook on High Pressure for 2 minutes. When ready, release the pressure quickly. Serve with sprinkled parsley.

## Chicken with Tomatoes and Capers

**(Ready in about:** 45 min | **Servings:** 4)

**Ingredients:**

- 4 chicken legs
- 1 onion; diced
- 2 garlic cloves; minced
- ⅓ cup red wine
- 2 cups diced tomatoes
- ⅓ cup capers
- ¼ cup fresh basil
- 2 pickles; chopped
- 2 tablespoon olive oil
- sea salt and fresh ground black pepper to taste

**Directions:**

1. Sprinkle pepper and salt over the chicken. Warm oil on Sear/Sauté. Add in onion and cook for 3 minutes until fragrant; add in garlic and cook for 30 seconds until softened.
2. Mix the chicken with vegetables and cook for 6 to 7 minutes until lightly browned.
3. Add red wine to the pan to deglaze, scrape the pan's bottom to get rid of any browned bits of food; stir in tomatoes. Seal the pressure lid, choose Pressure, set to High, and set the timer to 12 minutes; press Start.
4. When ready, release the pressure quickly. To the chicken mixture, add basil, capers and pickles. Serve the chicken in plates covered with the tomato sauce mixture.

## Asian Chicken

**(Ready in about:** 35 min | **Servings:** 4)

**Ingredients:**

- 1 lb. chicken; cut in stripes
- 1 large onion
- 3 green peppers; cut in stripes
- 2 tomatoes; cubed
- 1 pinch fresh and chopped coriander
- 1 pinch ginger
- 1 tablespoon mustard
- 1 tablespoon cumin powder
- 2 tablespoon oil
- Salt and black pepper

**Directions:**

1. Heat the oil in a deep pan. Add in the mustard, onion, ginger, cumin and green chili peppers. Sauté the mixture for 2-3 minutes. Then, add the tomatoes, coriander, and salt and keep stirring.
2. Coat the chicken with oil, salt, and pepper and cook for 25 minutes on Air Crisp mode at 380 F. Remove from the Foodi and pour the sauce over and around.

## Chicken with Black Beans

**(Ready in about:** 25 min | **Servings:** 4)

**Ingredients:**

- 4 boneless; skinless chicken drumsticks
- 2 green onions, thinly sliced
- 3 garlic cloves, grated
- 2 cups canned black beans
- ½ cup soy sauce
- ½ cup chicken broth
- 1 (1 inch) piece fresh ginger, grated
- 1 tablespoon sriracha
- 1 tablespoon sesame oil
- 1 tablespoon cornstarch
- 1 tablespoon water
- 2 tablespoon toasted sesame seeds; divided
- 3 tablespoon honey
- 2 tablespoon tomato paste

**Directions:**

1. In your Foodi, mix the soy sauce, honey, ginger, tomato paste, chicken broth, sriracha, and garlic. Stir well until smooth; toss in the chicken to coat.
2. Seal the pressure lid, choose Pressure, set to High, and set the timer to 3 minutes. Press Start. Release the pressure immediately.
3. Open the lid and Press Sear/Sauté. In a small bowl, mix water and cornstarch until no lumps remain; stir into the sauce and cook for 5 minutes until thickened.
4. Stir sesame oil and 1½ tablespoon sesame seeds through the chicken mixture; garnish with extra sesame seeds and green onions. Serve with black beans.

## Herby Chicken with Asparagus Sauce

**(Ready in about:** 1 hr | **Servings:** 4)

**Ingredients:**

- 1 (3 ½ pounds) Young Whole Chicken
- 8 ounces asparagus, trimmed and chopped
- 1 onion; chopped
- 1 cup chicken stock
- 4 fresh thyme; minced
- 3 fresh rosemary; minced
- 4 garlic cloves; minced
- 2 lemons, zested and quartered
- 1 fresh thyme sprig
- 1 tablespoon flour
- 1 tablespoon soy sauce
- 2 tablespoon olive oil
- 1 teaspoon olive oil
- Cooking spray
- salt and freshly ground black pepper to taste
- Chopped parsley to garnish

**Directions:**

1. Rub all sides of the chicken with garlic, rosemary, black pepper, lemon zest; minced thyme, and salt. Into the chicken cavity, insert lemon wedges.
2. Warm oil on Sear/Sauté. Add in onion and asparagus, and cook for 5 minutes until softened. Mix in chicken stock, 1 thyme sprig, black pepper, soy sauce, and salt.
3. Into the inner pot, set trivet over asparagus mixture. On top of the trivet, place your chicken with breast-side up.
4. Seal the pressure lid, choose Pressure, set to High, and set the timer to 20 minutes. Press Start. Once ready, do a quick release. Remove the chicken to a serving platter.
5. In the inner pot, sprinkle flour over asparagus mixture and blend the sauce with an immersion blender until desired consistency. Top the chicken with asparagus sauce and garnish with parsley.

## Greek Style Turkey Meatballs

**(Ready in about:** 30 min | **Servings:** 6)

**Ingredients:**

- 1 pound ground turkey
- 1 carrot; minced
- ½ celery stalk; minced
- 1 onion; minced and divided
- 1 egg, lightly beaten
- 3 cups tomato puree
- 2 cups water
- ½ cup plain bread crumbs
- ⅓ cup feta cheese, crumbled
- 1 tablespoon olive oil
- 2 teaspoon salt; divided
- ½ teaspoon dried oregano
- ¼ teaspoon ground black pepper

**Directions:**

1. In a mixing bowl, thoroughly combine half the onion, oregano, ground turkey, salt, bread crumbs, pepper, and egg and stir until everything is well incorporated.
2. Heat oil on Sear/Sauté, and cook celery, remaining onion, and carrot for 5 minutes until soft. Pour in water, and tomato puree. Adjust the seasonings as necessary.
3. Roll the mixture into meatballs, and drop into the sauce. Seal the pressure lid, choose Pressure, set to High, and set the timer to 5 minutes. Press Start. Allow the cooker to cool and release pressure naturally for 20 minutes. Serve topped with feta cheese.

## Spicy Chicken Wings.

**(Ready in about:** 25 min | **Servings:** 2)

**Ingredients:**
- 10 chicken wings
- ½ tablespoon honey
- 2 tablespoon hot chili sauce
- ½ tablespoon lime juice
- ½ teaspoon kosher salt
- ½ teaspoon black pepper

**Directions:**
1. Mix the lime juice, honey, and chili sauce. Toss the mixture over the chicken wings.
2. Put the wings in the fryer's basket, close the crisping lid and cook for 25 minutes on Air Crisp mode at 350 F. Shake the basket every 5 minutes.

## Greek Chicken with Potatoes

**(Ready in about:** 40 min | **Servings:** 4)

**Ingredients:**
- 4 potatoes, peeled and quartered
- 4 boneless skinless chicken drumsticks
- 2 lemons, zested and juiced
- 1 cucumber, thinly sliced
- 2 Serrano peppers, stemmed, cored, and chopped
- 1 cup packed watercress
- ½ cup cherry tomatoes, quartered
- ¼ cup Kalamata olives, pitted
- ¼ cup hummus
- ¼ cup feta cheese, crumbled
- 4 cups water
- 3 tablespoon finely chopped parsley
- 1 tablespoon olive oil
- 2 teaspoon fresh oregano
- ¼ teaspoon freshly ground black pepper
- Lemon wedges; for serving
- Salt to taste

**Directions:**
1. In the cooker, add water and potatoes. Set trivet over them. In a baking bowl, mix lemon juice, olive oil, black pepper, oregano, zest, salt, and red pepper flakes. Add chicken drumsticks in the marinade and stir to coat.
2. Set the bowl with chicken on the trivet in the inner pot. Seal the lid, select Pressure and set the time to 15 minutes on High pressure. Press Start.
3. When ready, do a quick pressure release. Take out the bowl with chicken and the trivet from the pot. Drain potatoes and add parsley and salt.
4. Split the potatoes among four serving plates and top with watercress, cucumber slices, hummus, cherry tomatoes, chicken, olives, and feta cheese. Each bowl should be garnished with a lemon wedge.

## Sweet Garlicky Chicken Wings

**(Ready in about:** 20 min | **Servings:** 4)

**Ingredients:**
- 16 chicken wings
- 4 garlic cloves; minced
- ¾ cup potato starch
- ¼ cup butter
- ¼ cup honey
- ½ teaspoon salt

**Directions:**
1. Rinse and pat dry the wings, and place them in a bowl. Add the starch to the bowl, and mix to coat the chicken.
2. Place the chicken in a baking dish that has been previously coated lightly with cooking oil. Close the crisping lid and cook for 5 minutes on Air Crisp mode at 370 F.
3. Meanwhile, whisk the rest of the ingredients together in a bowl. Pour the sauce over the wings and cook for another 10 minutes.

## Greek Chicken

**(Ready in about:** 45 min | **Servings:** 6)

**Ingredients:**
- 1 whole chicken (3 lb); cut in pieces
- ½ cup olive oil
- 3 garlic cloves; minced
- Juice from 1 lemon
- ½ cup white wine
- 1 tablespoon chopped fresh oregano
- 1 tablespoon fresh thyme
- 1 tablespoon fresh rosemary
- Salt and black pepper, to taste

**Directions:**
1. In a large bowl, combine the garlic, rosemary, thyme, olive oil, lemon juice, oregano, salt, and pepper. Mix all ingredients very well and spread the mixture into the Foodi basket.
2. Stir in the chicken. Sprinkle with wine and cook for 45 minutes on Air Crisp mode at 380 F.

## Chicken Tenders with Rice and Broccoli

**(Ready in about:** 60 min | **Servings:** 3)

**Ingredients:**
- 1 pound chicken tenderloins
- 1 can condensed cream chicken soup
- 1 package instant long grain rice
- 1 cup chopped broccoli
- 2 cups water
- 1 tablespoon minced garlic

**Directions:**
1. Place the chicken quarters in the Foodi. Season with salt, pepper and a tablespoon of oil and cook for 30 minutes on Roast mode at 390 F. Meanwhile, in a bowl, mix rice, water; minced garlic, soup, and broccoli. Combine the mixture very well. Remove the chicken from the Foodi and place it on a platter to drain.
2. Spread the rice mixture on the bottom of the dish and place the chicken on top of the rice. Close the crisping lid and cook for 30 minutes on Roast mode at 390 F.

## Rosemary Lemon Chicken

**(Ready in about:** 60 min | **Servings:** 2)

**Ingredients:**
- 2 chicken breasts
- 2 rosemary sprigs
- ½ lemon; cut into wedges
- 1 tablespoon oyster sauce
- 3 tablespoon brown sugar
- 1 tablespoon soy sauce
- ½ tablespoon olive oil
- 1 teaspoon minced ginger

**Directions:**
1. Place the ginger, soy sauce, and olive oil, in a bowl. Add the chicken and coat well. Cover the bowl and refrigerate for 30 minutes. Transfer the marinated chicken to the Foodi basket.
2. Close the crisping lid and cook for about 6 minutes on Air Crisp mode at 370 F.
3. Mix the oyster sauce, rosemary and brown sugar in a small bowl. Pour the sauce over the chicken. Arrange the lemon wedges in the dish. Return to the Foodi and cook for 13 more minutes on Air Crisp mode.

## Buttered Turkey

**(Ready in about:** 25 min | **Servings:** 6)

**Ingredients:**

- 6 turkey breasts, boneless and skinless
- 1 stick butter, melted
- 2 cups panko breadcrumbs
- ½ teaspoon cayenne pepper
- ½ teaspoon black pepper
- 1 teaspoon salt

**Directions:**

1. In a bowl, combine the panko breadcrumbs, half of the black pepper, the cayenne pepper, and half of the salt.
2. In another bowl, combine the melted butter with salt and pepper. Brush the butter mixture over the turkey breast.
3. Coat the turkey with the panko mixture. Arrange on a lined Foodi basket. Close the crisping lid and cook for 15 minutes at 390 F on Air Crisp mode, flipping the meat after 8 minutes.

## Thyme Turkey Nuggets

**(Ready in about:** 20 min | **Servings:** 2)

**Ingredients:**

- 8 oz. turkey breast, boneless and skinless
- 1 cup breadcrumbs
- 1 egg, beaten
- 1 tablespoon dried thyme
- ½ teaspoon dried parsley
- Salt and pepper, to taste

**Directions:**

1. Mince the turkey in a food processor. Transfer to a bowl. Stir in the thyme and parsley, and season with salt and pepper.
2. Take a nugget-sized piece of the turkey mixture and shape it into a ball, or another form. Dip it in the breadcrumbs, then egg, then in the breadcrumbs again. Place the nuggets onto a prepared baking dish. Close the crisping lid and cook for 10 minutes on Air Crisp mode at 350 F.

## Korean Barbecued Satay

**(Ready in about:** 4h 15 min | **Servings:** 4)

**Ingredients:**

- 1 lb. boneless; skinless chicken tenders
- ½ cup pineapple juice
- ½ cup soy sauce
- ⅓ cup sesame oil
- 4 scallions; chopped
- 1 pinch black pepper
- 4 cloves garlic; chopped
- 2 teaspoon sesame seeds, toasted
- 1 teaspoon fresh ginger, grated

**Directions:**

1. Skew each tender and trim any excess fat. Mix the other ingredients in one large bowl. Add the skewered chicken and place in the fridge for 4 to 24 hours.
2. Preheat the Foodi to 370 degrees F. Using a paper towel, pat the chicken dry. Fry for 10 minutes on Air Crisp mode.

## Crumbed Sage Chicken Scallopini

**(Ready in about:** 12 min | **Servings:** 4)

**Ingredients:**

- 4 chicken breasts; skinless and boneless
- 2 oz. flour
- 3 oz. breadcrumbs
- 2 eggs, beaten
- 2 tablespoon grated Parmesan cheese
- 1 tablespoon fresh; chopped sage
- Cooking spray

**Directions:**

1. Place some plastic wrap underneath and on top of the chicken breasts. Using a rolling pin beat the meat until it becomes fragile.
2. In a small bowl, combine the Parmesan, sage, and breadcrumbs. Dip the chicken in the egg first, and then in the sage mixture.
3. Spray with cooking oil and arrange the meat in the Foodi. Cook for 7 minutes on Air Crisp mode at 370 F.

## Buttermilk Chicken Thighs

**(Ready in about:** 4 hours 40 min | **Servings:** 6)

**Ingredients:**

- 1 ½ lb. chicken thighs
- 2 cups buttermilk
- 2 cups flour
- 1 tablespoon paprika
- 1 tablespoon baking powder
- 2 teaspoon black pepper
- 1 teaspoon cayenne pepper
- 3 teaspoon salt divided

**Directions:**

1. Rinse and pat dry the chicken thighs. Place the chicken thighs in a bowl. Add cayenne pepper, 2 teaspoon salt, black pepper, and buttermilk, and stir to coat well.
2. Refrigerate for 4 hours. Preheat the Foodi to 350 degrees F. In another bowl, mix the flour, paprika, 1 teaspoon salt, and baking powder.
3. Dredge half of the chicken thighs, one at a time, in the flour, and then place on a lined dish. Close the crisping lid and cook for 18 minutes on Air Crisp mode, flipping once halfway through. Repeat with the other batch.

# Beef, Pork & Lamb

## Beef Stew with Beer

**(Ready in about:** 60 min | **Servings:** 4)

**Ingredients:**
- 2 lb. beef stewed meat; cut into bite-size pieces
- 1 packet dry onion soup mix
- 2 cloves garlic; minced
- 2 cups beef broth
- ¼ cup flour
- 1 medium bottle beer
- 3 tablespoon butter
- 2 tablespoon Worcestershire sauce
- 1 tablespoon tomato paste
- Salt and black pepper to taste

**Directions:**
1. In a zipper bag, add beef, salt, all-purpose flour, and pepper. Close the bag up and shake it to coat the meat well with the mixture. Select Sear/Sauté mode on the Foodi. Melt the butter, and brown the beef on both sides, for 5 minutes.
2. Pour the broth to deglaze the bottom of the pot. Stir in tomato paste, beer, Worcestershire sauce, and the onion soup mix.
3. Close the lid, secure the pressure valve, and select Pressure mode on High pressure for 25 minutes. Press Start/Stop to start cooking.
4. Once the timer is done, do a natural pressure release for 10 minutes, and then a quick pressure release to let out any remaining steam.
5. Open the pressure lid and close the crisping lid. Cook on Broil mode for 10 minutes. Spoon the beef stew into serving bowls and serve with over a bed of vegetable mash with steamed greens.

## Chorizo Stuffed Yellow Bell Peppers

**(Ready in about:** 40 min | **Servings:** 4)

**Ingredients:**
- ¾ pound chorizo
- 1 small onion; diced
- ⅔ cup diced fresh tomatoes
- 1½ cups cooked rice
- 1 cup shredded Mexican blend cheese; divided
- 4 large yellow bell peppers
- 2 teaspoon olive oil

**Directions:**
1. Cut about ¼ to ⅓ inch off the top of each pepper. Cut through the ribs inside the peppers and pull out the core and remove as much of the ribs as possible.
2. On the Foodi, choose Sear/Sauté and adjust to Medium. Press Start to preheat the inner pot for 5 minutes. Heat the oil in the pot until shimmering and cook in the chorizo while breaking the meat with a spatula. Cook until just starting to brown, about 2 minutes.
3. Add the onion and sauté until the vegetables soften and the chorizo has now browned, about 3 minutes.
4. Turn the Foodi off and scoop the chorizo and vegetables into a medium bowl. Add the tomatoes, rice, and ½ cup of cheese to the bowl. Mix to combine well.
5. Spoon the filling mixture into the bell peppers to the brim. Clean the inner pot with a paper towel and return the pot to the base. Pour 1 cup of water into the pot and fix the rack in the pot in the lower position. Put the peppers on the rack and cover the tops loosely with a piece of foil.
6. Lock the pressure lid into place and set to Seal. Choose Pressure; adjust the pressure to High and the time to 12 minutes. Press Start.
7. After cooking, perform a quick pressure release and carefully open the lid. Remove the foil from the top of the peppers and sprinkle the remaining ½ cup of cheese on the peppers.
8. Close the crisping lid; choose Broil, adjust the time to 5 minutes, and press Start to broil the cheese. After 4 minutes, open the lid and check the peppers. The cheese should have melted and browned a bit. If not, close the lid and continue cooking. Let the peppers cool for several minutes before serving.

## Beef Bourguignon

**(Ready in about:** 45 min | **Servings:** 4)

**Ingredients:**

- 2 lb. stewing beef; cut in large chunks
- ½ lb. mushrooms; sliced
- 2 carrots, peeled and chopped
- 1 onion; sliced
- 2 cloves garlic, crushed
- 1 cup red wine
- ½ cup cognac
- 2 cups beef broth
- 1 bunch thyme
- ¼ cup pearl onion
- 2 ½ tablespoon olive oil
- 2 tablespoon flour
- 3 teaspoon tomato paste
- ¼ teaspoon red wine vinegar
- Salt and pepper, to taste

**Directions:**

1. Select Sear/Sauté mode. Season the beef with salt, pepper, and a light sprinkle of flour. Heat the oil in the pot, and brown the meat on all sides. Pour the cognac into the pot and stir the mixture with a spoon to deglaze the bottom. Stir in thyme, red wine, broth, paste, garlic, mushrooms, onion, and pearl onions.
2. Close the lid, secure the pressure valve, and select Pressure mode on High for 25 minutes. Press Start/Stop.
3. Once the timer is off, do a natural pressure release for 10 minutes, then a quick pressure release to let out the remaining steam. Close the crisping lid and cook for 10 minutes on Broil mode. When ready, open the lid.
4. Use the spoon to remove the thyme, adjust the taste with salt and pepper, and add the vinegar. Stir the sauce and serve hot, with a side of rice.

## Caribbean Ropa Vieja

**(Ready in about:** 1 hr 10 min | **Servings:** 6)

**Ingredients:**

- 2 pounds beef skirt steak
- ¼ cup cheddar cheese, shredded
- 1 cup tomato sauce
- 3½ cups beef stock
- 1 cup dry red wine
- ¼ cup minced garlic
- ¼ cup olive oil
- 1 green bell pepper, thinly sliced
- 1 red bell pepper, thinly sliced
- 2 bay leaves
- 1 red onion, halved and thinly sliced
- 1 tablespoon vinegar
- 1 teaspoon dried oregano
- 1 teaspoon ground cumin
- Salt and ground black pepper to taste

**Directions:**

1. Season the skirt steak with pepper and salt. Add water into Foodi; mix in bay leaves and flank steak. Seal the pressure lid, choose Pressure, set to High, and set the timer to 35 minutes. Press Start. When ready, release the pressure quickly.
2. Remove skirt steak to a cutting board and allow to sit for about 5 minutes. Press Start. When cooled, shred the beef using two forks. Drain the pressure cooker, and reserve the bay leaves and 1 cup liquid.
3. Warm the oil on Sear/Sauté. Add onion, red bell pepper, cumin, garlic, green bell pepper, and oregano and continue cooking for 5 minutes until vegetables are softened.
4. Stir in reserved liquid, tomato sauce, bay leaves and red wine. Return shredded beef to the pot with vinegar; season with pepper and salt.
5. Seal the pressure lid, choose Pressure, set to High, and set the timer to 15 minutes. Press Start. Release pressure naturally for 10 minutes, then turn steam vent valve to Venting to release the remaining pressure quickly. Serve with shredded cheese.

## Thai Roasted Beef

**(Ready in about:** 4 hours 20 min | **Servings:** 2)

**Ingredients:**

- 1 lb. ground beef
- Thumb-sized piece of ginger; chopped
- 3 chilies, deseeded and chopped
- 4 garlic cloves; chopped
- Juice of 1 lime
- 2 tablespoon oil
- 2 tablespoon fish sauce
- 2 tablespoon soy sauce
- 2 tablespoon mirin
- 2 tablespoon coriander; chopped
- 2 tablespoon basil; chopped
- ½ teaspoon salt
- ½ teaspoon pepper
- 1 teaspoon brown sugar

**Directions:**

1. Place all ingredients, except beef, salt, and pepper, in a blender; pulse until smooth. Season the beef with salt and pepper. Place the meat and Thai mixture in a zipper bag. Shake well to combine and let marinate in the fridge for about 4 hours.
2. Place the beef in the Foodi basket and cook for about 12 minutes, or a little more for well done, on Air Crisp mode at 350 F. Let sit for 5 minutes before serving.

## Smoky Horseradish Spare Ribs

**(Ready in about:** 55 min | **Servings:** 4)

**Ingredients:**

- 1 spare rack ribs
- 1 cup smoky horseradish sauce
- 1 teaspoon salt

**Directions:**

1. Season all sides of the rack with salt and cut into 3 pieces. Cut the rack into 3 pieces. Pour 1 cup of water into the Foodi's inner pot. Fix the reversible rack in the pot in the lower position and put the ribs on top, bone-side down.
2. Seal the pressure lid, choose Pressure; adjust the pressure to High and the cook time to 18 minutes. Press Start. After cooking, perform a quick pressure release and carefully open the lid.
3. Take out the rack with ribs and pour out the water from the pot. Return the inner pot to the base. Set the reversible rack and ribs in the pot in the lower position. Close the crisping lid and Choose Air Crisp; adjust the temperature to 400°F and the cook time to 20 minutes. Press Start.
4. After 10 minutes, open the lid and turn the ribs. Lightly baste the bony side of the ribs with the smoky horseradish sauce and close the lid to cook further. After 4 minutes, open the lid and turn the ribs again. Baste the meat side with the remaining sauce and close the lid to cook until the ribs are done.

## Teriyaki Pork Noodles

**(Ready in about:** 60 min | **Servings:** 4)

**Ingredients:**

- 1 pork tenderloin, trimmed and cut into 1-inch pieces
- 1 pound green beans, trimmed
- 1 cup teriyaki sauce
- 8 ounces egg noodles
- 1 tablespoon olive oil
- ¼ teaspoon salt
- ¼ teaspoon black pepper
- Cooking spray
- Sesame seeds, for garnish

**Directions:**

1. Pour the egg noodles and cover with enough water in the pot. Seal the pressure lid, choose Pressure, set to High, and set the time to 2 minutes. Choose Start/Stop.
2. In a large bowl, toss the green beans with the olive oil, salt, and black pepper. In another bowl, toss the pork with the teriyaki sauce. When the egg noodles are ready, perform a quick pressure release, and carefully open the lid.

3. Fix the reversible rack in the upper position of the pot, which will be over the egg noodles. Oil the rack with cooking spray and place the pork in the rack. Also, lay the green beans around the pork.
4. Close the crisping lid. Choose Broil and set the time to 12 minutes. Press Start/Stop to begin cooking the pork and vegetables.
5. When done cooking, check for your desired crispiness and take the rack out of the pot. Serve the pork and green beans over the drained egg noodles and garnish with sesame seeds.

## Pot Roast with Biscuits

**(Ready in about:** 75 min | **Servings:** 6)

**Ingredients:**

- 1 (3-pound) chuck roast
- 1 pound small butternut squash; diced
- 1 small red onion, peeled and quartered
- 2 carrots, peeled and cut into 1-inch pieces
- 6 refrigerated biscuits
- 1 bay leaf
- ⅔ cup dry red wine

- ⅔ cup beef broth
- ¾ cup frozen pearl onions
- 2 tablespoon olive oil
- 1½ teaspoon salt
- 1 teaspoon dried oregano leaves
- ¼ teaspoon black pepper

**Directions:**

1. On the Foodi, choose Sear/Sauté and adjust to Medium-High. Press Start to preheat the pot. Heat the olive oil until shimmering. Season the beef on both sides with salt and add to the pot. Cook, undisturbed, for 3 minutes or until deeply browned. Flip the roast over and brown the other side for 3 minutes. Transfer the beef to a wire rack.
2. Pour the oil out of the pot and add the wine to the pot. Stir with a wooden spoon, scraping the bottom of the pot to let off any browned bits. Bring to a boil and cook for 1 to 2 minutes or until the wine has reduced by half.
3. Mix in the beef broth, oregano, bay leaf, black pepper, and red onion. Stir to combine and add the beef with its juices. Seal the pressure lid and choose Pressure; adjust the pressure to High and the cook time to 35 minutes. Press Start to begin cooking.
4. After cooking, perform a quick pressure release. Carefully open the pressure lid.
5. Add the butternut squash, carrots, and pearl onions to the pot. Lock the pressure lid into place, set to Seal position and Choose Pressure; adjust the pressure to High and the cook time to 2 minutes. Press Start to cook the vegetables.
6. After cooking, perform a quick pressure release, and open the lid. Transfer the beef to a cutting board and cover with aluminum foil.
7. Put the reversible rack in the upper position of the pot and cover with a circular piece of aluminum foil. Put the biscuits on the rack and put the rack in the pot.
8. Close the crisping lid and Choose Bake/Roast; adjust the temperature to 300°F and the cook time to 15 minutes. Press Start. After 8 minutes, open the lid and carefully flip the biscuits over. After baking, remove the rack and biscuits. Allow the biscuits to cool for a few minutes before serving.
9. While the biscuits cook, remove the foil from the beef and cut it against the grain into slices. Remove and discard the bay leaf and transfer the beef to a serving platter. Spoon the vegetables and the sauce over the beef. Serve with the biscuits.

## Baked Rigatoni with Beef Tomato Sauce

**(Ready in about:** 75 min | **Servings:** 4)

**Ingredients:**

- 2 pounds ground beef
- 2 (24-ounce) cans tomato sauce
- 16-ounce dry rigatoni
- 1 cup cottage cheese
- 1 cup shredded mozzarella cheese
- ½ cup chopped fresh parsley

- 1 cup water
- 1 cup dry red wine
- 1 tablespoon butter
- ½ teaspoon garlic powder
- ½ teaspoon salt

**Directions:**
1. Choose Sear/Sauté and set to High. Choose Start/Stop to preheat the pot. Melt the butter, add the beef and cook for 5 minutes, or until browned and cooked well. Stir in the tomato sauce, water, wine, and rigatoni; season with the garlic powder and salt.
2. Put the pressure lid together and lock in the Seal position. Choose Pressure, set to Low, and set the time to 2 minutes. Choose Start/Stop to begin cooking.
3. When the timer is done, perform a natural pressure release for 10 minutes, then a quick pressure release and carefully open the lid. Stir in the cottage cheese and evenly sprinkle the top of the pasta with the mozzarella cheese. Close the crisping lid.
4. Choose Broil, and set the time to 3 minutes. Choose Start/Stop to begin. Cook for 3 minutes, or until the cheese has melted, slightly browned, and bubbly. Garnish with the parsley and serve immediately.

## Cheese burgers in Hoagies

### (**Ready in about:** 65 min | **Servings:** 4)

**Ingredients:**
- 1 lb. chuck beef roast
- 1 (14 oz) can French onion soup
- 3 slices Provolone cheese
- 3 hoagies, halved
- 1 onion; sliced
- 2 Cups beef broth
- 1 tablespoon olive oil
- 2 tablespoon Worcestershire sauce
- 1 teaspoon garlic powder
- 3 teaspoon mayonnaise
- Salt and black pepper to taste

**Directions:**
1. Season the beef with garlic powder, salt, and pepper. On Foodi, select Sear/Sauté mode. Heat the olive oil and brown the beef on both sides for about 5 minutes. Remove the meat onto a plate.
2. Into the pot, add the onions and cook until soft. Then, pour the beef broth and stir, while scraping the bottom off every stuck bit. Add the onion soup, Worcestershire sauce, and beef. Close the lid, secure the pressure valve, and select Pressure mode on High pressure for 20 minutes. Press Start/Stop.
3. Once the timer has stopped, do a natural pressure release for 10-15 minutes, and then a quick pressure release to let out any remaining steam.
4. Use two forks to shred the meat. Close the crisping lid and cook on Bake/Roast for 10 minutes at 350 F. When ready, open the lid and strain the juice of the pot through a sieve into a bowl. Assemble the burgers by slathering mayo on halved hoagies, spoon the shredded meat over and top each hoagie with cheese.

## Beef Congee

### (**Ready in about:** 1 hr | **Servings:** 6)

**Ingredients:**
- 2 pounds ground beef
- 1 (1 inch) piece fresh ginger; minced
- 2 cloves garlic; minced
- 6 cups beef stock
- 1 cup jasmine rice
- 1 cup kale, roughly chopped
- 1 cups water
- salt and ground black pepper to taste
- Fresh cilantro; chopped

**Directions:**
1. Run cold water and rinse rice. Add garlic, rice, and ginger into the Foodi. Pour water and stock into the pot and spread the beef on top of rice.
2. Seal the pressure lid, choose Pressure, set to High, and set the timer to 30 minutes. Press Start. Once ready, release pressure naturally for 10 minutes.
3. Stir in kale to obtain the desired consistency. Add pepper and salt for seasoning. Divide into serving plates and top with cilantro.

# Calzones with Sausage and Mozzarella

**(Ready in about:** 35 min | **Servings:** 4)

**Ingredients:**

- 1 pound frozen bread dough
- 1 small green bell pepper, seeded and chopped
- 2 or 3 Italian sausages
- ¼ cup tomato sauce
- 1 cup shredded mozzarella cheese
- 2 tablespoon olive oil

**Directions:**

1. On your Foodi, choose Sear/Sauté, and adjust to Medium-High to preheat the inner pot. Press Start to preheat the pot. Heat 1 tablespoon of olive oil in the pot and sauté the bell pepper for 1 minute or until just starting to soften. Remove the pepper into a plate and set aside. Brown the sausages for 2 to 3 minutes on one side. Turn the sausages and brown the other side.
2. Add ¾ cup of water to the inner pot. Then, lock the pressure lid into place and set to seal. Choose Pressure; adjust the pressure to High and the cook time to 4 minutes. Press Start. After cooking, perform a quick pressure release and carefully open the pressure lid.
3. Remove the sausages from the pot onto a cutting board and cool for several minutes. Discard the water in the pot, wipe the pot dry with a clean napkin, and return the pot to the base. When the sausages have cooled, slice into ¼-inch rounds.
4. Cut four pieces of parchment paper about 8 inches and divide the dough into four equal pieces. One at a time and on a piece of parchment, use your hands to press each dough into a circle about 6 to 7 inches in diameter.
5. Close the crisping lid. Choose Bake/Roast and adjust the temperature to 400°F. Press Start to preheat the pot for 5 minutes.
6. While the preheats, make the calzones. One after the other, spread 1 tablespoon of tomato sauce over half a dough circle, leaving a ½-inch clear border. Arrange the sausage rounds in a single layer and sprinkle a quarter of the green peppers over the top.
7. Top with a quarter cup of cheese. Use the parchment to pull the other side of the dough over the filling and pinch the edges together to seal. Repeat the process with another dough.
8. Cut the parchment around each calzone, so it is about ½ inch larger than the calzone. Brush the calzones with some of the remaining olive oil. With a large spatula, transfer the two calzones to the reversible rack set in the lower position in the pot. Open the lid and place the rack in the pot.
9. Close the crisping lid and choose Bake/Roast; adjust the temperature to 400°F and the cook time to 12 minutes. Press Start.
10. After 6 minutes, check the calzones, which will be a dark golden brown. Remove the rack and turn the calzones over. Remove the parchment paper and brush the tops with a little olive oil. Return the rack to the pot. Close the lid and continue cooking for the last 6 minutes.
11. While the first two calzones bake, assemble the remaining two. When the first set of calzones are done, transfer to a wire rack to cool and bake the second batch.

## Braised Short Ribs with Mushrooms

**(Ready in about:** 1 hr | **Servings:** 4)

**Ingredients:**

- 2 pounds beef short ribs
- 1 small onion; sliced
- 1 bell pepper; diced
- 4 garlic cloves, smashed
- ⅓ cup beef broth
- 1 cup beer
- 1 cup crimini mushrooms; sliced
- 1 tablespoon olive oil
- 1 tablespoon soy sauce
- 1 teaspoon smoked paprika
- ½ teaspoon dried oregano
- ½ teaspoon cayenne pepper
- salt and ground black pepper to taste

**Directions:**

1. In a small bowl, combine pepper, paprika, cayenne pepper, salt, and oregano. Rub the seasoning mixture on all sides of the short ribs.
2. Warm oil on Sear/Sauté. Add mushrooms and cook until browned, about 6-8 minutes; set aside. Add short ribs to the Foodi, and cook for 3 minutes for each side until browned; set aside on a plate.
3. Throw in garlic and onion to the oil and stir-fry for 2 minutes until fragrant. Add in beer to deglaze, scrape the pot's bottom to get rid of any browned bits of food; bring to a simmer and cook for 2 minutes until reduced slightly.
4. Stir in soy sauce, bell pepper and beef broth. Dip short ribs into the liquid in a single layer. Seal the pressure lid, choose Pressure, set to High, and set the timer to 40 minutes. Press Start. Release pressure naturally for about 10 minutes. Divide the ribs with the sauce into bowls and top with fried mushrooms.

## Ground Beef Stuffed Empanadas

**(Ready in about:** 60 min | **Servings:** 2)

**Ingredients:**

- ¼ pound ground beef
- 2 small tomatoes; chopped
- 8 square gyoza wrappers
- 1 egg, beaten
- 1 garlic clove; minced
- ½ white onion; chopped
- 6 green olives, pitted and chopped
- 1 tablespoon olive oil
- ¼ teaspoon cumin powder
- ¼ teaspoon paprika
- ⅛ teaspoon cinnamon powder

**Directions:**

1. Choose Sear/Sauté on the pot and set to Medium High. Choose Start/Stop to preheat the pot. Put the oil, garlic, onion, and beef in the preheated pot and cook for 5 minutes, stirring occasionally, until the fragrant and the beef is no longer pink.
2. Stir in the olives, cumin, paprika, and cinnamon and cook for an additional 3 minutes. Add the tomatoes and cook for 1 more minute.
3. Spoon the beef mixture into a plate and allow cooling for a few minutes.
4. Meanwhile, put the Crisping Basket in the pot. Close the crisping lid; choose Air Crisp, set the temperature to 400°F, and the time to 5 minutes. Press Start.
5. Lay the gyoza wrappers on a flat surface. Place 1 to 2 tablespoons of the beef mixture in the middle of each wrapper. Brush the edges of the wrapper with egg and fold in half to form a triangle. Pinch the edges together to seal.
6. Place 4 empanadas in a single layer in the preheated Basket. Close the crisping lid. Choose Air Crisp, set the temperature to 400°F, and set the time to 7 minutes. Choose Start/Stop to begin frying.
7. Once the timer is done, remove the empanadas from the basket and transfer to a plate. Repeat with the remaining empanadas.

## Chunky Pork Meatloaf with Mashed Potatoes

**(Ready in about:** 55 min | **Servings:** 4)

**Ingredients:**

- 2 pounds potatoes; cut into large chunks
- 12 ounces pork meatloaf
- 2 garlic cloves; minced
- 2 large eggs
- 12 individual saltine crackers, crushed
- 1¾ cups full cream milk; divided
- 1 cup chopped white onion
- ½ cup heavy cream
- ¼ cup barbecue sauce
- 1 tablespoon olive oil
- 3 tablespoon chopped fresh cilantro
- 3 tablespoon unsalted butter
- ¼ teaspoon dried rosemary
- 1 teaspoon yellow mustard
- 1 teaspoon Worcestershire sauce
- 2 teaspoon salt
- ½ teaspoon black pepper

**Directions:**

1. Select Sear/Sauté and adjust to Medium. Press Start to preheat the pot for 5 minutes. Heat the olive oil until shimmering and sauté the onion and garlic in the oil. Cook for about 2 minutes until the onion softens. Transfer the onion and garlic to a plate and set aside.
2. In a bowl, crumble the meatloaf mix into small pieces. Sprinkle with 1 teaspoon of salt, the pepper, cilantro, and thyme. Add the sautéed onion and garlic. Sprinkle the crushed saltine crackers over the meat and seasonings.
3. In a small bowl, beat ¼ cup of milk, the eggs, mustard, and Worcestershire sauce. Pour the mixture on the layered cracker crumbs and gently mix the ingredients in the bowl with your hands. Shape the meat mixture into an 8-inch round.
4. Cover the reversible rack with aluminum foil and carefully lift the meatloaf into the rack. Pour the remaining 1½ cups of milk and the heavy cream into the inner pot. Add the potatoes, butter, and remaining salt. Place the rack with meatloaf over the potatoes in the upper position in the pot.
5. Seal the pressure lid, choose Pressure; adjust the pressure to High and the cook time to 25 minutes; press Start. After cooking, perform a quick pressure release, and carefully open the pressure lid. Brush the meatloaf with the barbecue sauce.
6. Close the crisping lid; choose Broil and adjust the cook time to 7 minutes. Press Start to begin grilling. When the top has browned, remove the rack, and transfer the meatloaf to a serving platter. Mash the potatoes in the pot. Slice the meatloaf and serve with the mashed potatoes.

## Beef and Bacon Chili

**(Ready in about:** 1 hr | **Servings:** 6)

**Ingredients:**

- 2 pounds stewing beef, trimmed
- 29 ounces canned whole tomatoes
- 15 ounces canned kidney beans, drained and rinsed
- 4 ounces smoked bacon; cut into strips
- 1 chipotle in adobo sauce, finely chopped
- 1 onion; diced
- 2 bell peppers; diced
- 3 garlic cloves; minced
- 2 cups beef broth
- 1 tablespoon ground cumin
- 2 teaspoon olive oil; divided
- 1 teaspoon chili powder
- ½ teaspoon cayenne pepper
- 4 teaspoon salt; divided
- 1 teaspoon freshly ground black pepper; divided

**Directions:**

1. Set on Sear/Sauté, set to Medium High, and choose Start/Stop to preheat the pot and fry the bacon until crispy, about 5 minutes. Set aside.
2. Rub the beef with ½ teaspoon black pepper and 1 teaspoon salt. In the bacon fat, brown beef for 5-6 minutes; transfer to a plate.

3. Warm the oil. Add in garlic, peppers and onion and cook for 3 to 4 minutes until soft. Stir in cumin, cayenne pepper, the extra pepper and salt; chopped chipotle, and chili powder and cook for 30 seconds until soft.
4. Return beef and bacon to the pot with vegetables and spices; add in tomatoes and broth.
5. Seal the pressure lid, choose Pressure, set to High, and set the timer to 45 minutes. Press Start. When ready, release the pressure quickly. Stir in beans. Let simmer on Keep Warm for 10 minutes until flavors combine.

## Honey Short Ribs with Rosemary Potatoes

**(Ready in about:** 105 min | **Servings:** 4)

**Ingredients:**

- 4 bone-in beef short ribs, silver skin
- 2 potatoes, peeled and cut into 1-inch pieces
- ½ cup beef broth
- 3 garlic cloves; minced
- 1 onion; chopped
- 2 tablespoon olive oil
- 2 tablespoon honey
- 2 tablespoon minced fresh rosemary
- 1 teaspoon salt
- 1 teaspoon black pepper

**Directions:**

1. Choose Sear/Sauté on the pot and set to High. Choose Start/Stop to preheat the pot. Season the short ribs on all sides with ½ teaspoon of salt and ½ teaspoon of pepper. Heat 1 tablespoon of olive oil and brown the ribs on all sides, about 10 minutes total. Stir in the onion, honey, broth, 1 tablespoon of rosemary, and garlic.
2. Seal the pressure lid, choose Pressure, set to High, and set the time to 40 minutes. Choose Start/Stop to begin. In a large bowl, toss the potatoes with the remaining oil, rosemary, salt, and black pepper.
3. When the ribs are ready, perform a quick pressure release and carefully open the lid.
4. Fix the reversible rack in the higher position of the pot, which is over the ribs. Put the potatoes on the rack. Close the crisping lid. Choose Bake/Roast, set the temperature to 350°F, and set the time to 15 minutes. Choose Start/Stop to begin roasting.
5. Once the potatoes are tender and roasted, use tongs to pick the potatoes and the short ribs into a plate; set aside. Choose Sear/Sauté and set to High. Simmer the sauce for 5 minutes and spoon the sauce into a bowl.
6. Allow sitting for 2 minutes and scoop off the fat that forms on top. Serve the ribs with the potatoes and sauce.

## Sweet Potato Gratin with Bacon and Peas

**(Ready in about:** 30 min | **Servings:** 4)

**Ingredients:**

- 1½ pounds sweet potatoes, peeled and quartered
- 10 ounces prosciutto, cooked and diced
- ½ cup heavy cream, or more to taste
- 1 cup shredded Provolone cheese
- ¾ cup frozen peas; thawed
- ½ cup grated Pecorino Romano
- 3 tablespoon chopped fresh chives
- ½ teaspoon salt or to taste
- ⅛ teaspoon freshly ground black pepper

**Directions:**

1. Place the sweet potatoes on the reversible rack. Pour 1 cup of water into the inner pot and put the rack in the lower position in the pot.
2. Seal the pressure lid, choose Pressure; adjust the pressure to High and the cook time to 4 minutes. Press Start to begin cooking. After cooking, perform a quick pressure release, and carefully open the lid.
3. Remove the rack. Empty the water out of the pot and return the pot to the base. Put the potatoes back in the pot and season with the salt and pepper. Use a large fork to break the potatoes into pieces about ½ inch on a side. Mix in the heavy cream, Provolone cheese, and prosciutto. Gently stir in the peas. Sprinkle the mixture with the Pecorino Romano.

4. Close the crisping lid and Choose Bake/Roast; adjust the temperature to 400°F and the cook time to 10 minutes. Press Start to begin browning. When the top of the gratin has browned, sprinkle with chives and serve.

## Herbed Lamb Chops

**(Ready in about:** 30 min | **Servings:** 4)

**Ingredients:**
- 4 lamb chops
- 1 garlic clove, peeled
- ½ tablespoon oregano
- 1 tablespoon plus
- ½ tablespoon thyme
- 2 teaspoon olive oil
- ½ teaspoon salt
- ¼ teaspoon black pepper

**Directions:**
1. Coat the garlic clove with 1 teaspoon of olive oil and cook in the Foodi for 10 minutes on Air Crisp mode. Meanwhile, mix the herbs and seasonings with the remaining olive oil.
2. Using a towel, squeeze the hot roasted garlic clove into the herb mixture and stir to combine. Coat the lamb chops with the mixture well, and place in the Foodi.
3. Close the crisping lid and cook for about 8 to 12 minutes on Air Crisp mode at 390 F, until crispy on the outside.

## Beef and Broccoli Sauce

**(Ready in about:** 35 min | **Servings:** 4)

**Ingredients:**
- 2 lb. chuck roast, boneless and cut into thin strips
- 4 cloves garlic; minced
- 1 cup beef broth
- ¾ cup soy sauce
- 7 cups broccoli florets
- 1 tablespoon cornstarch
- 1 tablespoon olive oil
- Salt to taste

**Directions:**
1. Open the lid of Foodi, and select Sear/Sauté mode. Add the olive oil, and once heated, add the beef and minced garlic. Cook the meat until brown. Stir in soy sauce and beef broth.
2. Close the lid, secure the pressure valve, and select Pressure mode on High pressure for 10 minutes. Press Start/Stop to start cooking.
3. Once the timer has ended, do a quick pressure release and remove the meat and set aside.
4. Use a soup spoon to fetch out a quarter of the liquid into a bowl, add the cornstarch, and mix it until it is well dissolved.
5. Pour the starch mixture into the pot and place the reversible rack. Place the broccoli florets on it and seal the pressure lid. Select Steam mode on LOW for 5 minutes.
6. When ready, do a quick pressure release and open the lid. Remove the rack, stir the sauce, add the meat and close the crisping lid.
7. Cook for 5 minutes on Broil mode. The sauce should be thick enough when you finish cooking. Dish the beef broccoli sauce into a serving bowl and serve with a side of cooked pasta.

## Gingery Beef and Broccoli

**(Ready in about:** 70 min | **Servings:** 4)

**Ingredients:**

- 2 pounds skirt steak; cut into strips
- 1 head broccoli, trimmed into florets
- 3 scallions, thinly sliced
- 4 garlic cloves; minced
- ½ cup coconut aminos

- ½ cup water, plus 3 tbsp.
- ⅔ cup dark brown sugar
- 1 tablespoon olive oil
- 2 tablespoon cornstarch
- ½ teaspoon ginger puree

**Directions:**

1. Choose Sear/Sauté on the pot and set to Medium High; hit Start/Stop to preheat the pot. Pour the oil and beef in the preheated pot and brown the beef strips on both sides, about 5 minutes in total. Remove the beef from the pot and set aside.
2. Add the garlic to the oil and Sear/Sauté for 1 minute or until fragrant. Stir in the coconut aminos, ½ cup of water, brown sugar, and ginger to the pot. Mix evenly and add the beef. Seal the pressure lid, choose Pressure, set to High, and set the time to 10 minutes. Choose Start/Stop to begin cooking.
3. Meanwhile, in a small bowl whisk combine the cornstarch and the remaining water.
4. When done cooking, perform a quick pressure release. Choose Sear/Sauté and set to Medium Low. Choose Start/Stop. Pour in the cornstarch mixture and stir continuously until the sauce becomes syrupy. Add the broccoli, stir to coat in the sauce, and cook for another 5 minutes. Once ready, garnish with scallions, and serve.

## Steak and Chips

**(Ready in about:** 50 min | **Servings:** 4)

**Ingredients:**

- 4 potatoes; cut into wedges
- 4 rib eye steaks
- 1 tablespoon olive oil
- 1 teaspoon sweet paprika

- 1 teaspoon salt; divided
- 1 teaspoon ground black pepper
- Cooking spray

**Directions:**

1. Put the Crisping Basket in the pot. Close the crisping lid. Choose Air Crisp, set the temperature to 390°F, and set the time to 5 minutes. Press Start. Meanwhile, rub all over with olive oil. Put the potatoes in the preheated Crisping Basket and season with ½ teaspoon of salt and ½ teaspoon of black pepper and sweet paprika.
2. Close the crisping lid. Choose Air Crisp, set the temperature to 400°F, and set the time to 35 minutes. Choose Start/Stop to begin baking.
3. Season the steak on both sides with the remaining salt and black pepper. When done cooking, remove potatoes to a plate.
4. Grease the Crisping Basket with cooking spray and put the steaks in the basket.
5. Close the crisping lid. Choose Air Crisp, set the temperature to 400°F, and set the time to 8 minutes. Choose Start/Stop to begin grilling.
6. When ready, check the steaks for your preferred doneness and cook for a few more minutes if needed. Take out the steaks from the basket and rest for 5 minutes. Serve the steaks with the potato wedges and the steak sauce.

## Braised Short Ribs with Creamy Sauce

**(Ready in about:** 1 hr 55 min | **Servings:** 6)

**Ingredients:**

- 3 pounds beef short ribs
- 1 (14.5 ounces) can diced tomatoes
- 1 celery stalk; chopped
- 3 garlic cloves; chopped
- 1 onion; chopped
- 1 large carrot; chopped
- 2 cups beef broth
- ½ cup cheese cream
- ½ cup dry red wine
- ¼ cup red wine vinegar
- 2 bay leaves
- 2 tablespoon olive oil
- 2 tablespoon chopped parsley
- ¼ teaspoon red pepper flakes
- 2 teaspoon salt; divided
- 1½ teaspoon freshly ground black pepper; divided

**Directions:**

1. Season your short ribs with 1 teaspoon black pepper and 1 teaspoon salt. Warm olive oil on Sear/Sauté. Add in short ribs and sear for 3 minutes each side until browned. Set aside on a bowl.
2. Drain everything only to be left with 1 tablespoon of the remaining fat from the pot. Set on Sear/Sauté, and stir-fry garlic, carrot, onion, and celery in the hot fat for 4 to 6 minutes until fragrant.
3. Stir in broth, wine, red pepper flakes, vinegar, tomatoes, bay leaves, and remaining pepper and salt; turn the Foodi to Sear/Sauté on Low and bring the mixture to a boil.
4. With the bone-side up, lay short ribs into the braising liquid. Seal the pressure lid, choose Pressure, set to High, and set the timer to 40 minutes. Press Start.
5. When ready, release the pressure quickly. Set the short ribs on a plate. Get rid of bay leaves. Skim and get rid of the fat from the surface of braising liquid.
6. Using an immersion blender, blend the liquid for 1 minute; add cream cheese, pepper and salt and blitz until smooth Arrange the ribs onto a serving plate, pour the sauce over and top with parsley.

## Carbonnade Flamande

**(Ready in about:** 70 min | **Servings:** 4)

**Ingredients:**

- 2 pounds brisket; cut into 2 or 3 pieces
- ¼ cup beef broth
- 1 large onion; sliced
- 8 fluid ounces stout
- 1 tablespoon olive oil
- 2 tablespoon chopped fresh chervil
- ½ teaspoon salt
- ½ teaspoon Dijon-style mustard
- ½ teaspoon brown sugar to taste
- ¼ teaspoon dried rosemary leaves

**Directions:**

1. Season the brisket with salt on all sides. On the Foodi, choose Sear/Sauté and adjust to Medium to preheat the inner pot. Press Start. Allow the pot to preheat for 5 minutes. Heat the olive oil in the pot until shimmering and sear the brisket. Cook, without turning, for 4 minutes or until browned. Use tongs to turn the beef and move to the side.
2. Add the onion on the other side. Cook, stirring, for 1 to 2 minutes or until slightly softened. Pour in the stout, scraping off any browned bits from the bottom of the pot. Simmer and cook until the stout has reduced by about half. Stir in the rosemary and broth.
3. Seal the pressure lid, choose pressure; adjust the pressure to High and the cook time to 35 minutes; press Start. After cooking, perform a natural pressure release for 10 minutes, then a quick release and carefully open the pressure lid.
4. Remove the beef onto a cutting board. Scoop off any excess fat on the sauce and stir in the mustard and brown sugar.
5. Choose Sear/Sauté and adjust to Medium. Press Start. Simmer the sauce and cook until reduced to a thin gravy. Taste and adjust the seasoning.
6. Slice the beef and return to the sauce to reheat. Serve over mashed potatoes or noodles and garnish with chervil.

## Sticky Barbeque Baby Back Ribs

**(Ready in about:** 35 min | **Servings:** 4)

**Ingredients:**

- 1 (3-pound) rack baby back ribs; cut into quarters
- 1 cup beer
- 1 cup barbecue sauce
- 3 tablespoon brown sugar
- 1½ tablespoon smoked paprika
- 1 tablespoon salt
- 1 tablespoon black pepper
- 2 teaspoon garlic powder

**Directions:**

1. In a bowl, mix the paprika, brown sugar, garlic, salt, and black pepper. Season all sides of the ribs with the rub. Pour the beer into the pot, put the ribs in the Crisping Basket, and place the basket in the pot. Seal the pressure lid, choose Pressure, set to High, and set the time to 10 minutes. Choose Start/Stop.
2. When done cooking, perform a quick pressure release, and carefully the open the lid. Close the crisping lid. Choose Air Crisp, set the temperature to 400°F, and the time to 15 minutes. Choose Start/Stop to begin crisping.
3. After 10 minutes, open the lid, and brush the ribs with the barbecue sauce. Close the lid to cook further for 5 minutes.

## Barbecue Juicy Pork Chops

**(Ready in about:** 100 min | **Servings:** 4)

**Ingredients:**

- 4 bone-in pork chops
- 1½ cups chicken broth
- 1 tablespoon freshly ground black pepper
- 1 tablespoon olive oil
- 4 tablespoon barbecue sauce
- 3 tablespoon brown sugar
- 1 tablespoon salt
- 1½ tablespoon smoked paprika
- 2 teaspoon garlic powder

**Directions:**

1. Choose Sear/Sauté and set to High. Choose Start/Stop to preheat the pot. In a small bowl, mix the brown sugar, salt, paprika, garlic powder, and black pepper. Season both sides of the pork with the rub. Heat the oil in the preheated pot and sear the pork chops, one at a time, on both sides, about 5 minutes per chop. Set aside.
2. Pour the chicken broth into the pot and with a wooden spoon, scrape the bottom of the pot of any browned bits. Place the Crisping Basket in the upper position of the pot. Put the pork chops in the basket and brush with 2 tablespoons of barbecue sauce.
3. Seal the pressure lid, choose Pressure and set to High. Set the time to 5 minutes, then Choose Start/Stop to begin cooking. When the timer is done, perform a natural pressure release for 10 minutes, then a quick pressure release, and carefully open the lid.
4. Apply the remaining barbecue sauce on both sides of the pork and close the crisping lid. Choose Broil and set the time to 3 minutes. Press Start/Stop to begin. When ready, check for your desired crispiness and remove the pork from the basket.

## Beef and Pepperoncini Peppers

**(Ready in about:** 55 min | **Servings:** 4)

**Ingredients:**

- 2 lb. beef roast; cut into cubes
- 1 pack brown gravy mix
- 1 pack Italian salad dressing mix
- 14 oz. jar pepperoncini peppers, with liquid
- ½ cup water

**Directions:**

1. Place the beef, pepperoncini peppers, brown gravy mix, Italian salad dressing mix, and water, in Foodi's inner pot.
2. Close the lid, secure the pressure valve, and select Pressure mode on High pressure for 35 minutes. Press Start/Stop to start cooking.
3. Once the timer has stopped, do a quick pressure release, and open the pot. Close the crisping lid and cook on Bake/Roast mode for 15 to 20 minutes at 380 F, until nice and tender.
4. When ready, dish the ingredients into a bowl and use two forks to shred the beef. Serve beef sauce in plates with a side of a veggie mash, or bread.

## Sausage with Noodles and Braised Cabbage

**(Ready in about:** 35 min | **Servings:** 4)

**Ingredients:**

- 1½ pounds smoked sausage; cut into 4 pieces
- 3 ounces serrano ham; diced
- 5 ounces wide egg noodles
- 4 cups shredded green cabbage
- 1 small onion; sliced
- ⅓ cup dry white wine
- 1 cup chicken stock
- 1 teaspoon salt
- ¼ teaspoon black pepper
- Cooking spray

**Directions:**

1. On the Foodi, choose Sear/Sauté and adjust to Medium. Press Start to preheat the pot for 5 minutes. Put the ham in the pot and cook for 6 minutes until crisp. Using a slotted spoon, transfer the ham to a paper towel-lined plate to drain, leaving the fat in the pot.
2. Sauté the onion to the pot for about 2 minutes or until the onion starts to soften. Pour in the wine and simmer until the wine reduces slightly while scraping the bottom of the pot with a wooden spoon to let off any browned bits.
3. Pour in the chicken stock, salt, black pepper, and noodles. Stir, while pushing the noodles as much as possible into the sauce. Put the cabbage on top of the noodles and the sausages on the cabbage.
4. Lock the pressure lid into place and seal. Choose Pressure; adjust the pressure to High and the cook time to 3 minutes.
5. When the cooking time is over, do a quick pressure release, and carefully open the lid. Stir the noodles and cabbage and adjust the taste with seasoning.
6. Grease the reversible rack with cooking spray and fix in the upper position of the pot. Transfer the sausages to the rack.
7. Close the crisping lid and Choose Bake/Roast; adjust the temperature to 390°F and the cook time to 8 minutes; press Start.
8. After 4 minutes, open the lid and check the sausages. When browned, turn the sausages, close the lid, and cook to brown the other side. Ladle the cabbage and noodles into a bowl and top with the bacon. Serve with the sausages.

## Greek Beef Gyros

(**Ready in about:** 55 min | **Servings:** 4)

**Ingredients:**
- 1 pound beef sirloin; cut into thin strips
- 1 onion, thinly sliced
- 4 slices pita bread
- 1 clove garlic; minced
- 1 cup Greek yogurt
- ⅓ cup beef broth
- 2 tablespoon fresh dill; chopped
- 2 tablespoon fresh lemon juice
- 2 tablespoon olive oil
- 2 teaspoon dry oregano
- salt and ground black pepper to taste

**Directions:**
1. In the Foodi, mix beef, beef broth, oregano, garlic, lemon juice, pepper, onion, olive oil, and salt.
2. Seal the pressure lid, choose Pressure, set to High, and set the timer to 30 minutes. Press Start. Release pressure naturally for 15 minutes, then turn steam vent valve to Venting to release the remaining pressure quickly. Divide the beef mixture between the pita bread slices, top with yogurt and dill, and roll up to serve.

## Bolognese Pizza

(**Ready in about:** 70 min | **Servings:** 4)

**Ingredients:**
- ½ lb. ground pork, meat cooked and crumbled
- 1 cup shredded mozzarella cheese
- ½ cup canned crushed tomatoes
- 1 yellow bell pepper; sliced; divided
- 4 pizza crusts
- 1 tablespoon chopped fresh basil, for garnish
- 1 teaspoon red chili flakes; divided
- Cooking spray

**Directions:**
1. Place the reversible rack in the pot. Close the crisping lid; choose Air Crisp, set the temperature to 400°F, and the time to 5 minutes.
2. Grease one side of a pizza crust with cooking spray and lay on the preheated rack, oiled side up. Close the crisping lid. Choose Air Crisp, set the temperature to 400°F, and set the time to 4 minutes. Choose Start/Stop to begin baking.
3. Remove the crust from the rack and flip so the crispy side is down. Top the crust with 2 tablespoons of crushed tomatoes, a quarter of bell pepper, 2 ounces of ground pork, ¼ cup of mozzarella cheese, and ¼ tablespoon of red chili flakes.
4. Close the crisping lid. Choose Broil and set the time to 3 minutes. Choose Start/Stop to continue baking. When done baking and crispy as desired, remove the pizza from the rack. Repeat with the remaining pizza crusts and ingredients. Top each pizza with some basil and serve.

## Beef Carnitas

(**Ready in about:** 55 min | **Servings:** 4)

**Ingredients:**
- 2½ pounds bone-in country ribs
- 1 small onion; cut into 8 wedges
- 3 garlic cloves, smashed and peeled
- ¼ cup orange juice
- 2 tablespoon beef stock
- 1 tablespoon lime juice
- 1 teaspoon salt
- Cooking spray

**Directions:**
1. Season the ribs with salt on all sides. In the Foodi's inner pot, combine the orange juice, stock, and lime juice. Drop in the onion and garlic; stir. Put the ribs in the pot,
2. Seal the pressure lid, choose Pressure; adjust the pressure to High and the cook time to 25 minutes. Press Start/Stop to begin cooking.

3. After cooking, do a natural pressure release for 12 minutes. Transfer the ribs to a plate to cool slightly. Remove and discard the bones.
4. Run the juice in the pot through a fat separator and set aside for a few minutes. Pour the sauce back into the pot and reserve the fat.
5. Close the crisping lid and Choose Air Crisp; adjust the temperature to 400°F and the time to 3 minutes to preheat; press Start. Oil the reversible rack with cooking spray and lay the ribs in a single layer on the rack. Baste with the reserved fat.
6. When the Foodi is heated, put the rack in the pot in the upper position. Close the crisping lid and Choose Air Crisp; adjust the temperature to 375°F and the cook time to 6 minutes; press Start.
7. After crisping, put the beef back in the sauce and use long forks to shred the meat. Stir the beef into the sauce. Serve the carnitas with flat bread or on rice.

## Peanut Sauce Beef Satay

(**Ready in about:** 60 min | **Servings:** 4)

### Ingredients:
- 1 pound flank steak
- 1 tablespoon coconut aminos
- 1 tablespoon lime juice
- 1 tablespoon coconut oil
- 1½ teaspoon red curry paste
- ½ teaspoon salt

### For the Cucumber Relish
- 1 serrano chile; cut into thin rounds
- ½ cucumber
- ½ cup rice vinegar
- ¼ cup water
- 2 tablespoon sugar
- 1 teaspoon salt

### For the Sauce
- 1 cup coconut milk
- ½ cup peanut butter
- ⅓ cup water
- 1 tablespoon lime juice
- 1 tablespoon onion; minced
- 1 tablespoon coconut oil
- 1 teaspoon garlic; minced
- 2 teaspoons red curry paste
- 1 teaspoon brown sugar

### Directions:
1. Season both sides of the steak with salt. Put in a resealable plastic bag, set aside, and make the marinade. In a small bowl, whisk the lime juice, curry paste, coconut aminos, and coconut oil. Pour the marinade over the steak, seal the bag, and massage the bag to coat the meat. Set aside for 20 minutes. While the steak marinates; cut the cucumber into ¼-inch slices, then into quarters.
2. In a bowl, whisk the vinegar, water, sugar, and salt until the sugar and salt dissolve. Add the cucumber pieces. Refrigerate until needed.
3. To make the sauce, on the Foodi, choose Sear/Sauté and adjust to Medium-High. Press Start to preheat the pot for 5 minutes. Then, heat the coconut oil until shimmering and sauté the onion and garlic in the pot. Cook for 1 to 2 minutes or until fragrant. Stir in the coconut milk, curry paste, and brown sugar.
4. Seal the pressure lid, choose Pressure; adjust the pressure to High and the cook time to 0 minutes. Press Start. After cooking, perform a quick pressure release, and carefully open the lid. Pour in the water and mix.
5. Remove the meat from the marinade, holding the meat above the bag for a while to drain the excess marinade, put on the reversible rack, and put the rack with the steak in the upper position of the pot above the sauce.
6. Close the crisping lid; choose Broil, adjust the cook time to 14 minutes, and press Start to begin cooking. After about 7 minutes, open the lid and turn the steak. Close the lid and begin broiling.
7. Transfer the steak to a cutting board and allow resting for a few minutes. While the steak cools, mix the peanut butter and lime juice into the sauce. Taste and adjust the seasoning. Cut the steak into thin slices and serve with the peanut sauce and cucumber relish.

## Short Ribs with Egg Noodles

(**Ready in about:** 65 min | **Servings:** 4)

**Ingredients:**

- 4 pounds bone-in short ribs
- 1 garlic clove; minced
- 1½ cups panko bread crumbs
- Low-sodium beef broth
- 6 ounces egg noodles

- 3 tablespoon melted unsalted butter
- 2 tablespoon prepared horseradish
- 6 tablespoon Dijon mustard
- 2½ teaspoon salt
- ½ teaspoon freshly ground black pepper

**Directions:**

1. Season the short ribs on all sides with 1½ teaspoons of salt. Pour 1 cup of broth into the inner pot. Put the reversible rack in the lower position in the pot, and place the short ribs on top. Seal the pressure lid, choose Pressure; adjust the pressure to High and the time to 25 minutes; press Start. After cooking, perform a natural pressure release for 5 minutes, then a quick pressure release, and carefully open the lid. Remove the rack and short ribs.
2. Pour the cooking liquid into a measuring cup to get 2 cups. If lesser than 2 cups, add more broth and season with salt and pepper.
3. Add the egg noodles and the remaining salt. Stir and submerge the noodles as much as possible. Seal the pressure lid, choose Pressure; adjust the pressure to High and the cook time to 4 minutes; press Start.
4. In a bowl, combine the horseradish, Dijon mustard, garlic, and black pepper. Brush the sauce on all sides of the short ribs and reserve any extra sauce.
5. In a bowl, mix the butter and breadcrumbs. Coat the ribs with the crumbs. Put the ribs back on the rack. After cooking, do a quick pressure release, and carefully open the lid. Stir the noodles, which may not be quite done but will continue cooking.
6. Return the rack and beef to the pot in the upper position.
7. Close the crisping lid and Choose Bake/Roast; adjust the temperature to 400°F and the cook time to 15 minutes. Press Start. After 8 minutes, open the lid and turn the ribs over. Close the lid and continue cooking. Serve the beef and noodles, with the extra sauce on the side, if desired.

## Beef and Cabbage Stew

(**Ready in about:** 30 min | **Servings:** 4)

**Ingredients:**

- 1 lb. ground beef
- 1 large head cabbage; cut in chunks
- 1 cup diced tomatoes
- 1 ½ cup beef broth
- ¼ cup Plain vinegar
- 1 cup rice
- ½ cup chopped onion
- 4 cloves garlic; minced

- 1 bay leaf
- 2 tablespoon Worcestershire sauce
- 2 tablespoon butter
- 1 tablespoon paprika powder
- 1 tablespoon dried oregano
- Salt and black pepper to taste
- Chopped parsley to garnish

**Directions:**

1. Set the Foodi on Sear/Sauté mode. Melt the butter and add the beef. Brown it for about 6 minutes and add in the onions, garlic, and bay leaf. Stir and cook for 2 more minutes.
2. Stir in the oregano, paprika, salt, pepper, rice, cabbage, vinegar, broth, and Worcestershire sauce. Cook for 3 minutes, stirring occassionally.
3. Add the tomatoes but don't stir. Close the lid, secure the pressure valve, and select Pressure Cook mode on High for 5 minutes. Press Start/Stop.
4. Once the timer is done, let the pot sit closed for 5 minutes and then do a quick pressure. Open the lid. Stir the sauce, remove the bay leaf, and adjust the seasoning with salt. Dish the cabbage sauce in serving bowls and serve with bread rolls.

## Asian Beef Curry

**(Ready in about:** 40 min | **Servings:** 4)

**Ingredients:**

- 1 ½ lb. beef brisket; cut in cubes
- 1 Potato, peeled and chopped
- 2 cloves garlic; minced
- ¼-inch ginger, peeled and sliced
- 2 bay leaves
- 2 star anises
- 1 large carrot; chopped
- 1 medium onion; chopped
- 1 cup milk
- 3 tablespoon water
- 1 tablespoon sugar
- 2 tablespoon red curry paste
- 1 tablespoon olive oil
- 2 teaspoon flour
- 2 teaspoon oyster sauce

**Directions:**

1. Select Sear/Sauté mode. Heat oil, add garlic, ginger, and red curry paste. Stir-fry them for 1 minute. Stir in onion and beef. Cook for 4 minutes.
2. Add the carrots, bay leaves, potato, star anises, sugar, and water. Stir. Close the lid, secure the pressure valve, and select Pressure mode on High for 25 minutes. Press Start/Stop to start cooking.
3. Once the timer goes off, do a quick pressure release. In a bowl, add the flour and 4 tablespoons of milk. Mix well with a spoon and pour it in the pot along with the oyster sauce and remaining milk. Stir it gently not to break the potato.
4. Close the crisping lid and cook on Broil mode for about 3 minutes, until the sauce thickens and meat is tender. After, turn off the pot. Spoon the sauce into soup bowls and serve with a side of rice.

## Beef and Bell Pepper with Onion Sauce

**(Ready in about:** 62 min | **Servings:** 6)

**Ingredients:**

- 2 lb. round steak pieces, about 6 to 8 pieces
- ½ yellow bell pepper, finely chopped
- 1 yellow onion, finely chopped
- 2 cloves garlic; minced
- ½ green bell pepper, finely chopped
- ½ red bell pepper, finely chopped
- ¼ cup flour
- ½ cup water
- 2 tablespoons olive oil
- Salt and pepper, to taste

**Directions:**

1. Wrap the steaks in plastic wrap, place on a cutting board, and use a rolling pin to pound flat of about 2-inch thickness. Remove the plastic wrap and season them with salt and pepper. Set aside.
2. Put the chopped peppers, onion, and garlic in a bowl, and mix them evenly. Spoon the bell pepper mixture onto the flattened steaks and roll them to have the peppers inside.
3. Use some toothpicks to secure the beef rolls and dredge the steaks in all-purpose flour while shaking off any excess flour. Place them in a plate.
4. Select Sear/Sauté mode on Foodi and heat the oil. Add the beef rolls and brown them on both sides, for about 6 minutes.
5. Pour the water over the meat, close the lid, secure the pressure valve, and select Pressure mode on High pressure for 20 minutes. Press Start/Stop.
6. Once the timer has stopped, do a natural pressure release for 10 minutes. Close the crisping lid and cook for 10 minutes on Broil mode. When ready, Remove the meat to a plate and spoon the sauce from the pot over. Serve the stuffed meat rolls with a side of steamed veggies.

## Beef and Green Bell Pepper Pot

### (**Ready in about:** 55 min | **Servings:** 4)

**Ingredients:**

- 2 lb. beef chuck roast
- 1 cup beef broth
- 1 medium white onion; sliced
- 1 green bell pepper, seeded and sliced
- 1 red bell pepper, seeded and sliced
- 1 tablespoon garlic powder
- 1 tablespoon onion powder
- 2 tablespoon olive oil
- 1 tablespoon Italian Seasoning
- Salt and black pepper to taste; cut in 4 pieces

**Directions:**

1. Rub the beef with pepper, salt, garlic powder, Italian seasoning, and onion powder. Select Sear/Sauté mode on Foodi. Heat 1 tablespoon oil, add the beef pieces and sear them on both sides until brown, for about 5 minutes. Use a pair of tongs to remove them onto a plate after. (You can do this in 2 batches).
2. Pour the beef broth and fish sauce into the pot to deglaze the bottom while you use a spoon to scrape any stuck beef bit at the bottom. Add the meat back to the pot, close the lid, secure the pressure valve, and select Pressure mode on High pressure for 30 minutes. Press Start/Stop.
3. Once the timer has stopped, do a quick pressure release, and open the pot.
4. Use two forks to shred the beef, inside the pot. Close the crisping lid and select Broil mode for 10 minutes. When ready, set aside the meat and discard the liquid. Wipe clean the pot.
5. Select Sear/Sauté mode, heat the remaining oil, add the beef with onions and peppers. Sauté them for 3 minutes and season with salt and pepper. Turn off the pot and dish the stir-fried beef into serving plates. Serve as a side to rice with sauce dish.

## Meatballs with Marinara Sauce

### (**Ready in about:** 35 min | **Servings:** 6)

**Ingredients:**

- 1½ pounds ground beef
- 1 egg
- 3 cups marinara sauce
- ⅓ cup warm water
- ¾ cup grated Parmigiano-Reggiano cheese
- ½ cup bread crumbs
- ½ cup capers
- 2 tablespoon fresh parsley
- ¼ teaspoon dried oregano
- ¼ teaspoon garlic powder
- 1 teaspoon olive oil
- salt and ground black pepper to taste

**Directions:**

1. In a large bowl, mix ground beef, garlic powder, pepper, oregano, bread crumbs, egg, and salt; shape into meatballs. Warm the oil on Sear/Sauté. Add meatballs to the oil and brown for 2-3 minutes and all sides.
2. Pour water and marinara sauce over the meatballs. Seal the pressure lid, choose Pressure, set to High, and set the timer to 10 minutes. Press Start.
3. When ready, release the pressure quickly. Serve in large bowls topped with capers and Parmigiano-Reggiano cheese.

## Spiced Beef Chili

**(Ready in about:** 40 min | **Servings:** 4)

**Ingredients:**

- 2 lb. ground beef
- 2 carrots; cut in little bits
- 1 large yellow bell pepper, seeded and chopped
- 1 white onion; chopped
- 1 large red bell pepper, seeded and chopped
- 2 cups chopped tomatoes
- 2 cups beef broth
- 2 tablespoon Worcestershire sauce
- 2 tablespoon chopped parsley
- 2 tablespoon olive oil
- 2 teaspoon onion powder
- 2 teaspoon garlic powder
- 5 teaspoon chili powder
- 2 teaspoon paprika
- ½ teaspoon cumin powder
- Salt and black pepper to taste

**Directions:**

1. Select Sear/Sauté mode, and add the olive oil and ground beef. Cook the meat until brown, stirring occasionally, for about 8 minutes.
2. Top with the remaining ingredients and mix well. Seal the lid, and cook on Pressure mode on High for 15 minutes. Press Start/Stop to start cooking.
3. Once the timer has ended, do a quick pressure release, and open the lid.
4. Stir the stew and close the crisping lid. Cook on Broil mode for 10 minutes. Dish into serving bowls. Serve this beef chili with crackers or potato mash.

## Peppercorn Meatloaf

**(Ready in about:** 35 min | **Servings:** 8)

**Ingredients:**

- 4 lb. ground beef
- 10 whole peppercorns, for garnishing
- 1 onion; diced
- 1 cup breadcrumbs
- 1 tablespoon parsley
- 1 tablespoon Worcestershire sauce
- 3 tablespoon ketchup
- 1 tablespoon basil
- 1 tablespoon oregano
- ½ teaspoon salt
- 1 teaspoon ground peppercorns

**Directions:**

1. Place the beef in a large bowl. Add all of the ingredients except the whole peppercorns and the breadcrumbs. Mix with your hand until well combined. Stir in the breadcrumbs.
2. Put the meatloaf on a lined baking dish. Insert in the Foodi, close the crisping lid and cook for 25 minutes on Air Crisp mode at 350 F.
3. Garnish the meatloaf with the whole peppercorns and let cool slightly before serving.

## Mississippi Pot Roast with Potatoes

**(Ready in about:** 1 hr 40 min | **Servings:** 6)

**Ingredients:**

- 2 pounds chuck roast
- 5 potatoes, peeled and sliced
- 10 pepperoncini
- 2 bay leaves
- 1 onion, finely chopped
- ½ cup pepperoncini juice
- 6 cups beef broth
- ¼ cup butter
- 1 tablespoon canola oil
- ½ teaspoon dried thyme
- ½ teaspoon dried parsley
- 1 teaspoon onion powder
- 1 teaspoon garlic powder
- 2 teaspoon salt
- ½ teaspoon black pepper

**Directions:**

1. Warm oil on Sear/Sauté. Season chuck roast with pepper and salt, then sear in the hot oil for 2 to 4 minutes for each side until browned. Set aside.
2. Melt butter and cook onion for 3 minutes until fragrant. Sprinkle with dried parsley, onion powder, dried thyme, and garlic powder and stir for 30 seconds.
3. Into the pot, stir bay leaves, beef broth, pepperoncini juice, and pepperoncini. Nestle chuck roast down into the liquid. Seal the pressure lid, choose Pressure, set to High, and set the timer to 60 minutes. Press Start.
4. Release pressure naturally for about 10 minutes. Set the chuck roast to a cutting board and use two forks to shred. Serve immediately.

## Beef and Vegetable Stew

**(Ready in about:** 70 min | **Servings:** 4)

**Ingredients:**

- 2 lb. brisket; cut into 2-inch pieces
- 1 lb. small potato, quartered
- ¼ lb. carrots; cut in 2-inch pieces
- 1 large red onion, quartered
- 3 cloves garlic; minced
- 1 bay leaf
- 2 fresh thyme sprigs
- 4 cups beef broth
- 3 tablespoon chopped cilantro to garnish
- 1 tablespoon Dijon mustard
- 1 tablespoon olive oil
- 2 tablespoon cornstarch
- Salt and black pepper to taste

**Directions:**

1. Pour broth, cornstarch, mustard, ½ teaspoon salt, and ½ teaspoon pepper in a bowl. Whisk them and set aside. Season the beef with salt and pepper.
2. On the Foodi, select Sear/Sauté mode. Add the olive oil, and once heated, add the beef strips. Flip halfway through to brown evenly. That should take 7 to 10 minutes.
3. Then, add potato, carrots, onion, garlic, thyme, mustard mixture, and bay leaf. Stir once more. Close the lid, secure the pressure valve, and select Pressure mode on High pressure for 35 minutes. Press Start/Stop.
4. Once the timer has ended, do a quick pressure release. Stir the stew and remove the bay leaf. Season the stew with pepper and salt. Close the crisping lid and cook for 10 minutes on Broil mode. Serve the soup with a bread of your choice.

## Meatballs with Spaghetti Sauce

**(Ready in about:** 20 min | **Servings:** 6)

**Ingredients:**

- 2 lb. ground beef
- 1 cup grated Parmesan cheese
- 4 cups spaghetti sauce
- 1 cup breadcrumbs
- 1 cup water
- 2 cloves garlic; minced
- 2 eggs, cracked into a bowl
- 1 onion, finely chopped
- 3 tablespoon milk
- 1 tablespoon olive oil
- 1 teaspoon dried oregano
- Salt and pepper, to taste

**Directions:**

1. In a bowl, add beef, onion, breadcrumbs, parmesan, eggs, garlic, milk, salt, oregano, and pepper. Mix well with hands and shape bite-size balls.
2. Open the pot, and add the spaghetti sauce, water and the meatballs. Close the lid, secure the pressure valve, and select Steam mode on High pressure for 6 minutes. Press Start/Stop.
3. Once the timer is done, do a natural pressure release for 5 minutes, then do a quick pressure release to let out any extra steam, and open the lid. Dish the meatball sauce over cooked pasta and serve.

## Beef Soup with Tortillas

**(Ready in about:** 30 min | **Servings:** 8)

**Ingredients:**
- 3 lb. ground beef, grass fed
- 2 medium yellow onion; chopped
- 6 green bell pepper; diced
- 6 cups chopped tomatoes
- ½ cup chopped green chilies
- 3 cups bone broth
- 3 cups milk
- 2 tablespoon cumin powder
- 2 tablespoon olive oil
- 3 tablespoon chili powder
- 1 teaspoon cinnamon
- 1 teaspoon onion powder
- 2 teaspoon paprika
- 1 teaspoon garlic powder
- Salt and black pepper to taste

**Topping:**
- Chopped Jalapenos, cilantro and green onions; sliced Avocados, lime juice

**Directions:**
1. Select Sear/Sauté mode and set High on your Foodi. Pour in the oil, once it has heated, add the yellow onion and green peppers. Sauté until they are soft for about 5 minutes. Include the ground beef, stir the ingredients, and let the beef cook for about 8 minutes until it browns.
2. Next, add the chili powder, cumin powder, black pepper, paprika, cinnamon, garlic powder, onion powder, and green chilies. Give them a good stir.
3. Top with tomatoes, milk, and bone broth. Close the lid, secure the pressure valve, and select Pressure mode on High for 20 minutes. Press Start.
4. Once the timer has ended, do a quick pressure release. Adjust the taste with salt and pepper. Dish the taco soup into serving bowls and add the toppings. Serve warm with a side of tortillas.

## Pot Roast with Broccoli

**(Ready in about:** 35 min | **Servings:** 4)

**Ingredients:**
- 2 lb. beef chuck roast
- 1 packet onion soup mix
- 2 red bell peppers, seeded and quartered
- 1 yellow onion, quartered
- 1 cup chopped broccoli
- 1 cup beef broth
- 3 tablespoon olive oil; divided into 2
- Salt to taste

**Directions:**
1. Season the chuck roast with salt and set aside. Select Sear/Sauté mode on the Foodi cooker. Add the olive oil, and once heated, add the chuck roast. Sear for 5 minutes on each side. Then, pour in the beef broth.
2. In a zipper bag, add broccoli, onions, peppers, the remaining olive oil, and onion soup. Close the bag and shake the mixture to coat the vegetables well. Use tongs to remove the vegetables into the pot and stir with a spoon.
3. Close the lid, secure the pressure valve, and select Pressure mode on High pressure for 18 minutes. Press Start/Stop.
4. Once the timer has stopped, do a quick pressure release, and open the pressure lid. Make cuts on the meat inside the pot and close the crisping lid.
5. Cook on Air Crisp mode for about 10 minutes, at 380 F, until nice and crispy. Plate and serve with the vegetables and a drizzle of the sauce in the pot.

# Beef and Pumpkin Stew

**(Ready in about:** 35 min | **Servings:** 6)

**Ingredients:**

- 2 pounds stew beef; cut into 1-inch chunks
- 3 carrots; sliced
- 1 onion; chopped
- 3 whole cloves
- 1 bay leaf
- ½ butternut pumpkin; sliced
- 1 cup red wine
- 2 tablespoon cornstarch
- 2 tablespoon canola oil
- 3 tablespoon water
- 1 teaspoon garlic powder
- 1 teaspoon salt

**Directions:**

1. Warm oil on Sear/Sauté. Add beef and brown for 5 minutes on each side. Deglaze the pot with wine, scrape the bottom to get rid of any browned beef bits. Add in onion, salt, bay leaf, cloves, and garlic powder. Seal the pressure lid, choose Pressure, set to High, and set the timer to 15 minutes. Press Start.
2. When ready, release the pressure quickly. Add in pumpkin and carrots without stirring. Seal the pressure lid again, choose Pressure, set to High, and set the timer to 5 minutes. Press Start.
3. When ready, release the pressure quickly. In a bowl, mix water and cornstarch until cornstarch dissolves completely; mix into the stew. Allow the stew to simmer while uncovered on Keep Warm for 5 minutes until you attain the desired thickness.

# Swedish Meatballs with Mashed Cauliflower

**(Ready in about:** 1 hr | **Servings:** 6)

**Ingredients:**

- ¾ pound ground pork
- ¾ pound ground beef
- 1 head cauliflower; cut into florets
- 1 large egg, beaten
- ½ onion; minced
- 1 ¾ cup heavy cream; divided
- ¼ cup bread crumbs
- ¼ cup sour cream
- 2 cups beef stock
- ¼ cup fresh chopped parsley
- 1 tablespoon water
- 4 tablespoon butter; divided
- 3 tablespoon flour
- ½ teaspoon red wine vinegar
- salt and freshly ground black pepper to taste

**Directions:**

1. In a mixing bowl, mix ground beef, onion, salt, bread crumbs, ground pork, egg, water, and pepper; shape meatballs. Warm 2 tablespoon of butter on Sear/Sauté.
2. Add meatballs and cook until browned, about 5-6 minutes. Set aside to a plate. Pour beef stock in the pot to deglaze, scrape the pan to get rid of browned bits of food.
3. Stir vinegar and flour with the liquid in the pot until smooth; bring to a boil. Stir ¾ cup heavy cream into the liquid. Arrange meatballs into the gravy. Place trivet onto meatballs. Arrange cauliflower florets onto the trivet.
4. Seal the pressure lid, choose Pressure, set to High, and set the timer to 8 minutes. Press Start. When ready, release the pressure quickly.
5. Set the cauliflower in a mixing bowl. Add in the remaining 1 cup heavy cream, pepper, sour cream, salt, and 2 tablespoon butter and use a potato masher to mash the mixture until smooth.
6. Spoon the mashed cauliflower onto serving bowls; place a topping of gravy and meatballs. Add parsley for garnishing.

## Philippine Pork Chops

**(Ready in about:** 2 hours 20 min | **Servings:** 6)

**Ingredients:**

- 2 lb. pork chops
- 5 garlic cloves, coarsely chopped
- 2 bay leaves
- 1 tablespoon peanut oil
- 2 tablespoon soy sauce
- 1 tablespoon peppercorns
- 1 teaspoon salt

**Directions:**

1. Combine the bay leaves, soy sauce, garlic, salt, peppercorns, and oil, in a bowl. Rub the mixture onto meat. Wrap the pork with a plastic foil and refrigerate for 2h.
2. Place the pork in the Foodi, close the crisping lid and cook for 10 minutes on Air Crisp mode at 350 F. Increase the temperature to 370 F, flip the chops, and cook for another 10 minutes. Discard bay leaves before serving.

## Beef and Cherry Tagine

**(Ready in about:** 1 hr 20 min | **Servings:** 4)

**Ingredients:**

- 1 ½ pounds stewing beef, trimmed
- 1 onion; chopped
- 1-star anise
- ¼ cup toasted almonds, slivered
- 1 cup dried cherries, halved
- 1 cup water
- 1 tablespoon honey
- 2 tablespoon olive oil
- ¼ teaspoon ground allspice
- 1 teaspoon ground cinnamon
- ½ teaspoon paprika
- ½ teaspoon turmeric
- ½ teaspoon salt
- ¼ teaspoon ground ginger

**Directions:**

1. Set your Foodi to Sear/Sauté, set to Medium High, and choose Start/Stop to preheat the pot. Warm olive oil. Add in onions and cook for 3 minutes until fragrant. Mix in beef and cook for 2 minutes each side until browned.
2. Stir in anise, cinnamon, turmeric, allspice, salt, paprika, and ginger; cook for 2 minutes until aromatic.
3. Add in honey and water. Seal the pressure lid, choose Pressure, set to High, and set the timer to 50 minutes. Press Start.
4. Meanwhile, in a bowl, soak dried cherries in hot water until softened. Once ready, release pressure naturally for 15 minutes. Drain cherries and stir into the tagine. Top with toasted almonds before serving.

## Pork Tenderloin with Ginger and Garlic

**(Ready in about:** 23 min | **Servings:** 4)

**Ingredients:**

- 2 lb. pork tenderloin
- ½ cup water + 2 tablespoon water
- ½ cup soy sauce
- ¼ cup sugar
- 2 cloves garlic; minced
- 3 tablespoon grated ginger
- 2 tablespoon sesame oil
- 2 teaspoon cornstarch
- Chopped scallions to garnish
- Sesame seeds to garnish

**Directions:**

1. In the Foodi's inner pot, add soy sauce, sugar, half cup of water, ginger, garlic, and sesame oil. Use a spoon to stir them. Then, add the pork. Close the lid, secure the pressure valve, and select Pressure mode on High pressure for 12 minutes. Press Start/Stop.
2. Once the timer has ended, do a quick pressure release, and open the pot. Remove the pork and set aside.

3. In a bowl, mix the cornstarch with the remaining water until smooth and pour it into the pot. Bring back the pork. Close the crisping lid and press Broil.
4. Cook for 5 minutes, until the sauce has thickened. Stir the sauce frequently, every 1-2 minutes, to avoid burning. Once the sauce is ready, serve the pork with a side endive salad or steamed veggies. Spoon the sauce all over it.

## Beef and Garbanzo Bean Chili

(**Ready in about:** 45 min | **Servings:** 10)

**Ingredients:**
- 1 pound garbanzo beans; soaked overnight, rinsed
- 2 ½ pounds ground beef
- 1 (6 ounces) can tomato puree
- 1 small jalapeño with seeds; minced
- 6 garlic cloves; minced
- 2 onions, finely chopped
- 2 ½ cups beef broth
- ¼ cup chili powder
- 2 tablespoon ground cumin
- 1 tablespoon olive oil
- 1 teaspoon garlic powder
- ¼ teaspoon cayenne pepper
- 1 teaspoon dried oregano
- 2 teaspoon salt
- 1 teaspoon smoked paprika

**Directions:**
1. Add the garbanzo beans to the Foodi and pour in cold water to cover 1 inch. Seal the pressure lid, choose Pressure, set to High, and set the timer to 20 minutes. Press Start. When ready, release the pressure quickly.
2. Drain beans and rinse with cold water. Set aside. Wipe clean the Foodi and set to Sear/Sauté, set to Medium High, and choose Start/Stop to preheat the pot. Press Start. Warm olive oil, add in onion, and cook for 3 minutes until soft.
3. Add jalapeño, ground beef, and minced garlic, and stir-fry for 5 minutes until everything is cooked through. Stir in chili powder, kosher salt, garlic powder, paprika, cumin, oregano, and cayenne pepper, and cook until soft, about 30 seconds. Pour beef broth, garbanzo beans, and tomato paste into the pot.
4. Seal the pressure lid, choose Pressure, set to High, and set the timer to 20 minutes; press Start. When ready, release pressure naturally for about 10 minutes. Open the lid, press Sear/Sauté, and cook as you stir until desired consistency is attained. Spoon chili into bowls and serve.

## Apple and Onion Topped Pork Chops

(**Ready in about:** 25 min | **Servings:** 3)

**Ingredients:**
**Topping:**
- 1 small onion; sliced
- 1 cup sliced apples
- 1 tablespoon apple cider vinegar
- 2 tablespoon olive oil
- ¼ teaspoon brown sugar
- 2 teaspoon rosemary
- 2 teaspoon thyme

**Meat:**
- 3 pork chops
- 1 tablespoon olive oil
- 1 tablespoon apple cider vinegar
- ¼ teaspoon smoked paprika
- Salt and pepper, to taste

**Directions:**
1. Place all topping ingredients in a baking dish, and then in the Foodi. Cook for 4 minutes on Air Crisp mode. Meanwhile, place the pork chops in a bowl. Add olive oil, vinegar, paprika, and season with salt and pepper. Stir to coat them well. Remove the topping from the dish.
2. Add the pork chops in the dish, close the crisping lid and cook for 10 minutes on Air Crisp mode at 350 F. Place the topping on top, return to the Foodi and cook for 5 more minutes.

## Cheddar Cheese burgers

**(Ready in about:** 20 min | **Servings:** 4)

**Ingredients:**

- 1 lb. ground beef
- 1 (1 oz) packet dry onion soup mix
- 4 burger buns
- 4 tomato slices
- 4 Cheddar cheese slices
- 4 small leaves lettuce
- 1 cup water
- Mayonnaise
- Ketchup
- Mustard

**Directions:**

1. In a bowl, add beef and onion mix, and mix well with hands. Shape in 4 patties and wrap each in foil paper. Pour the water into the inner steel insert of Foodi, and fit in the steamer rack. Place the wrapped patties on the trivet, close the lid, and secure the pressure valve, and cook on 10 minutes on Pressure mode on High pressure.
2. Once the timer has stopped, do a natural pressure release for 5 minutes, then a quick pressure release to let out the remaining steam.
3. Use a set of tongs to remove the wrapped beef onto a flat surface and carefully unwrap the patties.

**To assemble the burgers:**

4. In each half of the buns, put a lettuce leaf, then a beef patty, a slice of cheese, and a slice of tomato. Top it with the other halves of buns. Serve with some ketchup, mayonnaise, and mustard.

## Beef and Cheese Stuffed Mushrooms

**(Ready in about:** 10 min | **Servings:** 3)

**Ingredients:**

- 6 large white mushrooms, stems removed
- 2 oz. cream cheese, softened
- 2 cups cooked leftover beef; cut in very small cubes
- 1 cup shredded Cheddar cheese
- ½ cup vegetable broth
- 2 teaspoon garlic salt
- 1 teaspoon olive oil

**Directions:**

1. In a bowl, add the beef, garlic salt, cream cheese, and cheddar cheese. Use a spoon to mix them. Spoon the beef mixture into the mushrooms and place the mushrooms in the inner pot of Foodi. Drizzle them with olive oil, and add the broth.
2. Close the lid, secure the pressure valve, and select Pressure mode on High pressure for 3 minutes. Press Start/Stop to start cooking.
3. Once the timer is off, do a quick pressure release and open the pressure lid, discard the liquid, and remove the mushrooms.
4. Place the reversible rack and lay the mushrooms on it. Close the crisping lid and cook for 2 to 3 minutes on Air Crisp mode at 350 F. Remove the stuffed mushrooms onto a plate, and serve hot with a side of steamed green veggies.

## Barbeque Sticky Baby Back Ribs with

**(Ready in about:** 40 min | **Servings:** 6)

**Ingredients:**

- 1 reversible rack baby back ribs; cut into bones
- 1/3 cup ketchup
- 1 cup barbecue sauce
- ½ cup apple cider
- 1 tablespoon mustard powder
- 1 tablespoon smoked paprika
- 2 tablespoon olive oil
- 1 tablespoon dried oregano
- ½ teaspoon ground black pepper
- ½ teaspoon salt

**Directions:**

1. In a bowl, thoroughly combine salt, mustard powder, smoked paprika, oregano, and black pepper. Rub the mixture over the ribs. Warm oil on Sear/Sauté.
2. Add in the ribs and sear for 1 to 2 minutes for each side until browned. Pour apple cider and barbecue sauce into the pot. Turn the ribs to coat.
3. Seal the pressure lid, choose Pressure, set to High, and set the timer to 30 minutes. Press Start. When ready, release the pressure quickly.
4. Place the Cook & Crisp Basket in the pot. Close the crisping lid, choose Air Crisp, set the temperature to 390°F, and the time to 5 minutes.
5. Place the ribs with the sauce in the Cook & Crisp Basket. Close the Crisping Lid. Preheat the unit by selecting Air Crisp, setting the temperature to 390°F, and setting the time to 7 minutes. Press Start. When ready, the ribs should be sticky with a brown dark color. Transfer the ribs to a serving plate. Baste with the sauce to serve.

## Beef Pho with Swiss Chard

**(Ready in about:** 1 hr 10 min | **Servings:** 6)

**Ingredients:**

- 2 pounds Beef Neck Bones
- 10 ounces sirloin steak
- 8 ounces rice noodles
- 1 yellow onion, quartered
- A handful of fresh cilantro; chopped
- 2 scallions; chopped
- 2 jalapeño peppers; sliced
- ¼ cup minced fresh ginger
- 9 cups water
- 2 cups Swiss chard; chopped
- 2 teaspoon coriander seeds
- 2 teaspoon ground cinnamon
- 2 teaspoon ground cloves
- 2 tablespoon coconut oil
- 3 tablespoon sugar
- 2 tablespoon fish sauce
- 2 ½ teaspoon kosher salt
- Freshly ground black pepper to taste

**Directions:**

1. Melt the oil on Sear/Sauté. Add ginger and onions and cook for 4 minutes until the onions are softened. Stir in cloves, cinnamon and coriander seeds and cook for 1 minute until soft. Add in water, salt, beef meat and bones.
2. Seal the pressure lid, choose Pressure, set to High, and set the timer to 30 minutes. Press Start. Release pressure naturally for 10 minutes.
3. Transfer the meat to a large bowl; cover with it enough water and soak for 10 minutes. Drain the water and slice the beef. In hot water, soak rice noodles for 8 minutes until softened and pliable; drain and rinse with cold water. Drain liquid from cooker into a separate pot through a fine-mesh strainer; get rid of any solids.
4. Add fish sauce and sugar to the broth; transfer into the Foodi and simmer on Sear/Sauté. Place the noodles in four separate soup bowls. Top with steak slices, scallions, swiss chard; sliced jalapeño pepper, cilantro, red onion, and pepper. Spoon the broth over each bowl to serve.

## Beef and Turnip Chili

**(Ready in about:** 30 min | **Servings:** 6)

**Ingredients:**

- 1 pound turnips, peeled and cubed
- 1 pound ground beef meat
- 1 (28 ounces) can whole tomatoes
- 1 bell pepper; chopped
- 1 yellow onion; chopped
- 4 garlic cloves; minced
- 2 cups beef stock
- 2 tomatoes; chopped
- 1 tablespoon chili powder
- 1 tablespoon olive oil
- 2 tablespoon tomato puree
- ½ teaspoon ground turmeric
- 2 teaspoon ground cumin
- 1 teaspoon dried oregano
- 1 pinch cayenne pepper
- salt to taste

**Directions:**

1. Warm oil on Sear/Sauté. Add in onion with a pinch of salt and cook for 3 to 5 minutes until softened. Stir in garlic, chili powder, turmeric, cumin, tomato puree, oregano, and cayenne pepper; cook for 2 to 3 minutes as you stir until very soft and sticks to the pot's bottom; add beef and cook for 5 minutes until completely browned. Mix in tomatoes, turnips, bell pepper, and beef stock.
2. Seal the pressure lid, choose Pressure, set to High, and set the timer to 15 minutes; press Start. When ready, release the pressure quickly.

## Crunchy Cashew Lamb Rack

**(Ready in about:** 30 min | **Servings:** 4)

**Ingredients:**

- 1 ½ lb. rack of lamb
- 3 oz. chopped cashews
- 1 garlic clove; minced
- 1 egg, beaten
- 1 tablespoon chopped rosemary
- 1 tablespoon olive oil
- 1 tablespoon breadcrumbs
- Salt and pepper, to taste

**Directions:**

1. Combine the olive oil with the garlic and brush this mixture onto the lamb. Combine the rosemary, cashews, and breadcrumbs, in a small bowl. Brush the egg over the lambs, and then coat it with the cashew mixture.
2. Place the lamb in the Foodi, close the crisping lid and cook for 25 minutes on Air Crisp at 320 F. Then increase to 390 degrees F, and cook for 5 more minutes. Cover with a foil and let sit for a couple of minutes before serving.

## Chipotle Beef Brisket

**(Ready in about:** 1 hr 10 min | **Servings:** 4)

**Ingredients:**

- 2 pounds, beef brisket
- 1 cup beef broth
- ¼ cup red wine
- 2 tablespoon olive oil
- 1 tablespoon Worcestershire sauce
- ½ teaspoon ground cumin
- ½ teaspoon garlic powder
- 1 teaspoon chipotle powder
- ¼ teaspoon cayenne pepper
- 2 teaspoon smoked paprika
- ½ teaspoon dried oregano
- ½ teaspoon salt
- ½ teaspoon ground black pepper
- A handful of parsley; chopped

**Directions:**

1. In a bowl, combine oregano, cumin, cayenne pepper, garlic powder, salt, paprika, pepper, Worcestershire sauce and chipotle powder; rub the seasoning mixture on the beef to coat. Warm olive oil on Sear/Sauté. Add in beef and cook for 3 to 4 minutes each side until browned completely. Pour in beef broth and red wine.

2. Seal the pressure lid, choose Pressure, set to High, and set the timer to 50 minutes. Press Start. Release the pressure naturally, for about 10 minutes.
3. Place the beef on a cutting board and Allow cooling for 10 minutes before slicing. Arrange the beef slices on a serving platter, pour the cooking sauce over and scatter with parsley to serve.

## Spiced Beef Shapes

**(Ready in about:** 40 min | **Servings:** 12)

**Ingredients:**

- 1 ½ lb. ground beef
- 3 garlic cloves; minced
- ½ cup minced onion
- 2 tablespoon chopped mint leaves
- 1 tablespoon chopped parsley
- 2 teaspoon paprika
- 2 teaspoon cumin
- ½ teaspoon ground ginger
- 2 teaspoon coriander seeds
- ½ teaspoon cayenne pepper
- 1 teaspoon salt

**Directions:**

1. Soak 24 skewers in water, until ready to use. Combine all ingredients in a large bowl. Make sure to mix well with your hands until the herbs and spices are evenly distributed, and the mixture is well incorporated.
2. Shape the beef mixture into 12 shapes around 2 skewers. Close the crisping lid and cook for 12 - 15 minutes on Air Crisp mode at 330 F, or until preferred doneness. Serve with tzatziki sauce and enjoy.

## Italian Sausage with Onion Gravy Potato and Mash

**(Ready in about:** 40 min | **Servings:** 4)

**Ingredients:**

- 2 lb. potatoes, peeled and halved
- 1 onion; sliced thinly
- 4 Italian sausages
- ¼ cup + 2 tablespoon + 2 tablespoon butter
- 1 cup + 2 tablespoon beef broth
- 1 cup water + 2 tablespoon water
- ⅓ cup green onion; sliced
- 1 tablespoon cornstarch
- 3 tablespoon balsamic vinegar
- 4 tablespoon milk
- Salt and pepper, to taste

**Directions:**

1. Put the potatoes in the inner pot and pour the water over. Seal the lid; select Steam mode on High for 15 minutes and press Start/Stop. Do a quick pressure release, and remove the potatoes to a bowl. Add in a quarter cup butter and use a masher to mash them until the butter is well mixed. Slowly add the milk and mix it using a spoon. Add the green onions, season with pepper and salt and fold it in with the spoon. Set aside.
2. Pour out the liquid in the Foodi, and use paper towels to wipe inside the pot dry. Select Sear/Sauté mode and melt two tablespoons of butter.
3. Brown the sausages on each side for 3 minutes. Remove to the potato mash and cover with aluminium foil to keep warm. Set aside Back into the pot, add the two tablespoons of the beef broth to deglaze the bottom of the pot while stirring and scraping the bottom with a spoon. Add the remaining butter and onions; sauté the onions until translucent, then pour in the balsamic vinegar. Stir for another minute.
4. In a bowl, mix the cornstarch with water and pour into the pot. Add the remaining beef broth. Allow the sauce to thicken and adjust the seasoning. Turn off the heat once a slurry is formed. Dish the mashed potatoes and sausages in serving plates. Spoon the gravy over it and serve immediately with steamed green beans.

## Beef Stew with Veggies

**(Ready in about:** 1 hr 15 min | **Servings:** 6)

**Ingredients:**

- 2 pounds beef chuck; cubed
- 1 cup dry red wine
- 3 cups carrots; chopped
- ¼ cup flour
- 2 cups beef stock
- 4 cups potatoes; diced
- 1 onion; diced
- 3 garlic cloves; minced
- 2 celery stalks; chopped
- 3 tomatoes; chopped
- 2 bell pepper, thinly sliced
- 1 tablespoon dried Italian seasoning
- 2 tablespoon olive oil
- 2 tablespoon butter
- 2 teaspoon salt; divided
- 1 teaspoon paprika
- 1 teaspoon ground black pepper
- 2 teaspoon Worcestershire sauce
- A handful of fresh parsley; chopped
- salt and ground black pepper to taste

**Directions:**

1. In a bowl, mix black pepper, beef, flour, paprika, and 1 teaspoon salt. Toss the ingredients and ensure the beef is coated. Warm butter and oil on Sear/Sautét. Add in beef and cook for 8- 10 minutes until browned. Set aside on a plate.
2. To the same fat, add garlic, onion, and celery, bell peppers, and cook for 4-5 minutes until tender.
3. Deglaze with wine, scrape the bottom to get rid of any browned beef bits. Pour in remaining salt, beef stock, Worcestershire sauce, and Italian seasoning. Return beef to the pot; add carrots, tomatoes, and potatoes.
4. Seal the pressure lid, choose Pressure, set to High, and set the timer to 35 minutes. Press Start. Release pressure naturally for 10 minutes. Taste and adjust the seasonings as necessary. Serve on plates and scatter over the parsley.

## Italian Beef Sandwiches with Pesto

**(Ready in about:** 1 hr | **Servings:** 4)

**Ingredients:**

- 1 ½ pounds beef steak; cut into strips
- 8 slices mozzarella cheese
- 4 hoagie rolls, halved
- ½ cup sliced pepperoncini peppers
- 1/4 cup dry red wine
- 1 cup beef broth
- 4 tablespoon pesto
- 1 tablespoon oregano
- 1 tablespoon olive oil
- 1 teaspoon onion powder
- 1 teaspoon garlic powder
- salt and ground black pepper

**Directions:**

1. Sprinkle pepper and salt to season the beef cubes and bring to room temperature. Warm oil on Sear/Sauté. Add in the beef and sear for 2 to 3 minutes for each side until browned.
2. Add wine into the pot to deglaze, scrape the bottom to get rid of any browned beef bits.
3. Stir garlic powder, beef broth, onion powder, and oregano into the pot. Seal the pressure lid, choose Pressure, set to High, and set the timer to 25 minutes. Press Start.
4. Release pressure naturally for 10 minutes. Spread each bread half with pesto, put beef on top, place pepperoncini slices over, add mozzarella cheese slices and cover with the second half of bread to serve.

# Brisket Chili con Carne

(**Ready in about:** 1 hr 25 min | **Servings:** 6)

**Ingredients:**

- 1 (4 pounds) beef brisket
- 14 ounces canned black beans, drained and rinsed
- 1 cup beef broth
- 2 bay leaves
- 2 tablespoon Worcestershire sauce
- 1 tablespoon ground black pepper
- 2 teaspoon salt
- 1 teaspoon cayenne pepper
- ½ teaspoon onion powder
- 1 teaspoon sweet paprika
- 1 teaspoon chili powder
- ½ teaspoon garlic salt

**Directions:**

1. In a bowl, combine pepper, paprika, chili powder, cayenne pepper, salt, onion powder and garlic salt; rub onto brisket pieces to coat. Add the brisket to your Foodi. Cover with Worcestershire sauce and water.
2. Seal the pressure lid, choose Pressure, set to High, and set the timer to 50 minutes. Press Start. Release pressure naturally for 10 minutes.
3. Transfer the brisket to a cutting board. Drain any liquid present in the pot using a fine-mesh strainer; get rid of any solids and fat.
4. Slice brisket, arrange the slices onto a platter add the black beans on side and spoon the cooking liquid over the slices and beans to serve.

# Savory Pork Loin with Carrot and Celery Sauce

(**Ready in about:** 35 min | **Servings:** 4)

**Ingredients:**

- 2 lb. pork loin roast
- 3 stalks celery; chopped
- 3 carrots; chopped
- 3 cloves garlic; minced
- 1 medium onion; diced
- ¼ cup water
- 1 cup vegetable broth
- 2 tablespoon Worcestershire sauce
- 2 tablespoon butter
- ½ tablespoon sugar
- 1 tablespoon cornstarch
- 1 teaspoon yellow mustard
- 2 teaspoon dried basil
- 2 teaspoon dried thyme
- Salt and pepper, to taste

**Directions:**

1. Select Sear/Sauté mode, and heat oil. Season the pork with salt and pepper. Sear the pork to golden brown on both sides, about 4 minutes.
2. Then, add the garlic and onions, and cook them until soft, for about 4 minutes. Top with the celery, carrots, broth, Worcestershire sauce, mustard, thyme, basil, and sugar.
3. Close the lid, secure the pressure valve, and select Pressure mode on High pressure for 15 minutes. Press Start/Stop to start cooking.
4. Once the timer is off, do a quick pressure release. Next, add the cornstarch to the water, in a bowl, and mix with a spoon, until nice and smooth. Add it to the pot, close the crisping lid, and cook on Broil mode, for 3 - 5 minutes, until the sauce becomes a slurry with a bit of thickness, and the pork is nice and tender.
5. Adjust the seasoning, and ladle to a serving platter. Serve with a side of steamed almond garlicky rapini mix.

## Beef Roast with Peanut Satay Sauce

**(Ready in about:** 40 min | **Servings:** 4)

**Ingredients:**

- 1 lb. beef roast; cut into cubes
- ½ cup Peanut Satay sauce
- 2 cups diced carrots
- ½ cup coconut milk, light
- Salt and black pepper to taste

**Directions:**

1. Place the beef inside Foodi. In a bowl, mix in coconut milk, salt, pepper, and satay sauce. Pour over the beef. Add the carrots too. Close the lid, secure the pressure valve, and select Pressure mode on High pressure for 15 minutes. Press Start/Stop to start cooking.
2. Once the timer has ended, do a natural pressure release, then a quick pressure release to let out any remaining steam, and open the pot.
3. Give it a stir and close the crisping lid. Cook for 10 minutes on Bake/Roast mode at 400 F. Use a spoon to dish the meat into a serving plate, and serve with a side of steamed greens.

## Ranch Flavored Pork Roast with Gravy

**(Ready in about:** 25 min | **Servings:** 4)

**Ingredients:**

- 2 lb. pork roast; cut into 2-inch slabs
- 1 small onion; chopped
- 2 cloves garlic; minced
- 2 cups vegetable broth
- 2 tablespoon cornstarch
- 2 tablespoon water
- 1 tablespoon Italian Seasoning
- 1 tablespoon Ranch Dressing
- 1 tablespoon olive oil
- 2 teaspoon onion powder
- 1 teaspoon red wine vinegar
- ½ teaspoon paprika
- Salt and pepper, to taste
- Chopped parsley to garnish

**Directions:**

1. Season the pork roast with salt and pepper, and set aside. In a bowl, add Italian seasoning, ranch dressing, red wine vinegar, garlic, onion powder, and paprika.
2. Open the pot, select Sear/Sauté mode, and heat the oil. Sauté the onion, until translucent. Pour the gravy mixture and broth over and add the pork. Close the lid, secure the pressure valve, and select Pressure mode on High pressure for 15 minutes. Press Start/Stop to start cooking.
3. Once the timer has ended, do a quick pressure release, and open the pot. Remove the pork roast with a slotted spoon onto a serving plate. Mix the cornstarch with the water in a small bowl and add it to the sauce. Select Sear/Sauté. Stir and cook the sauce for 4 minutes, until thickens.
4. Once the gravy is ready, turn off the pot and spoon the sauce over the pork. Garnish with parsley and serve with a turnip mash.

## Traditional Beef Stroganoff

**(Ready in about:** 1 hr 15 min | **Servings:** 6)

**Ingredients:**

- 2 pounds beef stew meat
- 8 ounces sour cream
- 2 garlic cloves; minced
- 1 onion; chopped
- 3 cups fresh mushrooms; chopped
- 1 cup long-grain rice, cooked
- 1 cup beef broth
- ¼ cup flour
- 2 tablespoon olive oil
- 1 tablespoon chopped fresh parsley
- salt and ground black pepper to taste

**Directions:**

1. In a large bowl, combine salt, pepper and flour. Add beef and massage to coat beef in flour mixture. Warm oil on Sear/Sauté. Brown the beef for 4 to 5 minutes. Add garlic and onion and cook for 3 minutes until fragrant. Add beef broth to the pot.

2. Seal the pressure lid, choose Pressure, set to High, and set the timer to 35 minutes. Press Start. When ready, release the pressure quickly.
3. Open the lid and stir mushrooms and sour cream into the beef mixture. Seal the pressure lid again, choose Pressure, set to High, and set the timer to 2 minutes. Press Start.
4. When ready, release the pressure quickly. Season the stroganoff with pepper and salt; scoop over cooked rice before serving.

## Italian Pot Roast

**(Ready in about:** 1 hr 30 min | **Servings:** 5)

**Ingredients:**

- 2 ½ pounds beef brisket, trimmed
- 4 ounces pancetta; chopped
- 6 carrots; chopped
- 1 bay leaf
- 1 onion; chopped
- 3 garlic cloves; minced
- 1 cup beef broth
- ¾ cup dry red wine
- 2 fresh thyme sprigs
- 2 fresh rosemary sprigs
- 2 tablespoon olive oil
- salt and freshly ground black pepper
- A handful of parsley; chopped

**Directions:**

1. Warm olive oil on Sear/Sauté. Fry the pancetta for 4-5 minutes until crispy. Set aside. Season the beef with pepper and salt and add it to the pot and brown for 5 to 7 minutes for each; remove and set aside on a plate.
2. In the same oil, fry garlic and onion for 3 minutes until softened. Pour in red wine and beef broth to deglaze the bottom, scrape the bottom of the pot to get rid of any browned bits of food.
3. Return the beef and pancetta to the Foodi and add rosemary sprigs and thyme. Seal the pressure lid, choose Pressure, set to High, and set the timer to 50 minutes. Press Start.
4. When ready, release the pressure quickly. Add carrots and bay leaf to the pot. Seal the pressure lid again, choose Pressure, set to High, and set the timer to an additional 4 minutes. Press Start. When ready, release the pressure quickly. Get rid of the thyme, bay leaf and rosemary sprigs. Place beef on a serving plate and sprinkle with parsley to serve.

## Pork Tenderloin with Potatoes and Sweet Pepper Sauce

**(Ready in about:** 35 min | **Servings:** 4)

**Ingredients:**

- 1 pound russet potatoes, quartered
- 1 large (about 1¼-pound) beef tenderloin; cut into 2 pieces
- 1 small roasted red bell pepper; cut into strips
- 6 pickled pimientos, stemmed, seeded, and quartered
- 1 thyme sprig
- 2 medium garlic cloves, finely minced
- ¼ cup chicken stock
- ½ cup dry white wine
- 2 tablespoon unsalted butter
- 2 tablespoon olive oil
- 2 teaspoon pickling liquid from the peppers
- 2 teaspoon salt
- ¼ teaspoon freshly ground black pepper

**Directions:**

1. Season the beef pieces with the salt and black pepper on all sides. On your Foodi, choose Sear/Sauté and adjust to Medium-High. Press Start to preheat the pot for 5 minutes.
2. Pour in the oil into the pot and heat until shimmering. Add the beef pieces, sear for 3 minutes or until browned. Turn and brown the other side. Remove the beef to a plate.
3. Pour in the wine into the pot and scrape off any browned bits at the bottom. Let the wine cook until reduced by one-third. Stir in the potatoes, chicken stock, thyme, and garlic. Return the beef to the pot.

4. Seal the pressure lid, choose Pressure; adjust the pressure to High and the cook time to 20 minutes; press Start. After cooking, perform a natural pressure release for 5 minutes, then a quick pressure release, and carefully open the pressure lid.
5. Remove the beef and allow resting while you finish the sauce. Remove and discard the thyme. Choose Sear/Sauté and adjust to Medium. Press Start to simmer the sauce. Cook the potatoes for 2 to 4 minutes or until tender. Stir in the roasted pepper, pimiento, and the pickling liquid. Taste and adjust the seasoning.
6. Right before serving, turn off the heat and stir in the butter. Slice the tenderloin and lay the pieces on a platter. Ladle the peppers and potatoes around the pork and spoon the sauce over.

## Crispy Roast Pork

**(Ready in about:** 50 min | **Servings:** 4)

**Ingredients:**
- 4 pork tenderloins
- ¾ teaspoon garlic powder
- 1 teaspoon five spice seasoning
- ½ teaspoon white pepper
- 1 teaspoon salt
- Cooking spray

**Directions:**
1. Place the pork, white pepper, garlic powder, five seasoning, and salt into a bowl and toss to coat. Leave to marinate at room temperature for 30 minutes.
2. Place the pork into the Foodi basket, greased with cooking spray, close the crisping lid and cook for 20 minutes at 360 F. After 10 minutes, turn the tenderloins. Serve hot.

## Barbecue Pork Ribs

**(Ready in about:** 4 h 35 min | **Servings:** 2)

**Ingredients:**
- 1 lb. pork ribs
- 3 garlic cloves; chopped
- 1 tablespoon honey, plus more for brushing
- 4 tablespoon barbecue sauce
- 1 teaspoon black pepper
- 1 teaspoon sesame oil
- ½ teaspoon five spice powder
- 1 teaspoon salt
- 1 teaspoon soy sauce

**Directions:**
1. Chop the ribs into smaller pieces and place in a large bowl. In a separate bowl, whisk together all of the other ingredients. Add to the bowl with the pork, and mix until the pork is thoroughly coated. Cover the bowl, place it in the fridge, and let it marinade for about 4 hours.
2. Place the ribs in the basket of the Foodi. Close the crisping lid and cook for 15 minutes on Air Crisp mode at 350 F. After, brush the ribs with some honey and cook for 15 more minutes.

## Pork Sandwiches with Slaw

**(Ready in about:** 20 min | **Servings:** 8)

**Ingredients:**
- 2 lb. chuck roast
- 1 white onion; sliced
- 2 cups beef broth
- ¼ cup sugar
- 1 teaspoon Spanish paprika
- 1 teaspoon garlic powder
- 2 tablespoon apple cider vinegar
- Salt to taste

**Assembling:**
- 4 Buns, halved
- 1 cup red cabbage, shredded
- 1 cup white cabbage, shredded
- 1 cup white Cheddar cheese, grated
- 4 tablespoon mayonnaise

**Directions:**
1. Place the pork roast on a clean flat surface and sprinkle with paprika, garlic powder, sugar, and salt. Use your hands to rub the seasoning on the meat.

2. Open the Foodi, add beef broth, onions, pork, and apple cider vinegar. Close the lid, secure the pressure valve, and select Pressure mode on High pressure for 12 minutes. Press Start/Stop.
3. Once the timer has ended, do a quick pressure release. Remove the roast to a cutting board, and use two forks to shred them. Return to the pot, close the crisping lid, and cook for 3 minutes on Air Crisp at 300 F.
4. In the buns, spread the mayo, add the shredded pork, some cooked onions from the pot, and shredded red and white cabbage. Top with the cheese.

## Pork Carnitas Lettuce Cups

(**Ready in about:** 30 min + overnight refrigerated | **Servings:** 6)

**Ingredients:**

- 3 lb. pork shoulder
- 1 small head lettuce, leaves removed, washed and dried
- 1 onion; chopped
- 2 Limes; cut in wedges
- 2 carrots, grated
- 1 ½ cup water
- 2 tablespoon olive oil
- 1 teaspoon white pepper
- 2 teaspoon dried oregano
- 1 teaspoon red pepper flakes
- ½ teaspoon Cayenne pepper
- ½ teaspoon coriander powder
- 1 teaspoon cumin powder
- 1 teaspoon garlic powder
- Salt to taste

**Directions:**

1. In a bowl, add onion, cayenne, coriander, garlic, cumin, white pepper, dried oregano, red pepper flakes, and salt. Mix them well with a spoon.
2. Drizzle over the pork and rub to coat. Then, wrap the meat in plastic wrap and refrigerate overnight.
3. On the next day, open the Foodi lid, and select Sear/Sauté mode. Pour 2 tablespoons of olive oil in the pot and while heating, take the pork out from the fridge, remove the wraps and place it in the pot.
4. Brown it on both sides for 6 minutes and then pour the water. Close the lid, secure the pressure valve, and select Pressure mode on High pressure for 15 minutes. Press Start/Stop to start cooking.
5. Once the timer has stopped, do a quick pressure release. Use two forks to shred the pork, inside the pot. Close the crisping lid, and select Bake/Roast mode. Set for 10 minutes at 350 F. When ready, turn off the heat and begin assembling.
6. Arrange double layers of lettuce leaves on a flat surface, make a bed of grated carrots in them, and spoon the pulled pork on them.
7. Drizzle a sauce of choice (I used mustardy sauce) over them, and serve with lime wedges for freshness.

## Short Ribs with Mushroom and Asparagus Sauce

(**Ready in about:** 1 hr 15 min | **Servings:** 6)

**Ingredients:**

- 3½ pounds boneless beef short ribs; cut into pieces
- 10 ounces mushrooms, quartered
- 2 carrots, peeled and chopped
- 2 garlic cloves; minced
- 5 sprigs parsley; chopped
- 2 sprigs rosemary; chopped
- 3 sprigs oregano; chopped
- 1 onion; diced
- 4 cups beef stock
- 1 cup dry red wine
- 1 cup asparagus, trimmed and roughly chopped
- ¼ cup cold water
- 1 tablespoon cornstarch
- 3 tablespoon olive oil
- 1 tablespoon tomato puree
- 2 teaspoon salt
- 1 teaspoon ground black pepper

**Directions:**

1. Apply a seasoning of black pepper and salt to the ribs. Warm oil on Sear/Sauté. In batches, add the short ribs to the oil and cook for 3 to 5 minutes each side until browned. Set aside on a bowl. Add onions to the hot oil and cook for 3 to 5 minutes until soft.

2. Add tomato puree and red wine into the pot to deglaze, scrape the bottom to get rid of any browned beef bits. Cook for 2 minutes until wine reduces slightly. Return the ribs to pot and top with carrots, oregano, rosemary, and garlic. Add in beef broth.
3. Seal the pressure lid, choose Pressure, set to High, and set the timer to 35 minutes. Press Start. Release pressure naturally for 10 minutes. Transfer ribs to a plate. Strain and get rid of herbs and vegetables, and return cooking broth to inner pot. Add mushrooms and asparagus to the broth.
4. Press Sear/Sauté and cook for 2 to 4 minutes until vegetables are soft. In a bowl, mix water and cornstarch until cornstarch dissolves completely. Add the cornstarch mixture into the broth as you stir for 1 to 3 minutes until the broth thickens slightly. Season the sauce with black pepper and salt. Pour the sauce over ribs, add chopped parsley for garnish before serving.

## Holiday Honey Glazed Ham

**(Ready in about:** 30 min | **Servings:** 10)

**Ingredients:**
- 1 (5 pounds) ham, bone-in
- ¼ cup brown sugar
- ½ cup apple cider
- ¼ cup honey
- 1 pinch ground cloves

- 2 tablespoon orange juice
- 1 tablespoon Dijon mustard
- 2 tablespoon pineapple juice (optional)
- ¼ teaspoon grated nutmeg
- ½ teaspoon ground cinnamon

**Directions:**
1. Set on Sear/Sauté, set to Medium High, and choose Start/Stop to preheat the pot. Press Start. Mix in apple cider, mustard, pineapple juice, cloves, cinnamon, brown sugar, honey, orange juice, and nutmeg; cook until sauce becomes warm and the sugar and spices are completely dissolved.
2. Lay ham into the sauce. Seal the pressure lid, choose Pressure, set to High, and set the timer to 10 minutes; press Start. When ready, release the pressure quickly.
3. As the ham cooks, preheat the oven's broiler. Line aluminum foil to a baking sheet. Transfer the ham to the prepared baking sheet. On Sear/Sauté, cook the remaining liquid for 4 to 6 minutes until you have a thick and syrupy glaze. Brush the glaze onto ham.
4. Set the glazed ham in the preheated broiler and bake for 3 to 5 minutes until the glaze is caramelized. Place the ham on a cutting board and slice. Transfer to a serving bowl and drizzle glaze over the ham.

## Sour and Sweet Pork

**(Ready in about:** 40 min | **Servings:** 4)

**Ingredients:**
- 1 pound pork loin; cut into chunks
- 15 ounces canned peaches
- ¼ cup water
- ¼ cup beef stock
- 2 tablespoon sweet chili sauce

- 2 tablespoon soy sauce
- 2 tablespoon cornstarch
- 2 tablespoon white wine
- 2 tablespoon honey

**Directions:**
1. Into the pot, mix soy sauce, beef stock, white wine, juice from the canned peaches, and sweet chili sauce; stir in pork to coat.
2. Seal the pressure lid, choose Pressure, set to High, and set the timer to 5 minutes. Press Start. Release pressure naturally for 10 minutes, then release the remaining pressure quickly. Remove the pork to a serving plate. Chop the peaches into small pieces.
3. In a bowl, mix water and cornstarch until cornstarch dissolves completely; stir the mixture into the pot. Press Sear/Sauté and cook for 5 more minutes until you obtain the desired thick consistency; add in the chopped peaches and stir well. Serve the pork topped with peach sauce and enjoy.

## Char Siew Pork Ribs

(**Ready in about:** 4 hours 55 min | **Servings:** 6)

**Ingredients:**
- 2 lb. pork ribs
- 2 tablespoon char siew sauce
- 2 tablespoon minced ginger
- 2 tablespoon hoisin sauce
- 2 tablespoon sesame oil
- 1 tablespoon honey
- 4 garlic cloves; minced
- 1 tablespoon soy sauce

**Directions:**
1. Whisk together all marinade ingredients, in a small bowl. Coat the ribs well with the mixture. Place in a container with a lid, and refrigerate for 4 hours.
2. Place the ribs in the basket but do not throw away the liquid from the container. Close the crisping lid and cook for 40 minutes on Air Crisp at 350 F. Stir in the liquid, increase the temperature to 350 F, and cook for 10 minutes.

## Tomatillo and Sweet Potato pork Chili

(**Ready in about:** 70 min | **Servings:** 6)

**Ingredients:**
- 1 ½ lb. pork roast; cut into 1-inch cubes
- 1 lb. tomatillos, husks removed
- 1 bay leaf
- 1 bunch cilantro; chopped and divided into 2
- 2 sweet potatoes, peeled and cut into ½-inch cubes
- 1 bulb garlic, tail sliced off, peeled
- 2 green chilies
- 3 cups chicken broth
- 1 green bell pepper, seeded and roughly chopped
- 2 tablespoon olive oil; divided into 2
- ½ teaspoon cumin powder
- 1 teaspoon dried oregano
- Salt and pepper, to taste

**Directions:**
1. Put the garlic bulb in a baking dish that fits in your reversible rack, inside the inner pot. Drizzle a bit of 1 portion of olive oil over the garlic bulb. Place the green bell peppers, onion, green chilies, and tomatillos on the dish in a single layer.
2. Close the crisping lid and cook for 15 minutes at 400 F on Air Crisp mode. Then, remove them, and set aside to cool. Wipe clean the pot if needed.
3. Place the garlic in a blender. Add green bell pepper, tomatillos, onions, and green chilies. Pulse for a few minutes not to be smooth but slightly chunky.
4. Now, open the lid of the Foodi, and select Sear/Sauté mode.
5. Pour in the remaining olive oil and while is heating, season the pork cubes with salt and pepper. Then, brown the pork, for about 5 minutes.
6. Stir in oregano, cumin, bay leaf, pour in the blended green sauce, potatoes, and add the chicken broth. Stir well.
7. Close the lid, secure the pressure valve, and select Pressure mode on High pressure for 25 minutes. Press Start/Stop to start cooking.
8. Once the timer has ended, let the pot sit closed for 10 minutes.
9. After, do a natural pressure release for 5 minutes, and then a quick pressure release to let the remaining steam out.
10. Open the pot. Remove and discard the bay leaf, add half of the cilantro, adjust with salt and pepper, and stir. Close the crisping lid to give it nice and tender taste. Cook on Broil mode for 10 minutes.
11. Dish the chili into serving bowls and garnish it with the remaining chopped cilantro. Serve topped with a side of chips or crusted bread.

## Pork Chops with Mushroom Sauce

**(Ready in about:** 35 min | **Servings:** 4)

**Ingredients:**

- 4 pork chops
- 1 (10 oz) can mushroom soup
- 8 oz. Cremini mushrooms; sliced
- 3 cloves garlic; minced
- 1 small onion; chopped
- 1 cup beef broth
- 1 sprig fresh thyme
- 1 tablespoon olive oil
- 1 teaspoon garlic powder
- Salt and pepper, to taste
- Chopped parsley to garnish

**Directions:**

1. Select Sear/Sauté mode. Add oil, mushrooms, garlic, and onion. Sauté them, stirring occasionally with a spoon, until nice and translucent, for 3 minutes.
2. Season the pork chops with salt, garlic powder, and pepper, and add them to the pot followed by the thyme and broth. Seal the lid and select Pressure mode on High pressure for 10 minutes. Press Start/Stop to start cooking.
3. Once the timer has ended, do a natural pressure release for about 10 minutes, then a quick pressure release to let the remaining steam out. Close the crisping lid and cook on Broil mode for 5 minutes.
4. When ready, add the mushroom soup. Stir it until the mixture thickens a little bit. Dish the pork and gravy into a serving bowl and garnish with parsley. Serve with a side of creamy sweet potato mash.

## Pork Carnitas Wraps

**(Ready in about:** 1 hr 15 min | **Servings:** 12)

**Ingredients:**

- 1 (4 to 5 pounds) boneless pork shoulder
- 12 corn tortillas, warmed
- 1 avocado; sliced
- 1 onion; sliced
- 2 garlic cloves; minced
- 2 jalapeños; sliced
- 2 oranges, juiced
- 2 limes, juiced
- Fresh cilantro leaves; chopped
- 2 tablespoon sweet smoked paprika
- 1 tablespoon dried oregano
- 1 tablespoon salt
- 2 teaspoon grapeseed oil
- 2 teaspoon ground black pepper

**Directions:**

1. Warm oil on Sear/Sauté. Add in pork and cook for 5 minutes until golden brown. Transfer the pork to a plate. Add garlic and onions to the inner pot and cook for 2 to 3 minutes until soft.
2. Add lime and orange juices into the pot to deglaze, scrape the bottom to get rid of any browned bits of food.
3. Stir in pepper, paprika, salt and oregano. Return the pork to pot; stir to coat in seasoning and liquid. Seal the pressure lid, choose Pressure, set to High, and set the timer to 35 minutes. Press Start. When ready, release the pressure quickly.
4. Press Sear/Sauté. When the liquid starts to simmer, use two forks to shred the pork. Cook for 10 more minutes until liquid is reduced by half. Serve in warmed tortillas topped with jalapeños, avocado slices and cilantro.

# Spicy Pork Roast with Peanut Sauce.

**(Ready in about:** 30 min | **Servings:** 6)

**Ingredients:**

- 3 lb. pork roast
- 1 large white onion; sliced
- 1 large red bell pepper, seeded and sliced
- 2 chilies, deseeded; chopped
- 1 cup Hot water
- ½ cup soy sauce
- ½ cup peanut butter
- 1 tablespoon plain vinegar
- 1 tablespoon lime juice
- 1 tablespoon garlic powder
- 1 teaspoon ginger puree
- Salt and pepper to taste

**To Garnish:**

- Chopped green onions
- Chopped Peanuts
- Lime Wedges

**Directions:**

1. Add the soy sauce, vinegar, peanut butter, lime juice, garlic powder, chilies, and ginger puree, to a bowl. Whisk together and even. Add a few pinches of salt and pepper, and mix it.
2. Open the Foodi lid, and place the pork in the inner pot. Pour the hot water and peanut butter mixture over it.
3. Close the lid, secure the pressure valve, and select Pressure mode on High pressure for 15 minutes. Press Start/Stop to start cooking.
4. Once the timer has stopped, do a quick pressure release. Use two forks to shred it, inside the pot, and close the crisping lid.
5. Cook on Broil mode for 4 - 5 minutes, until the sauce thickens. On a bed of cooked rice, spoon the meat with some sauce and garnish it with the chopped peanuts, green onions, and the lemon wedges.

# Sweet Garlic Pork Tenderloin

**(Ready in about:** 30 min | **Servings:** 4)

**Ingredients:**

- 2 lb. pork tenderloin
- ¼ cup Balsamic vinegar
- ¼ cup honey
- ½ cup chicken broth
- 1 clove garlic; minced
- 1 tablespoon Dijon mustard
- 1 tablespoon Worcestershire sauce
- ½ tablespoon cornstarch
- 4 tablespoon water
- 2 tablespoon olive oil
- 1 teaspoon sage powder
- Salt and black pepper to taste

**Directions:**

1. Put the pork on a clean flat surface and pat dry using paper towels. Season with salt and pepper. Select Sear/Sauté mode.
2. Heat the oil and brown the pork on both sides, for about 4 minutes in total. Remove the pork onto a plate and set aside. Add in honey, chicken broth, balsamic vinegar, garlic, Worcestershire sauce, mustard, and sage. Stir the ingredients and return the pork to the pot.
3. Close the lid, secure the pressure valve, and select Pressure mode on High for 15 minutes. Once the timer has ended, do a quick pressure release.
4. Remove the pork with tongs onto a plate and wrap it in aluminum foil. Next, mix the cornstarch with water and pour it into the pot. Select Sear/Sauté mode, stir the mixture and cook until it thickens. Then, turn the pot off after the desired thickness is achieved.
5. Unwrap the pork and use a knife to slice it with 3 to 4-inch thickness. Arrange the slices on a serving platter and spoon the sauce all over it. Serve with a syrupy sautéed Brussels sprouts and red onion chunks.

## Hot Dogs with Peppers

**(Ready in about:** 15 min | **Servings:** 6)

**Ingredients:**

- 6 sausages pork sausage links
- 1 green bell pepper; sliced into strips
- 1 red bell pepper; sliced into strips
- 1 yellow bell pepper; sliced into strips
- 2 spring onions; sliced
- 1 ½ cups beer
- 6 hot dog rolls
- 1 tablespoon olive oil

**Directions:**

1. Warm oil on Sear/Sauté. Add in sausage links and sear for 5 minutes until browned; set aside on a plate. Into the Foodi, pile peppers. Lay the sausages on top. Add beer into the pot.
2. Seal the pressure lid, choose Pressure, set to High, and set the timer to 5 minutes. Press Start. When ready, release the pressure quickly. Serve sausages in buns topped with onions and peppers.

## Pork Chops with Squash Purée and Mushroom Gravy

**(Ready in about:** 45 min | **Servings:** 4)

**Ingredients:**

- 4 pork chops
- 1 pound butternut squash; cubed
- 2 sprigs rosemary, leaves removed and chopped
- 2 sprigs thyme, leaves removed and chopped
- 4 cloves garlic; minced
- 1 cup mushrooms; chopped
- 1 cup chicken broth
- 1 tablespoon olive oil
- 2 tablespoon olive oil
- 1 tablespoon soy sauce
- 1 teaspoon cornstarch

**Directions:**

1. Set on Sear/Sauté, set to Medium High, and choose Start/Stop to preheat the pot and heat rosemary, thyme and 1 tablespoon of olive oil. Add the pork chops and sear for 1 minute for each side until lightly browned.
2. Sauté garlic and mushrooms in the pressure cooker for 5-6 minutes until mushrooms are tender. Add soy sauce and chicken broth. Transfer pork chops to a wire trivet and place it into the pressure cooker. Over the chops, place a cake pan. Add butternut squash in the pot and drizzle with 1 tablespoon olive oil.
3. Seal the pressure lid, choose Pressure, set to High, and set the timer to 10 minutes. Press Start. When ready, release the pressure quickly. Remove the pan and trivet from the pot. Stir cornstarch into the mushroom mixture for 2 to 3 minutes until the sauce thickens.
4. Transfer the mushroom sauce to an immersion blender and blend until you attain the desired consistency. Scoop sauce into a cup with a pour spout. Smash the squash into a purée. Set pork chops on a plate and ladle squash puree next to them. Top the pork chops with gravy.

## Mediterranean Tender Pork Roast

**(Ready in about:** 60 min | **Servings:** 6)

**Ingredients:**

- 3 lb. pork roast; cut into 3-inch pieces
- ½ cup Kalamata olives, pitted
- ¼ cup fresh lemon juice
- 1 cup beef broth
- 3 tablespoon Cavender's Greek Seasoning to taste
- 1 teaspoon onion powder
- Salt to taste

**Directions:**

1. Put the pork chunks in the inner pot of the Foodi. In a bowl, add greek seasoning, onion powder, beef broth, lemon juice, olives, and salt to taste. Mix using a spoon and pour the sauce over the pork.
2. Close the lid, secure the pressure valve, and select Pressure mode on High pressure for 35 minutes. Press Start/Stop to start cooking.

3. Once the timer is off, do a natural pressure release for 10 minutes, then do a quick pressure release to let out any more steam, and open the pot.
4. Use two forks to shred the roast inside to pot and close the crisping lid. Cook on Broil mode for 10 minutes, until nice and tender. Serve with a green salad, potatoes or rice.

## Sausage with Celeriac and Potato Mash

**(Ready in about:** 45 min | **Servings:** 4)

### Ingredients:
- 4 potatoes, peeled and diced
- 4 pork sausages
- 1 onion
- 2 cups vegetable broth
- 1 cup celeriac; chopped
- ¼ cup milk
- ½ cup water
- 1 tablespoon heavy cream
- 1 tablespoon olive oil
- 2 tablespoon butter
- 1 teaspoon Dijon mustard
- ½ teaspoon dry mustard powder
- Fresh flat-leaf parsley; chopped
- salt and ground black pepper to taste

### Directions:
1. Warm oil on Sear/Sauté. Add in sausages and cook for 1 to 2 minutes for each side until browned. Set the sausages to a plate. To the same pot, add onion and cook for 3 minutes until fragrant.
2. Add sausages on top of onions and pour water and broth over them. Place a trivet over onions and sausages. Put potatoes and celeriac in the steamer basket and transfer it to the trivet.
3. Seal the pressure lid, choose Pressure, set to High, and set the timer to 11 minutes. Press Start. When ready, release the pressure quickly.
4. Transfer potatoes and celeriac to a bowl and set sausages on a plate and cover them with aluminum foil. Using a potato masher, mash potatoes and celeriac together with black pepper, milk, salt and butter until mash becomes creamy and fluffy. Adjust the seasonings.
5. Set your Foodi to Sear/Sauté. Add the onion mixture and bring to a boil. Cook for 5 to 10 minutes until the mixture is reduced and thickened. Into the gravy, stir in dry mustard, salt, pepper, mustard and cream. Place the mash in 4 bowls in equal parts, top with a sausage or two, and gravy. Add parsley for garnishing.

## Lamb Chops and Potato Mash

**(Ready in about:** 40 min | **Servings:** 8)

### Ingredients:
- 5 potatoes, peeled and chopped
- 4 cilantro leaves, for garnish
- 8 lamb cutlets
- 1 green onion; chopped
- ⅓ cup milk
- 1 cup beef stock
- 3 sprigs rosemary leaves; chopped
- 3 tablespoon butter, softened
- 1 tablespoon olive oil
- 1 tablespoon tomato puree
- salt to taste

### Directions:
1. Rub rosemary leaves and salt to the lamb chops. Warm oil and 2 tablespoon of butter on Sear/Sauté. Add in the lamb chops and cook for 1 minute for each side until browned; set aside on a plate.
2. In the pot, mix tomato puree and green onion; cook for 2-3 minutes. Add beef stock into the pot to deglaze, scrape the bottom to get rid of any browned bits of food.
3. Return lamb cutlets alongside any accumulated juices to the pot. Set a reversible rack on lamb cutlets. Place steamer basket on the reversible rack. Arrange potatoes in the steamer basket.
4. Seal the pressure lid, choose Pressure, set to High, and set the timer to 4 minutes. Press Start.
5. When ready, release the pressure quickly. Remove trivet and steamer basket from pot. In a high speed blender, add potatoes, milk, salt, and remaining tablespoon butter. Blend well until you obtain a smooth consistency.

6. Divide the potato mash between serving dishes. Lay lamb chops on the mash. Drizzle with cooking liquid obtained from pressure cooker; apply cilantro sprigs for garnish.

## Jamaican Pulled Pork with Mango Sauce

(**Ready in about:** 1 hr 15 min | **Servings:** 6)

### Ingredients:
- 3 pounds pork shoulder
- 1 mango; cut into chunks
- ½ cup water
- 1 tablespoon olive oil
- 2 tablespoon fresh cilantro, finely minced
- 1 ½ teaspoon onion powder
- ½ teaspoon ground nutmeg
- 1 teaspoon cayenne pepper
- 1 teaspoon ground allspice
- ½ teaspoon ground cinnamon
- 1 teaspoon sea salt
- 1 teaspoon dried thyme
- 1 teaspoon ground black pepper

### Directions:
1. In a bowl, combine onion powder, thyme, allspice, cinnamon, sugar, pepper, sea salt, cayenne, and nutmeg. Coat the pork shoulder with olive oil; season with seasoning mixture. Warm oil on Sear/Sauté. Add in the pork and cook for 5 minutes until browned completely.
2. To the pot, add water and mango chunks. Seal the pressure lid, choose Pressure, set to High, and set the timer to 45 minutes. Press Start. Release pressure naturally for 15 minutes, then release the remaining pressure quickly.
3. Transfer the pork to a cutting board and allow cooling. To make the sauce, pour the cooking liquid in a food processor and pulse until smooth. Use two forks to shred the pork and arrange on a serving platter. Serve the pulled pork topped with mango salsa and fresh cilantro.

## Garlicky Pork Neck Bones

(**Ready in about:** 40 min | **Servings:** 6)

### Ingredients:
- 3 lb. pork neck bones
- ½ cup red wine
- 1 cup beef broth
- 2 cloves garlic, smashed
- 1 white onion; sliced
- 4 tablespoon olive oil
- 1 tablespoon tomato paste
- 1 teaspoon dried thyme
- Salt and black pepper to taste

### Directions:
1. Open the lid and select Sear/Sauté mode. Warm the olive oil. Meanwhile, season the pork neck bones with salt and pepper. After, place them in the oil to brown on all sides. Work in batches.
2. Each batch should cook in about 5 minutes. Then, remove them onto a plate. Add the onion and season with salt to taste. Stir with a spoon and cook the onions until soft, for a few minutes.
3. Then, add garlic, thyme, pepper, and tomato paste. Cook them for 2 minutes, constant stirring to prevent the tomato paste from burning.
4. Next, pour the red wine into the pot to deglaze the bottom. Add the pork neck bones back to the pot and pour the beef broth over it.
5. Close the lid, secure the pressure valve, and select Pressure mode on High pressure for 10 minutes. Press Start/Stop to start cooking.
6. Once the timer has ended, let the pot sit for 10 minutes before doing a quick pressure release. Close the crisping lid and cook on Broil mode for 5 minutes, until nice and tender.
7. Dish the pork neck into a serving bowl and serve with the red wine sauce spooned over and a right amount of broccoli mash.

# Ranch Pork with Mushroom Sauce

**(Ready in about:** 22 min | **Servings:** 4)

**Ingredients:**
- 4 pork loin chops
- 1 oz. Ranch Dressing and Seasoning mix
- 1 (15 oz) can mushroom soup cream
- ½ cup chicken broth
- Chopped parsley to garnish

**Directions:**
1. Add pork, mushroom soup cream, ranch dressing and seasoning mix, and chicken broth, inside the inner pot of your Foodi. Close the lid, secure the pressure valve, and select Pressure mode on High pressure for 10 minutes. Press Start/Stop.
2. Once the timer has ended, do a natural pressure release for 10 minutes, then a quick pressure release to let the remaining steam out.
3. Close the crisping lid and cook for 5 minutes on Broil mode, until tender. Serve with well-seasoned sautéed cremini mushrooms, and the sauce.

# Ginger Garlic Pork with Coconut Sauce

**(Ready in about:** 45 min | **Servings:** 6)

**Ingredients:**
- 3 lb. shoulder roast
- 2 cups coconut milk
- ½ cup beef broth
- 1 onion, peeled and quartered
- Parsley leaves (unchopped), to garnish
- 1 tablespoon olive oil
- 3 tablespoon grated ginger
- 1 teaspoon Coriander powder
- 1 teaspoon cumin powder
- 3 teaspoon minced garlic
- Salt and black pepper to season

**Directions:**
1. In a bowl, add coriander, salt, pepper, and cumin. Use a spoon to mix them. Season the pork with the spice mixture. Rub the spice onto meat, with hands. Open the lid of Foodi, add olive oil, pork, onions, ginger, garlic, broth and coconut milk.
2. Close the lid, secure the pressure valve, and select Pressure mode on High for 30 minutes. Press Start/Stop to start cooking.
3. Once the timer has stopped, do a quick pressure release. Give it a good stir and close the crisping lid. Cook for 10 minutes on Broil mode, until you perfect texture and creaminess.
4. Dish the meat with the sauce into a serving bowl, garnish it with the parsley and serve with a side of bread or cooked shrimp.

# Ham with Collard Greens

**(Ready in about:** 10 min | **Servings:** 4)

**Ingredients:**
- 20 oz. collard greens, washed and cut
- ½ cup diced sweet onion
- 2 ½ cups diced ham
- 2 cubes of chicken bouillon
- 4 cups water

**Directions:**
1. Place the ham at the bottom of the inner pot. Add collard greens and onion. Then, add chicken cubes to the water and dissolve it. Pour the mixture into the pot. Close the lid, secure the pressure valve, to seal properly.
2. Select Steam mode on High pressure for 5 minutes. Press Start/Stop. Once the timer has ended, do a quick pressure release, and open the lid.
3. Spoon the vegetables and the ham with sauce into a serving platter. Serve with a side of steak dish of your choice.

# Apricot Lemon Ham

**(Ready in about:** 1 hr | **Servings:** 12)

**Ingredients:**

- 5 pounds smoked ham
- ¾ cup apricot jam
- ¼ cup water
- ½ cup brown sugar
- Juice from 1 Lime

- ½ teaspoon ground cardamom
- ¼ teaspoon ground nutmeg
- 2 teaspoon mustard
- freshly ground black pepper to taste

**Directions:**

1. Into the pot, add water and ham to the steel pot of a pressure cooker. In a bowl, combine jam, lemon juice, cardamom, pepper, nutmeg, mustard, and brown sugar; pour the mixture over the ham. Seal the pressure lid, choose Pressure, set to High, and set the timer to 10 minutes. Press Start.
2. When ready, release the pressure quickly. Transfer the ham to a cutting board; allow to sit for 10 minutes. Press Sear/Sauté.
3. Simmer the liquid and cook for 4 to 6 minutes until thickened into a sauce. Slice ham and place onto a serving bowl. Drizzle with sauce before serving.

# Pork Chops with Broccoli

**(Ready in about:** 45 min | **Servings:** 6)

**Ingredients:**
**Pork Chops:**

- 6 boneless pork chops
- 1 broccoli head, broken into florets
- ¼ cup butter, melted
- 1 cup chicken stock
- ¼ cup milk

- 1 teaspoon garlic powder
- 1 teaspoon onion powder
- 1 teaspoon red pepper flakes
- 1 ½ teaspoon salt
- 1 teaspoon ground black pepper

**Gravy:**

- ½ cup heavy cream
- 3 tablespoon flour

- salt and ground black pepper to taste

**Directions:**

1. Combine salt, garlic powder, red pepper flakes, onion powder, and black pepper; rub the mixture to the pork chops. Place stock and broccoli into the Foodi. Lay the pork chops on top.
2. Seal the pressure lid, choose Pressure, set to High, and set the timer to 15 minutes. Press Start.When ready, release the pressure quickly.
3. Transfer the pork chops and broccoli to a plate. Press Sear/Sauté and simmer the liquid remaining in the pot. Mix cream and flour; pour into the simmering liquid and cook for 5 to 7 minutes until thickened and bubbly; season with pepper and salt. Top the chops with gravy before, drizzle melted butter over broccoli and serve.

# Italian Sausage and Cannellini Stew

**(Ready in about:** 45 min | **Servings:** 6)

**Ingredients:**

- 1 pound Italian sausages, halved
- 2 cups vegetable stock
- 3 cups fresh spinach
- 1 cup Cannellini Beans; soaked and rinsed
- 1 carrot; chopped
- 1 onion; chopped

- 1 celery stalk; chopped
- 1 sprig fresh rosemary
- 1 bay leaf
- 1 sprig fresh sage
- 1 tablespoon olive oil
- 1 teaspoon salt

**Directions:**

1. Warm oil on Sear/Sauté. Add in sausage pieces and sear for 5 minutes until browned; set aside on a plate. To the pot, add celery, onion, bay leaf, sage, carrot, and rosemary; cook for 3 minutes to soften slightly.
2. Stir in vegetable stock and beans. Arrange seared sausage pieces on top of the beans. Seal the pressure lid, choose Pressure, set to High, and set the timer to 10 minutes. Press Start. Release pressure naturally for 20 minutes,
3. Once ready, do a quick release. Get rid of bay leaf, rosemary and sage. Mix spinach into the mixture to serve.

## Cuban Pork

(**Ready in about:** 2 hr 30 min | **Servings:** 8)

**Ingredients:**
- 3 pounds pork shoulder
- ¼ cup lime juice
- ½ cup orange juice
- ¼ cup canola oil
- ¼ cup chopped fresh cilantro
- 8 cloves garlic; minced
- 1 tablespoon fresh oregano
- 1 tablespoon ground cumin
- 1 teaspoon red pepper flakes
- 2 teaspoon ground black pepper
- 1 teaspoon salt

**Directions:**
1. In a bowl, mix orange juice, olive oil, cumin, salt, pepper, oregano, lime juice, and garlic; add into a large plastic bag alongside the pork. Seal and massage the bag to ensure the marinade covers the pork completely.
2. Place in the refrigerator for an hour to overnight. In the Foodi, set your removed pork from bag. Add the marinade on top. Seal the pressure lid, choose Pressure, set to High, and set the timer to 50 minutes. Press Start.
3. Release pressure naturally for 15 minutes. Transfer the pork to a cutting board; use a fork to break into smaller pieces.
4. Skim and get rid of the fat from liquid in the cooker. Serve the liquid with pork and sprinkle with cilantro.

## Red Pork and Chickpea Stew

(**Ready in about:** 40 min | **Servings:** 6)

**Ingredients:**
- 1 (3 pounds) boneless pork shoulder, trimmed and cubed
- 15 ounces canned chickpeas, drained and rinsed
- 1½ cups water
- ½ cup sweet paprika
- 1 bay leaf
- 2 red bell peppers; chopped
- 6 cloves garlic; minced
- 1 white onion; chopped
- 1 tablespoon cornstarch
- 1 tablespoon olive oil
- 1 tablespoon chilli powder
- 1 tablespoon water
- 2 teaspoon salt

**Directions:**
1. Set on Sear/Sauté, set to Medium High, and choose Start/Stop to preheat the pot; add pork and oil and allow cooking for 5 minutes until browned.
2. Add in the onion, paprika, bay leaf, salt, water, chickpeas, and chili powder. Seal the pressure lid, choose Pressure, set to High, and set the timer to 8 minutes. Press Start.
3. Do a quick release and discard bay leaf. Remove 1 cup of cooking liquid from the Foodi; add to a blender alongside garlic, water, cornstarch, and red bell peppers; blend well until smooth. Add the blended mixture into the stew and mix well.

## Pork Chops with Plum Sauce

**(Ready in about:** 20 min | **Servings:** 4)

**Ingredients:**
- 4 pork chops
- 2 cups firm plums, pitted and sliced
- ¾ cup vegetable stock
- 1 tablespoon vegetable oil
- 1 teaspoon ground black pepper
- 1 teaspoon cumin seeds
- 1 teaspoon salt

**Directions:**
1. Sprinkle salt, cumin, and pepper on the pork chops. Set your Foodi to Sear/Sauté, set to Medium High, and choose Start/Stop to preheat the pot. Warm oil. Add the chops and cook for 3 to 5 minutes until browned and set aside on a bowl.
2. Arrange plum slices on the bottom of your Foodi. Place the pork chops on top of the plumes. Add any juice from the plate over the pork and apply stock around the edges.
3. Seal lid and cook on High pressure for 8 minutes. When ready, do a quick pressure release. Transfer the pork chops to a serving plate and spoon over the plum sauce before serving.

## Crispy Pork Fajitas

**(Ready in about:** 1 hr 30 min | **Servings:** 5)

**Ingredients:**
- 3 pounds boneless pork shoulder
- 1 lime, juiced
- 4 cloves garlic, crushed
- 2 bay leaves
- 5 corn tortillas, warmed
- ¾ cup vegetable broth
- ½ cup queso Cotija, crumbled
- ¼ cup pineapple juice
- 1 tablespoon ground cumin
- ½ teaspoon ground cinnamon
- 1 teaspoon paprika
- 1 teaspoon onion powder
- 2 teaspoon dried oregano
- 1 teaspoon salt
- 1 teaspoon ground black pepper

**Directions:**
1. In a bowl, combine cumin, paprika, pepper, onion powder, oregano, salt, and cinnamon; toss in pork to coat. Place the pork in the Foodi and allow settling for 15 to 30 minutes.
2. Add in chicken broth, garlic, lime juice, bay leaves, and pineapple juice. Seal the pressure lid, choose Pressure, set to High, and set the timer to 50 minutes; press Start. When ready, release pressure naturally for 15 minutes, then release the remaining pressure quickly.
3. Transfer the pork to a rimmed baking sheet and use two forks to shred the meat. Reserve the juices in a bowl. Place the Cook & Crisp Basket into the inner pot. Close the crisping lid and choose Air Crisp; adjust the temperature to 380°F and the time to 4 minutes to preheat. Press Start.
4. Add the baking sheet to the Cook & Crisp basket. Close the crisping lid. Select Air Crisp; adjust the temperature to 375°F and the cook time to 10 minutes. Press Start. After 5 minutes, open the lid and toss the meat. Continue cooking until the pork is done. Skim and get rid of fat from the liquid remaining. Dispose of the bay leaves. Over the pork, pour the liquid and serve alongside warm corn tortillas and queso fresco.

# Barbeque Pork Ribs

**(Ready in about:** 45 min | **Servings:** 2)

**Ingredients:**
- ½ lb. rack baby back ribs
- ½ cup Barbecue sauce
- ¼ cup beef broth
- 3 tablespoon apple cider vinegar
- Salt and pepper to season

**Directions:**
1. Select Sear/Sauté mode. Heat the oil into the pot. Meanwhile, season the ribs with salt and pepper. Cook them to brown, for 1 to 2 minutes per side. Pour the barbecue sauce, broth, and apple cider vinegar over the ribs and use tongs to flip so they are well coated.
2. Close the lid and pressure valve and set to Pressure mode on High pressure for 30 minutes. Press Start/Stop to start cooking.
3. Once the timer goes off, do a natural pressure release for 12 minutes, then a quick pressure release to let out the remaining steam.
4. Close the crisping lid and set to Air Crisp mode for 5 minutes at 350 F. Make sure the sauce is thick enough.
5. Use a knife to slice the ribs and over the sauce all over it. Serve the ribs with a generous side of steamed but crunchy green beans.

# Baby Back Ribs with Barbeque Sauce

**(Ready in about:** 45 min | **Servings:** 4)

**Ingredients:**
- 2 pounds baby back pork ribs
- Juice from 1 lemon
- 4 cups orange juice

**For BBQ sauce:**
- ½ cup ketchup
- Juice from ½ lemon
- 1 tablespoon Worcestershire sauce
- 2 tablespoon honey
- 2 teaspoon paprika
- ½ teaspoon cayenne pepper
- 1teaspoon mustard
- Salt to taste

**Directions:**
1. Mix all the BBQ sauce ingredients in a bowl until well incorporated. Set aside. Place ribs in your Foodi pot; add in lemon juice and orange juice.
2. Seal the pressure lid, choose Pressure, set to High, and set the timer to 20 minutes. Press Start. Release pressure naturally for 15 minutes. Meanwhile, preheat oven to 400° F. Line the sheet pan with aluminum foil.
3. Transfer the ribs to the prepared sheet. Do away with the cooking liquid. Onto both sides of ribs, brush barbecue sauce. Bake ribs in the oven for 10 minutes until sauce is browned and caramelized; set the ribs aside and cut into individual bones to serve.

**(Ready in about:** 1 hr 25 min | **Servings:** 5)

**Ingredients:**

- 2 pounds pork shoulder, trimmed; cut into chunks
- 3 cups shredded cabbage
- 5 taco tortillas
- 1 cup beer
- 1 cup vegetable broth
- 1/4 cup plus 2 tablespoon lemon juice
- 1/4 cup mayonnaise
- 3 tablespoon sugar
- 2 tablespoon honey
- 3 teaspoon taco seasoning
- 1 teaspoon ground black pepper
- 2 teaspoon mustard

**Directions:**

1. In a bowl, combine sugar, taco seasoning, and black pepper; rub the mixture onto pork pieces to coat well. Allow to settling for 30 minutes. Into the Foodi, add 1/4 cup lemon juice, broth, pork and beer.

2. Seal the pressure lid, choose Pressure, set to High, and set the timer to 50 minutes. Press Start. Meanwhile in a large bowl, mix mayonnaise, mustard, 2 tablespoon lemon juice, cabbage and honey until well coated.

3. Release pressure naturally for 15 minutes before doing a quick release. Transfer the pork to a cutting board and Allow cooling before using two forks to shred. Skim and get rid of fat from liquid in the pressure cooker. Return pork to the pot and mix with the liquid. Top the pork with slaw on taco tortillas before serving.

# Fish & Seafood Mains

## Herb Salmon with Barley Haricot Verts

**(Ready in about:** 50 min **| Servings:** 4)

**Ingredients:**

- 4 salmon fillets
- 8 ounces green beans haricot verts, trimmed
- 2 garlic cloves, minced
- 1 cup pearl barley
- 2 cups water
- ½ tablespoon brown sugar
- ½ tablespoon freshly squeezed lemon juice
- 1 tablespoon olive oil
- 4 tablespoons melted butter
- ½ teaspoon dried thyme
- ½ teaspoon dried rosemary
- 1 teaspoon salt; divided
- 1 teaspoon freshly ground black pepper; divided

**Directions:**

1. Pour the barley and water in the pot and mix to combine. Place the reversible rack in the pot. Lay the salmon fillets on the rack. Seal the pressure lid, choose Pressure, set to High and set the time to 2 minutes. Press Start.
2. In a bowl, toss the green beans with olive oil, ½ teaspoon of black pepper, and ½ teaspoon of salt.
3. Then, in another bowl, mix the remaining black pepper and salt, the butter, brown sugar, lemon juice, rosemary, garlic, and rosemary.
4. When done cooking the rice and salmon, perform a quick pressure release. Gently pat the salmon dry with a paper towel, then coat with the buttery herb sauce.
5. Position the haricots vert around the salmon. Close the crisping lid; choose Broil and set the time to 7 minutes; press Start/Stop. When ready, remove the salmon from the rack, and serve with the barley and haricots vert.

## Fried Salmon

**(Ready in about:** 13 min **| Servings:** 1)

**Ingredients:**

- 1 salmon fillet.
- ¼ teaspoon garlic powder
- 1 tablespoon soy sauce
- Salt and pepper

**Directions:**

1. Combine the soy sauce with the garlic powder, salt, and pepper. Brush the mixture over the salmon. Place the salmon onto a sheet of parchment paper and inside the Ninja Foodi.
2. Close the crisping lid and cook for 10 minutes on Air Crisp at 350 F, until crispy on the outside and tender on the inside.

## Shrimp and Sausage Paella

**(Ready in about:** 70 min **| Servings:** 4)

**Ingredients:**

- 1 pound andouille sausage; sliced
- 1 pound baby squid, cut into ¼-inch rings
- 1 pound jumbo shrimp, peeled and deveined
- 1 white onion; chopped
- 4 garlic cloves, minced
- 1 red bell pepper; diced
- 2 cups Spanish rice
- 4 cups chicken stock
- ½ cup dry white wine
- 1 tablespoon melted butter
- 1 teaspoon turmeric powder
- 1½ teaspoons sweet paprika
- ½ teaspoon freshly ground black pepper
- ½ teaspoon salt

**Directions:**

1. Choose Sear/Sauté on the pot and set to Medium High. Choose Start/Stop to preheat the pot. Melt the butter and add the sausage. Cook until browned on both sides, about 3 minutes while stirring frequently. Remove the sausage to a plate and set aside.
2. Sauté the onion and garlic in the same fat for 3 minutes until fragrant and pour in the wine. Use a wooden spoon to scrape the bottom of the pot of any brown bits and cook for 2 minutes or until the wine reduces by half.
3. Stir in the rice and water. Season with the paprika, turmeric, black pepper, and salt. Seal the pressure lid, choose Pressure and set to High. Set the time to 5 minutes, then Choose Start/Stop. When done cooking, do a quick pressure release and carefully open the lid.
4. Choose Sear/Sauté, set to Medium High, and choose Start/Stop. Add the squid and shrimp to the pot and stir gently without mashing the rice.
5. Seal the pressure lid again and cook for 6 minutes, until the shrimp are pink and opaque. Return the sausage to the pot and mix in the bell pepper. Warm through for 2 minutes. Dish the paella and serve immediately.

## Lemon Cod Goujons and Rosemary Chips

(**Ready in about:** 100 min | **Servings:** 4)

**Ingredients:**

- 4 cod fillets, cut into strips
- 2 potatoes, cut into chips
- 4 lemon wedges to serve
- 2 eggs
- 1 cup arrowroot starch
- 1 cup flour
- 2 tablespoons olive oil
- 3 tablespoon fresh rosemary; chopped
- 1 tablespoon cumin powder
- ½ tablespoon cayenne powder
- 1 teaspoon black pepper, plus more for seasoning
- 1 teaspoon salt, plus more for seasoning
- Zest and juice from 1 lemon
- Cooking spray

**Directions:**

1. Fix the Crisping Basket in the pot and close the crisping lid. Choose Air Crisp, set the temperature to 375°F, and the time to 5 minutes. Choose Start/Stop to preheat the pot.
2. In a bowl, whisk the eggs, lemon zest, and lemon juice. In another bowl, combine the arrowroot starch, flour, cayenne powder, cumin, black pepper, and salt.
3. Coat each cod strip in the egg mixture, and then dredge in the flour mixture, coating well on all sides. Grease the preheated basket with cooking spray. Place the coated fish in the basket and oil with cooking spray.
4. Close the crisping lid. Choose Air Crisp, set the temperature to 375°F, and the time to 15 minutes; press Start/Stop. Toss the potatoes with oil and season with salt and pepper.
5. After 15 minutes, check the fish making sure the pieces are as crispy as desired. Remove the fish from the basket.
6. Pour the potatoes in the basket. Close the crisping lid; choose Air Crisp, set the temperature to 400°F, and the time to 24 minutes; press Start/Stop.
7. After 12 minutes, open the lid, remove the basket and shake the fries. Return the basket to the pot and close the lid to continue cooking until crispy.
8. When ready, sprinkle with fresh rosemary. Serve the fish with the potatoes and lemon wedges.

## Potato Chowder with Peppery Prawns

**(Ready in about:** 80 min | **Servings:** 4)

**Ingredients:**

- 4 slices serrano ham; chopped
- 16 ounces frozen corn
- 16 prawns, peeled and deveined
- 1 onion; chopped
- 2 Yukon Gold potatoes; chopped
- ¾ cup heavy cream
- 2 cups vegetable broth
- 2 tablespoons olive oil
- 4 tablespoons minced garlic; divided
- 1 teaspoon dried rosemary
- 1 teaspoon salt; divided
- 1 teaspoon freshly ground black pepper; divided
- ½ teaspoon red chili flakes

**Directions:**

1. Choose Sear/Sauté on the pot and set to Medium High. Choose Start/Stop to preheat the pot. Add 1 tablespoon of the olive oil and cook the serrano ham, 2 tablespoons of garlic, and onion, stirring occasionally; for 5 minutes. Fetch out one-third of the serrano ham into a bowl for garnishing.
2. Add the potatoes, corn, vegetable broth, rosemary, half of the salt, and half of the black pepper to the pot.
3. Seal the pressure lid, hit Pressure and set to High. Set the time to 10 minutes, and press Start.
4. In a bowl, toss the prawns in the remaining garlic, salt, black pepper, the remaining olive oil, and the red chili flakes. When done cooking, do a quick pressure release and carefully open the pressure lid.
5. Stir in the heavy cream and fix the reversible rack in the pot over the chowder.
6. Spread the prawn in the rack. Close the crisping lid. Choose Broil and set the time to 8 minutes. Choose Start/Stop. When the timer has ended, remove the rack from the pot.
7. Ladle the corn chowder into serving bowls and top with the prawns. Garnish with the reserved ham and serve immediately.

## Tuna Salad with Potatoes and Asparagus

**(Ready in about:** 60 minutes | **Servings:** 4)

**Ingredients:**

- 1½ pounds potatoes, quartered
- 8 ounces asparagus, cut into three
- 2 cans tuna, drained
- ½ cup pimento stuffed green olives
- ½ cup coarsely chopped roasted red peppers
- 1 cup water
- 2 tablespoons chopped fresh parsley
- 2 tablespoons red wine vinegar; divided
- 3 tablespoons olive oil
- ¼ teaspoon freshly ground black pepper
- 1 teaspoon salt; divided, plus more as needed

**Directions:**

1. Pour the water into the inner pot and set the reversible rack. Place the potatoes on the rack. Lock the pressure lid into place and set to Seal. Choose Pressure; adjust the pressure to High and the cook time to 4 minutes. Press Start/Stop.
2. After pressure cooking, perform a quick pressure release and carefully open the pressure lid. Take out the rack, empty the water in the pot, and return the pot to the base.
3. Arrange the potatoes and asparagus on the Crisping Basket. Drizzle the half of olive oil on them, and season with salt.
4. Place the basket in the pot. Close the crisping lid; choose Air Crisp, adjust the temperature to 375°F, and the cook time to 12 minutes. Press Start.
5. After 8 minutes, open the lid, and check the veggies. The asparagus will have started browning and crisping. Gently toss with the potatoes and close the lid. Continue cooking for the remaining 4 minutes.
6. Take out the basket, pour the asparagus and potatoes into a salad bowl. Sprinkle with 1 tablespoon of red wine vinegar and mix to coat.
7. In a bowl, pour the remaining oil, remaining vinegar, salt, and pepper. Whisk to combine.

8. To the potatoes and asparagus, add the roasted red peppers, olives, parsley, and tuna. Drizzle the dressing over the salad and mix to coat. Adjust the seasoning and serve immediately.

## Scottish Seafood Curry

**(Ready in about:** 45 min | **Servings:** 8)

**Ingredients:**
**Seafood:**
- ½ lb. squid, trimmed and cut into 1-inch rings
- ½ lb. Scallop meat
- ½ lb. mussel meat
- ½ lb. langoustine tall meat

**Curry:**
- 2 cups shellfish stock
- 1 ½ cups coconut milk
- 1 cup milk
- 2 curry leaves
- 2 tablespoon ginger paste
- 2 tablespoon garlic paste
- 4 tablespoon olive oil
- 2 tablespoon Shallot puree
- 3 tablespoon yellow curry paste
- 1 ½ tablespoon chili powder
- 1 ½ tablespoon chili paste
- 2 tablespoon lemongrass paste
- 1 tablespoon Grants Scotch Whiskey
- 2 tablespoon fish curry powder
- 2 teaspoon shrimp powder
- 1 teaspoon shrimp paste
- ½ teaspoon turmeric powder
- Salt to taste

**Vegetables:**
- ¼ cup chopped okra
- ¼ cup diced tomatoes
- ¼ cup chopped onion
- ¼ cup chopped eggplants

**Directions:**
1. Add olive oil, shallot paste, yellow curry paste, ginger puree, garlic paste, lemongrass paste, chili paste, shrimp paste, and curry leaves. Stir-fry for 10 minutes on Sear/Sauté mode, until well combined and aromatic.
2. Next, add turmeric powder, fish curry powder, and shrimp powder. Stir-fry for another minute. Pour in the shellfish stock and close the crisping lid. Cook on Broil mode for 15 minutes.
3. Open the lid, and add the scallops, squid; chopped onion, okra, tomatoes, and aubergine. Stir lightly.
4. Close the pressure lid, secure the pressure valve, and select Steam mode on High pressure for 5 minutes. Press Start/Stop to start cooking.
5. Once the timer has ended, do a quick pressure release, and open the lid.
6. Add milk, coconut milk, scotch whiskey, and salt. Stir carefully not to mash the aubergine.
7. Select Sear/Sauté and add mussel meat and langoustine. Stir carefully.
8. Simmer the sauce for 3 minutes, press Stop, and turn off the Ninja Foodi. Dish the seafood with sauce and veggies into serving bowls. Serve with a side of broccoli mash.

## Salmon with Creamy Grits

**(Ready in about:** 100 min | **Servings:** 4)

**Ingredients:**
- 4 salmon fillets, skin removed
- 1½ cups vegetable stock
- ¾ cup corn grits
- 1½ cups coconut milk
- 3 tablespoons Cajun
- 1 tablespoon packed brown sugar
- 3 tablespoons butter; divided
- 2 teaspoons salt
- Cooking spray

**Directions:**
1. Pour the grits into a heatproof bowl. Add the coconut milk, stock, 1 tablespoon of butter, and ½ teaspoon of salt. Stir and cover the bowl with foil. Pour the water into the inner pot. Put the reversible rack in the pot and place the bowl on top.

2. Seal the pressure lid, choose Pressure; adjust the pressure to High and the cook time to 15 minutes. Press Start to begin cooking.
3. In a bowl combine the Cajun, brown sugar, and remaining salt.
4. Oil the fillets on one side with cooking spray and place one or two at a time with sprayed-side down into the spice mixture. Oil the other sides and turn over to coat that side in the seasoning. Repeat the process with the remaining fillets.
5. Once the grits are ready, perform a natural pressure release for 10 minutes. Remove the rack and bowl from the pot.
6. Add the remaining butter to the grits and stir to combine well. Cover again with aluminum foil and return the bowl to the pot (without the rack).
7. Fix the rack in the upper position of the pot and put the salmon fillets on the rack.
8. Close the crisping lid and Choose Bake/Roast; adjust the temperature to 400°F and the cook time to 12 minutes. Press Start. After 6 minutes, open the lid and use tongs to turn the fillets over. Close the lid and continue cooking.
9. When the salmon is ready, take out the rack. Remove the bowl of grits and take off the foil. Stir and serve immediately with the salmon.

## Penne all Arrabbiata with Seafood and Chorizo

**(Ready in about:** 50 min | **Servings:** 4)

**Ingredients:**
- 16 ounces penne
- 8 ounces shrimp, peeled and deveined
- 8 ounces scallops
- 12 clams, cleaned and debearded
- 1 (24-ounce) jar Arrabbiata sauce
- 1 onion; diced
- 3 cups fish broth
- 1 chorizo; sliced
- 1 tablespoon olive oil
- ½ teaspoon freshly ground black pepper
- ½ teaspoon salt

**Directions:**
1. Choose Sear/Sauté on the pot and set to Medium High. Choose Start/Stop to preheat the pot. Heat the oil and add the chorizo, onion, and garlic; sauté them for about 5 minutes. Stir in the penne, Arrabbiata sauce, and broth.
2. Season with the black pepper and salt and mix. Seal the pressure lid, choose Pressure, set to High and set the time to 2 minutes; press Start. When the time is over, do a quick pressure release and carefully open the lid.
3. Choose Sear/Sauté and set to Medium High. Choose Start/Stop. Stir in the shrimp, scallops, and clams. Put the pressure lid together and set to the Vent position.
4. Cover and cook for 5 minutes, until the clams have opened and the shrimp and scallops are opaque and cooked through.
5. Discard any unopened clams. Spoon the seafood and chorizo pasta into serving bowls and serve warm.

## Italian Flounder

**(Ready in about:** 70 min | **Servings:** 4)

**Ingredients:**
- 4 flounder fillets
- 3 slices prosciutto; chopped
- 2 (6-ounce) bags baby kale
- ½ small red onion; chopped
- ½ cup whipping cream
- 1 cup panko breadcrumbs
- 2 tablespoons chopped fresh parsley
- 3 tablespoons unsalted butter, melted and divided
- ¼ teaspoon fresh ground black pepper
- ½ teaspoon salt; divided

**Directions:**

1. On the Foodi, choose Sear/Sauté and adjust to Medium. Press Start to preheat the inner pot. Add the prosciutto and cook until crispy, about 6 minutes. Stir in the red onions and cook for about 2 minutes or until the onions start to soften. Sprinkle with half of the salt.
2. Fetch the kale into the pot and cook, stirring frequently until wilted and most of the liquid has evaporated, about 4-5 minutes. Mix in the whipping cream.
3. Lay the flounder fillets over the kale in a single layer. Brush 1 tablespoon of the melted butter over the fillets and sprinkle with the remaining salt and black pepper.
4. Close the crisping lid and choose Bake/Roast. Adjust the temperature to 300°F and the cook time to 3 minutes. Press Start.
5. Combine the remaining butter, the parsley and breadcrumbs in a bowl.
6. When done cooking, open the crisping lid. Spoon the breadcrumbs mixture on the fillets.
7. Close the crisping lid and Choose Bake/Roast. Adjust the temperature to 400°F and the cook time to 6 minutes. Press Start.
8. After about 4 minutes, open the lid and check the fish. The breadcrumbs should be golden brown and crisp. If not, close the lid and continue to cook for an additional two minutes.

## Haddock with Sanfaina

**(Ready in about:** 40 min | **Servings:** 4)

**Ingredients:**

- 4 haddock fillets
- 1 (14.5-ounce) can diced tomatoes, drained
- ½ small onion; sliced
- 1 small jalapeño pepper, seeded and minced
- 2 large garlic cloves, minced
- 1 eggplant; cubed
- 1 bell pepper; chopped
- 1 bay leaf
- ⅓ cup sliced green olives
- ¼ cup chopped fresh chervil; divided
- 3 tablespoons olive oil
- 3 tablespoons capers; divided
- ½ teaspoon dried basil
- ¼ teaspoon salt

**Directions:**

1. Season the fish on both sides with salt, place in the refrigerator, and make the sauce. Press Sear/Sauté and set to Medium. Press Start. Melt the butter until no longer foaming. Add onion, eggplant, bell pepper, jalapeño, and garlic; sauté for 5 minutes.
2. Stir in the tomatoes, bay leaf, basil, olives, half of the chervil, and half of the capers. Remove the fish from the refrigerator and lay on the vegetables in the pot.
3. Seal the pressure lid, choose Pressure; adjust the pressure to Low and the cook time to 3 minutes; press Start. After cooking, do a quick pressure release and carefully open the lid. Remove and discard the bay leaf.
4. Transfer the fish to a serving platter and spoon the sauce over. Sprinkle with the remaining chervil and capers. Serve.

## Cod on Lentils

**(Ready in about:** 65 min | **Servings:** 4)

**Ingredients:**

- 4 cod fillets
- 1 lemon, juiced
- 1 yellow bell pepper; diced
- 1 red bell pepper; diced
- 4 cups vegetable broth
- 1 cup panko breadcrumbs
- ¼ cup minced fresh cilantro
- 2 cups lentils, soaked
- 1 tablespoon olive oil
- 4 tablespoons melted butter
- 1 teaspoon lemon zest
- 1 teaspoon salt

**Directions:**

1. Choose Sear/Sauté on the pot and set to Medium High. Choose Start/Stop to preheat the pot. Combine the oil, lentils, yellow and red bell peppers in the preheated pot and cook for 1 minute. Mix in the vegetable broth.
2. Seal the pressure lid, choose Pressure, set to High, and set the time to 6 minutes. Choose Start/Stop.
3. In a small bowl, combine the breadcrumbs, butter, cilantro, lemon zest, lemon juice, and salt. Spoon the breadcrumb mixture evenly on the cod fillet.
4. When cooking ended, perform a quick pressure release, and carefully open the pressure lid.
5. Fix the reversible rack in the pot, which will be over the lentils. Lay the cod fillets on the rack.
6. Close the crisping lid. Choose Air Crisp, set the temperature to 350°F, and set the time to 12 minutes; press Start/Stop.
7. When ready, share the lentils into four serving plates, and top with salmon.

## Crabmeat with Broccoli Risotto

(**Ready in about:** 80 min | **Servings:** 4)

**Ingredients:**

- 1 pound broccoli, cut into florets and chopped into 1-inch pieces
- 8 ounces lump crabmeat
- 1 small onion; chopped (about ½ cup)
- 2 cups vegetable stock
- ⅓ cup grated Pecorino Romano cheese
- 1 cup short grain rice
- ⅓ cup white wine
- 1 tablespoon olive oil
- 1 teaspoon salt; divided
- 2 tablespoons ghee

**Directions:**

1. Preheat your Foodi by closing the crisping lid. Choose Air Crisp; adjust the temperature to 375°F and the time to 2 minutes. Press Start. Add the broccoli in the crisping basket and drizzle with the olive oil. Season with ½ teaspoon of salt and toss.
2. Put the basket in the inner pot. Close the crisping lid; choose Air Crisp, adjust the temperature to 375°F and the cook time to 10 minutes. Press Start.
3. After 5 minutes, open the lid and stir the broccoli, then resume cooking. When done cooking, take out the basket and set aside.
4. Choose Sear/Sauté and adjust to Medium. Press Start and melt the ghee. Add and sauté the onion for 5 minutes until softened.
5. Stir in the rice and cook for 1 minute. Add the wine and cook for 2 to 3 minutes, stirring frequently, until the liquid has almost completely evaporated.
6. Pour in vegetable stock and the remaining salt. Stir to combine. Seal the pressure lid, choose Pressure, adjust the pressure to High, and the cook time to 8 minutes. Press Start.
7. After cooking, perform a quick pressure release and carefully open the pressure lid. Gently stir in the crabmeat, and cheese. Taste and adjust the seasoning. Serve immediately.

## Mackerel en Papillote with Vegetables

(**Ready in about:** 25 min + 2 h for marinating | **Servings:** 6)

**Ingredients:**

- 3 large whole mackerel, cut into 2 pieces
- 1 pound asparagus, trimmed
- 1 carrot, cut into sticks
- 1 celery stalk, cut into sticks
- 3 cloves garlic, minced
- 2 lemons, cut into wedges
- 6 medium tomatoes, quartered
- 1 large brown onion; sliced thinly
- 1 Orange Bell pepper, seeded and cut into sticks
- ½ cup butter; at room temperature
- 1 ½ cups water
- 2 ½ tablespoon Pernod
- Salt and black pepper to taste

**Directions:**

1. Cut out 6 pieces of parchment paper a little longer and wider than a piece of fish with kitchen scissors. Then, cut out 6 pieces of foil slightly longer than the parchment papers.
2. Lay the foil wraps on a flat surface and place each parchment paper on each aluminium foil.
3. In a bowl, add tomatoes, onions, garlic, bell pepper, pernod, butter, asparagus, carrot, celery, salt, and pepper. Use a spoon to mix them.
4. Place each fish piece on the layer of parchment and foil wraps. Spoon the vegetable mixture on each fish. Then, wrap the fish and place the fish packets in the refrigerator to marinate for 2 hours. Remove the fish to a flat surface.
5. Open the Ninja Foodi, pour the water in, and fit the reversible rack at the bottom of the pot. Put the packets on the trivet.
6. Seal the lid and select Steam mode on High pressure for 3 minutes. Press Start/Stop to start cooking.
7. Once the timer has ended, do a quick pressure release, and open the lid.
8. Remove the trivet with the fish packets onto a flat surface. Carefully open the foil and using a spatula. Return the packets to the pot, on top of the rack.
9. Close the crisping lid and cook on Air Crisp for 3 minutes at 300 F. Then, remove to serving plates. Serve with lemon wedges.

## Salmon with Dill Chutney

**(Ready in about:** 15 min | **Servings:** 2)

**Ingredients:**

- 2 salmon fillets
- Juice from ½ lemon
- 2 cups water

- ¼ teaspoon paprika
- salt and freshly ground pepper to taste

**For Chutney:**

- ¼ cup extra virgin olive oil
- ¼ cup fresh dill

- Juice from ½ lemon
- Sea salt to taste

**Directions:**

1. In a food processor, blend all the chutney Ingredients until creamy. Set aside. To your Foodi, add the water and place a reversible rack.
2. Arrange salmon fillets skin-side down on the steamer basket. Drizzle lemon juice over salmon and apply a seasoning of paprika.
3. Seal the pressure lid, choose Pressure, set to High, and set the timer to 3 minutes; press Start. When ready, release the pressure quickly. Season the fillets with pepper and salt, transfer to a serving plate and top with the dill chutney.

## Cod Cornflakes Nuggets

**(Ready in about:** 25 min | **Servings:** 4)

**Ingredients:**

- 1 ¼ lb. cod fillets, cut into chunks
- 1 egg
- 1 cup cornflakes
- ½ cup flour

- 1 tablespoon olive oil
- 1 tablespoon water
- Salt and pepper, to taste

**Directions:**

1. Add the oil and cornflakes in a food processor, and process until crumbed. Season the fish chunks with salt and pepper.
2. Beat the egg along with 1 tablespoon water. Dredge the chunks in flour first, then dip in the egg, and coat with cornflakes. Arrange on a lined sheet. Close the crisping lid and cook at 350 F for 15 minutes on Air Crisp mode.

# Mussel Chowder with Oyster Crackers

(**Ready in about:** 75 min | **Servings:** 4)

**Ingredients:**

- 1 pound parsnips, peeled and cut into chunks
- 3 (6-ounce) cans chopped mussels, drained, liquid reserved
- 1½ cups heavy cream
- 2 cups oyster crackers
- ¼ cup white wine
- ¼ cup finely grated Pecorino Romano cheese
- 1 cup clam juice
- 2 thick pancetta slices, cut into thirds
- 1 bay leaf
- 2 celery stalks; chopped
- 1 medium onion; chopped
- 1 tablespoon flour
- 2 tablespoons chopped fresh chervil
- 2 tablespoons melted ghee
- ½ teaspoon garlic powder
- 1 teaspoon salt; divided
- 1 teaspoon dried rosemary

**Directions:**

1. To preheat the Foodi, close the crisping lid and Choose Air Crisp; adjust the temperature to 375°F and the time to 2 minutes; press Start. In a bowl, pour in the oyster crackers. Drizzle with the melted ghee, add the cheese, garlic powder, and ½ teaspoon of salt. Toss to coat the crackers. Transfer to the crisping basket.
2. Once the pot is ready, open the pressure lid and fix the basket in the pot. Close the lid and Choose Air Crisp; adjust the temperature to 375°F and the cook time to 6 minutes; press Start.
3. After 3 minutes, carefully open the lid and mix the crackers with a spoon. Close the lid and resume cooking until crisp and lightly browned. Take out the basket and set aside to cool.
4. On the pot, choose Sear/Sauté and adjust to Medium. Press Start. Add the pancetta and cook for 5 minutes, turning once or twice, until crispy.
5. Remove the pancetta to a paper towel-lined plate to drain fat; set aside.
6. Sauté the celery and onion in the pancetta grease for 1 minute or until the vegetables start softening. Mix the flour into the vegetables to coat evenly and pour the wine over the veggies. Cook for about 1 minute or until reduced by about one-third.
7. Pour in the clam juice, the reserved mussel liquid, parsnips, remaining salt, rosemary, and bay leaf. Seal the pressure lid, choose Pressure; adjust the pressure to High and the cook time to 4 minutes. Press Start.
8. After cooking, perform a natural pressure release for 5 minutes. Stir in the mussels and heavy cream. Choose Sear/Sauté and adjust to Medium. Press Start to simmer to the chowder and heat the mussels. Carefully remove and discard the bay leaf after.
9. Spoon the soup into bowls and crumble the pancetta over the top. Garnish with the chervil and a handful of oyster crackers, serving the remaining crackers on the side.

# Spaghetti with Scallops and Arugula

(**Ready in about:** 50 min | **Servings:** 4)

**Ingredients:**

- 1¼ pounds scallops, peeled and deveined
- 10 ounces spaghetti
- 2 large garlic cloves, minced; divided
- 6 cups arugula
- ¼ cup white wine
- 2½ cups water
- ⅓ cup tomato puree
- 1 tablespoon lemon juice
- 1 tablespoon melted butter
- ½ teaspoon red chili flakes or to taste
- 1 teaspoon grated lemon zest
- 1½ teaspoons salt; divided

**Directions:**

1. Arrange the scallops in the Crisping Basket. Season with ½ teaspoon salt, melted butter, and 1 minced garlic clove. Toss to coat and put the basket in the inner pot.
2. Close the crisping lid; choose Air Crisp, adjust the temperature to 400°F and the cook time to 6 minutes.

3. Press Start. After 3 minutes, open the lid and use tongs to turn the scallops. Close the lid and resume cooking. Remove onto a plate and set aside.
4. On the pot, choose Sear/Sauté and adjust to High. Press Start to preheat the pot. Pour in the white wine and simmer for 1 to 2 minutes until reduced by half.
5. Add the spaghetti, water, remaining salt, garlic, puréed tomato, and chili flakes. Stir to combine.
6. Lock the pressure lid into place and set to Seal. Choose Pressure; adjust the pressure to High and the cook time to 5 minutes. Press Start.
7. After cooking, perform a quick pressure release and carefully open the lid. Stir in the lemon zest, juice, and arugula until wilted and soft. Add the scallops and heat through for a few minutes. Serve immediately.

## Seafood Gumbo

**(Ready in about:** 90 min | **Servings:** 4)

**Ingredients:**

- 1 pound jumbo shrimp
- 8 ounces lump crabmeat
- 1 medium onion; chopped
- 2 green onions, finely sliced
- 1 small banana pepper, seeded and minced
- 1 small red bell pepper; chopped (about ⅔ cup)
- 2 celery stalks; chopped
- 2 garlic cloves, minced
- 3 cups chicken broth
- ¼ cup olive oil, plus 2 teaspoons
- ⅓ cup all-purpose flour
- 1 cup jasmine rice
- ¾ cup water
- 1½ teaspoons Cajun Seasoning
- 1½ teaspoons salt divided

**Directions:**

1. Lay the shrimp in the Crisping Basket. Season with ½ teaspoon of salt and 2 teaspoons of olive oil. Toss to coat and fix the basket in the inner pot. Close the crisping lid and Choose Air Crisp; adjust the temperature to 400°F and the cook time to 6 minutes. Press Start.
2. After 3 minutes, open the lid and toss the shrimp. Close the lid and resume cooking. When ready, the shrimp should be opaque and pink. Remove the basket and set aside.
3. Choose Sear/Sauté and adjust to High. Press Start. Heat the remaining ¼ cup of olive oil. Whisk in the flour with a wooden spoon and cook the roux that forms for 3 to 5 minutes, stirring constantly, until the roux has the color of peanut butter. Turn the pot off.
4. Stir in the Cajun, onion, bell pepper, celery, garlic, and banana pepper for about 5 minutes until the mixture slightly cools. Add the chicken broth and crabmeat, stir.
5. Put the rice into a heatproof bowl. Add the water and the remaining salt. Cover the bowl with foil. Put the reversible rack in the lower position of the pot and set the bowl in the rack.
6. Seal the pressure lid, choose Pressure; adjust the pressure to High and the cook time to 6 minutes; press Start. After cooking, perform a natural pressure for 8 minutes. Take out the rack and bowl and set aside. Stir the shrimp into the gumbo to heat it up for 3 minutes.
7. Fluff the rice with a fork and divide into the center of four bowls. Spoon the gumbo around the rice and garnish with the green onions.

## Cajun Salmon with Lemon

**(Ready in about:** 10 min | **Servings:** 1)

**Ingredients:**

- 1 salmon fillet
- Juice of ½ lemon
- 2 lemon wedges
- 1 tablespoon Cajun seasoning
- 1 tablespoon chopped parsley; for garnishing
- ¼ teaspoon brown sugar

**Directions:**

1. Meanwhile, combine the sugar and lemon and coat the salmon with this mixture thoroughly. Coat the salmon with the Cajun seasoning as well.

2. Place a parchment paper into the Ninja Foodi, close the crisping lid and cook the salmon for 7 minutes on Air Crisp mode at 350 F. If you use a thicker fillet, cook no more than 6 minutes. Serve with lemon wedges and chopped parsley.

## Chorizo and Shrimp Boil

**(Ready in about:** 30 min | **Servings:** 4)

**Ingredients:**
- 4 chorizo sausages; sliced
- 1 pound shrimp, peeled and deveined
- 1 lemon, cut into wedges
- 3 red potatoes
- 3 ears corn, cut into 1½-inch rounds
- ¼ cup butter, melted
- 1 cup white wine
- 2 cups water
- 2 tablespoon of seafood seasoning
- salt to taste

**Directions:**
1. To your Foodi add all Ingredients except butter and lemon wedges. Do not stir. Seal the pressure lid, choose Pressure, set to High, and set the timer to 2 minutes; press Start. When ready, release the pressure quickly.
2. Drain the mixture through a colander. Transfer to a serving platter. Serve with melted butter and lemon wedges.

## Traditional Mahi Mahi

**(Ready in about:** 10 min | **Servings:** 4)

**Ingredients:**
- 4 Mahi Mahi fillets, fresh
- 1 lime, juiced
- 4 cloves garlic, minced
- 1 ¼ -inch ginger, grated
- 1 cup water
- 1 ½ tablespoon maple syrup
- 2 tablespoon chili powder
- 1 tablespoon Sriracha sauce
- Salt and black pepper

**Directions:**
1. Place mahi mahi on a plate and season with salt and pepper on both sides. In a bowl, add garlic, ginger, chili powder, sriracha sauce, maple syrup, and lime juice. Use a spoon to mix it. With a brush, apply the hot sauce mixture on the fillet.
2. Then, open the Ninja Foodi's lid, pour the water it and fit the rack at the bottom of the pot. Put the fillets on the trivet. Close the lid, secure the pressure valve, and select Steam mode on High pressure for 5 minutes. Press Start/Stop to start cooking.
3. Once the timer has ended, do a quick pressure release, and open the lid. Use a set of tongs to remove the mahi mahi onto serving plates.
4. Serve with steamed or braised asparagus. For a crispier taste, cook them for 2 minutes on Air Crisp mode; at 300 degrees F.

## Smoked Salmon Pilaf with Walnuts

**(Ready in about:** 60 min | **Servings:** 4)

**Ingredients:**
- 4 green onions; chopped (white part separated from the green part)
- 1 smoked salmon fillet, flaked
- 1 medium tomato, seeded and diced
- 1 cup basmati rice
- 1 cup frozen corn, thawed
- 2 cups water
- ½ cup walnut pieces
- 1 tablespoon ghee
- 1 teaspoon salt
- 2 teaspoons prepared horseradish

**Directions:**
1. Pour the walnuts into a heatproof bowl. Put the Crisping basket in the inner pot and the bowl in the basket.

2. Close the crisping lid and Choose Air Crisp; adjust the temperature to 375°F and the time to 5 minutes. Press Start to begin toasting the walnuts.
3. After the cooking time is over, carefully take the bowl and basket out of the pot and set aside.
4. On the Foodi, choose Sear/Sauté and adjust to Medium to preheat the inner pot. Add the ghee to melt and sauté the white part of the green onions for about a minute, or until starting to soften.
5. Stir in the rice and corn, stirring occasionally for 2 to 3 minutes, or until starting to be fragrant. Add the water and salt.
6. Seal the pressure lid, choose Pressure; adjust the pressure to High and the cook time to 3 minutes; press Start.
7. After cooking, perform a natural pressure release for 5 minutes, then a quick pressure and carefully open the lid.
8. Fluff the rice gently with a fork. Stir in the flaked salmon, green parts of the green onions, and the horseradish.
9. Add the tomato and allow sitting a few minutes to warm through. Spoon the pilaf into serving bowls and top with the walnuts. Serve.

## Farfalle Tuna Casserole with Cheese

(**Ready in about:** 60 min | **Servings:** 4)

**Ingredients:**

- 6 ounces farfalle
- 1 (12-ounce) can full cream milk; divided
- 2 (5- to 6-ounce) cans tuna, drained
- 1 medium onion; chopped
- 1 large carrot; chopped
- 1 cup vegetable broth
- 2 cups shredded Monterey Jack cheese
- 1 cup chopped green beans
- 2½ cups panko bread crumbs
- 3 tablespoons butter, melted
- 1 tablespoon olive oil
- 1 teaspoon salt
- 2 teaspoons corn starch

**Directions:**

1. On the Foodi, Choose Sear/Sauté and adjust to Medium. Press Start to preheat the pot.
2. Heat the oil until shimmering and sauté the onion and carrots for 3 minutes, stirring, until softened.
3. Add the farfalle, ¾ cup of milk, broth, and salt to the pot. Stir to combine and submerge the farfalle in the liquid with a spoon.
4. Seal the pressure lid, choose pressure; adjust the pressure to Low and the cook time to 5 minutes; press Start. After cooking, do a quick pressure release and carefully open the pressure lid.
5. Choose Sear/Sauté and adjust to Less for low heat. Press Start. Pour the remaining milk on the farfalle.
6. In a medium bowl, mix the cheese and cornstarch evenly and add the cheese mixture by large handfuls to the sauce while stirring until the cheese melts and the sauce thickens. Add the tuna and green beans, gently stir. Heat for 2 minutes.
7. In another bowl, mix the crumbs and melted butter well. Spread the crumbs over the casserole. Close the crisping lid and press Broil. Adjust the cook time to 5 minutes; press Start. When ready, the topping should be crisp and brown. If not, broil for 2 more minutes. Serve immediately.

## Pistachio Crusted Salmon

(**Ready in about:** 15 min | **Servings:** 1)

**Ingredients:**

- 1 salmon fillet
- 3 tablespoon pistachios
- 1 teaspoon grated Parmesan cheese
- 1 teaspoon lemon juice
- 1 teaspoon mustard
- 1 teaspoon olive oil
- Pinch of sea salt
- Pinch of garlic powder
- Pinch of black pepper

**Directions:**

1. Whisk the mustard and lemon juice together. Season the salmon with salt, pepper, and garlic powder. Brush the olive oil on all sides.
2. Brush the mustard-lemon mixture on top of the salmon. Chop the pistachios finely, and combine them with the Parmesan cheese.
3. Sprinkle them on top of the salmon. Place the salmon in the Ninja Foodi basket with the skin side down.
4. Close the crisping lid and cook for 10 minutes on Air Crisp mode at 350 F.

## Succotash with Basil Crusted Fish

**(Ready in about:** 65 min | **Servings:** 4)

**Ingredients:**

- 4 firm white fish fillets; at least 1 inch thick
- 1 large tomato, seeded and chopped
- ½ small onion; chopped
- 1 bay leaf
- 1 garlic clove, minced
- 1 medium red chili, seeded and chopped
- ¼ cup mayonnaise
- 1 ½ cups breadcrumbs
- ¼ cup chicken stock
- ¼ cup chopped fresh basil
- 1 cup frozen corn
- 1 cup frozen mixed beans
- 1 cup butternut squash; cubed
- 1 tablespoon olive oil
- 1 tablespoon Dijon-style mustard
- ¼ teaspoon cayenne pepper
- ½ teaspoon Worcestershire sauce
- 1 teaspoon salt; divided
- Cooking spray

**Directions:**

1. Press Sear/Sauté and adjust to Medium. Press Start to preheat the pot. Heat the oil and sauté the onion, garlic, and red chili pepper in the oil for 4 minutes or until the vegetables are soft.
2. Stir in the corn, squash, mixed beans, bay leaf, cayenne, chicken stock, Worcestershire sauce, and ½ teaspoon salt. Seal the pressure lid, choose Pressure; adjust the pressure to High and the cook time to 5 minutes. Press Start.
3. Season the fish fillets with the remaining salt. In a small bowl, mix the mayonnaise and mustard. Pour the breadcrumbs and basil into another bowl.
4. Use a brush to spread the mayonnaise mixture on all sides of the fish and dredge each piece in the basil breadcrumbs to be properly coated.
5. Once the succotash is ready, perform a quick pressure release and carefully open the pressure lid. Stir in the tomato and remove the bay leaf.
6. Set the reversible rack in the upper position of the pot, line with aluminum foil, and carefully lay the fish in the rack. Oil the top of the fish with cooking spray.
7. Close the crisping lid and Choose Bake/Roast; adjust the temperature to 375°F and the cook time to 8 minutes. Press Start.
8. After 4 minutes, open the lid. Use tongs to turn them over and oil the other side with cooking spray. Close the lid and continue cooking. Serve the fillets with the succotash.

## Mediterranean Cod

**(Ready in about:** 20 min | **Servings:** 4)

**Ingredients:**

- 4 fillets cod
- 1 bunch fresh thyme sprigs
- 1 pound cherry tomatoes, halved
- 1 clove garlic, pressed
- 1 cup white rice
- 2 cups water
- 1 cup Kalamata olives
- 2 tablespoon pickled capers
- 1 tablespoon olive oil; divided
- 1 teaspoon olive oil
- 1 pinch ground black pepper
- 3 pinches salt

**Directions:**

1. Line a parchment paper to the steamer basket of your Foodi. Place about half the tomatoes in a single layer on the paper. Sprinkle with thyme, reserving some for garnish. Arrange cod fillets on the top of tomatoes. Sprinkle with a little bit of olive oil.
2. Spread the garlic, pepper, salt, and remaining tomatoes over the fish. In the pot, mix rice and water. Lay a trivet over the rice and water. Lower steamer basket onto the trivet.
3. Seal the pressure lid, choose Pressure, set to High, and set the timer to 7 minutes. Press Start. When ready, release the pressure quickly.
4. Remove the steamer basket and trivet from the pot. Use a fork to fluff rice. Plate the fish fillets and apply a garnish of olives, reserved thyme, pepper, remaining olive oil, and capers. Serve with rice.

## Steamed Sea Bass with Turnips

**(Ready in about:** 15 min | **Servings:** 4)

**Ingredients:**

- 4 sea bass fillets
- 4 sprigs thyme
- 1 lemon; sliced
- 2 turnips; sliced
- 1 white onion; sliced into thin rings
- 1½ cups water
- 2 teaspoon olive oil
- 2 pinches salt
- 1 pinch ground black pepper

**Directions:**

1. Add water to the Foodi. Set a reversible rack into the pot. Line a parchment paper to the bottom of steamer basket. Place lemon slices in a single layer on the reversible rack.
2. Arrange fillets on the top of the lemons, cover with onion and thyme sprigs and top with turnip slices.
3. Drizzle pepper, salt, and olive oil over the mixture. Put steamer basket onto the reversible rack. Seal lid and cook on Low for 8 minutes; press Start.
4. When ready, release pressure quickly. Serve over the delicate onion rings and thinly sliced turnips.

## White Wine Mussels

**(Ready in about:** 15 min | **Servings:** 5)

**Ingredients:**

- 2 pounds mussels, cleaned and debearded
- 1 cup white wine
- ½ cup water
- 1 teaspoon garlic powder
- Juice from 1 lemon

**Directions:**

1. In the Foodi, mix garlic powder, water and wine. Put the mussels into the steamer basket, rounded-side should be placed facing upwards to fit as many as possible.
2. Insert reversible rack in the Foodi and lower steamer basket onto the reversible rack.
3. Seal lid and cook on Low pressure for 1 minute. When ready, release the pressure quickly.
4. Remove unopened mussels. Coat the mussels with the wine mixture. Serve with a side of French fries or slices of toasted bread.

## Crab Cakes

**(Ready in about:** 55 min | **Servings:** 4)

**Ingredients:**

- ½ cup cooked crab meat
- ¼ cup breadcrumbs
- ¼ cup chopped celery
- ¼ cup chopped red pepper
- ¼ cup chopped red onion
- Zest of ½ lemon
- 3 tablespoon mayonnaise
- 1 tablespoon chopped basil
- 2 tablespoon chopped parsley
- Old Bay seasoning, as desired
- Cooking spray

**Directions:**

1. Place all Ingredients in a large bowl and mix well until thoroughly incorporated. Make 4 large crab cakes from the mixture and place on a lined sheet. Refrigerate for 30 minutes, to set.
2. Spay the air basket with cooking spray and arrange the crab cakes in it.
3. Close the crisping lid and cook for 7 minutes on each side on Air Crisp at 390 F.

## Alaskan Cod with Fennel and Beans

(**Ready in about:** 25 min | **Servings:** 4)

**Ingredients:**

- 2 (18 oz) Alaskan cod, cut into 4 pieces each
- 2 cloves garlic, minced
- 2 small onions; chopped
- 1 head fennel, quartered
- ½ cup olive brine
- 1 cup Pinto beans, soaked, drained and rinsed
- 1 cup green olives, pitted and crushed
- ½ cup basil leaves
- ½ cup tomato puree
- 3 cups chicken broth
- 4 tablespoon olive oil
- Salt and black pepper to taste
- Lemon slices to garnish

**Directions:**

1. Heat the olive oil and add the garlic and onion. Stir-fry on Sear/Sauté mode until the onion softens. Pour in chicken broth and tomato puree. Let simmer for about 3 minutes.
2. Add fennel, olives, beans, salt, and pepper. Seal the lid and select Steam mode on High pressure for 10 minutes. Press Start/Stop to start cooking.
3. Once the timer has stopped, do a quick pressure release, and open the lid.
4. Transfer the beans to a plate with a slotted spoon. Adjust broth's taste with salt and pepper and add the cod pieces to the cooker.
5. Close the lid again, secure the pressure valve, and select Steam mode on Low pressure for 3 minutes. Press Start/Stop.
6. Once the timer has ended, do a quick pressure release, and open the lid. Remove the cod into soup plates, top with the beans and basil leaves, and spoon the broth over them. Serve with a side of crusted bread.

## Seared Scallops with Butter Caper Sauce

(**Ready in about:** 18 min | **Servings:** 6)

**Ingredients:**

- 2 lb. sea scallops, foot removed
- 1 cup dry white wine
- 10 tablespoon butter, unsalted
- 4 tablespoon olive oil
- 4 tablespoon capers, drained
- 3 teaspoon lemon zest

**Directions:**

1. Melt the butter to caramel brown on Sear/Sauté. Use a soup spook to fetch the butter out into a bowl. Next, heat the oil in the pot, once heated add the scallops and sear them on both sides to golden brown which is about 5 minutes. Remove to a plate and set aside.
2. Pour the white wine in the pot to deglaze the bottom while using a spoon to scrape the bottom of the pot of any scallop bits.
3. Add the capers, butter, and lemon zest. Use a spoon to stir the mixture once gently.
4. After 40 seconds, spoon the sauce with capers over the scallops. Serve with a side of braised asparagus.

## Monk Fish with Greens

**(Ready in about:** 22 min | **Servings:** 4)

**Ingredients:**

- 4 (8 oz) monk fish fillets, cut in 2 pieces each
- ½ lb. baby bok choy, stems removed and chopped largely
- 2 cloves garlic; sliced
- 1 lemon, zested and juiced
- ½ cup chopped green beans
- 1 cup kale leaves
- 2 tablespoon olive oil
- Lemon wedges to serve
- Salt and white pepper to taste

**Directions:**

1. Pour in the coconut oil, garlic, red chili, and green beans. Stir fry for 5 minutes on Sear/Sauté mode. Add the kale leaves, and cook them to wilt, about 3 minutes.
2. Meanwhile, place the fish on a plate and season with salt, white pepper, and lemon zest. After, remove the green beans and kale into a plate and set aside.
3. Back to the pot, add the olive oil and fish. Brown the fillets on each side for about 2 minutes and then add the bok choy in.
4. Pour the lemon juice over the fish and gently stir. Cook for 2 minutes and then press Start/Stop to stop cooking.
5. Spoon the fish with bok choy over the green beans and kale. Serve with a side of lemon wedges and there, you have a complete meal.

## Creamy Crab Soup

**(Ready in about:** 45 min | **Servings:** 4)

**Ingredients:**

- 2 lb. Crabmeat Lumps
- 2 celery stalk; diced
- 1 white onion; chopped
- ¾ cup heavy cream
- ½ cup Half and Half cream
- 1 ½ cup chicken broth
- ¾ cup Muscadet
- 6 tablespoon butter
- 6 tablespoon flour
- 3 teaspoon Worcestershire sauce
- 3 teaspoon old bay Seasoning
- 2 teaspoon Hot sauce
- 3 teaspoon minced garlic
- Salt to taste
- Lemon juice to serve
- Chopped dill to serve

**Directions:**

1. Melt the butter on Sear/Sauté mode, and mix in the all-purpose flour, in a fast motion to make a rue. Add celery, onion, and garlic.
2. Stir and cook until soft and crispy; for 3 minutes. While stirring, gradually add the half and half cream, heavy cream, and broth.
3. Let simmer for 2 minutes. Add Worcestershire sauce, old bay seasoning, Muscadet, and hot sauce. Stir and let simmer for 15 minutes. Add the crabmeat and mix it well into the sauce.
4. Close the crisping lid and cook on Broil mode for 10 minutes to soften the meat.
5. Dish into serving bowls, garnish with dill and drizzle squirts of lemon juice over. Serve with a side of garlic crusted bread.

# Tuna Patties

**(Ready in about:** 50 min | **Servings:** 2)

**Ingredients:**
- 5 oz. of canned tuna
- 1 small onion; diced
- 2 eggs
- ¼ cup flour
- ½ cup milk
- 1 teaspoon lime juice
- 1 teaspoon paprika
- 1 teaspoon chili powder, optional
- ½ teaspoon salt

**Directions:**
1. Place all Ingredients in a bowl, and mix to combine. Make two large patties, or a few smaller ones, out of the mixture. Place them on a lined sheet and refrigerate for 30 minutes.
2. Close the crisping lid and cook the patties for about 6 minutes on each side on Roast mode at 350 F.

# Parmesan Tilapia

**(Ready in about:** 15 min | **Servings:** 4)

**Ingredients:**
- ¾ cup grated Parmesan cheese
- 4 tilapia fillets
- 1 tablespoon olive oil
- 1 tablespoon chopped parsley
- ¼ teaspoon garlic powder
- 2 teaspoon paprika
- ¼ teaspoon salt

**Directions:**
1. Mix parsley, Parmesan, garlic, salt, and paprika, in a shallow bowl. Brush the olive oil over the fillets, and then coat them with the Parmesan mixture.
2. Place the tilapia onto a lined baking sheet, and then into the Ninja Foodi.
3. Close the crisping lid and cook for about 4 to 5 minutes on all sides on Air Crisp mode at 350 F.

# Black Mussels

**(Ready in about:** 45 min | **Servings:** 4)

**Ingredients:**
- 1 ½ lb. black mussels, cleaned and de-bearded
- 1 white onion; chopped finely
- 10 tomatoes, skin removed and chopped
- 3 large chilies, seeded and chopped
- 3 cloves garlic, peeled and crushed
- 1 cup dry white wine
- 3 cups vegetable broth
- ⅓ cup fresh basil leaves
- 1 cup fresh parsley leaves
- 4 tablespoon tomato paste
- 3 tablespoon olive oil

**Directions:**
1. Heat the olive oil on Sear/Sauté mode, and stir-fry the onion, until soft. Add the chilies and garlic, and cook for 2 minutes, stirring frequently. Stir in the tomatoes and tomato paste, and cook for 2 more minutes. Then, pour in the wine and vegetable broth. Let simmer for 5 minutes.
2. Add the mussels, close the lid, secure the pressure valve, and press Steam mode on High pressure for 3 minutes. Press Start/Stop to start cooking.
3. Once the timer has ended, do a natural pressure release for 15 minutes, then a quick pressure release, and open the lid.
4. Remove and discard any unopened mussels. Then, add half of the basil and parsley, and stir. Close the crisping lid and cook on Broil mode for 5 minutes.
5. Dish the mussels with sauce in serving bowls and garnish it with the remaining basil and parsley. Serve with a side of crusted bread.

## Paella Señorito

(**Ready in about:** 25 min | **Servings:** 5)

**Ingredients:**

- 1 pound frozen shrimp, peeled and deveined
- 2 garlic cloves, minced
- 1 onion; chopped
- 1 lemon, cut into wedges
- 1 red bell pepper; diced
- 2 cups fish broth
- ¼ cup olive oil
- 1 cup bomba rice
- ¼ cup frozen green peas
- 1 teaspoon paprika
- 1 teaspoon turmeric
- salt and ground white pepper to taste
- chopped fresh parsley

**Directions:**

1. Warm oil on Sear/Sauté. Add in bell pepper and onions and cook for 5 minutes until fragrant. Mix in garlic and cook for one more minute until soft.
2. Add paprika, ground white pepper, salt and turmeric to the vegetables and cook for 1 minute.
3. Stir in fish broth and rice. Add shrimp in the rice mixture. Seal the pressure lid, choose Pressure, set to High, and set the timer to 5 minutes; press Start. When ready, release the pressure quickly.
4. Stir in green peas and let sit for 5 minutes until green peas are heated through. Serve warm garnished with parsley and lemon wedges.

## Oyster Stew

(**Ready in about:** 12 min | **Servings:** 4)

**Ingredients:**

- 3 (10 oz) jars shucked oysters in liqueur
- 3 Shallots, minced
- 3 cloves garlic, minced
- 2 cups chopped celery
- 2 cups bone broth
- 2 cups heavy cream
- 3 tablespoon olive oil
- 3 tablespoon chopped parsley
- Salt and white pepper to taste

**Directions:**

1. Add oil, garlic, shallot, and celery. Stir-fry them for 2 minutes on Sear/Sauté mode, and add the heavy cream, broth, and oysters. Stir once or twice.
2. Close the lid, secure the pressure valve, and select Steam mode on High pressure for 3 minutes. Press Start/Stop. Once the timer has stopped, do a quick pressure release, and open the lid.
3. Season with salt and white pepper. Close the crisping lid and cook for 5 minutes on Broil mode. Stir and dish the oyster stew into serving bowls. Garnish with parsley and top with some croutons.

## Fish Finger Sandwich

(**Ready in about:** 20 min | **Servings:** 4)

**Ingredients:**

- 4 cod fillets
- 2 oz. breadcrumbs
- 10 capers
- 4 bread rolls
- 4 lettuce leaves
- 2 tablespoon flour
- 4 tablespoon pesto sauce
- Salt and pepper, to taste

**Directions:**

1. Season the fillets with some salt and pepper, and coat them with the flour, and then dip in the breadcrumbs.
2. You should get at the layer of breadcrumbs, that's why we don't use eggs for this recipe. Arrange the fillets onto a baking mat.
3. Close the crisping lid and cook for about 10 to 15 minutes on Air Crisp mode at 370 F. Cut the bread rolls in half.

4. Place a lettuce leaf on top of the bottom halves; place the fillets over. Spread a tablespoon of pesto sauce on top of each fillet; top with the remaining halves.

## Paprika and Garlic Salmon

**(Ready in about:** 10 min | **Servings:** 4)

**Ingredients:**

- 4 (5 oz) salmon fillets
- 2 cloves garlic, minced
- 1 lime, juiced
- 1 cup water
- 2 tablespoon chopped parsley
- 2 tablespoon hot water
- 1 tablespoon maple syrup
- 2 tablespoon olive oil
- 2 teaspoon cumin powder
- 1 ½ teaspoon paprika
- Salt and black pepper to taste

**Directions:**

1. In a bowl, add cumin, paprika, parsley, olive oil, hot water, maple syrup, garlic, and lime juice. Mix with a whisk. Set aside.
2. Open the Ninja Foodi and pour the water in. Then, fit the rack. Season the salmon with pepper and salt; and place them on the rack.
3. Close the lid, secure the pressure valve, and select Steam mode on High pressure for 3 minutes. Press Start/Stop. Once the timer has ended, do a quick pressure release, and open the pot.
4. Close the crisping lid and cook on Air Crisp mode for 3 minutes at 300 F. Use a set of tongs to transfer the salmon to a serving plate and drizzle the lime sauce all over it. Serve with steamed swiss chard.

## Coconut Shrimp

**(Ready in about:** 30 min | **Servings:** 2)

**Ingredients:**

- 8 large shrimp
- ½ cup orange jam
- ½ cup shredded coconut
- ½ cup breadcrumbs
- 8 oz. coconut milk
- 1 tablespoon honey
- ½ teaspoon cayenne pepper
- ¼ teaspoon hot sauce
- 1 teaspoon mustard
- ¼ teaspoon salt
- ¼ teaspoon pepper

**Directions:**

1. Combine the breadcrumbs, cayenne pepper, shredded coconut, salt, and pepper in a small bowl. Dip the shrimp in the coconut milk, first, and then in the coconut crumbs.
2. Arrange in the lined Ninja Foodi basket, close the crisping lid and cook for 20 minutes on Air Crisp mode at 350 F.
3. Meanwhile whisk the jam, honey, hot sauce, and mustard. Serve the shrimp with the sauce.

# Snacks, Appetizers & Sides

## Cheesy Smashed Sweet Potatoes

**(Ready in about:** 70 min | **Servings:** 4)

**Ingredients:**

- 2 slices bacon, cooked and crumbled
- 12 oz. baby sweet potatoes
- ¼ cup shredded Monterey Jack cheese
- ¼ cup sour cream
- 1 tablespoon chopped scallions
- 1 teaspoon melted butter
- Salt to taste

**Directions:**

1. Put the Crisping Basket in the pot and close the crisping lid. Choose Air Crisp, set the temperature to 350°F, and the time to 5 minutes. Press Start/Stop to begin preheating.
2. Meanwhile, toss the sweet potatoes with the melted butter until evenly coated. Once the pot and basket have preheated, open the lid and add the sweet potatoes to the basket. Close the lid, Choose Air Crisp, set the temperature to 350°F, and set the time to 30 minutes; press Start.
3. After 15 minutes, open the lid, pull out the basket and shake the sweet potatoes. Return the basket to the pot and close the lid to continue cooking. When ended, check the sweet potatoes for your desired crispiness, which should also be fork tender.
4. Take out the sweet potatoes from the basket and use a large spoon to crush the soft potatoes just to split lightly. Top with the cheese, sour cream, bacon, and scallions, and season with salt.

## Mouthwatering Meatballs

**(Ready in about:** 30 min | **Servings:** 6)

**Ingredients:**

- 2 lb. ground beef
- 1 potato, shredded
- 2 eggs, beaten
- ½ cup Parmesan cheese, grated
- 2 cups tomato sauce to serve
- 2 tablespoon chopped chives
- ¼ teaspoon pepper
- ½ teaspoon garlic powder
- ½ teaspoon salt
- 1 package cooked spaghetti to serve
- Basil leaves to serve
- Cooking spray

**Directions:**

1. In a large bowl, combine the potato, salt, pepper, garlic powder, eggs, and chives. Form 12 balls out of the mixture. Spray with cooking spray. Arrange half of the balls onto a lined Ninja Foodi basket.
2. Close the crisping lid and cook for 14 minutes on Air Crisp mode at 330 F. After 7 minutes, turn the meatballs.
3. Repeat with the other half. Serve over cooked spaghetti mixed with tomato sauce, sprinkled with Parmesan cheese and basil leaves.

## Artichoke Bites

**(Ready in about:** 70 min | **Servings:** 8)

**Ingredients:**

- ¼ cup frozen chopped kale
- ¼ cup finely chopped artichoke hearts
- ¼ cup goat cheese
- ¼ cup ricotta cheese
- 4 (13-by-18-inch) sheets frozen phyllo dough, thawed
- 1 lemon, zested
- 1 large egg white
- 1 tablespoon olive oil
- 2 tablespoons grated Parmesan cheese
- 1 teaspoon dried basil
- ½ teaspoon salt
- ½ teaspoon freshly ground black pepper

**Directions:**

1. In a bowl, mix the kale, artichoke hearts, ricotta cheese, parmesan cheese, goat cheese, egg white, basil, lemon zest, salt, and pepper. Put the Crisping Basket in the pot. Close the crisping lid, choose Air Crisp, set the temperature to 375°F, and the time to 5 minutes; press Start/Stop.
2. Then, place a phyllo sheet on a clean flat surface. Brush with olive oil, place a second phyllo sheet on the first, and brush with oil. Continue layering to form a pile of four oiled sheets.
3. Working from the short side, cut the phyllo sheets into 8 strips. Cut the strips in half to form 16 strips.
4. Spoon 1 tablespoon of filling onto one short side of every strip. Fold a corner to cover the filling to make a triangle; continue repeatedly folding to the end of the strip, creating a triangle-shaped phyllo packet. Repeat the process with the other phyllo bites.
5. Open the crisping lid and place half of the pastry in the basket in a single layer. Close the lid, Choose Air Crisp, set the temperature to 350°F, and the timer to 12 minutes; press Start/Stop.
6. After 6 minutes, open the lid, and flip the bites. Return the basket to the pot and close the lid to continue baking. When ready, take out the bites into a plate. Serve warm.

## Eggplant Chips with Honey

**(Ready in about:** 20 min | **Servings:** 4)

**Ingredients:**

- 2 eggplants
- ⅓ cup cornstarch
- ½ cup water
- ⅓ cup olive oil
- 2 teaspoon honey
- 1 teaspoon dry thyme
- A pinch of salt

**Directions:**

1. Cut the eggplants in slices of ½ -inch each. In a big bowl, mix the cornstarch, water, olive oil, and eggplant slices, until evenly coated. Line the Ninja Foodi basket with baking paper and spray with olive oil.
2. Place the eggplants in the basket, scatter with thyme and cook for 15 minutes on Air Crisp mode, shaking every 5 minutes at 370 F. When ready, transfer the eggplants to a serving platter and drizzle with honey. Serve with yogurt dip.

## Rosemary and Garlic Mushrooms

**(Ready in about:** 20 min | **Servings:** 4)

**Ingredients:**

- 12 oz. button mushrooms
- 2 rosemary sprigs
- 3 garlic cloves, minced
- ¼ cup melted butter
- ½ teaspoon salt
- ¼ teaspoon black pepper

**Directions:**

1. Wash and pat dry the mushrooms and cut them in half. Place in a large bowl. Add the remaining Ingredients to the bowl and toss well to combine.
2. Transfer the mushrooms to the basket of the Ninja Foodi. Close the crisping lid and cook for 12 minutes on Air Crisp mode, shaking once halfway through; at 350 F.

## Cheesy Tangy Arancini

(**Ready in about:** 105 min | **Servings:** 6)

**Ingredients:**

- ½ cup olive oil, plus 1 tablespoon
- 2 large eggs
- 2 garlic cloves, minced
- 1 small white onion; diced
- ½ cup apple cider vinegar
- 2 cups short grain rice
- 2 cups fresh panko bread crumbs
- 5 cups chicken stock
- 1½ cups grated Parmesan cheese, plus more for garnish
- 1 cup chopped green beans
- 1 teaspoon salt
- 1teaspoon freshly ground black pepper

**Directions:**

1. Choose Sear/Sauté on the pot and set to Medium High. Choose Start/Stop to preheat the pot. Add 1 tablespoon of oil and the onion, cook the onion until translucent, add the garlic and cook further for 2 minutes or until the garlic starts getting fragrant.
2. Stir in the stock, vinegar, and rice. Seal the pressure lid, choose pressure, set to High, and set the time to 7 minutes; press Start.
3. After cooking, perform a natural pressure release for 10 minutes, then a quick pressure release and carefully open the pressure lid.
4. Stir in the Parmesan cheese, green beans, salt, and pepper to mash the rice until a risotto forms. Spoon the mixture into a bowl and set aside to cool completely.
5. Clean the pot and in a bowl, combine the breadcrumbs and the remaining olive oil. In another bowl, lightly beat the eggs.
6. Form 12 balls out of the risotto or as many as you can get. Dip each into the beaten eggs, and coat in the breadcrumb mixture.
7. Put half of the rice balls in the Crisping Basket in a single layer. Close the crisping lid, hit Air Crisp, set the temperature to 400°F, and set the time to 10 minutes; press Start. Leave to cool before serving.

## Crispy Cheesy Straws

(**Ready in about:** 45 min | **Servings:** 8)

**Ingredients:**

- 2 cups cauliflower florets, steamed
- 5 oz. cheddar cheese
- 3 ½ oz. oats
- 1 egg
- 1 red onion; diced
- 1 teaspoon mustard
- Salt and pepper, to taste

**Directions:**

1. Add the oats in a food processor and process until they resemble breadcrumbs. Place the steamed florets in a cheesecloth and squeeze out the excess liquid.
2. Put the florets in a large bowl, and add the rest of the Ingredients to the bowl.
3. Mix well with your hands, to combine the Ingredients thoroughly.
4. Take a little bit of the mixture and twist it into a straw. Place in the lined Ninja Foodi basket; repeat with the rest of the mixture.
5. Close the crisping lid and cook for 10 minutes on Air Crisp mode at 350 F. After 5 minutes, turn them over and cook for an additional 10 minutes.

# Green Vegan Dip

**(Ready in about:** 20 min | **Servings:** 4)

**Ingredients:**
- 10 ounces canned green chiles, drained with liquid reserved
- 2 cups broccoli florets
- ¼ cup raw cashews
- ¼ cup soy sauce
- 1 cup water
- ¾ cup green bell pepper; chopped
- ¼ teaspoon garlic powder
- ½ teaspoon sea salt
- ¼ teaspoon chili powder

**Directions:**
1. In the cooker, add cashews, broccoli, green bell pepper, and water. Seal the pressure lid, choose Pressure, set to High, and set the timer to 5 minutes. Press Start. When ready, release the pressure quickly.
2. Drain water from the pot; add reserved liquid from canned green chilies, sea salt, garlic powder, chili powder, soy sauce, and cumin.
3. Use an immersion blender to blend the mixture until smooth; set aside in a mixing bowl. Stir green chilies through the dip; add your desired optional additions.

# Creamy Tomato Parsley Dip

**(Ready in about:** 18 min | **Servings:** 6)

**Ingredients:**
- 10 oz. shredded Parmesan cheese
- 10 oz. cream cheese
- ½ cup heavy cream
- 1 cup chopped tomatoes
- 1 cup water
- ¼ cup chopped parsley

**Directions:**
1. Open the Ninja Foodi and pour in the tomatoes, parsley, heavy cream, cream cheese, and water. Close the lid, secure the pressure valve, and select Pressure for 3 minutes at High. Press Start/Stop.
2. Once the timer has ended, do a natural pressure release for 10 minutes.
3. Stir the mixture with a spoon while mashing the tomatoes with the back of the spoon. Add the parmesan cheese and Close the crisping lid.
4. Select Bake/Roast mode, set the temperature to 370 degrees F and the time to 3 minutes. Dish the dip into a bowl and serve with chips or veggie bites.

# Cheesy Tomato Bruschetta

**(Ready in about:** 15 min | **Servings:** 2)

**Ingredients:**
- 1 Italian Ciabatta Sandwich Bread
- 2 tomatoes; chopped
- 2 garlic cloves, minced
- 1 cup grated mozzarella cheese
- Olive oil to brush
- Basil leaves; chopped
- Salt and pepper to taste

**Directions:**
1. Cut the bread in half, lengthways, then each piece again in half. Drizzle each bit with olive oil and sprinkle with garlic. Top with the grated cheese, salt, and pepper.
2. Place the bruschetta pieces into the Ninja Foodi basket, close the crisping lid and cook for 12 minutes on Air Crisp mode at 380 F. At 6 minutes, check for doneness.
3. Once the Ninja Foodi beeps, remove the bruschetta to a serving platter, spoon over the tomatoes and chopped basil to serve.

## Wrapped Asparagus in Bacon

**(Ready in about:** 30 min | **Servings:** 6)

**Ingredients:**

- 1 lb. bacon; sliced
- 1 lb. asparagus spears, trimmed
- ½ cup Parmesan cheese, grated
- Cooking spray
- Salt and pepper, to taste

**Directions:**

1. Place the bacon slices out on a work surface, top each one with one asparagus spear and half of the cheese. Wrap the bacon around the asparagus.
2. Line the Ninja Foodi basket with parchment paper. Arrange the wraps into the basket, scatter over the remaining cheese, season with salt and black pepper, and spray with cooking spray. Close the crisping lid and cook for 8 to 10 minutes on Roast mode at 370 F. If necessary work in batches. Serve hot!

## Fried Pin Wheels

**(Ready in about:** 50 min | **Servings:** 6)

**Ingredients:**

- 1 sheet puff pastry
- 1 ½ cups Gruyere cheese, grated
- 8 ham slices
- 4 teaspoon Dijon mustard

**Directions:**

1. Place the pastry on a lightly floured flat surface. Brush the mustard over and arrange the ham slices; top with cheese. Start at the shorter edge and roll up the pastry.
2. Wrap it in a plastic foil and place in the freezer for about half an hour, until it becomes firm and comfortable to cut.
3. Meanwhile, slice the pastry into 6 rounds. Line the Ninja Foodi basket with parchment paper, and arrange the pinwheels on top.
4. Close the crisping lid and cook for 10 minutes on Air Crisp mode at 370 F. Leave to cool on a wire rack before serving.

## Fried Beef Dumplings

**(Ready in about:** 45 min | **Servings:** 8)

**Ingredients:**

- 8 ounces ground beef
- 20 wonton wrappers
- 1 carrot, grated
- 1 large egg, beaten
- 1 garlic clove, minced
- ½ cup grated cabbage
- 2 tablespoons olive oil
- 2 tablespoons coconut aminos
- ½ tablespoon melted ghee
- ½ tablespoon ginger powder
- ½ teaspoon salt
- ½ teaspoon freshly ground black pepper

**Directions:**

1. Put the Crisping Basket in the pot. Close the crisping lid, choose Air Crisp, set the temperature to 400°F, and the time to 5 minutes; press Start/Stop. In a large bowl, mix the beef, cabbage, carrot, egg, garlic, coconut aminos, ghee, ginger, salt, and black pepper.
2. Put the wonton wrappers on a clean flat surface and spoon 1 tablespoon of the beef mixture into the middle of each wrapper.
3. Run the edges of the wrapper with a little water; fold the wrapper to cover the filling into a semi-circle shape and pinch the edges to seal. Brush the dumplings with olive oil.
4. Lay the dumplings in the preheated basket, choose Air Crisp, set the temperature to 400°F, and set the time to 12 minutes. Choose Start/Stop to begin frying.
5. After 6 minutes, open the lid, pull out the basket and shake the dumplings. Return the basket to the pot and close the lid to continue frying until the dumplings are crispy to your desire.

## Cheesy Cabbage Side Dish

(**Ready in about:** 30 min | **Servings:** 4)

**Ingredients:**
- ½ head of cabbage, cut into 4 wedges
- 2 cup Parmesan cheese
- 4 tablespoon butter, melted
- 1 teaspoon smoked paprika
- Salt and pepper, to taste

**Directions:**
1. Line the basket with parchment paper. Brush the butter over the cabbage wedges; season with salt and pepper. Coat the cabbage with the Parmesan cheese. Arrange in the basket and sprinkle with paprika.
2. Close the crisping lid and cook for 15 minutes on Air Crisp mode, flip over and cook for an additional 10 minutes; at 330 F.

## Buttery Chicken Meatballs

(**Ready in about:** 90 min | **Servings:** 6)

**Ingredients:**
- 1 pound ground chicken
- 1 green bell pepper, minced
- 1 egg
- 2 celery stalks, minced
- ¼ cup hot sauce
- ½ cup water
- ¼ cup panko bread crumbs
- ¼ cup crumbled queso fresco
- 2 tablespoons melted butter

**Directions:**
1. Choose Sear/Sauté on the pot and set to High. Choose Start/Stop to preheat the pot. Meanwhile, in a bowl, evenly combine the chicken, bell pepper, celery, queso fresco, hot sauce, breadcrumbs, and egg. Form meatballs out of the mixture.
2. Then, pour the melted butter into the pot and fry the meatballs in batches until lightly browned on all sides. Use a slotted spoon to remove the meatballs onto a plate.
3. Put the Crisping Basket in the pot. Pour in the water and put all the meatballs in the basket. Seal the pressure lid, choose Pressure, set to High, and set the timer to 5 minutes. Choose Start/Stop to begin cooking.
4. When done cooking, perform a quick pressure release and carefully open the lid. Close the crisping lid. Choose Air Crisp, set the temperature to 360°F, and set the time to 10 minutes; press Start.
5. After 5 minutes, open the lid, lift the basket and shake the meatballs. Return the basket to the pot and close the lid to continue cooking until the meatballs are crispy.

## Honey Mustard Hot Dogs

(**Ready in about:** 22 min | **Servings:** 4)

**Ingredients:**
- 20 Hot Dogs, cut into 4 pieces
- ¼ cup honey
- ¼ cup red wine vinegar
- ½ cup tomato puree
- ¼ cup water
- 1½ teaspoon soy sauce
- 1 teaspoon Dijon mustard
- Salt and black pepper to taste

**Directions:**
1. Add the tomato puree, red wine vinegar, honey, soy sauce, Dijon mustard, salt, and black pepper in a medium bowl. Mix them with a spoon.
2. Put sausage weenies in the crisp basket, and close the crisping lid. Select Air Crisp mode. Set the temperature to 370 degrees F and the timer to 4 minutes. Press Start/Stop. At the 2-minute mark, turn the sausages.
3. Once ready, open the lid and pour the sweet sauce over the sausage weenies.
4. Close the pressure lid, secure the pressure valve, and select Pressure mode on High for 3 minutes. Press Start/Stop. Once the timer has ended, do a quick pressure release. Serve and enjoy.

# Turkey Scotch Eggs

**(Ready in about:** 20 min | **Servings:** 6)

**Ingredients:**
- 10 oz. ground turkey
- 4 eggs, soft boiled, peeled
- 2 garlic cloves, minced
- 2 eggs, lightly beaten
- 1 white onion; chopped
- ½ cup flour
- ½ cup breadcrumbs
- 1 teaspoon dried mixed herbs
- Salt and pepper to taste
- Cooking spray

**Directions:**
1. Mix together the onion, garlic, salt, and pepper. Shape into 4 balls. Wrap the turkey mixture around each egg, and ensure the eggs are well covered.
2. Dust each egg ball in flour, then dip in the beaten eggs and finally roll in the crumbs, until coated. Spray with cooking spray.
3. Lay the eggs into your Ninja Foodi's basket. Set the temperature to 390 degrees F, close the crisping lid and cook for 15 minutes. After 8 minutes, turn the eggs. Slice in half and serve warm.

# Steak and Minty Cheese

**(Ready in about:** 15 min | **Servings:** 4)

**Ingredients:**
- 2 New York strip steaks
- 8 oz. halloumi cheese
- 12 kalamata olives
- Juice and zest of 1 lemon
- Olive oil
- 2 tablespoon chopped parsley
- 2 tablespoon chopped mint
- Salt and pepper, to taste

**Directions:**
1. Season the steaks with salt and pepper, and gently brush with olive oil. Place into the Ninja Foodi, close the crisping lid and cook for 6 minutes (for medium rare) on Air Crisp mode at 350 F. When ready, remove to a plate and set aside.
2. Drizzle the cheese with olive oil and place it in the Ninja Foodi; cook for 4 minutes.
3. Remove to a serving platter and serve with sliced steaks and olives, sprinkled with herbs, and lemon zest and juice.

# Teriyaki Chicken Wings

**(Ready in about:** 30 min | **Servings:** 6)

**Ingredients:**
- 2 lb. chicken wings
- 1 cup teriyaki sauce
- 1 tablespoon honey
- 2 tablespoon cornstarch
- 2 tablespoon cold water
- 1 teaspoon finely ground black pepper
- 1 teaspoon sesame seeds

**Directions:**
1. In the pot, combine honey, teriyaki sauce and black pepper until the honey dissolves completely; toss in chicken to coat. Seal the pressure lid, choose Pressure, set to High, and set the timer to 10 minutes. Press Start.
2. When ready, release the pressure quickly. Transfer chicken wings to a platter. Mix cold water with the cornstarch.
3. Press Sear/Sauté and stir in cornstarch slurry into the sauce and cook for 3 to 5 minutes until thickened. Top the chicken with thickened sauce. Add a garnish of sesame seeds, and serve.

# Herby Fish Skewers

**(Ready in about:** 75 min | **Servings:** 4)

**Ingredients:**
- 1 pound cod loin, boneless, skinless; cubed
- 2 garlic cloves, grated
- 1 lemon, juiced and zested
- 1 lemon, cut in wedges to serve
- 3 tablespoon olive oil
- 1 teaspoon dill; chopped
- 1 teaspoon parsley; chopped
- Salt to taste

**Directions:**
1. In a bowl, combine the olive oil, garlic, dill, parsley, salt, and lemon juice. Stir in the cod and place in the fridge to marinate for 1 hour. Thread the cod pieces onto halved skewers.
2. Arrange into the oiled Ninja Foodi basket; close the crisping lid and cook for 10 minutes at 390 F. Flip them over halfway through cooking. When ready, remove to a serving platter, scatter lemon zest and serve with wedges.

# Cheesy Cauliflower Tater Tots

**(Ready in about:** 35 min | **Servings:** 10)

**Ingredients:**
- 2 lb. cauliflower florets, steamed
- 5 oz. cheddar cheese
- 1 egg, beaten
- 1 onion; diced
- 1 cup breadcrumbs
- 1 teaspoon chopped chives
- 1 teaspoon garlic powder
- 1 teaspoon chopped parsley
- 1 teaspoon chopped oregano
- Salt and pepper, to taste

**Directions:**
1. Mash the cauliflower and place it in a large bowl. Add the onion, parsley, oregano, chives, garlic powder, salt, and pepper, and cheddar cheese. Mix with hands until thoroughly combined.
2. Form 12 balls out of the mixture. Line a baking sheet with paper. Dip half of the tater tots into the egg and then coat with breadcrumbs.
3. Arrange them on the baking sheet, close the crisping lid and cook in the Ninja Foodi at 350 F for 15 minutes on Air Crisp mode. Repeat with the other half.

# Zesty Brussels Sprouts with Raisins

**(Ready in about:** 45 min | **Servings:** 4)

**Ingredients:**
- 14 oz. Brussels sprouts, steamed
- 2 oz. toasted pine nuts
- 2 oz. raisins
- 1 tablespoon olive oil
- Juice and zest of 1 orange

**Directions:**
1. Soak the raisins in the orange juice and let sit for about 20 minutes. Drizzle the Brussels sprouts with the olive oil, and place them in the basket of the Ninja Foodi.
2. Close the crisping lid and cook for 15 minutes on Air Crisp mode at 370 F. Remove to a bowl and top with pine nuts, raisins, and orange zest.

# Barbecue Chicken Drumsticks

**(Ready in about:** 30 min **| Servings:** 6)

**Ingredients:**
- 3 lb. chicken drumsticks
- 1 cup Barbecue sauce
- ¼ cup butter, melted
- ½ cup water
- 3 tablespoon garlic powder
- Salt to taste

**Directions:**
1. Season drumsticks with garlic powder and salt. Open the Ninja Foodi, pour in the water, and fit in the reversible rack. Arrange the drumsticks on top, close the lid, secure the pressure valve, and select Pressure mode for 5 minutes. Press Start/Stop to start cooking.
2. Once the timer has ended, do a natural pressure release for 10 minutes, and then a quick pressure release to let out any more steam. Open the lid.
3. Remove the drumsticks to a crisp basket and add the butter and half of the barbecue sauce. Stir the chicken until well coated in the sauce.
4. Insert the basket in the pot and close the crisping lid. Select Air Crisp, set to 380 degrees F, and cook for 10 minutes. Select Start/Stop. Once nice and crispy, remove drumsticks to a bowl, and top with the remaining barbecue sauces. Stir and serve the chicken with a cheese dip.

# Asparagus Wrapped in Prosciutto with Garbanzo Dip.

**(Ready in about:** 15 min **| Servings:** 6)

**Ingredients:**
- 1 lb. asparagus, stalks trimmed
- 10 oz. Prosciutto, thinly sliced
- Cooking spray

**For the Dip:**
- 1 medium onion; diced
- 2 medium jalapeños; chopped
- 2 cloves of garlic, minced
- 1 cup canned garbanzo beans
- 1 cup crushed tomatoes
- 1 cup vegetable broth
- 1 ½ tablespoon olive oil
- 1 teaspoon paprika
- ¾ teaspoon sea salt
- ½ teaspoon chili powder

**Directions:**
1. Open the Ninja Foodi and add the garbanzo beans, onion, jalapeños, garlic, tomatoes, broth, oil, paprika, chili powder, and salt. Close the lid, secure the pressure valve, and select Pressure mode on High for 8 minutes. Press Start/Stop.
2. Once the timer has ended, do a quick pressure release, and open the pot.
3. Transfer the Ingredients to a food processor, and blend until creamy and smooth. Set aside. Wrap each asparagus with a slice of prosciutto from top to bottom.
4. Grease the crisp basket with cooking spray, and add in the wrapped asparagus.
5. Close the crisping lid, select Air Crisp mode at 370 degrees F and set the time to 8 minutes. Press Start/Stop. At the 4-minute mark, turn the bombs. Remove the wrapped asparagus onto a plate and serve with bean dip.

# Chicken Wings

**(Ready in about:** 60 min | **Servings:** 4)

**Ingredients:**
- 2 lb. chicken wings, frozen
- ½ (1-ounce) ranch salad mix
- ½ cup sriracha sauce
- ½ cup water
- 2 tablespoon butter, melted
- 1 tablespoon lemon juice
- ½ teaspoon paprika
- Non-stick cooking spray

**Directions:**
1. Mix the water, sriracha, butter and lemon juice or vinegar in the pot. In the Crisping Basket, put the wings, and then the basket into the pot.
2. Seal the pressure lid, choose Pressure, set to High, set the timer at 5 minutes, and press Start. When the timer is done reading, perform a quick pressure release, and carefully open the lid.
3. Pour the paprika and ranch dressing all over the chicken and oil with cooking spray. Cover the crisping lid. Choose Air Crisp, set the temperature to 370 F, and the timer to 15 minutes. Choose Start to commence frying.
4. After half the cooking time, open the lid, remove the basket and shake the wings. Oil the chicken again with cooking spray and return the basket to the pot. Close the lid and continue cooking until the wings are crispy to your desire.

# Chicken Meatballs with Ranch Dip

**(Ready in about:** 34 min | **Servings:** 4)

**Ingredients:**
- 1 lb. ground chicken
- 1 egg, beaten
- Green onions for garnish
- 2 tablespoon minced garlic
- 2 tablespoon olive oil
- 2 tablespoon chopped green onions
- 5 tablespoon Hot sauce
- 2 tablespoon Buffalo wing sauce
- Salt and pepper, to taste

**For the dip:**
- ½ cup Roquefort cheese, crumbled
- 2 tablespoon olive oil
- 2 tablespoon mayonnaise
- ¼ tablespoon heavy cream
- Juice from ½ lemon

**Directions:**
1. Mix all salsa Ingredients in a bowl until uniform and creamy, and refrigerate. Add the ground chicken, salt, garlic, and two tablespoons of green onions. Mix well with your hands.
2. Rub your hands with some oil and form bite-size balls out of the mixture. Lay onto your crisp basket fryer basket. Spray with cooking spray.
3. Select Air Crisp, set the temperature to 385 degrees F and the time to 14minutes. At the 7-minute mark, turn the meatballs.
4. Meanwhile, add the hot sauce and butter to a bowl and microwave them until the butter melts. Mix the sauce with a spoon.
5. Pour the hot sauce mixture and a half cup of water over the meatballs.
6. Close the lid, secure the pressure valve, and select Sear/Sauté mode on High Pressure for 10 minutes. Press Start/Stop.
7. Once the timer has ended, do a quick pressure release. Dish the meatballs. Garnish with green onions, and serve with Roquefort sauce.

## Rosemary Potato Fries

**(Ready in about:** 30 min | **Servings:** 4)

**Ingredients:**

- 4 russet potatoes, cut into sticks
- 2 garlic cloves, crushed
- 2 tablespoon butter, melted
- 1 teaspoon fresh rosemary; chopped
- Salt and pepper, to taste

**Directions:**

1. Add butter, garlic, salt, and pepper to a bowl; toss until the sticks are well-coated. Lay the potato sticks into the Ninja Foodi's basket. Close the crisping lid and cook for 15 minutes at 370 F. Shake the potatoes every 5 minutes.
2. Once ready, check to ensure the fries are golden and crispy all over if not, return them to cook for a few minutes.
3. Divide standing up between metal cups lined with nonstick baking paper, and serve sprinkled with rosemary.

## Egg Brulee

**(Ready in about:** 12 min | **Servings:** 8)

**Ingredients:**

- 8 large eggs
- 1 cup water
- Salt to taste
- Ice bath

**Directions:**

1. Open the Ninja Foodi, pour the water in, and fit the reversible rack in it. Put the eggs on the rack in a single layer, close the lid, secure the pressure valve, and select Pressure on High Pressure for 5 minutes. Press Start/Stop.
2. Once the timer has ended, do a quick pressure release, and open the pot.
3. Remove the eggs into the ice bath and peel the eggs. Put the peeled eggs in a plate and slice them in half.
4. Sprinkle a bit of salt on them and then followed by the sugar. Lay onto your crisp basket fryer basket. Select Air Crisp mode, set the temperature to 390 degrees F and the time to 3 minutes.

## Cumin Baby Carrots

**(Ready in about:** 25 min | **Servings:** 4)

**Ingredients:**

- 1 ¼ lb. baby carrots
- 1 handful cilantro; chopped
- 2 tablespoon olive oil
- ½ teaspoon cumin powder
- ½ teaspoon garlic powder
- 1 teaspoon cumin seeds
- 1 teaspoon salt
- ½ teaspoon black pepper

**Directions:**

1. Place the baby carrots in a large bowl. Add cumin seeds, cumin, olive oil, salt, garlic powder, and pepper, and stir to coat them well.
2. Put the carrots in the Ninja Foodi's basket, close the crisping lid and cook for 20 minutes on Roast mode at 370 F. Remove to a platter and sprinkle with chopped cilantro, to serve.

## Chicken and Cheese Bake

**(Ready in about:** 1 hour 18 min | **Servings:** 6)

**Ingredients:**
- 1 lb. chicken breast
- 10 oz. Cheddar cheese
- 10 oz. cream cheese
- ½ cup sour cream
- ½ cup breadcrumbs
- ½ cup water

**Directions:**
1. Open the Ninja Foodi and add the chicken, water, and cream cheese. Close the lid, secure the pressure valve, and select Pressure mode on High for 10 minutes. Press Start/Stop.
2. Once the timer has ended, do a quick pressure release, and open the pot.
3. Shred the chicken with two forks and add the cheddar cheese. Sprinkle with breadcrumbs, and close the crisping lid. Select Bake/Roast, set the temperature to 380 degrees F and the timer to 3 minutes. Serve warm with veggie bites.

## Cheesy Brazilian Balls

**(Ready in about:** 35 min | **Servings:** 4)

**Ingredients:**
- 2 cups flour
- 2 cups grated mozzarella cheese
- ½ cup olive oil
- 1 cup milk
- 2 eggs, cracked into a bowl
- A pinch of salt

**Directions:**
1. Grease the crisp basket with cooking spray and set aside. Put the Ninja Foodi on Medium and select Sear/Sauté mode. Add the milk, oil, and salt, and let boil. Add the flour and mix it vigorously with a spoon.
2. Let the mixture cool. Once cooled, use a hand mixer to mix the dough well, and add the eggs and cheese while still mixing. The dough should be thick and sticky.
3. Use your hands to make 14 balls out of the mixture, and put them in the greased basket. Put the basket in the pot and close the crisping lid.
4. Select Air Crisp, set the temperature to 380 degrees F and set the timer to 15 minutes. At the 7-minute mark, shake the balls. Serve with lemon aioli, garlic mayo or ketchup.

## Spinach Hummus

**(Ready in about:** 1 hr 10 min | **Servings:** 12)

**Ingredients:**
- 2 cups spinach; chopped
- ½ cup tahini
- 2 cups dried chickpeas
- 8 cups water
- 5 garlic cloves, crushed
- 5 tablespoon grapeseed oil
- 2 teaspoon salt; divided
- 5 tablespoon lemon juice

**Directions:**
1. In the pressure cooker, mix 2 tablespoon oil, water, 1 teaspoon salt, and chickpeas. Seal the pressure lid, choose Pressure, set to High, and set the timer to 35 minutes. Press Start. When ready, release the pressure quickly. In a small bowl, reserve ½ cup of the cooking liquid and drain chickpeas.
2. Mix half the reserved cooking liquid and chickpeas in a food processor and puree until no large chickpeas remain; add remaining cooking liquid, spinach, lemon juice, remaining teaspoon salt, garlic, and tahini.
3. Process hummus for 8 minutes until smooth. Stir in the remaining 3 tablespoon of olive oil before serving.

# Cheesy Bacon Dip

**(Ready in about:** 10 min | **Servings:** 10)

**Ingredients:**

- 10 bacon slices; chopped roughly
- 4 chopped tomatoes
- 1 cup water
- 1¼ cup cream cheese
- 1¼ cup shredded Monterey Jack cheese

**Directions:**

1. Turn on the Ninja Foodi and select Air Crisp mode. Set the temperature to 370 degrees F and the time to 8 minutes. Add the bacon pieces and close the crisping lid. Press Start/Stop.
2. When ready, open the lid and add the water, cream cheese, and tomatoes. Do Not Stir. Close the lid, secure the pressure valve, and select Pressure mode on High for 5 minutes. Press Start/Stop.
3. Once the timer has ended, do a quick pressure release, and open the lid. Stir in the cheddar cheese and mix to combine. Serve with a side of chips.

# Cheese bombs wrapped in Bacon.

**(Ready in about:** 20 min | **Servings:** 8)

**Ingredients:**

- 8 bacon slices, cut in half
- 16 oz. Mozzarella cheese, cut into 8 pieces
- 3 tablespoon butter, melted

**Directions:**

1. Wrap each cheese string with a slice of bacon and secure the ends with toothpicks. Set aside. Grease the crisp basket with the melted butter and add in the bombs.
2. Close the crisping lid, select Air Crisp mode, and set the temperature to 370 degrees F and set the time to 10 minutes.
3. At the 5-minute mark, turn the bombs. When ready, remove to a paper-lined plate to drain the excess oil. Serve on a platter with toothpicks and tomato dip.

# Sweet Pickled Cucumbers

**(Ready in about:** 5 min | **Servings:** 6)

**Ingredients:**

- 1 pound small cucumbers; sliced into rings
- 1/4 cup green garlic, minced
- 2 cups white vinegar
- 1 cup sugar
- 1 cup water
- 2 tablespoon Dill Pickle Seasoning
- 2 teaspoon salt
- 1 teaspoon cumin

**Directions:**

1. Into the pot, add sliced cucumber, vinegar and pour water on top. Sprinkle sugar over cucumbers. Add cumin, dill pickle seasoning, and salt.
2. Stir well to dissolve the sugar. Seal the pressure lid, choose Pressure, set to High, and set the timer to 4 minutes. Press Start.
3. When ready, release the pressure quickly. Ladle cucumbers into a large storage container and pour cooking liquid over the top. Chill for 1 hour.

# Rice, Grains & Pasta

## Black Eyed Peas with Kale

**(Ready in about:** 30 min | **Servings:** 6)

**Ingredients:**

- 1 (15 ounces) can fire roasted tomatoes
- 1 cup fire-roasted red peppers; diced
- 1 ½ cups dried black-eyed peas; soaked and rinsed
- 1 ½ cups vegetable broth
- 2 cups chopped kale
- 2 garlic cloves; minced
- 1 bay leaf
- 1 onion, thinly sliced
- ½ teaspoon ground allspice
- 1 teaspoon olive oil
- ½ teaspoon red pepper, crushed
- Salt to taste

**Directions:**

1. Warm oil on Sear/Sauté. Add onion and cook for 5 minutes until fragrant; add garlic and fire roasted red peppers and cook for 1 more minute until softened.
2. To the vegetable mixture, add a seasoning of salt, crushed red pepper, and allspice.
3. Add vegetable broth, bay leaf, and black-eyed peas to the pot. Seal the pressure lid, choose Pressure, set to High, and set the timer to 5 minutes. Press Start. When ready, do a quick pressure release.
4. Remove the bay leaf and discard. Mix the peas with kale and tomatoes.
5. Seal the pressure lid again, choose Pressure, set to High, and set the timer to 1 minute. Press Start. When ready, release the pressure quickly. Adjust the seasoning and serve.

## Vegan Sloppy Joes

**(Ready in about:** 45 min | **Servings:** 6)

**Ingredients:**

- 1 cup pearl barley, rinsed
- 1 cup green onion; chopped
- 2 cups tomato sauce
- 1 clove garlic; minced
- 6 brioche buns
- 2 cups water
- 2 tablespoon brown sugar
- 2 tablespoon Worcestershire sauce
- 1 teaspoon Dijon mustard
- 1 teaspoon smoked paprika
- 1 teaspoon chili powder
- Dill Pickles for garnish

**Directions:**

1. In the pot, mix Worcestershire sauce, water, onion, garlic, brown sugar, barley, tomato sauce, and spices. Seal the pressure lid, choose Pressure, set to High, and set the timer to 25 minutes. Press Start. When ready, release the pressure quickly.
2. Press Sear/Sauté and cook until the mixture becomes thick. Transfer the sloppy joe mixture to the brioche buns and add a topping of dill pickles.

## Cheese and Spinach Stuffed Shells

**(Ready in about:** 1 hr | **Servings:** 6)

**Ingredients:**

- 2 cups onion; chopped
- 1 cup shredded cheddar cheese
- 1 cup carrot; chopped
- 2 cups ricotta cheese, crumbled
- 1 ½ cup feta cheese, crumbled
- 2 cups spinach; chopped
- ¾ cup grated Pecorino Romano cheese
- 1 (28 ounces) canned tomatoes, crushed
- 12 ounces jumbo shell pasta
- 3 garlic cloves; minced
- 2 tablespoon chopped fresh chives
- 1 tablespoon chopped fresh dill
- 3 ½ tablespoon olive oil,
- 1 tablespoon olive oil
- Salt and ground black pepper to taste

**Directions:**

1. Warm olive oil on Sear/Sauté. Add in onion, carrot, and garlic, and cook for 5 minutes until tender; stir in tomatoes and cook for another 10 minutes. Remove to a bowl and set aside.
2. Wipe the pot with a damp cloth, add pasta and cover with enough water. Seal the pressure lid, choose Pressure, set to High, and set the timer to 5 minutes. Press Start.
3. Do a quick pressure and drain the pasta. Lightly grease olive oil to a baking sheet. In a bowl, combine feta and ricotta cheese. Add in spinach, Pecorino Romano cheese, dill, and chives, and stir well. Adjust the seasonings. Using a spoon, fill the shells with the mixture.
4. Spread 4 cups tomato sauce on the baking sheet. Place the stuffed shells over with seam-sides down and sprinkle cheddar cheese atop. Use aluminum foil to the cover the baking dish.
5. Pour 1 cup of water in the pot of the Foodi and insert the trivet. Lower the baking dish onto the trivet.
6. Seal the pressure lid, choose Pressure, set to High, and set the timer to 15 minutes. Press Start. Once ready, do a quick release. Take away the foil. Place the stuffed shells to serving plates and top with tomato sauce before serving.

## Grana Padano Risotto

**(Ready in about:** 25 min | **Servings:** 6)

**Ingredients:**

- 1 white onion; chopped
- 2 cups Carnaroli rice, rinsed
- ¼ cup dry white wine
- 4 cups chicken stock
- 2 tablespoon Grana Padano cheese, grated
- ¼ tablespoon Grana Padano cheese, flakes
- 1 tablespoon butter
- 1 tablespoon olive oil
- 1 teaspoon salt
- ½ teaspoon ground white pepper

**Directions:**

1. Warm oil on Sear/Sauté. Stir-fry onion for 3 minutes until soft and translucent. Add in butter and rice and cook for 5 minutes stirring occasionally.
2. Pour wine into the pot to deglaze, scrape away any browned bits of food from the pan. Stir in stock, pepper, and salt to the pot.
3. Seal the pressure lid, choose Pressure, set to High, and set the timer to 15 minutes. Press Start. When ready, release the pressure quickly. Sprinkle with grated Parmesan cheese and stir well. Top with flaked cheese for garnish before serving.

## Cherry Tomato Basil Linguine

**(Ready in about:** 22 min | **Servings:** 4)

**Ingredients:**

- 1 pound Linguine noodles, halved
- 1 ½ cups vegetable stock
- ¼ cup julienned basil leaves
- ½ cup Parmigiano-Reggiano cheese, grated
- 1 cup cherry tomatoes, halved
- 1 small onion; diced
- 2 garlic cloves; minced
- 2 tablespoon olive oil
- ¼ teaspoon red chili flakes
- 1 teaspoon salt
- ½ teaspoon ground black pepper
- Fresh basil leaves for garnish

**Directions:**

1. Warm oil on Sear/Sauté. Add onion and cook for 2 minutes until soft. Mix garlic and tomatoes and sauté for 4 minutes. To the pot, add vegetable stock, salt, julienned basil, red chili flakes and pepper.
2. Add linguine to the tomato mixture until covered. Seal the pressure lid, choose Pressure, set to High, and set the timer to 5 minutes. Press Start.
3. When ready, naturally release the pressure for 5 minutes. Stir the mixture to ensure it is broken down. Divide into plates. Top with basil and Parmigiano-Reggiano cheese and serve.

# Lemony Wild Rice Pilaf

**(Ready in about:** 25 min | **Servings:** 6)

**Ingredients:**
- 2 cups white wild rice, rinsed and drained
- 4 cups vegetable broth
- Zest and juice from 1 lemon
- 1 tablespoon butter
- ½ teaspoon salt
- ½ teaspoon ground black pepper

**Directions:**
1. In your Foodi, mix rice, lemon zest, butter, and water. Seal the pressure lid, choose Pressure, set to High, and set the timer to 3 minutes. Press Start. When ready, release pressure naturally for 10 minutes.
2. Sprinkle salt, lemon juice, and pepper over the pilaf and use a fork to gently fluff.

# Easy Jasmine Rice

**(Ready in about:** 25 min | **Servings:** 4)

**Ingredients:**
- 2 cups jasmine rice
- 3 ½ cups of water
- Salt and black pepper to taste

**Directions:**
1. Stir rice and water together in the Foodi. Season with salt to taste. Seal the pressure lid, press Pressure, set to High, and set the timer to 15 minutes; press Start.
2. When ready, release pressure naturally for 10 minutes. Use a fork to fluff rice. Season with black pepper before serving.

# Spicy Lentils with Chorizo.

**(Ready in about:** 50 min | **Servings:** 10)

**Ingredients:**
- 7 ounces chorizo; sliced
- 1 onion; diced
- 2 garlic cloves, crushed
- ½ cup cider vinegar
- 2 cups brown sugar
- 2 cups lentils, drained and rinsed
- 2 cups tomato sauce
- 2 cups vegetable broth
- ½ cup mustard
- 2 tablespoon maple syrup
- 3 tablespoon Worcestershire sauce
- 2 tablespoon liquid smoke
- 1 tablespoon lime juice
- 1 tablespoon salt
- 1 tablespoon black pepper
- 1 teaspoon chili powder
- 1 teaspoon paprika
- ¼ teaspoon cayenne pepper

**Directions:**
1. Set on Sear/Sauté, set to Medium High, and choose Start/Stop to preheat the pot; add in chorizo and cook for 3 minutes as you stir until crisp; add garlic and onion and cook for 2 more minutes until translucent.
2. Mix tomato sauce, broth, cider vinegar, liquid smoke, Worcestershire sauce, lime juice, mustard, and maple syrup in a mixing bowl.
3. Pour the mixture in the Foodi to deglaze the pan, scrape the bottom of the pan to do away with any browned bits of food. Add pepper, chili powder, brown sugar, paprika, salt, and cayenne into the sauce mixture as you stir to mix.
4. Stir in lentils to coat. Seal the pressure lid, choose Pressure, set to High, and set the timer to 30 minutes. Press Start. Release pressure naturally for 10 minutes.

## Veggie Quinoa Bowls with Pesto

**(Ready in about:** 30 min | **Servings:** 2)

**Ingredients:**

- 1 potato, peeled; cubed
- 1 avocado, thinly sliced
- 1 head broccoli; cut into small florets
- 1 bunch baby heirloom carrots, peeled
- ¼ cabbage; sliced
- 2 eggs
- 2 cups vegetable broth
- ¼ cup pesto sauce
- 1 cup quinoa, rinsed and drained
- Salt and ground black pepper to taste
- Lemon wedges; for serving

**Directions:**

1. In the Foodi, mix broth, pepper, quinoa and salt. Set trivet to the inner pot on top of quinoa and add a steamer basket to the top of the trivet. Mix carrots, potato, eggs and broccoli in the steamer basket. Add pepper and salt for seasoning.
2. Seal the pressure lid, choose Pressure, set to High, and set the timer to 1 minute. Press Start. Quick-release the pressure.
3. Take away the trivet and steamer basket from pot. Set the eggs in a bowl of ice water. Then peel and halve the eggs. Use a fork to fluff quinoa. Adjust the seasonings. In two bowls, equally divide avocado, quinoa, broccoli, eggs, carrots, potato, and a dollop of pesto. Serve alongside a lemon wedge.

## Mix Bean Veggie Chili

**(Ready in about:** 1 hr | **Servings:** 8)

**Ingredients:**

- ½ cup dried pinto beans; soaked, drained and rinsed
- ½ cup dried black beans; soaked, drained and rinsed
- ½ cup dried cannellini beans; soaked, drained and rinsed
- 4 cups vegetable broth
- 1 (28 ounces) can tomatoes, crushed
- 1 head broccoli; chopped into florets
- 1 bay leaf
- 1 onion; chopped
- 3 stalks of celery; chopped
- 1 green bell pepper; chopped
- 1 tablespoon canola oil
- 2 tablespoon minced garlic
- 2 tablespoon chili powder
- 2 teaspoon ground cumin
- Salt to taste
- Fresh parsley; chopped for garnish

**Directions:**

1. Warm oil on Sear/Sauté. Add onion and bell pepper, broccoli, and celery, and cook for about 8 minutes until softened. Mix in cumin, chili powder, and garlic and cook for another 1 minute.
2. Add vegetable broth, tomatoes, black beans, salt, cannellini beans, pinto beans, and bay leaf to the pot.
3. Seal the pressure lid, choose Pressure, set to High, and set the timer to 25 minutes. Press Start. When ready, do a quick pressure release. Dispose of the bay leaf. Taste and adjust the seasonings. Sprinkle with fresh parsley and serve.

## American Black Bean Chili

**(Ready in about:** 1 hr 10 min | **Servings:** 8)

**Ingredients:**

- 1 jalapeño pepper, deseeded and diced
- 6 cups vegetable broth
- 2 cups dried black beans; soaked, drained and rinsed
- 1 onion; chopped
- 3 cloves garlic; minced
- 1 teaspoon dried oregano
- 1 teaspoon olive oil
- 1 teaspoon dried chili flakes
- Cotija Cheese, crumbled for garnish
- Salt to taste
- Fresh cilantro for garnish

**Directions:**

1. Warm oil on Sear/Sauté. Add in garlic and onion and cook for 3 to 4 minutes until fragrant. Add beans, vegetable broth, oregano, chili flakes, salt and jalapeño pepper.
2. Seal the pressure lid, choose Pressure, set to High, and set the timer to 35 minutes. Press Start. When ready, quick-release pressure. Divide between serving plates. Apply a topping of cilantro and cotija cheese to serve.

## Beef Stuffed Pasta Shells

**(Ready in about:** 35 min | **Servings:** 4)

**Ingredients:**

- 1 pound ground beef
- 16 ounces pasta shells
- 10 ounces red enchilada sauce
- 4 ounces diced green chiles
- 15 ounces tomato sauce
- 15-ounce can black beans, drained and rinsed
- 15-ounces canned corn, drained
- 1 cup shredded mozzarella cheese
- 2 cups water
- 2 tablespoon olive oil
- Finely chopped parsley for garnish
- additional cheese for topping if desired
- salt and ground black pepper to taste

**Directions:**

1. Heat oil on Sear/Sauté. Add ground beef and cook for 7 minutes until it starts to brown. Mix in pasta, tomato sauce, enchilada sauce, black beans, water, corn, and green chiles and stir to coat well. Add more water if desired.
2. Seal the pressure lid, choose Pressure, set to High, and set the timer to 10 minutes. Press Start. When ready, do a quick pressure release. Into the pasta mixture, mix in mozzarella cheese until melted; add black pepper and salt. Garnish with parsley to serve.

## Creamed Kale Parmesan Farro

**(Ready in about:** 35 min | **Servings:** 2)

**Ingredients:**

- 1 cup kale; chopped
- 2 cups vegetable broth
- ½ cup grated Parmesan cheese, plus 1 tablespoon for topping
- 1 cup pearl barley, rinsed and drained
- 1 small onion; diced
- 2 garlic cloves, smashed
- 1 tablespoon butter
- Juice of ½ lemon, juiced
- Salt and freshly ground black pepper to taste

**Directions:**

1. Warm butter on Sear/Sauté. Add in onion and cook for 3 minutes until soft. Stir in garlic and barley, and cook for 1-2 minutes until barley is toasted; mix in broth.
2. Seal the pressure lid, choose Pressure, set to High, and set the timer to 9 minutes. Press Start. Release pressure naturally for 10 minutes, then quick-release the remaining pressure.
3. Add Parmesan cheese into barley mixture and stir until fully melted. Just before serving, add lemon juice and kale into barley mixture. Add pepper and salt for seasoning.

## Pasta Caprese Ricotta Basil Fusilli

**(Ready in about:** 15 min | **Servings:** 3)

**Ingredients:**

- 2 ½ cups dried fusilli
- 1 (15 ounces) can tomato sauce
- 1 cup tomatoes, halved
- 1 cup water
- ¼ cup basil leaves
- 1 cup Ricotta cheese, crumbled
- 1 onion, thinly sliced
- 6 garlic cloves; minced
- 1 tablespoon olive oil
- 2 tablespoon chopped fresh basil
- 1 teaspoon red pepper flakes
- 1 teaspoon salt

**Directions:**

1. Warm the oil on Sear/Sauté. Add in red pepper flakes, garlic and onion and cook for 3 minutes until soft. Mix in fusilli, tomatoes, half of the basil leaves, water, tomato sauce, and salt.
2. Seal the pressure lid, choose Pressure, set to High, and set the timer to 4 minutes. Press Start. When ready, release the pressure quickly.
3. Transfer the pasta to a serving platter and top with the crumbled ricotta and remaining chopped basil.

## Parsley Lime Bulgur Bowl

**(Ready in about:** 30 min | **Servings:** 4)

**Ingredients:**

- 1small onion; chopped
- 10 black olives to garnish
- 1 handful fresh parsley, roughly chopped
- 2 cloves garlic; minced
- 2 ½ cups vegetable broth
- 1 cup bulgur wheat
- 1 pinch salt
- 1 tablespoon lime juice, or more to taste
- 1 tablespoon olive oil
- Salt and black pepper to taste

**Directions:**

1. Heat oil on Sear/Sauté, stir in garlic and onion and cook for 10 to 13 minutes until golden brown. Add in cilantro, bulgur, salt, 1 tablespoon lime juice, and vegetable broth.
2. Seal the pressure lid, choose Pressure, set to High, and set the timer to 1 minute. Once ready, do a quick release. Use a fork to fluff bulgur. Add fresh parsley as you stir. Season with additional lime salt, juice, and pepper if desired. Serve in bowls topped with black olives.

## Millet with Cherry Tomatoes

**(Ready in about:** 1 hr 15 min | **Servings:** 8

**Ingredients:**

- 2 cups millet, rinsed and drained
- ½ sweet onion; chopped
- 4 cups vegetable stock
- 1 cup cherry tomatoes; cut into halves
- 1 tablespoon fresh sage; chopped
- 1 teaspoon fresh thyme; chopped
- 1 teaspoon fresh parsley; chopped
- Salt and ground black pepper to taste

**Directions:**

1. Add millet, onion, and vegetable stock the inner pot of Foodi. Seal the pressure lid, choose Pressure, set to High, and set the timer to 10 minutes; press Start.
2. When ready, release pressure quickly. Fluff the millet with a fork, add in herbs and tomatoes and apply a seasoning of pepper and salt.

## Baked Garbanzo Beans and Pancetta

**(Ready in about:** 50 min | **Servings:** 6)

**Ingredients:**

- 3 strips pancetta; cut into strips
- 15 oz. canned garbanzo beans
- 2 garlic cloves; minced
- 1 onion; diced
- 2 cups water
- 1 cup apple cider
- ½ cup ketchup
- ¼ cup sugar
- 1 teaspoon ground black pepper
- 1 teaspoon ground mustard powder
- 1 teaspoon salt
- Fresh parsley to garnish

**Directions:**

1. Set your Foodi to Sear/Sauté, set to Medium High, and choose Start/Stop to preheat the pot. Cook pancetta for 5 minutes until crispy. Add onion and garlic, and cook for 3 minutes until soft.
2. Mix in garbanzo beans, ketchup, sugar, salt, apple cider, mustard powder, water, and pepper. Seal the pressure lid, press Pressure, set to High, and set the timer to 30 minutes; press Start.
3. Once done, release pressure naturally for 10 minutes, then turn steam vent valve to Venting to release the remaining pressure quickly. Serve in bowls garnished with parsley.

## Chicken Ragù Bolognese

**(Ready in about:** 50 min | **Servings:** 8)

**Ingredients:**

- 1 ½ pounds ground chicken
- 1 pound spaghetti
- 6 ounces bacon; cubed
- ½ cup white wine
- 1 cup milk
- ¼ cup tomato paste
- 1 cup chicken broth
- 1 onion; minced
- 1 carrot; minced
- 1 celery stalk; minced
- 2 garlic cloves, crushed
- 2 tablespoon olive oil
- ¼ teaspoon crushed red pepper flakes
- Salt to taste

**Directions:**

1. Warm oil on Sear/Sauté. Add in bacon and fry for 5 minutes until crispy. Add celery, carrot, garlic and onion and cook for 5 minutes until fragrant. Mix in red pepper flakes and tomato paste and cook for 2 minutes. Break chicken into small pieces and place in the pot. Cook for 10 minutes as you stir until browned. Pour in wine and simmer for 2 minutes. Add in chicken broth and milk.
2. Seal the pressure lid, choose Pressure, set to High, and set the timer to 15 minutes. Press Start. When ready, release the pressure quickly.
3. Add in the spaghetti and stir. Seal the pressure lid again, choose Pressure, set to High, and set the timer to another 5 minutes. Press Start.
4. When ready, release the pressure quickly. Check the pasta for doneness. If necessary press Sear/Sauté and cook for an additional 2 minutes. Adjust the seasoning and serve right away.

## Lentil and Spinach

**(Ready in about:** 35 min | **Servings:** 6)

**Ingredients:**

- 1 red jalapeño, seeded and minced
- 4 cloves garlic; minced
- 1 tomato; diced
- 1½ cups red lentils
- ¼ cup lemon juice
- 1 cup spinach; chopped
- 3 cups water
- 1 tablespoon cumin seeds
- 2 tablespoon olive oil
- 1 tablespoon coriander seeds
- 1 teaspoon ground turmeric
- ¼ teaspoon cayenne pepper
- 1 teaspoon fresh ginger, peeled and grated
- Fresh Cilantro; chopped for garnish
- Natural yogurt for garnish
- Salt to taste

**Directions:**

1. Heat oil on Sear/Sauté, add cayenne pepper, jalapeño pepper, ginger, turmeric, cumin, and garlic, and coriander and cook for 2-3 minutes until seeds become fragrant and begin to pop. Pour in water, tomato, and lentils into pot and stir. Seal the pressure lid, choose Pressure, set to High, and set the timer to 10 minutes; press Start.
2. Release pressure naturally for 10 minutes, then turn steam vent valve to Venting to release the remaining pressure quickly.
3. Stir in spinach until wilted. Add lemon juice and season to taste. Divide lentils between bowls and garnish with yogurt and cilantro.

## Shrimp Risotto with Vegetables

(**Ready in about:** 1 hr 15 min | **Servings:** 4)

**Ingredients:**

- 1 pound asparagus, trimmed and roughly chopped
- 16 shrimp, cleaned and deveined
- 1¼ cups chicken broth
- ¾ cup Parmesan cheese, shredded
- ¾ cup coconut milk
- 1 cup spinach; chopped
- 1½ cups mushrooms; sliced
- 1 cup rice, rinsed and drained
- 1 tablespoon avocado oil
- 1 tablespoon coconut oil
- Salt and ground black pepper to taste

**Directions:**

1. Warm the oil on Sear/Sauté. Add spinach, mushrooms and asparagus and cook for 10 minutes until cooked through; press Start. Add rice, coconut milk and broth to the pot as you stir.
2. Seal the pressure lid, choose Pressure, set to High, and set the timer to 40 minutes. Press Start. Do a quick release, open the lid and put the rice on a serving plate.
3. Take back the empty pot to the Foodi, add coconut oil and press Sear/Sauté. Add shrimp and cook each side taking 4 minutes until cooked through and turns pink.
4. Set the shrimp over rice, add pepper and salt for seasoning. Serve topped with shredded parmesan cheese.

## Quinoa with Onion and Carrots

(**Ready in about:** 15 min | **Servings:** 6)

**Ingredients:**

- 1 cup quinoa, rinsed until the water runs clear
- 2 carrots; cut into sticks
- 1 large onion; sliced
- 2 cups water
- 2 tablespoon olive oil
- Salt to taste
- Fresh cilantro; chopped for garnish

**Directions:**

1. Heat oil on Sear/Sauté. Add in onion and carrots and stir-fry for about 10 minutes until tender and crispy; remove to a plate. Add water, salt and quinoa to the steel pot of the Foodi.
2. Seal the pressure lid, choose Pressure, set to High, and set the timer to 1 minute. Press Start. Once ready, do a quick release. Fluff the cooked quinoa with a fork. Transfer to a serving plate and top with the carrots and onion. Serve scattered with cilantro.

# Turkey Fajita Tortiglioni

**(Ready in about:** 35 min | **Servings:** 6)

**Ingredients:**

- 1 ½ pounds turkey breast; cut into strips
- 16 ounces tortiglioni
- 1 red bell pepper; sliced diagonally
- 1 yellow bell pepper; sliced diagonally
- 1 green bell pepper; sliced diagonally
- 1 medium red onion; cut into wedges
- 4 garlic cloves; minced
- 3 cups chicken broth
- ½ cup sour cream
- ½ cup chopped parsley
- 1 cup salsa
- 1 cup shredded Gouda cheese
- 1 tablespoon olive oil
- 2 teaspoon chili powder
- 1 teaspoon salt
- 1 teaspoon cumin
- 1 teaspoon onion powder
- 1 teaspoon garlic powder
- ½ teaspoon thyme

**Directions:**

1. In a bowl, mix chili powder, cumin, garlic powder, onion powder, salt, and oregano. Reserve 1 teaspoon seasoning. Coat turkey with the remaining seasoning.
2. Warm the oil on Sear/Sauté. Add in turkey strips and cook for 4 to 5 minutes until browned. Place the turkey in a bowl.
3. Cook the onion and garlic lightly for 1 minute until soft. In the Foodi, mix salsa and chicken broth, scrape the bottom of any brown bits.
4. Into the broth mixture, stir in tortiglioni pasta and cover with bell peppers and turkey. Seal the pressure lid, choose Pressure, set to High, and set the timer to 5 minutes. Press Start. When ready, do a quick pressure release.
5. Open the lid and sprinkle with shredded gouda cheese and reserved seasoning and stir well. Add more salt if desired. Divide into plates and top with sour cream. Add parsley for garnishing and serve.

# Chipotle Mac and Cheese

**(Ready in about:** 15 min | **Servings:** 6)

**Ingredients:**

- 12 ounces macaroni
- 4 cups sharp Cheddar cheese, grated
- 2 cups Pecorino Romano cheese, grated
- 1½ cup milk
- 4 cups cold water
- 2 eggs
- 1 tablespoon chipotle chili powder
- 4 tablespoon butter
- 1 teaspoon salt
- ½ teaspoon ground black pepper
- Salt and black pepper to taste

**Directions:**

1. In your Foodi, add salt, water and macaroni. Seal the pressure lid, choose Pressure, set to High, and set the timer to 4 minutes. Press Start.
2. As the pasta cooks, take a bowl and beat eggs, chipotle chili powder, and black pepper, to mix well. When ready, release the pressure quickly. Add butter to the pasta and stir until melts. Stir in milk and egg mixture.
3. Pour in Pecorino Romano and Cheddar cheeses until well melted. You can do so in batches. Add pepper and salt to season.

## Asian Yellow Lentils

**(Ready in about:** 30 min | **Servings:** 6)

**Ingredients:**

- 1 tablespoon ghee
- 2 teaspoon cumin seeds
- 1 onion; chopped
- 4 garlic cloves; minced
- 1-inch piece of ginger, peeled; minced
- Sea salt salt
- 1 tomato; chopped
- 2 cups split yellow lentils; soaked and drained
- 2 tablespoon garam masala
- ½ teaspoon ground turmeric
- ½ teaspoon cayenne pepper
- 6 cups water
- 1 tablespoon fresh cilantro, finely chopped

**Directions:**

1. Warm ghee on Sear/Sauté, set to Medium High, and choose Start/Stop to preheat the pot. Press Start. Add cumin seeds and cook for 10 seconds until they begin to pop; stir in onion and cook for 2 to 3 minutes until softened. Mix in ginger and garlic and cook for 1 minute as you stir. Add salt for seasoning.
2. Mix in tomato and cook for 3 to 5 minutes until the mixture breaks down. Stir in turmeric, lentils, garam masala, and cayenne and cover with water. Seal the pressure lid, choose Pressure, set to High, and set the timer to 8 minutes. Press Start. When ready, release pressure quickly. Serve in bowls sprinkled with fresh cilantro.

## Asian Beef with Rice

**(Ready in about:** 40 min | **Servings:** 5)

**Ingredients:**

- 2 pounds beef stew meat; cut into bite-sized cubes
- 1 (14-ounce) can puréed tomatoes
- 1 onion; chopped
- 2 cloves garlic, smashed
- 1 lime, juiced
- ½ bunch fresh cilantro; chopped
- ¼ cup yogurt
- ½ cup beef broth
- 2 cups basmati rice, rinsed
- 2 cups water
- ½ cup heavy cream
- 1 tablespoon garam masala
- 1 tablespoon fresh ginger, grated
- 3 tablespoon butter
- 1 tablespoon olive oil
- 1 ½ teaspoon smoked paprika
- 1 teaspoon ground cumin
- ¼ teaspoon cayenne pepper
- Salt and black pepper to taste

**Directions:**

1. In a bowl, mix garlic, lime juice, olive oil, pepper, salt and yogurt. Stir in the beef to coat. In a different bowl, thoroughly mix paprika, garam masala, cumin, ginger, and cayenne pepper.
2. Melt butter on Sear/Sauté; stir-fry the onion for 7 to 9 minutes, until translucent. Sprinkle spice mixture over onion; cook for about 30 seconds until soft.
3. To the onion, add in the beef-yogurt mixture; cook for 3 to 4 minutes until meat is slightly cooked. Mix in broth and puréed tomatoes. Set trivet over beef in the pressure cooker's inner pot.
4. In an oven-proof bowl, mix water and rice. Set the bowl onto the trivet. Seal the pressure lid, press Pressure, set to High, and set the timer to 10 minutes; press Start. When ready, release pressure quickly.
5. Remove the bowl with rice and trivet. Add pepper, salt and cream into beef and stir. Use a fork to fluff rice and divide into serving plates; apply a topping of beef. Use cilantro to garnish.

## Rice Pilaf with Mushrooms

**(Ready in about:** 35 min | **Servings:** 6)

**Ingredients:**

- 4 cups vegetable stock
- 2 cups white rice
- 2 cups button mushrooms, thinly sliced
- 2 cloves garlic; minced
- 1 yellow onion, finely chopped
- 2 sprigs parsley; chopped
- 1 tablespoon olive oil
- 1 teaspoon salt

**Directions:**

1. Select Sear/Sauté, set to Medium High, choose Start/Stop to preheat the pot and heat oil.
2. Add mushrooms, onion, and garlic, and stir-fry for 5 minutes until tender. Mix in rice, stock, and salt. Seal the pressure lid, choose Pressure, set to High, and set the timer to 20 minutes. Press Start. When ready, release pressure naturally for 10 minutes. Use a fork to fluff the rice and add parsley for garnishing before serving.

## Chili Garlic Rice Noodles with Tofu

**(Ready in about:** 20 min | **Servings:** 6)

**Ingredients:**

- 8 ounces rice noodles
- 20 ounces extra firm tofu, pressed and cubed
- 1/4 cup chopped fresh chives, for garnish
- ½ cup soy sauce
- 2 cups water
- 1 tablespoon sweet chili sauce
- 1 tablespoon sesame oil
- 2 tablespoon brown sugar
- 2 tablespoon rice vinegar
- 1 teaspoon fresh minced garlic

**Directions:**

1. Heat the oil on Sear/Sauté and fry the tofu for 5 minutes until golden brown. Set aside. To the pot, add water, garlic, olive oil, vinegar, brown sugar, soy sauce, and chili sauce and mix well until smooth; stir in rice noodles.
2. Seal the pressure lid, choose Pressure, set to High, and set the timer to 3 minutes. Press Start. When ready, release the pressure quickly. Split the noodles between bowls. Top with fried tofu and sprinkle with fresh chives before serving.

## Pork Spaghetti with Tomatoes and Spinach

**(Ready in about:** 35 min | **Servings:** 4)

**Ingredients:**

- 1 pound pork sausage meat
- 1 fresh jalapeño chile, stemmed, seeded, and minced
- 8 ounces dried spaghetti, halved
- 1 garlic clove; minced
- 1 (14 ounces) can diced tomatoes, drained
- 1 cup spinach
- ½ cup onion; chopped
- 2 cups water
- ½ cup sun-dried tomatoes
- 2 tablespoon olive oil
- 1 tablespoon dried oregano
- 1 teaspoon Italian seasoning
- 1 teaspoon salt

**Directions:**

1. Warm oil on Sear/Sauté. Add in onion and garlic and cook for 2 minutes until softened.
2. Stir in sausage meat and cook for 5 minutes. Stir in jalapeño, water, sun-dried tomatoes, Italian seasoning, oregano; diced tomatoes, and salt; mix spaghetti and press to submerge into the sauce.
3. Seal the pressure lid, choose Pressure, set to High, and set the timer to 9 minutes. Press Start. When ready, release the pressure quickly. Stir in spinach, close lid again, and simmer on Keep Warm for 5 minutes until spinach is wilted.

## Quinoa and Pinto Bean Bowl

**(Ready in about:** 30 min | **Servings:** 5)

**Ingredients:**

- 14 ounces canned pinto beans, drained and rinsed
- 1 green bell pepper; diced
- 1 onion; diced
- 1 cup red salsa
- 1 cup vegetable broth
- 1 cup organic Tri-Color Quinoa, rinsed
- 1 teaspoon extra-virgin olive oil
- 1 teaspoon ground cumin
- ½ teaspoon salt

**Directions:**

1. Warm oil on Sear/Sauté. Add red onion and green bell pepper as you stir. Add salt and cumin for seasoning and cook for 7-8 minutes until fragrant.
2. To the vegetable mixture, add quinoa, broth, salsa, and pinto beans. Seal the pressure lid, choose Pressure, set to High, and set the timer to 12 minutes. Press Start. When ready, do a quick pressure release.
3. Use a fork to fluff quinoa and divide between serving bowls to serve.

## Shrimp Lo Mein

**(Ready in about:** 20 min | **Servings:** 2)

**Ingredients:**

- 1 lb. shrimp, peeled and deveined
- 10 ounces lo mein egg noodles
- 2 cups vegetable stock
- 1 cup carrots; cut into strips
- ½ cup diced onion
- 1 cup green beans, washed
- 2 cloves garlic; minced
- 1 tablespoon sesame oil
- 3 tablespoon soy sauce
- 2 tablespoon rice wine vinegar
- ½ teaspoon toasted sesame seeds
- Sea salt and ground black pepper to taste

**Directions:**

1. Warm oil on Sear/Sauté. Stir-fry the shrimp for 5 minutes. Remove to a plate and set aside. Add in garlic and onion and cook for 3 minutes until fragrant. Mix in soy sauce, carrots, vegetable stock, green beans, and rice wine vinegar. Add noodles into the mixture and ensure they are covered. Season with pepper and salt.
2. Seal the pressure lid, choose Pressure, set to High, and set the timer to 5 minutes. Press Start. When ready, release the pressure quickly. Plate the lo mein, add the reserved shrimp, sprinkle with sesame seeds, and serve.

## Spinach Kidney Bean Stew

**(Ready in about:** 45 min | **Servings:** 4)

**Ingredients:**

- 1 cup white kidney beans; soaked, drained, rinsed
- 1 cup celery; chopped
- 4 cups vegetable broth
- 1 cup spinach, torn into pieces
- 1 bay leaf
- 1 onion; chopped
- 2 cloves garlic; minced
- 2 carrots, peeled and sliced
- 2 tablespoon olive oil
- 1 teaspoon dried thyme
- 1 teaspoon dried rosemary
- A pinch of salt
- Salt and black pepper to taste

**Directions:**

1. Set your Foodi to Sear/Sauté, set to Medium High, and choose Start/Stop to preheat the pot. Warm olive oil; stir in garlic and onion and cook for 3 minutes until tender and fragrant.
2. Mix in celery and carrots and cook for 2 to 3 minutes more until they start to soften. To the Foodi, add vegetable broth, bay leaf, thyme, rosemary, kidney beans, and salt.

3. Seal the pressure lid, choose Pressure, set to High, and set the timer to 30 minutes. Press Start. Quick release the pressure and add spinach to the beans as you stir and allow sit for 2 to 4 minutes until the spinach wilts; add pepper and salt for seasoning.

## Rigatoni with Spinach and Sausage

(**Ready in about:** 45 min | **Servings:** 4)

**Ingredients:**

- 12 ounces rigatoni pasta
- 4 sausage links; sliced
- 1 onion; chopped
- 3 cups vegetable broth
- ¼ cup tomato purée
- ½ cup diced red bell pepper
- 1 cup baby spinach
- ½ cup Parmesan cheese
- 1 tablespoon butter
- 2 teaspoon chili powder
- salt and ground black pepper to taste

**Directions:**

1. Warm the butter on Sear/Sauté. Add red bell pepper, onion, and sausage, and cook for 5 minutes. Mix in vegetable broth, chili powder, tomato paste, salt, and pepper to combine. Stir in rigatoni pasta.
2. Seal the pressure lid, choose Pressure, set to High, and set the timer to 12 minutes. Press Start. When ready, naturally release pressure for 20 minutes. Stir in spinach and let simmer until wilted. Top with Parmesan cheese and serve.

## Chicken and Chickpea Stew

(**Ready in about:** 40 min | **Servings:** 6)

**Ingredients:**

- 1 pound boneless; skinless chicken legs
- 1 (24 ounces) can crushed tomatoes
- 2 (14 ounces) cans chickpeas, drained and rinsed
- 3 garlic cloves, crushed
- 1 onion; minced
- 2 jalapeño peppers, deseeded and minced
- ⅔ cup coconut milk
- ¼ cup fresh parsley; chopped
- 2 cups hot cooked basmati rice
- ¼ cup chicken stock
- 2 tablespoon olive oil
- 2 teaspoon ground cumin
- 2 teaspoon freshly grated ginger
- 1 teaspoon salt
- ½ teaspoon cayenne pepper
- Salt to taste

**Directions:**

1. Season the chicken with 1 teaspoon salt, cayenne pepper, and cumin. Set your Foodi to Sear/Sauté, set to Medium High, and choose Start/Stop to preheat the pot. Warm oil.
2. Add in jalapeño peppers and onion and cook for 5 minutes until soft; mix in ginger and garlic and cook for 3 minutes until tender.
3. Add ¼ cup chicken stock into the Foodi to ensure the pan is deglazed, from the pan's bottom scrape any browned bits of food.
4. Mix the onion mixture with chickpeas, tomatoes, and salt. Stir in the chicken to coat in sauce.
5. Seal the pressure lid, choose Pressure, set to High, and set the timer to 20 minutes. Press Start. When ready, release the pressure quickly.
6. Transfer the chicken from the cooker and slice into chunks.
7. Into the remaining sauce, mix in coconut milk; simmer for 5 minutes on Keep Warm. Split rice into 6 bowls. Top with chicken, then sauce and add cilantro for garnish.

## Black Beans Tacos

(**Ready in about:** 1 hr 30 min | **Servings:** 6)

**Ingredients:**

- 2 cups black beans; soaked overnight
- 1 cup shallots; chopped
- 4 cups water
- 6 soft Taco tortillas
- 1 avocado; sliced
- 1 tablespoon dried oregano
- 1 teaspoon chili powder
- Salt to taste
- Fresh Cilantro for garnish

**Directions:**

1. Drain the beans and add to the Foodi. Mix in the onion, oregano and chili powder. Pour water.
2. Seal the pressure lid, choose Pressure, set to High, and set the timer to 60 minutes. Press Start.
3. Do a quick release, carefully open the lid and Allow cooling for a few minutes. Serve with taco tortillas, avocado slices and cilantro.

## Spicy Corn and Pinto Bean Stew

(**Ready in about:** 1 hr 5 min | **Servings:** 6)

**Ingredients:**

- 2 cups dried pinto beans, rinsed
- 3 cups vegetable stock
- ½ cup fresh chives; chopped
- ¼ cup fresh corn kernels
- 14 ounces canned tomatoes; chopped
- 1 onion; chopped
- 1 red bell pepper; chopped
- 1 tablespoon white wine vinegar
- 1 tablespoon dried oregano
- 2 tablespoon olive oil
- 1 tablespoon ground cumin
- 1 teaspoon sea salt
- 1 teaspoon red pepper flakes

**Directions:**

1. Set your Foodi to Sear/Sauté, set to Medium High, and choose Start/Stop to preheat the pot. Press Start. Stir in oil, bell pepper, pepper flakes, oregano, onion, and cumin. Cook for 3 minutes until soft.
2. Mix in pinto beans, vegetable stock, and tomatoes. Seal the pressure lid, choose Pressure, set to High, and set the timer to 30 minutes. Press Start. Release pressure naturally for 20 minutes. Add in salt and vinegar. Divide in serving plates and top with corn and fresh chives.

## Easy Brown Rice

(**Ready in about:** 30 min| **Servings:** 6)

**Ingredients:**

- 3 cups chicken broth
- 1 ½ cups brown rice
- 2 teaspoon sesame olive oil
- 2 teaspoon lemon juice
- 1 tablespoon toasted sunflower seeds

**Directions:**

1. Add broth and brown rice to the Foodi. Seal the pressure lid, choose Pressure, set to High, and set the timer to 15 minutes. Press Start. When ready, release the pressure quickly.
2. Do not open the lid for an additional 5 minutes. Use a fork to fluff rice. Add lemon juice, sunflower seeds and oil.

# Vegetables & Vegan

## Baked Cajun Turnips

**(Ready in about:** 85 min | **Servings:** 4)

**Ingredients:**
- 4 small turnips, scrubbed clean
- 4 green onions; chopped; divided
- ¼ cup whipping cream
- ¼ cup sour cream
- ½ cup chopped roasted red bell pepper
- 1½ cups shredded Monterey Jack cheese
- ⅓ cup grated Parmesan cheese
- 1 teaspoon Cajun seasoning mix

**Directions:**
1. Pour 1 cup of water into the inner pot. Put the reversible rack in the pot and place the turnips on top. Seal the pressure lid, choose Pressure, adjust the pressure to High, and the cook time to 10 minutes; press Start. After cooking, perform a natural pressure release for 5 minutes.
2. Remove the turnips to a cutting board and allow cooling. Slice off a ½-inch piece from the top and the longer side of each turnip. Scoop the pulp into a bowl, including the flesh from the sliced tops making sure not to rip the skin of the turnip apart.
3. In the bowl with the pulp, add the whipping cream and sour cream and use a potato mash to break the pulp and mix the Ingredients until fairly smooth. Stir in the roasted bell pepper, Cajun seasoning, and Monterey Jack cheese. Fetch out 2 tablespoons of green onions and stir the remaining into the mashed turnips.
4. Next, fill the turnip skins with the mashed mixture and sprinkle with the Parmesan. Pour the water into the inner pot and return the pot to the base.
5. Put the Crisping basket into the pot. Close the crisping lid; choose Air Crisp, adjust the temperature to 375°F, and the time to 2 minutes. Press Start.
6. When the timer is done, open the lid and put the turnips in the basket. Close the crisping lid; choose Air Crisp, adjust the temperature to 375°F, and the cook time to 15 minutes. Press Start. Cool for a few minutes and garnish with the reserved onions.

## Mashed Broccoli with Cream Cheese

**(Ready in about:** 12 min | **Servings:** 4)

**Ingredients:**
- 3 heads broccoli; chopped
- 2 cloves garlic, crushed
- 6 oz. cream cheese
- 2 cups water
- 2 tablespoon butter, unsalted
- Salt and black pepper to taste

**Directions:**
1. Turn on the Ninja Foodi and select Sear/Sauté mode, adjust to High. Drop in the butter, once it melts add the garlic and cook for 30 seconds while stirring frequently to prevent the garlic from burning.
2. Then, add the broccoli, water, salt, and pepper. Close the lid, secure the pressure valve, and select Pressure mode on High pressure for 5 minutes. Press Start/Stop.
3. Once the timer has ended, do a quick pressure release and use a stick blender to mash the Ingredients until smooth to your desired consistency and well combined.
4. Stir in Cream cheese. Adjust the taste with salt and pepper. Close the crisping lid and cook for 2 minutes on Broil mode. Serve warm.

# Carrot Gazpacho

(**Ready in about:** 2 hr 30 min | **Servings:** 4)

**Ingredients:**
- 1 pound trimmed carrots
- 1 pound tomatoes; chopped
- 1 red onion; chopped
- 2 cloves garlic
- 1 cucumber, peeled and chopped
- 1/4 cup extra-virgin olive oil
- 1 pinch salt
- 2 tablespoon lemon juice
- 2 tablespoon white wine vinegar
- salt and freshly ground black pepper to taste

**Directions:**
1. To the Foodi add carrots, salt and enough water. Seal the pressure lid, choose Pressure, set to High, and set the timer to 20 minutes. Press Start.
2. Once ready, do a quick release. Set the beets to a bowl and place in the refrigerator to cool.
3. In a blender, add carrots, cucumber, red onion, pepper, garlic, olive oil, tomatoes, lemon juice, vinegar, and salt.
4. Blend until very smooth. Place gazpacho to a serving bowl, chill while covered for 2 hours.

# Chipotle Vegetarian Chili

(**Ready in about:** 45 min | **Servings:** 12)

**Ingredients:**
- 1 (28 ounces) can diced tomatoes
- 3 chipotle peppers; chopped
- 3 garlic cloves, minced
- 1 (15 ounces) can black beans, rinsed and drained
- 1/4 cup fresh parsley; chopped
- 2 cups carrots; chopped
- 1 cup red lentils
- 1 cup red quinoa
- 2 cups cashews; chopped
- 1 cup onion; chopped
- 4½ cups water
- 2 tablespoon chili powder
- 1 teaspoon salt

**Directions:**
1. In the pot, mix tomatoes, onion, chipotle peppers, chili powder, lentils, walnuts, carrots, quinoa, garlic, and salt; stir in more water.
2. Seal the pressure lid, choose Pressure, set to High, and set the timer to 30 minutes. Press Start.
3. When ready, release the pressure quickly. Into the chili, add black beans; simmer on Keep Warm until heated through. Add ¼ cup to 1 cup water if you want a thinner consistency. Top with a garnish of parsley.

# Roasted Squash and Rice with Crispy Tofu

(**Ready in about:** 70 min | **Servings:** 4)

**Ingredients:**
- 1 small butternut squash, peeled and diced
- 1 (15-ounce) block extra-firm tofu, drained and cubed
- 1 cup jasmine rice, cooked
- ¾ cup water
- 1 tablespoon coconut aminos
- 2 tablespoons melted butter; divided
- 2 teaspoons arrowroot starch
- 1 teaspoon salt
- 1 teaspoon freshly ground black pepper

**Directions:**
1. Pour the rice and water into the pot and mix with a spoon. Seal the pressure lid, choose Pressure, set to High and set the time to 2 minutes. Choose Start/Stop to boil the rice.
2. in a bowl, toss the butternut squash with 1 tablespoon of melted butter and season with the salt and black pepper. Set aside.
3. In another bowl, mix the remaining butter with the coconut aminos, and toss the tofu in the mixture. Pour the arrowroot starch over the tofu and toss again to combine well.

4. When done cooking the rice, perform a quick pressure release, and carefully open the pressure lid. Put the reversible rack in the pot in the higher position and line with aluminum foil. Arrange the tofu and butternut squash on the rack.
5. Close the crisping lid. Choose Air Crisp, set the temperature to 400°F, and set the time to 20 minutes. Choose Start/Stop to begin cooking.
6. After 10 minutes, use tongs to turn the butternut squash and tofu. When done cooking, check for your desired crispiness and serve the tofu and squash with the rice.

## Risotto and Roasted Bell Peppers

**(Ready in about:** 80 min | **Servings:** 4)

**Ingredients:**
- 4 mixed bell peppers, seeds removed and chopped diagonally
- 1 garlic clove, minced
- 2 cups carnaroli rice
- 1½ cups grated Parmesan cheese, plus more for garnish
- 5 cups vegetable stock
- ¼ cup freshly squeezed lemon juice
- 2 tablespoons ghee; divided
- 2 tablespoons unsalted butter
- 1 teaspoon grated lemon zest
- 2 teaspoons salt; divided
- 1 teaspoon freshly ground black pepper

**Directions:**
1. On the pot, choose Sear/Sauté and set to Medium High. Choose Start/Stop to preheat the pot. Melt the ghee and cook the garlic until fragrant, about 1 minute.
2. Then, pour the stock, lemon juice, lemon zest, and rice into the pot. Sprinkle with 1 teaspoon of salt and stir to combine well.
3. Seal the pressure lid, hit Pressure, set to High, and the timer to 7 minutes; press Start. While the rice cooks, in a bowl, toss the peppers with the remaining ghee, salt, and black pepper.
4. When the timer has ended, do a natural pressure release for 10 minutes, then a quick pressure release. Stir the butter into the rice until properly mixed.
5. Then, put the reversible rack inside the pot in the higher position, which will be over the risotto. Arrange the bell peppers on the rack.
6. Close the crisping lid. Choose Broil and set the time to 8 minutes; press Start/Stop.
7. When done cooking, take out the rack from the pot. Stir the Parmesan cheese into the risotto. To serve, spoon the risotto into serving plates, top with the bell peppers and garnish with extra Parmesan. Serve immediately.

## Olives and Rice Stuffed Mushrooms

**(Ready in about:** 70 min | **Servings:** 4)

**Ingredients:**
- 4 large Portobello mushrooms, stems and gills removed
- 1 green bell pepper, seeded and diced
- 1 lemon, juiced
- 1 tomato, seed removed and chopped
- ½ cup brown rice, cooked
- ¼ cup black olives, pitted and chopped
- ½ cup feta cheese, crumbled
- 2 tablespoons melted butter
- ½ teaspoon salt
- ½ teaspoon ground black pepper
- Minced fresh cilantro; for garnish

**Directions:**
1. Put the Crisping Basket in the pot. Close the crisping lid, choose Air Crisp, setting the temperature to 375°F, and setting the time to 5 minutes. Press Start/Stop to preheat the pot.
2. Brush the mushrooms with the melted butter. Open the crisping lid and arrange the mushrooms, open-side up and in a single layer in the preheated basket.
3. Close the crisping lid. Choose Air Crisp, set the temperature to 375°F, and set the time to 20 minutes. Choose Start/Stop.

4. In a bowl, combine the brown rice, tomato, olives, bell pepper, feta cheese, lemon juice, salt, and black pepper.
5. Open the crisping lid and spoon the rice mixture equally into the 4 mushrooms. Close the lid.
6. Choose Air Crisp, set the temperature to 350°F, and set the time to 8 minutes. Press Start/Stop to commence cooking.
7. When the mushrooms are ready, remove to a plate, garnish with fresh cilantro and serve immediately.

## Spinach, Tomatoes, and Butternut Squash Stew

**(Ready in about:** 65 min | **Servings:** 6)

**Ingredients:**

- 2 lb. butternut squash, peeled and cubed
- 1 (15-ounce) can sundried tomatoes, undrained
- 2 (15-ounce) cans chickpeas, drained
- 1 white onion; diced
- 4 garlic cloves, minced
- 4 cups baby spinach
- 4 cups vegetable broth
- 1 tablespoon butter
- ½ teaspoon smoked paprika
- 1 teaspoon coriander powder
- 1½ teaspoons cumin powder
- ½ teaspoon salt
- ½ teaspoon freshly ground black pepper

**Directions:**

1. Choose Sear/Sauté, set to Medium High, and the timer to 5 minutes; press Start/Stop to preheat the pot. Combine the butter, onion, and garlic in the pot. Cook, stirring occasionally; for 5 minutes or until soft and fragrant.
2. Add the butternut squash, vegetable broth, tomatoes, chickpeas, cumin, paprika, coriander, salt, and black pepper to the pot. Put the pressure lid together and lock in the Seal position.
3. Choose Pressure, set to High, and set the time to 8 minutes; press Start/Stop.
4. When the timer is done reading, perform a quick pressure release. Stir in the spinach to wilt, adjust the taste with salt and black pepper, and serve warm.

## Pesto with Cheesy Bread

**(Ready in about:** 60 min | **Servings:** 4)

**Ingredients:**

- 1 medium red onion; diced
- 1 celery stalk; diced
- 1 large carrot, peeled and diced
- 1 small yellow squash; diced
- 1 (14-ounce) can chopped tomatoes
- 1 (27-ounce) can cannellini beans, rinsed and drained
- 1 bay leaf
- 1 cup chopped zucchini
- ¼ cup shredded Pecorino Romano cheese
- ⅓ cup olive oil based pesto
- 3 cups water
- 1 Pecorino Romano rind
- 1 garlic clove, minced
- 4 slices white bread
- 3 tablespoons butter; at room temperature
- 3 tablespoons ghee
- 1 teaspoon mixed herbs
- ¼ teaspoon cayenne pepper
- ½ teaspoon salt

**Directions:**

1. On your Foodi, choose Sear/Sauté, and adjust to Medium to preheat the inner pot. Press Start. Add the ghee to the pot to melt and sauté the onion, celery, and carrot for 3 minutes or until the vegetables start to soften.
2. Stir in the yellow squash, tomatoes, beans, water, zucchini, bay leaf, mixed herbs, cayenne pepper, salt, and Pecorino Romano rind.
3. Seal the pressure lid, choose Pressure, adjust to High, and set the time to 4 minutes. Press Start. In a bowl, mix the butter, shredded cheese, and garlic. Spread the mixture on the bread slices.
4. After cooking the soup, perform a natural pressure release for 2 minutes, then a quick pressure release and carefully open the lid.

5. Adjust the taste of the soup with salt and black pepper, and remove the bay leaf. Put the reversible rack in the upper position of the pot and lay the bread slices in the rack with the buttered-side up.
6. Close the crisping lid. Choose Broil; adjust the cook time to 5 minutes, and Press Start/Stop to begin broiling.
7. When the bread is crispy, carefully remove the rack, and set aside. Ladle the soup into serving bowls and drizzle the pesto over. Serve with the garlic toasts.

## Steamed Artichokes with Lemon Aioli

### (Ready in about: 20 min | Servings: 4)

**Ingredients:**
- 4 artichokes, trimmed
- 1 small handful parsley; chopped
- 1 lemon, halved
- 3 cloves garlic, crushed
- ½ cup mayonnaise
- 1 cup water
- 1 teaspoon lemon zest
- 1 tablespoon lemon juice
- Salt to taste

**Directions:**
1. On the artichokes cut ends, rub with lemon. Add water into the pot of pressure cooker. Set the reversible rack over the water,
2. Place the artichokes into the steamer basket with the points upwards; sprinkle each with salt. Seal lid and cook on High pressure for 10 minutes. Press Start. When ready, release the pressure quickly.
3. In a mixing bowl, combine mayonnaise, garlic, lemon juice, and lemon zest. Season to taste with salt. Serve with warm steamed artichokes sprinkled with parsley.

## Rice Stuffed Zucchini Boats

### (Ready in about: 55 min| Servings: 4)

**Ingredients:**
- 2 small zucchini
- ½ cup chopped toasted cashew nuts
- ½ cup grated Parmesan cheese; divided
- ½ cup cooked white short grain rice
- ½ cup canned white beans, drained and rinsed
- ½ cup chopped tomatoes
- 2 tablespoons melted butter; divided
- ½ teaspoon salt
- ½ teaspoon freshly ground black pepper

**Directions:**
1. Cut each zucchini in half and then, cut in half lengthwise and scoop out the pulp. Chop the pulp roughly and place in a medium bowl. In the bowl, add the rice, beans, tomatoes, cashew nuts, ¼ cup of Parmesan cheese, 1 tablespoon of melted butter, the salt, and black pepper. Combine the mixture well but not to break the beans.
2. Put the Crisping Basket in the pot. Close the crisping lid, choose Air Crisp, set the temperature to 400°F, and the time to 5 minutes.
3. Spoon the mixed Ingredients into the zucchini boats and arrange the stuffed zucchinis in a single layer in the preheated basket. Close the crisping lid. Choose Air Crisp, set the temperature to 400°F, and the time to 15 minutes. Choose Start/Stop to begin cooking.
4. After 15 minutes, sprinkle the zucchini boats with the remaining Parmesan cheese and butter.
5. Close the crisping lid. Choose Broil, set the time to 5 minutes, and choose Start/Stop to broil.
6. When done cooking, ensure it is as crisp as you desire, otherwise broil for a few more minutes. Remove the zucchinis onto a plate, allow cooling for about a minute, and serve.

## Zucchini Quinoa Stuffed Red Peppers

**(Ready in about:** 40 min | **Servings:** 4)

**Ingredients:**

- 1 small zucchini; chopped
- 4 red bell peppers
- 2 large tomatoes; chopped
- 1 small onion; chopped
- 2 cloves garlic, minced
- 1 cup quinoa, rinsed
- 1 cup grated Gouda cheese
- ½ cup chopped mushrooms
- 1 ½ cup water
- 2 cups chicken broth
- 1 tablespoon olive oil
- ½ teaspoon smoked paprika
- Salt and black pepper to taste

**Directions:**

1. Select Sear/Sauté mode on High. Once it is ready, add the olive oil to heat and then add the onion and garlic. Sauté for 3 minutes to soften, stirring occasionally.
2. Include the tomatoes, cook for 3 minutes and then add the quinoa, zucchinis, and mushrooms. Season with paprika, salt, and black pepper and stir with a spoon. Cook for 5 to 7 minutes, then, turn the pot off.
3. Use a knife to cut the bell peppers in halves (lengthwise) and remove their seeds and stems.
4. Spoon the quinoa mixture into the bell peppers. Put the peppers in a greased baking dish and pour the broth over.
5. Wipe the pot clean with some paper towels, and pour the water into it. After, fit the steamer rack at the bottom of the pot.
6. Place the baking dish on top of the reversible rack, cover with aluminum foil, close the lid, secure the pressure valve, and select Pressure mode on High pressure for 15 minutes. Press Start/Stop.
7. Once the timer has ended, do a quick pressure release and open the lid. Remove the aluminum foil and sprinkle with the gouda cheese.
8. Close the crisping lid, select Bake/Roast mode and cook for 10 minutes on 375 degrees F. Arrange the stuffed peppers on a serving platter and serve right away or as a side to a meat dish.

## Cauliflower and Asparagus Farfalle

**(Ready in about:** 60 min | **Servings:** 4)

**Ingredients:**

- 1 bunch asparagus, trimmed, cut into 1-inch pieces
- 2 cups cauliflower florets
- 10 ounces farfalle
- 3 garlic cloves, minced
- ¼ cup chopped basil
- ½ cup grated Parmesan cheese
- 2½ cups vegetable stock
- ½ cup heavy cream
- 1 cup cherry tomatoes, halved
- 3 tablespoons melted butter; divided
- 3 teaspoons salt; divided

**Directions:**

1. Put the Crisping Basket in the Foodi. Close the crisping lid, choose Air Crisp; adjust the temperature to 375°F and the time to 2 minutes; press Start. Pour the asparagus, and cauliflower, in a large bowl and drizzle with 1 tablespoon of melted butter. Season with ½ teaspoon of salt and toss. Open the cooker and transfer the vegetables to the basket.
2. Close the crisping lid; choose Air Crisp, adjust the temperature to 375°F, and set the timer to 10 minutes. Press Start to begin roasting. After 5 minutes, carefully open the lid and mix the vegetables. Close the lid and continue cooking.
3. When done roasting, take out the basket, and cover the top with aluminum foil; set aside.
4. Place the farfalle into the inner pot and add the remaining butter. Using tongs, toss the farfalle to coat, and add the remaining salt, garlic, and water. Stir to combine.
5. Seal the pressure lid, choose Pressure; adjust the pressure to High and the cook time to 5 minutes; press Start. After cooking, do a quick pressure release and carefully open the lid.

6. Stir the heavy cream and tomatoes into the pasta, tossing well. Choose Sear/Sauté and adjust to Medium. Press Start to simmer the cream until the sauce has your desired consistency.
7. Gently mix in the asparagus, and cauliflower. Allow warming to soften the vegetables, then stir in the basil and Parmesan cheese. Dish the creamy farfalle and serve warm.

## Spicy Salmon with Wild Rice

(**Ready in about:** 50 min | **Servings:** 4)

**Ingredients:**

- 1 cup wild rice
- 1 cup vegetable stock
- 2 limes, juiced
- 2 jalapeño peppers, seeded and diced
- 4 garlic cloves, minced
- 4 skinless salmon fillets
- A bunch of asparagus, trimmed and cut diagonally
- 2 tablespoons chopped fresh parsley
- 3 tablespoons olive oil; divided
- 2 tablespoons honey
- 1 teaspoon sweet paprika
- 1 teaspoon salt
- 1 teaspoon freshly ground black pepper

**Directions:**

1. Pour the brown rice and vegetable stock in the pot; stir to combine. Put the reversible rack in the pot in the higher position and lay the salmon fillets on the rack.
2. Seal the pressure lid, choose Pressure, set to High, and set the time to 2 minutes; press Start. In a bowl, toss the broccoli with 1 tablespoon of olive oil and season with the salt and black pepper. In another bowl, evenly combine the remaining oil, the lime juice, honey, paprika, jalapeño, garlic, and parsley.
3. When done cooking, do a quick pressure release, and carefully open the pressure lid.
4. Pat the salmon dry with a paper towel and coat the fish with the honey sauce while reserving a little for garnishing.
5. Arrange the asparagus around the salmon. Close the crisping lid; choose Broil and set the time to 7 minutes. Choose Start/Stop.
6. When ready, remove the salmon from the rack. Dish the salmon with asparagus and rice. Garnish with parsley and remaining sauce. Serve immediately.

## Buttered Leafy Greens

(**Ready in about:** 10 min | **Servings:** 4)

**Ingredients:**

- 2 lb. baby spinach
- ½ lb. Swiss chard
- 1 lb. kale leaves
- ½ cup water
- 1 tablespoon dried basil
- ½ tablespoon butter
- Salt and black pepper to season

**Directions:**

1. Turn on the Ninja Foodi, add the water and fit the reversible rack at the bottom of the pot. Put the spinach, swiss chard, and kale on the rack.
2. Close the lid, secure the pressure valve, and select Steam mode on High pressure for 3 minutes. Press Start/Stop.
3. Once the timer has ended, do a quick pressure release and open the lid. Remove the trivet with the wilted greens onto a plate and discard the water in the pot.
4. Select Sear/Sauté mode on the pot and add the butter. Once it melts, add the spinach and kale back to the pot, and the dried basil.
5. Season with salt and pepper and stir it. Close the crisping lid and cook for 4 minutes on Bake/Roast mode on 380 degrees F. Dish the greens into serving plates and serve as a side dish.

## Eggplant Lasagna

**(Ready in about:** 25 min | **Servings:** 4)

**Ingredients:**

- 3 large eggplants; sliced in uniform ¼ inches
- ¼ cup Parmesan cheese, grated
- 4 ¼ cups Marinara sauce
- 1 ½ cups shredded Mozzarella cheese
- Cooking spray
- Chopped fresh basil to garnish

**Directions:**

1. Open the pot and grease it with cooking spray. Arrange the eggplant slices in a single layer on the bottom of the pot and sprinkle some cheese all over it.
2. Arrange another layer of eggplant slices on the cheese, sprinkle this layer with cheese also, and repeat the layering of eggplant and cheese until both Ingredients are exhausted.
3. Lightly spray the eggplant with cooking spray and pour the marinara sauce all over it. Close the lid and pressure valve, and select Pressure mode on High pressure for 8 minutes. Press Start/Stop.
4. Once the timer has stopped, do a quick pressure release, and open the lid. Sprinkle with grated parmesan cheese, close the crisping lid and cook for 10 minutes on Bake/Roast mode on 380 degrees F.
5. With two napkins in hand, gently remove the inner pot. Allow cooling for 10 minutes before serving. Garnish the lasagna with basil and serve warm as a side dish.

## Creamy Cauliflower and Butternut Squash

**(Ready in about:** 32 min | **Servings:** 4)

**Ingredients:**

- 1 (2 pounds) butternut squash, peeled, seeded, and cubed
- 1 large white onion; chopped
- 2 heads cauliflower, cut in florets
- 3 cups chicken broth
- 1 cup milk, full fat
- 4 cloves garlic, minced
- 3 teaspoon paprika
- 2 teaspoon olive oil
- Salt and black pepper to taste

**Topping:**

- Grated Cheddar cheese, crumbled bacon; chopped chives, pumpkin seeds

**Directions:**

1. Select Sear/Sauté mode and set to High. Heat olive oil, add the white onion and garlic and sauté for 3 minutes. Next, pour in the butternut squash, cauliflower florets, broth, paprika, pepper, and salt (if needed because of the broth). Stir the Ingredients with a spoon.
2. Close the lid, secure the pressure valve, select Pressure mode on High pressure and adjust the time for 8 minutes. Press Start button.
3. Once the timer has ended, do a quick pressure release, and open the lid. Stir in the milk and use a stick blender to puree the soup. Adjust the seasoning.
4. Stir in cheese, close the crisping lid and cook for 2 minutes on Broil mode. Dish the soup into serving bowls. Add the remaining toppings on the soup and serve warm.

## Noodles with Tofu and Peanuts

**(Ready in about:** 20 min | **Servings:** 4)

**Ingredients:**

- 1 package tofu; cubed
- 8 ounces egg noodles
- 2 bell peppers; sliced
- 3 scallions, thinly sliced
- ¼ cup roasted peanuts
- ¼ cup soy sauce
- ¼ cup orange juice
- 1 tablespoon fresh ginger, peeled and minced
- 2 tablespoon vinegar
- 1 tablespoon sesame oil
- 1 tablespoon sriracha

**Directions:**

1. In the pressure cooker, mix tofu, bell peppers, orange juice, sesame oil, ginger, egg noodles, soy sauce, vinegar, and sriracha; cover with enough water.
2. Seal the pressure lid, choose Pressure, set to High, and set the timer to 2 minutes. Press Start. When ready, release the pressure quickly. Place the mixture into four plates; apply a topping of scallions and peanuts before serving.

## Chipotle Chili

**(Ready in about:** 35 min | **Servings:** 4)

**Ingredients:**

- 4 celery stalks; chopped
- 2 (15 oz) cans diced tomatoes
- 1.5 oz. dark chocolate; chopped
- 1 small chipotle, minced
- 3 carrots; chopped
- 2 cloves garlic, minced
- 2 green bell pepper; diced
- 1 sweet onion; chopped
- 2 cups tomato sauce
- ½ cup water
- 1 ½ cups raw walnuts; chopped + extra to garnish
- 1 tablespoon cinnamon powder
- 1 tablespoon olive oil
- 1 tablespoon cumin powder
- 2 teaspoon smoked paprika
- Salt and pepper, to taste
- Chopped cilantro to garnish

**Directions:**

1. Turn on the Ninja Foodi, open the lid and select Sear/Sauté mode on Medium. Pour in the oil to heat and add the onion, celery, and carrots. Sauté for 4 minutes. Add the garlic, cumin, cinnamon, and paprika. Stir and let the sauce cook for 2 minutes.
2. Now, include the bell peppers, tomatoes, tomato sauce, chipotle, water, and walnuts Stir.
3. Close the lid, secure the pressure valve, and select Pressure mode on High pressure for 15 minutes. Press Start/Stop. Once the timer has ended, do a quick pressure release, and open the lid.
4. Pour the chopped chocolate in and stir it until it melts and is well incorporated into the chili. Adjust the taste with salt and pepper. Close the crisping lid and cook for 5 minutes on Broil mode.
5. Dish the chili into a serving bowl, garnish it with the remaining walnuts and cilantro. Serve with some noodles.

## Asian-Style Tofu Soup

**(Ready in about:** 25 min | **Servings:** 4)

**Ingredients:**

- 16 oz. firm Tofu, water- packed
- 6 ounces dry egg noodles
- 7 cloves garlic, minced
- 4 cups vegetable broth
- 1 cup sliced Shitake mushrooms
- ½ cup chopped cilantro
- ¼ cup soy sauce
- 3 cup sliced bok choy
- 1 tablespoon olive oil
- 2 tablespoon ginger paste
- 2 tablespoon Korean red pepper flakes (gochugaru)
- 1 tablespoon sugar

**Directions:**

1. Drain the liquid out of the tofu, pat the tofu dry with paper towels, and use a knife to cut them into 1-inch cubes.
2. Turn your Ninja Foodi on and select Sear/Sauté mode on Medium. Pour the oil to heat, add the garlic and ginger, and sauté for 2 minutes.
3. Add the sugar, broth, and soy sauce. Stir and cook for 30 seconds. Include the tofu and bok choy, close the lid, secure the pressure valve, and select Pressure mode on High pressure for 10 minutes. Press Start/Stop.
4. Once the timer has ended, do a quick pressure release and open the lid. Add the zucchini noodles, give it a good stir using a spoon, and close the crisping lid.

5. Let the soup cook for 4 minutes on Broil mode. Use a soup spoon to fetch the soup into soup bowls, top with cilantro and enjoy.

## Pasta with Roasted Veggies

### (**Ready in about:** 25 min | **Servings:** 6)

**Ingredients:**

- 1 lb. penne, cooked
- 1 acorn squash; sliced
- 4 oz. mushrooms; sliced
- 1 zucchini; sliced
- 1 pepper; sliced
- 1 cup grape tomatoes, halved
- ½ cup kalamata olives, pitted, halved
- ¼ cup olive oil
- 3 tablespoon balsamic vinegar
- 2 tablespoon chopped basil
- 1 teaspoon Italian seasoning
- Salt and pepper, to taste

**Directions:**

1. Combine the pepper, zucchini, squash, mushrooms, and olive oil, in a large bowl. Season with salt and pepper. Close the crisping lid and cook the veggies for 15 minutes on Air Crisp mode at 380 F.
2. In a large bowl, combine the penne, roasted vegetables, olives, tomatoes, Italian seasoning, and vinegar. Sprinkle basil and serve.

## Steamed Asparagus and Pine nuts

### (**Ready in about:** 15 min | **Servings:** 4)

**Ingredients:**

- 1 ½ lb. asparagus, ends trimmed
- ½ cup chopped Pine Nuts
- 1 cup water
- 1 tablespoon butter
- 1 tablespoon olive oil to garnish
- Salt and pepper, to taste

**Directions:**

1. Open the Ninja Foodi, pour the water in, and fit the reversible rack at the bottom. Place the asparagus on the rack, close the crisping lid, select Air Crisp mode, and set the time to 8 minutes on 380 degrees F. Press Start/Stop.
2. At the 4-minute mark, carefully turn the asparagus over. When ready, remove to a plate, sprinkle with salt and pepper, and set aside.
3. Select Sear/Sauté on your Ninja Foodi, set to Medium and melt the butter. Add the pine nuts and cook for 2-3 minutes until golden. Scatter over the asparagus the pine nuts, and drizzle olive oil.

## Quinoa Pesto Bowls with Veggies

### (**Ready in about:** 30 min | **Servings:** 2)

**Ingredients:**

- 1 cup quinoa, rinsed
- 1 cup broccoli florets
- ¼ cup pesto sauce
- 2 cups water
- ½ pound Brussels sprouts
- 2 eggs
- 1 small beet, peeled and cubed
- 1 carrot, peeled and chopped
- 1 avocado, thinly sliced
- lemon wedges; for serving
- salt and ground black pepper to taste

**Directions:**

1. In the pot, mix water, salt, quinoa and pepper. Set the reversible rack to the pot over quinoa. To the reversible rack, add eggs, Brussels sprouts, broccoli, beet cubes, carrots, pepper and salt.
2. Seal the pressure lid, choose Pressure, set to High, and set the timer to 1 minute. Press Start. Release pressure naturally for 10 minutes, then release any remaining pressure quickly.
3. Remove reversible rack from the pot and set the eggs to a bowl of ice water. Peel and halve the eggs. Use a fork to fluff quinoa.
4. Separate quinoa, broccoli, avocado, carrots, beet, Brussels sprouts, eggs, and a dollop of pesto into two bowls. Serve alongside a lemon wedge.

## Garlic Potatoes

**(Ready in about:** 30 min | **Servings:** 4)

**Ingredients:**

- 1½ pounds potatoes
- ½ cup vegetable broth
- 3 cloves garlic, thinly sliced
- 3 tablespoon butter
- 2 tablespoon fresh rosemary; chopped
- ½ teaspoon fresh parsley; chopped
- ½ teaspoon fresh thyme; chopped
- 1/4 teaspoon ground black pepper

**Directions:**

1. Use a small knife to pierce each potato to ensure there are no blowouts when placed under pressure. Melt butter on Sear/Sauté. Add in potatoes, rosemary, parsley, pepper, thyme, and garlic, and cook for 10 minutes until potatoes are browned and the mixture is aromatic.
2. In a bowl, mix miso paste and vegetable stock; stir into the mixture in the pressure cooker.
3. Seal the pressure lid, choose Pressure, set to High, and set the timer to 5 minutes. Press Start. Do a pressure quickly.

## Mushroom Risotto with Swiss Chard

**(Ready in about:** 60 min | **Servings:** 4)

**Ingredients:**

- 1 small bunch Swiss chard; chopped
- ½ cup sautéed mushrooms
- ½ cup caramelized onions
- ⅓ cup white wine
- 2 cups vegetable stock
- ⅓ cup grated Pecorino Romano cheese
- 1 cup short grain rice
- 3 tablespoons ghee; divided
- ½ teaspoon salt

**Directions:**

1. Press Sear/Sauté and adjust to Medium. Press Start to preheat the inner pot. Melt 2 tablespoons of ghee and sauté the Swiss chard for 5 minutes until wilted. Spoon into a bowl and set aside.
2. Use a paper towel to wipe out any remaining liquid in the pot and melt the remaining ghee. Stir in the rice and cook for about 1 minute.
3. Add the white wine and cook for 2 to 3 minutes, with occasional stirring until the wine has evaporated. Add in stock and salt; stir to combine.
4. Seal the pressure lid, choose Pressure; adjust the pressure to High and the cook time to 8 minutes; press Start. When the timer is done reading, perform a quick pressure release and carefully open the lid.
5. Stir in the mushrooms, swiss chard, and onions and let the risotto heat for 1 minute. Mix the cheese into the rice to melt, and adjust the taste with salt.Spoon the risotto into serving bowls and serve immediately.

## Vegan Curry

**(Ready in about:** 25 min | **Servings:** 3)

**Ingredients:**

- 1 (15 ounces) can chickpeas, drained and rinsed
- 1 onion; chopped
- 2 cloves garlic, minced
- 1 tomato; diced
- 5 cups collard greens; chopped
- ⅓ cup water
- 1 tablespoon butter
- 1 teaspoon ginger, grated
- 1 teaspoon ground cumin
- ½ teaspoon garam masala
- 1 teaspoon lemon juice
- 1 teaspoon red chilli powder
- 1 teaspoon salt
- ½ teaspoon ground turmeric

**Directions:**

1. Melt butter on Sear/Sauté. Toss in the onion to coat. Close the pressure lid and cook for 2 minutes until soft.
2. Mix in ginger, cumin powder, turmeric, red chili powder, garlic, and salt and cook for 30 seconds until crispy; stir in tomatoes. In the Foodi, mix in ⅓ water, tomato and chickpeas.
3. Seal the pressure lid, choose Pressure, set to High, and set the timer to 4 minutes. Press Start. When ready, release the pressure quickly.
4. Into the chickpea mixture, stir in lemon juice, collard greens and garam masala until well coated. Cook for 2 to 3 minutes until collard greens wilt. Serve over rice or naan.

## Crème de la Broc

**(Ready in about:** 25 min | **Servings:** 6)

**Ingredients:**

- 1 ½ cups grated yellow and white Cheddar cheese + extra for topping
- 1 ½ oz. cream cheese
- 1 medium Red onion; chopped
- 3 cloves garlic, minced
- 4 cups chopped broccoli florets, only the bushy tops
- 3 cups heavy cream
- 3 cups vegetable broth
- 4 tablespoon butter
- 4 tablespoon flour
- 1 teaspoon Italian Seasoning
- Salt and black pepper to taste

**Directions:**

1. Select Sear/Sauté mode, adjust to High and melt the butter once the pot is ready. Add the flour and use a spoon to stir until it clumps up. Gradually pour in the heavy cream while stirring until white sauce forms. Fetch out the butter sauce into a bowl and set aside.
2. Press Stop and add the onions, garlic, broth, broccoli, Italian seasoning, and cream cheese. Use a wooden spoon to stir the mixture.
3. Seal the lid, and select Pressure mode on High pressure for 12 minutes. Press Start/Stop. Once the timer has ended, do a quick pressure release.
4. Add in butter sauce and cheddar cheese, salt, and pepper. Close the crisping lid and cook on Broil mode for 3 minutes. Dish the soup into serving bowls, top it with extra cheese, to serve.

## Cheesy Squash and Linguine

**(Ready in about:** 75 min | **Servings:** 4)

**Ingredients:**

- 1 pound linguine
- 1 (24-ounce) tomato sauce
- 2 eggs
- 1 yellow squash, peeled and sliced
- 1 cup shredded mozzarella cheese
- ½ cup grated Parmesan cheese + more for garnish
- 1 cup seasoned panko breadcrumbs
- 1 cup flour
- 4 cups water + 2 tbsp.
- 2 tablespoons olive oil
- 2 teaspoons salt
- Minced fresh cilantro; for garnish

**Directions:**

1. Break the spaghetti in half and place in the pot. Pour 4 cups of water and 1 teaspoon of salt. Seal the pressure lid, choose Pressure, set to High, and set the time to 2 minutes; press Start.
2. In a bowl, combine the flour and the remaining salt evenly. In another bowl, whisk the eggs and 2 tablespoons of water. In a third bowl, mix the breadcrumbs and Parmesan cheese.
3. Coat each squash slice in the flour. Shake off the excess flour, dip the slice in the egg wash, and then dredge in the breadcrumbs. Place in a plate and set aside.
4. When ready, perform a quick pressure release. Drain the pasta through a colander and transfer to the pot. Pour all but ¼ cup of the tomato sauce over the linguine; mix gently.

5. Fix the reversible rack inside the pot over the linguine. Place the breaded squash on the rack and lightly brush with oil.
6. Close the crisping lid. Choose Air Crisp, set the temperature to 350°F, and set the time to 15 minutes. Press Start/Stop to cook.
7. When done cooking, spread the remaining tomato sauce on top of the squash, and sprinkle with the mozzarella cheese.
8. Close the crisping lid again, choose Broil, and set the time to 3 minutes; press Start/Stop. When ready, spoon the pasta into plates, place the breaded squash to the side, and garnish with fresh cilantro.

## Tasty Acorn Squash

**(Ready in about:** 30 min | **Servings:** 4)

### Ingredients:
- 1 lb. acorn squash, peeled and cut into chunks
- ½ cup water
- 2 tablespoon butter
- 1 tablespoon dark brown sugar
- 1 tablespoon cinnamon
- 3 tablespoon honey; divided
- salt and ground black pepper to taste

### Directions:
1. In a small bowl, mix 1 tablespoon honey and water; pour into the pressure cooker's pot. Add in squash. Seal the and cook on High pressure for 4 minutes. Press Start. When ready, release the pressure quickly.
2. Transfer the squash to a serving dish. Turn Foodi to Sear/Sauté.
3. Mix brown sugar, cinnamon, the remaining 2 tablespoon honey and the liquid in the pot; cook as you stir for 4 minutes to obtain a thick consistency and starts to turn caramelized and golden. Spread honey glaze over squash; add pepper and salt for seasoning.

## Aloo Gobi with Cilantro

**(Ready in about:** 40 min | **Servings:** 4)

### Ingredients:
- 1 head cauliflower, cored and cut into florets
- 1 potato, peeled and diced
- 4 garlic cloves, minced
- 1 tomato, cored and chopped
- 1 jalapeño pepper, deseeded and minced
- 1 onion, minced
- 1 cup water
- 1 tablespoon curry paste
- 1 tablespoon vegetable oil
- 1 tablespoon ghee
- 2 teaspoon cumin seeds
- 1 teaspoon ground turmeric
- ½ teaspoon chili pepper
- salt to taste
- A handful of cilantro leaves; chopped

### Directions:
1. Warm oil on Sear/Sauté. Add in potato and cauliflower and cook for 8 to 10 minutes until lightly browned; add salt for seasoning. Set the vegetables to a bowl.
2. Add ghee to the pot. Mix in cumin seeds and cook for 10 seconds until they start to pop; add onion and cook for 3 minutes until softened. Mix in garlic; cook for seconds.
3. Add in tomato, curry paste, chili pepper, jalapeño pepper, curry paste, and turmeric; cook for 3 to 5 minutes until the tomato starts to break down.
4. Return potato and cauliflower to the pot. Add water over the vegetables, add more salt if need be, and stir. Seal the pressure lid, choose Pressure, set to High, and set the timer to 4 minutes. Press Start. Release pressure naturally. Top with cilantro and serve.

# Spanish Rice

**(Ready in about:** 50 min | **Servings:** 4)

**Ingredients:**

- 1 small onion; chopped
- 1 (16-ounce) can pinto beans, drained and rinsed
- 2 garlic cloves, minced
- 1 banana pepper, seeded and chopped
- ¼ cup stewed tomatoes
- ½ cup vegetable stock
- 1 cup jasmine rice
- ⅓ cup red salsa
- 3 tablespoons ghee
- 1 tablespoon chopped fresh parsley
- 1 teaspoon Mexican Seasoning Mix
- 1 teaspoon salt

**Directions:**

1. On your Foodi, choose Sear/Sauté and adjust to Medium. Press Start to preheat the inner pot. Add the ghee to melt until no longer foaming and cook the onion, garlic, and banana pepper in the ghee. Cook for 2 minutes or until fragrant.
2. Stir in the rice, salsa, tomato sauce, vegetable stock, Mexican seasoning, pinto beans, and salt. Seal the pressure lid, choose Pressure and adjust the pressure to High and the cook time to 6 minutes; press Start.
3. After cooking, do a natural pressure release for 10 minutes. Stir in the parsley, dish the rice, and serve.

# Green Squash Gruyere

**(Ready in about:** 70 min | **Servings:** 4)

**Ingredients:**

- 1 large green squash; sliced
- 2 cups tomato sauce
- 1 cup shredded mozzarella cheese
- 1½ cups panko breadcrumbs
- ⅓ cup grated Gruyere cheese
- 3 tablespoons melted unsalted butter
- 2 teaspoons salt

**Directions:**

1. Season the squash slices on both sides with salt and place the slices on a wire rack to drain liquid for 5 to 10 minutes. In a bowl, combine the melted butter, breadcrumbs, and Gruyere cheese and set aside.
2. Rinse the squash slices with water and blot dry with paper towel. After, arrange the squash in the inner pot in a single layer as much as possible and pour the tomato sauce over the slices.
3. Seal the pressure lid, choose Pressure, set to High, and the time to 5 minutes. Press Start to commence cooking. When the timer has read to the end, perform a quick pressure release. Sprinkle the squash slices with the mozzarella cheese.
4. Close the crisping lid. Choose Bake/Roast; adjust the temperature to 375°F and the cook time to 2 minutes. Press Start to broil.
5. After, carefully open the lid and sprinkle the squash with the breadcrumb mixture. Close the crisping lid again, choose Bake/Roast, adjust the temperature to 375°F, and the cook time to 8 minutes. Press Start to continue broiling. Serve immediately.

# Green Cream Soup

**(Ready in about:** 22 min | **Servings:** 4)

**Ingredients:**

- ½ lb. kale leaves; chopped
- ½ lb. Swiss chard leaves; chopped
- ½ lb. spinach leaves; chopped
- 1 onion; chopped
- 4 cloves garlic, minced
- 4 cups vegetable broth
- 1 ¼ cup heavy cream
- 1 tablespoon olive oil
- 1 ½ tablespoon white wine vinegar
- Salt and pepper, to taste
- Chopped Peanuts to garnish

**Directions:**
1. Turn on the Ninja Foodi and select Sear/Sauté mode on Medium. Add the olive oil, once it has heated add the onion and garlic and sauté for 2-3 minutes until soft. Add greens and vegetable broth.
2. Close the lid, secure the pressure valve, and select Pressure mode on High pressure for 10 minutes. Press Start/Stop. Once the timer has ended, do a quick pressure release.
3. Add the white wine vinegar, salt, and pepper. Use a stick blender to puree the Ingredients in the pot. Close the crisping lid and cook for 3 minutes on Broil mode. Stir in the heavy cream. Spoon the soup into bowls, sprinkle with peanuts, and serve.

## Palak Paneer

**(Ready in about:** 20 min | **Servings:** 4)

**Ingredients:**
- 1 pound spinach; chopped
- 1 tomato; chopped
- 2 cups paneer; cubed
- 1 cup water
- ¼ cup milk
- 2 tablespoon butter
- 1 teaspoon minced fresh ginger
- 1 teaspoon minced fresh garlic
- 1 red onion; chopped
- 1 teaspoon cumin seeds
- 1 teaspoon coriander seeds
- 1 teaspoon salt, or to taste
- 1 teaspoon chilli powder

**Directions:**
1. Warm butter on Sear/Sauté, set to Medium High, and choose Start/Stop to preheat the pot. Press Start.
2. Add in garlic, cumin seeds, coriander seeds, chilli powder, ginger, and garlic and fry for 1 minute until fragrant; add onion and cook for 2 more minutes until crispy. Add in salt, water and chopped spinach.
3. Seal the pressure lid, choose Pressure, set to High, and set the timer to 1 minute. Press Start.
4. When ready, release the pressure quickly. Add spinach mixture to a blender and blend to obtain a smooth paste. Mix paneer and tomato with spinach mixture.

## Bok Choy and Zoddle Soup

**(Ready in about:** 35 min | **Servings:** 6)

**Ingredients:**
- 1 lb. baby bok choy, stems removed
- 2 zucchinis, spiralized
- 6 oz. Shitake mushrooms, stems removed and sliced to a 2-inch thickness
- 2-inch ginger; chopped
- 2 cloves garlic, peeled
- 3 carrots, peeled and sliced diagonally
- 2 sweet onion; chopped
- 6 cups water
- 2 tablespoon sesame oil
- 2 tablespoon soy sauce
- 2 tablespoon chili paste
- Salt to taste
- Sesame seeds to garnish
- Chopped green onion to garnish

**Directions:**
1. In a food processor, add the chili paste, ginger, onion, and garlic; and process them until they are pureed. Turn on the Ninja foodi and select Sear/Sauté mode to High.
2. Pour in the sesame oil, once it has heated add the onion puree and cook for 3 minutes while stirring constantly to prevent burning. Add the water, mushrooms, soy sauce, and carrots.
3. Close the lid, secure the pressure valve, and select Pressure mode on High pressure for 5 minutes. Press Start/Stop.
4. Once the timer has ended, do a quick pressure release and open the lid. Add the zucchini noodles and bok choy, and stir to ensure that they are well submerged in the liquid.
5. Adjust the taste with salt, cover the pot with the crisping lid, and let the vegetables cook for 10 minutes on Broil mode.
6. Use a soup spoon to dish the soup with veggies into soup bowls. Sprinkle with green onions and sesame seeds. Serve as a complete meal.

## Vegetarian Minestrone Soup

(**Ready in about:** 40 min | **Servings:** 4)

**Ingredients:**

- 1 (15.5 oz) can Cannellini beans
- 8 sage leaves; chopped finely
- 1 bay leaf
- 2 small Red onions, cut in wedges
- 1 Potato, peeled and diced
- 1 carrot, peeled and chopped
- 1 cup chopped butternut squash
- 1 cup chopped celery
- 4 cups vegetable broth
- 1 tablespoon chopped fresh rosemary
- 2 tablespoon chopped fresh parsley
- 2 teaspoon olive oil
- Salt and pepper, to taste

**Directions:**

1. Add the potato, carrot, squash, onion, celery, rosemary, sage leaves, bay leaf, vegetable broth, salt, pepper, and olive oil to the pot of your Ninja Foodi. Close the lid, secure the pressure valve, and select Pressure mode on High pressure for 7 minutes. Press Start/Stop.
2. Once the timer has ended, do a quick pressure release and open the lid. Add the cannellini beans and stir with a spoon. Close the crisping lid and cook for 5 minutes on Broil mode.
3. Use a soup spoon to fetch the soup into soup bowls. Garnish with fresh parsley and serve with a side of crusted bread.

## Chorizo Mac and Cheese

(**Ready in about:** 30 min | **Servings:** 6)

**Ingredients:**

- 1 pound macaroni
- 3 ounces chorizo; chopped
- 2 cups milk
- 2 cups Cheddar cheese, shredded
- 3 cups water
- 2 tablespoon minced garlic
- 1 tablespoon garlic powder
- salt to taste

**Directions:**

1. Put chorizo in the pot of your Foodi, select Sear/Sauté and stir-fry until crisp, about 5 minutes. Press Start. Set aside. Wipe the pot with kitchen paper. Add in water, macaroni, and salt to taste. Seal lid and cook on for 5 minutes High Pressure. Press Start.
2. When ready, release the pressure quickly. Stir in cheese and milk until the cheese melts. Divide the mac and cheese between serving bowls. Top with chorizo and serve.

## Cheese and Mushroom Tarts

(**Ready in about:** 75 min | **Servings:** 4)

**Ingredients:**

- 1 small white onion; sliced
- 1 sheet puff pastry, thawed
- 5 ounces oyster mushrooms; sliced
- 1 cup shredded Swiss cheese
- ¼ cup dry white wine
- 1 tablespoon thinly sliced fresh green onions
- 2 tablespoons melted butter; divided
- ¼ teaspoon salt
- ¼ teaspoon freshly ground black pepper

**Directions:**

1. Choose Sear/Sauté, set to High, and set the time to 5 minutes. Choose Start/Stop to preheat the pot. Add 1 tablespoon of butter, the onion, and mushrooms to the pot. Sauté for 5 minutes or until the vegetables are tender and browned.
2. Season with salt and black pepper, pour in the white wine, and cook until evaporated, about 2 minutes. Spoon the vegetables into a bowl and set aside.
3. Unwrap the puff pastry and cut into 4 squares. Pierce the dough with a fork and brush both sides with the remaining oil. Share half of the cheese evenly over the puff pastry squares, leaving a ½- inch border

around the edges. Also, share the mushroom mixture over the pastry squares and top with the remaining cheese.

4. Put the Crisping Basket in the pot. Close the crisping lid, choose Air Crisp, set the temperature to 400°F, and the time to 5 minutes.
5. Once the pot has preheated, put 1 tart in the Crisping Basket. Close the crisping lid, choose Air Crisp, set the temperature to 360°F, and set the time to 6 minutes; press Start.
6. After 6 minutes, check the tart for your preferred brownness. Take the tart out of the basket and transfer to a plate. Repeat the process with the remaining tarts. Garnish with the green onions and serve.

## Mashed Potatoes with Spinach

**(Ready in about:** 30 min | **Servings:** 6)

**Ingredients:**
- 3 pounds potatoes, peeled and quartered
- 2 cups spinach; chopped
- ½ cup milk
- ⅓ cup butter
- 1½ cups water
- 2 tablespoon chopped fresh chives
- ½ teaspoon salt
- fresh black pepper to taste

**Directions:**
1. In the cooker, mix water, salt and potatoes. Seal the pressure lid, choose Pressure, set to High, and set the timer to 8 minutes. Press Start. When ready, release the pressure quickly. Drain the potatoes, and reserve the liquid in a bowl. In a large bowl, mash the potatoes.
2. Mix with butter and milk; season with pepper and salt. With reserved cooking liquid, thin the potatoes to attain the desired consistency.
3. Put the spinach in the remaining potato liquid and stir until wilted; season with salt and pepper. Drain and serve with potato mash. Garnish with black pepper and chives.

## Pumpkin Soup

**(Ready in about:** 30 min | **Servings:** 4)

**Ingredients:**
- 1 lb. green beans, cut in 5 strips each
- 16 oz. pumpkin puree
- 1 celeriac, peeled and cubed
- 5 stalks celery; chopped
- 1 white onion; chopped
- 2 cups vegetable broth
- 3 cups spinach leaves
- 1 tablespoon chopped basil leaves
- ¼ teaspoon dried thyme
- ⅛ teaspoon rubbed sage
- Salt to taste

**Directions:**
1. Open the Ninja Foodi and pour in the celeriac, pumpkin puree, celery, onion, green beans, vegetable broth, basil leaves, thyme, sage, and a little salt.
2. Close the lid, secure the pressure valve, and select Steam mode on High pressure for 5 minutes. Press Start/Stop. Once the timer has ended, do a quick pressure release and open the lid.
3. Add in the spinach and stir using a spoon. Close the crisping lid and cook for 3 minutes on Broil mode. Use a soup spoon to fetch the soup into serving bowls.

# Mushroom Brown Rice Pilaf

**(Ready in about:** 15 min | **Servings:** 4)

**Ingredients:**

- 2 cups brown rice, rinsed
- 1 cup Portobello mushrooms, thinly sliced
- ¼ cup Romano cheese, grated
- 2 sprigs parsley, to garnish
- 4 cups vegetable broth
- 3 teaspoons olive oil
- Salt to taste

**Directions:**

1. Heat the oil on Sear/Sauté on Medium, and stir-fry the mushrooms for 3 minutes until golden. Season with salt, and add rice and broth.
2. Close the lid, secure the pressure valve, and select Pressure mode on High pressure for 5 minutes. Press Start/Stop to start cooking.
3. Once the timer has ended, do a quick pressure release and open the lid.
4. Spread the cheese over and close the crisping lid. Select Bake/Roast, adjust to 375°F and the timer to 2 minutes. Press Start/Stop to start cooking. To serve, plate the pilaf and top with freshly chopped parsley.

# Green Minestrone

**(Ready in about:** 30 min | **Servings:** 4)

**Ingredients:**

- 1 head broccoli, cut into florets
- 1 zucchini; chopped
- 2 cups chopped kale
- 1 cup green beans
- 2 cups vegetable broth
- 4 celery stalks; sliced thinly
- 1 leek; sliced thinly
- 3 whole black peppercorns
- 2 tablespoon olive oil
- water to cover
- salt to taste

**Directions:**

1. Into the pressure cooker, add broccoli, leek, green beans, salt, peppercorns, zucchini, and celery. Mix in vegetable broth, oil, and water.
2. Seal the pressure lid, choose Pressure, set to High, and set the timer to 4 minutes. Press Start.
3. Release pressure naturally for 5 minutes, then release the remaining pressure quickly. Add kale into the soup and stir; set to Keep Warm and cook until tender.

# Colorful Vegetable Medley

**(Ready in about:** 15 min | **Servings:** 4)

**Ingredients:**

- 16 asparagus, trimmed
- 1 small head broccoli, broken into florets
- 1 small head cauliflower, broken into florets
- 5 ounces green beans
- 2 carrots, peeled and cut on bias into 1/4-inch rounds
- 1 cup water
- salt to taste

**Directions:**

1. Into the pot, add water and set trivet on top of water and place steamer basket on top of the trivet. In an even layer, spread green beans, broccoli, cauliflower, asparagus, and carrots in the steamer basket.
2. Seal the pressure lid, choose Pressure, set to High, and set the timer to 3 minutes on High. When ready, release the pressure quickly. Remove steamer basket from cooker and add salt to vegetables for seasoning. Serve immediately.

## Veggie Mash with Parmesan

**(Ready in about:** 15 min | **Servings:** 6)

**Ingredients:**
- 3 pounds Yukon Gold potatoes, cut into 1-inch pieces
- 1 garlic clove, minced
- 1 cup Parmesan cheese, shredded
- ¼ cup butter, melted
- 1 ½ cups cauliflower, broken into florets
- 1 carrot; chopped
- ¼ cup milk
- 1 teaspoon salt
- Fresh parsley for garnish

**Directions:**
1. Into your pot, add veggies, salt and cover with enough water. Seal the pressure lid, choose Pressure, set to High, and set the timer to 10 minutes. Press Start. When ready, release the pressure quickly.
2. Drain the vegetables and mash them with a potato masher; add garlic, butter and milk, and whisk until everything is well incorporated. Serve topped with parmesan cheese and chopped parsley.

## Simple Fried Ravioli

**(Ready in about:** 15 min | **Servings:** 6)

**Ingredients:**
- 1 package cheese ravioli
- ¼ cup Parmesan cheese
- 1 cup buttermilk
- 2 cup Italian breadcrumbs
- ¼ teaspoon garlic powder
- 1 teaspoon olive oil

**Directions:**
1. In a bowl, combine the crumbs, Parmesan cheese, garlic powder, and olive oil. Dip the ravioli in the buttermilk and then coat them with the breadcrumb mixture.
2. Line a baking sheet with parchment paper and arrange the ravioli on it. Place in the Ninja Foodi and cook for 5 minutes on Air Crisp mode at 390 F. Serve the air-fried ravioli with marinara jar sauce.

## Tahini Sweet Potato Mash

**(Ready in about:** 25 min| **Servings:** 4)

**Ingredients:**
- 2 pounds sweet potatoes, peeled and cubed
- 1 cup water
- 2 tablespoon tahini
- 1 tablespoon sugar
- ¼ teaspoon ground nutmeg
- sea salt to taste
- Chopped fresh chives; for garnish

**Directions:**
1. In the Foodi, add 1 cup cold water and set a steamer basket into the pot. Add sweet potato cubes into the steamer basket. Seal the pressure lid, choose Pressure, set to High, and set the timer to 8 minutes. Press Start. When ready, release the pressure quickly.
2. In a large mixing bowl, add cooked sweet potatoes and slightly mash. Using a hand mixer, whip in nutmeg, sugar, and tahini until the sweet potatoes attain the consistency you desire; add salt for seasoning. Top with chives and serve.

## Stuffed Mushrooms

**(Ready in about:** 40 min **| Servings:** 4)

**Ingredients:**
- 10 large white mushrooms, stems removed
- 1 red bell pepper, seeded and chopped
- 1 small onion; chopped
- 1 green onion; chopped
- ¼ cup roasted red bell peppers; chopped
- ¼ cup grated Parmesan cheese
- ½ cup water
- 1 tablespoon butter
- ½ teaspoon dried oregano
- Salt and black pepper to taste

**Directions:**
1. Turn on the Ninja Foodi and select Sear/Sauté mode on Medium. Put in the butter to melt and add the roasted and fresh peppers, green onion, onion, oregano, salt, and pepper. Use a spoon to mix and cook for 2 minutes.
2. Spoon the bell pepper mixture into the mushrooms and use a paper towel to wipe the pot and place the stuffed mushrooms in it, 5 at a time. Pour in water.
3. Close the lid, secure the pressure valve, and select pressure mode on High pressure for 5 minutes. Press Start/Stop. Once the timer has ended, do a quick pressure release and open the lid.
4. Sprinkle with parmesan cheese and close the crisping lid. Select Bake/Roast, adjust the temperature to 380°F and the time to 2 minutes and press Start/Stop button.
5. Use a set of tongs to remove the stuffed mushrooms onto a plate and repeat the cooking process for the remaining mushrooms. Serve hot with a side of steamed green veggies and a sauce.

## Crispy Cheese Lings

**(Ready in about:** 15 min **| Servings:** 4)

**Ingredients:**
- 4 cups grated cheddar cheese
- 1 cup all-purpose flour
- 1 tablespoon baking powder
- 1 tablespoon butter
- 1-2 tablespoon water
- ¼ teaspoon chili powder
- ¼ teaspoon salt, to taste

**Directions:**
1. Mix the flour and the baking powder. Add the chili powder, salt, butter, cheese and 1-2 tablespoon of water to the mixture.
2. Make a stiff dough. Knead the dough for a while. Sprinkle a tablespoon or so of flour on the table. Take a rolling pin and roll the dough into ½ -inch thickness.
3. Cut the dough in any shape you want. Close the crisping lid and fry the cheese lings for 6 minutes at 370° F on Air Crisp mode.

## Crispy Kale Chips

**(Ready in about:** 9 min **| Servings:** 2)

**Ingredients:**
- 4 cups kale, stemmed and packed
- 1 tablespoon of yeast flakes
- 2 tablespoon of olive oil
- 1 teaspoon of vegan seasoning
- Salt to taste

**Directions:**
1. In a bowl, add the oil, the kale, the vegan seasoning, and the yeast and mix well. Dump the coated kale in the Ninja Foodi's basket.
2. Set the heat to 370°F, close the crisping lid and fry for a total of 6 minutes on Air Crisp mode. Shake it from time to time.

## Cauliflower Rice with Peas

(**Ready in about:** 15 min | **Servings:** 2)

**Ingredients:**
- 1 head cauliflower, cut into florets
- ¼ cup green peas
- 1 cup water
- 2 tablespoon olive oil
- 1 tablespoon chopped fresh parsley
- 1 teaspoon chili powder
- salt to taste

**Directions:**
1. Into the pressure cooker's pot, add water. Set the reversible rack over water. Add cauliflower into the steamer basket.
2. Seal the pressure lid, choose Pressure, set to High, and set the timer to 1 minute. Press Start.
3. When ready, release the pressure quickly. Remove reversible rack. Drain water from the pot, pat dry, and return to pressure cooker base.
4. Set on Sear/Sauté. Warm oil. Add in cauliflower and stir to break into smaller pieces like rice; stir in chili powder, peas and salt. Place the cauliflower rice into plates and add parsley for garnishing.

## Green Lasagna Soup

(**Ready in about:** 30 min | **Servings:** 4)

**Ingredients:**
- ½ pound broccoli; chopped
- 3 lasagna noodles
- 1 carrot; chopped
- 2 garlic cloves minced
- 1 cup tomato paste
- 1 cup tomatoes; chopped
- ¼ cup dried green lentils
- 2 cups vegetable broth
- 1 cup leeks; chopped
- 1 teaspoon olive oil
- 2 teaspoon Italian seasoning
- salt to taste

**Directions:**
1. Warm oil on Sear/Sauté. Add garlic and leeks and cook for 2 minutes until soft; add tomato paste, carrot, Italian seasoning, broccoli, tomatoes, lentils, and salt. Stir in vegetable broth and lasagna pieces.
2. Seal the pressure lid, choose Pressure, set to High, and set the timer to 3 minutes. Press Start.
3. Release pressure naturally for 10 minutes, then release the remaining pressure quickly. Divide soup into serving bowls and serve.

## Prawn Toast

(**Ready in about:** 12 min | **Servings:** 2)

**Ingredients:**
- 6 large prawns, shells removed; chopped
- 1 egg white, whisked
- 1 large spring onion, finely sliced
- ½ cup sweet corn
- 3 white slices of bread
- 1 tablespoon black sesame seeds

**Directions:**
1. In a bowl, place the prawns, corn, spring onion and the black sesame seeds. Add the whisked egg white, and mix the Ingredients. Spread the mixture over the bread slices.
2. Place the prawns in the Ninja Foodi's basket and sprinkle with oil.
3. Close the crisping lid and fry the prawns until golden; for 8-10 minutes at 370 F on Air Crisp mode. Serve with ketchup or chili sauce.

# Crispy Nachos

**(Ready in about:** 20 min | **Servings:** 2)

**Ingredients:**

- 1 cup sweet corn
- 1 cup all-purpose flour
- 1 tablespoon butter
- 2-3 tablespoon water
- ½ teaspoon chili powder
- Salt to taste

**Directions:**

1. Add a small amount of water to the sweet corn and grind until you obtain an excellent paste.
2. In a large bowl, add the flour, the salt, the chili powder, the butter and mix very well. Add the corn and stir well.
3. Start to knead with your palm until you obtain a stiff dough. Meanwhile, dust a little bit of flour and spread the batter with a rolling pin.
4. Make it around ½ inch thick. Cut it in any shape you want and cook in the Ninja Foodi for 10 minutes on Air Crisp mode at 350 F. Serve with guacamole salsa.

# Parsley Mashed Cauliflower

**(Ready in about:** 15 min | **Servings:** 4)

**Ingredients:**

- 1 head cauliflower
- 1/4 cup heavy cream
- 2 cups water
- 1 tablespoon fresh parsley, finely chopped
- 1 tablespoon butter
- ¼ teaspoon celery salt
- ⅛ teaspoon freshly ground black pepper

**Directions:**

1. Into the pot, add water and set trivet on top and lay cauliflower head onto the trivet. Seal the pressure lid, choose Pressure, set to High, and set the timer to 8 minutes. Press Start.
2. When ready, release the pressure quickly. Remove the trivet and drain liquid from the pot before returning to the base.
3. Take back the cauliflower to the pot alongside the pepper, heavy cream, salt and butter; use an immersion blender to blend until smooth. Top with parsley and serve.

# Garganelli with Cheese and Mushrooms

**(Ready in about:** 60 min | **Servings:** 4)

**Ingredients:**

- 1 large egg
- 8 ounces garganelli
- 8 ounces Swiss cheese, shredded
- 1 recipe sautéed mushrooms
- 1 (12–fluid ounce) can full fat evaporated milk
- 1½ cups panko breadcrumbs
- 1¼ cups water
- 2 tablespoons chopped fresh cilantro
- 3 tablespoons sour cream
- 3 tablespoons melted unsalted butter
- 3 tablespoons grated Cheddar cheese
- 1½ teaspoons salt
- 1½ teaspoons arrowroot starch

**Directions:**

1. Pour the garganelli into the inner pot, add half of the evaporated milk, the water, and salt. Seal the pressure lid, choose Pressure, set to High and the time to 4 minutes. Press Start.
2. In a bowl, whisk the remaining milk with the egg. In another bowl, combine the arrowroot starch with the Swiss cheese.
3. When the pasta has cooked, perform a natural pressure release for 3 minutes, then a quick pressure release and carefully open the lid. Pour in the milk-egg mixture and a large handful of the starch mixture. Stir to melt the cheese and then add the remaining cheese in 3 or 4 batches while stirring to melt. Mix in the mushrooms, cilantro, and sour cream.

4. In a bowl, mix the breadcrumbs, melted butter, and cheddar cheese. Then, sprinkle the mixture evenly over the pasta. Close the crisping lid. Choose Broil and adjust the time to 5 minutes. Press Start to begin crisping.
5. When done, the top should be brown and crispy, otherwise broil further for 3 minutes, and serve immediately.

## Cheesy Green Beans with Nuts

### (Ready in about: 15 min | Servings: 6)

**Ingredients:**
- 2 pounds green beans, trimmed
- 1 cup chopped toasted pine nuts
- 1 cup feta cheese, crumbled
- 1½ cups water
- Juice from 1 lemon
- 6 tablespoon olive oil
- ½ teaspoon salt
- freshly ground black pepper to taste

**Directions:**
1. Add water to the pot. Set the reversible rack over the water. Loosely heap green beans into the reversible rack.
2. Seal lid and cook on High Pressure for 5 minutes. Press Start. When the cooking cycle is complete, When ready, release pressure quickly. Drop green beans into a salad bowl; top with the olive oil, feta cheese, pepper, and pine nuts.

## Veggie and Quinoa Stuffed Peppers

### (Ready in about: 16 min | Servings: 1)

**Ingredients:**
- ¼ cup cooked quinoa
- ½ diced tomato, plus one tomato slice
- 1 bell pepper
- ½ tablespoon diced onion
- 1 teaspoon olive oil
- ¼ teaspoon smoked paprika
- ¼ teaspoon dried basil
- Salt and pepper, to taste

**Directions:**
1. Core and clean the bell pepper to prepare it for stuffing. Brush the pepper with half of the olive oil on the outside.
2. In a small bowl, combine all of the other Ingredients, except the tomato slice and reserved half-teaspoon olive oil. Stuff the pepper with the filling. Top with the tomato slice.
3. Brush the tomato slice with the remaining half-teaspoon of oil and sprinkle with basil. Close the crisping lid and cook for 10 minutes on Air Crisp mode at 350 F.

## Minestrone with Pancetta

### (Ready in about: 40 min | Servings: 6)

**Ingredients:**
- 2 ounces pancetta; chopped
- 1 (15 ounces) can diced tomatoes
- 1 (15 ounces) can chickpeas, rinsed and drained
- 1 onion; diced
- 1 parsnip, peeled and chopped
- 2 carrots, peeled and sliced into rounds
- 2 celery stalks,
- 2 garlic cloves, minced
- 6 cups chicken broth
- ½ cup grated Parmesan cheese
- 2 cups green beans, trimmed and chopped
- 1½ cups small shaped pasta
- 1 tablespoon dried basil
- 1 tablespoon dried oregano
- 2 tablespoon olive oil
- 1 tablespoon dried thyme
- salt and ground black pepper to taste

**Directions:**
1. Warm oil on Sear/Sauté. Add onion, carrots, garlic, pancetta, celery, and parsnip, and cook for 5 minutes until they become soft.

2. Stir in basil, oregano, green beans, broth, tomatoes, pepper, salt, thyme, vegetable broth, chickpeas, and pasta.
3. Seal the pressure lid, choose Pressure, set to High, and set the timer to 6 minutes. Press Start.
4. Release pressure naturally for 10 minutes then release the remaining pressure quickly. Ladle the soup into bowls and serve garnished with grated parmesan cheese.

## Carrots with Crumbled Bacon

**(Ready in about:** 30 min | **Servings:** 8)

**Ingredients:**
- 4 pounds carrots, peeled and sliced
- ½ cup fresh orange juice
- ¼ cup olive oil
- 3 slices bacon, crumbled
- 1 tablespoon cold water
- 3 tablespoon honey
- 1 teaspoon salt
- 2 teaspoon cornstarch

**Directions:**
1. Fry the bacon in your pressure cooker on Sear/Sauté until crisp, about 5 minutes. Set aside. In a bowl, mix salt, olive oil, orange juice, and maple syrup; add the mixture and carrots to the pot and mix well to coat. Seal the pressure lid, choose Pressure, set to High, and set the timer to 6 minutes. Press Start.
2. When ready, release the pressure quickly. Transfer carrots to a serving dish. Press Sear/Sauté. In a bowl, mix cold water and cornstarch until cornstarch dissolves completely; add to the liquid remaining in the pressure cooker.
3. Simmer sauce as you stir for 2 minutes to obtain a thick and smooth consistency. Ladle sauce over the carrots and scatter over the crumbled bacon.

## Paneer Cheese Balls

**(Ready in about:** 12 min | **Servings:** 2)

**Ingredients:**
- 2 oz. paneer cheese
- 1 green chili; chopped
- A 1-inch ginger piece; chopped
- 2 medium onions; chopped
- 2 tablespoon flour
- 1 tablespoon corn flour
- 1 tablespoon olive oil
- 1 teaspoon red chili powder
- a few leaves of coriander; chopped
- Salt to taste

**Directions:**
1. Mix all Ingredients except the oil and the cheese. Take a small part of the mixture, roll it up and slowly press to flatten it. Stuff in 1 cube of cheese and seal the edges. Repeat with the rest of the mixture.
2. Close the crisping lid and fry the balls in the Ninja Foodi for 12 minutes on Air Crisp mode and at 370 F. Serve hot, with ketchup.

## Pilau Rice with Veggies

**(Ready in about:** 30 min | **Servings:** 4)

**Ingredients:**
- 1 cup basmati rice, rinsed and drained
- 2 cups vegetable broth
- 1 cup onion; chopped
- 1 cup green peas
- 1 cup carrot; chopped
- 1 cup mushroom; chopped
- 1 cup broccoli; chopped
- 3 tablespoon olive oil
- 1 tablespoon ginger, minced
- 1 tablespoon chili powder
- ½ tablespoon ground cumin
- 1 tablespoon lemon juice
- 2 tablespoon chopped fresh cilantro
- 1 teaspoon garam masala
- ½ teaspoon turmeric powder

**Directions:**

1. Warm 1 tablespoon olive oil on Sear/Sauté. Add in onion and ginger and cook for 3 minutes until soft. Stir in broccoli, green peas, mushrooms, and carrots; cook for 1 more minute. Add turmeric powder, chili powder, garam masala, and cumin for seasoning; cook for 1 minute until soft.
2. Add ¼ cup water into the pan to deglaze; scrape the bottom to get rid of any browned bits. To the vegetables, add the remaining water and rice.
3. Seal the pressure lid, choose Pressure, set to High, and set the timer to 1 minute. Press Start. Release pressure naturally. Use a fork to fluff rice, sprinkle with lemon juice; divide onto plates and garnish with cilantro.

## Grilled Tofu Sandwich

(**Ready in about:** 20 min | **Servings:** 1)

**Ingredients:**

- 2 slices of bread
- ¼ cup red cabbage, shredded
- 1-inch thick Tofu slice
- 2 teaspoon olive oil divided
- ¼ teaspoon vinegar
- Salt and pepper, to taste

**Directions:**

1. Place the bread slices and toast for 3 minutes on Roast mode at 350 F; set aside. Brush the tofu with 1 teaspoon of oil, and place in the basket of the Ninja Foodi. Bake for 5 minutes on each side on Roast mode at 350 F.
2. Combine the cabbage, remaining oil, and vinegar, and season with salt and pepper.
3. Place the tofu on top of one bread slice, place the cabbage over, and top with the other bread slice.

## Baby Porcupine Meatballs

(**Ready in about:** 30 min | **Servings:** 4)

**Ingredients:**

- 1 lb. of ground beef
- 1 onion; chopped
- 1 green bell pepper, finely chopped
- 1 garlic clove, minced
- 1 cup rice
- 2 cups of tomato juice
- 2 tablespoon Worcestershire sauce
- 1 teaspoon celery salt
- 1 teaspoon oregano

**Directions:**

1. Combine the rice, ground beef, onion, celery, salt, green peppers, and garlic. Shape into balls of 1 inch each. Arrange the balls in the basket of the Ninja Foodi. Close the crisping lid and cook for 15 minutes at 320°F.
2. After 8 minutes, shape the balls. Heat the tomato juice, cloves, oregano, and Worcestershire sauce in a saucepan over medium heat.
3. Pour in the meatballs, bring to a boil, reduce the heat and simmer for 10 minutes, stirring often. Serve warm.

## Veggie Skewers

(**Ready in about:** 20 min | **Servings:** 4)

**Ingredients:**

- 2 boiled and mashed potatoes
- ¼ cup chopped fresh mint leaves
- ⅔ cup canned beans
- ⅓ cup grated carrots
- ½ cup paneer
- 1 green chili
- 1-inch piece of fresh ginger
- 3 garlic cloves
- 2 tablespoon corn flour
- ½ teaspoon garam masala powder
- Salt, to taste

**Directions:**

1. Soak 12 skewers until ready to use. Place the beans, carrots, garlic, ginger, chili, paneer, and mint, in a food processor and process until smooth; transfer to a bowl.
2. Add the mashed potatoes, corn flour, some salt, and garam masala powder to the bowl. Mix until fully incorporated. Divide the mixture into 12 equal pieces.
3. Shape each of the pieces around a skewer. Close the crisping lid and cook the skewers for 10 minutes on Air Crisp mode at 390 F.

## Turkey Stuffed Potatoes

(**Ready in about:** 30 min | **Servings:** 4)

**Ingredients:**

- 1 pound turkey breasts
- 4 potatoes
- 1 Fresno chili pepper; chopped
- 2 cups vegetable broth
- 2 tablespoon fresh cilantro; chopped
- 1 teaspoon ground cumin
- ½ teaspoon onion powder
- 1 teaspoon chili powder
- ½ teaspoon garlic powder

**Directions:**

1. In the pot, combine chicken broth, cumin, garlic powder, onion powder, and chili powder; toss in turkey to coat.
2. Place a reversible rack over the turkey. Use a fork to pierce the potatoes and set them into the reversible rack.
3. Seal the pressure lid, choose Pressure, set to High, and set the timer to 20 minutes. Press Start. When ready, release the pressure quickly. Remove reversible rack from the cooker. Place the potatoes on a plate.
4. Place turkey in a mixing bowl and use two forks to shred. Half each potato lengthwise. Stuff with shredded turkey; top with cilantro, onion, and fresno pepper and serve.

## Burrito Bowls

(**Ready in about:** 30 min | **Servings:** 4)

**Ingredients:**

- 1 (14.5 ounces) can diced tomatoes
- 1 (14.5 ounces) can black beans, drained and rinsed
- 1 ½ cups vegetable stock
- 1 cup frozen corn kernels
- 1 cup quinoa, rinsed
- 1 avocado; sliced
- 1 onion
- 2 garlic cloves, minced
- 2 tablespoon chopped cilantro
- 1 tablespoon roughly chopped fresh coriander
- 2 tablespoon olive oil
- 1 tablespoon chili powder
- 2 teaspoon ground cumin
- 2 teaspoon paprika
- 1 teaspoon salt
- ½ teaspoon black pepper
- ¼ teaspoon cayenne pepper
- Cheddar cheese, grated for garnish

**Directions:**

1. Warm oil on Sear/Sauté. Add in onion and cook for 3 to 5 minutes until fragrant. Add garlic and cook for 2 more minutes until soft and golden brown. Add in chili powder, paprika, cayenne pepper, salt, cumin, and black pepper and cook for 1 minute until spices are soft.
2. Pour quinoa into onion and spice mixture and stir to coat quinoa completely in spices. Add diced tomatoes, black beans, vegetable stock, and corn; stir to combine.
3. Seal the pressure lid, choose Pressure, set to High, and set the timer to 7 minutes. Press Start. When ready, release the pressure quickly. Open the lid and let sit for 6 minutes until flavors combine. Use a fork to fluff quinoa and season with pepper and salt if desired.
4. Into quinoa and beans mixture, stir in cilantro and divide among plates. Top with cheese and avocado slices.

# Italian Sausage with Garlic Mash

**(Ready in about:** 30 min | **Servings:** 6)

**Ingredients:**
- 6 Italian sausages
- 4 large potatoes, peeled and cut into 1½-inch chunks
- 2 garlic cloves, smashed
- ⅓ cup butter, melted
- ¼ cup milk; at room temperature, or more as needed
- 1 ½ cups water
- 1 tablespoon olive oil
- 1 tablespoon chopped chives
- salt and ground black pepper to taste

**Directions:**
1. Select Sear/Sauté, set to Medium High, and choose Start/Stop to preheat the pot and heat olive oil. Cook for 8-10 minutes, turning periodically until browned. Set aside. Wipe the pot with paper towels. Add in water and set the reversible rack over water. Place potatoes onto the reversible rack.
2. Seal the pressure lid, choose Pressure, set to High, and set the timer to 12 minutes. Press Start.
3. When ready, release the pressure quickly. Remove reversible rack from the pot. Drain water from the pot. Return potatoes to pot. Add in salt, butter, pepper, garlic, and milk and use a hand masher to mash until no large lumps remain.
4. Using an immersion blender, blend potatoes on Low for 1 minute until fluffy and light. Avoid over-blending to ensure the potatoes do not become gluey!
5. Transfer the mash to a serving plate, top with sausages and scatter chopped chives over to serve.

# Pepper and Sweet Potato Skewers

**(Ready in about:** 20 min | **Servings:** 1)

**Ingredients:**
- 1 large sweet potato
- 1 green bell pepper
- 1 beetroot
- 1 tablespoon olive oil
- 1 teaspoon chili flakes
- ¼ teaspoon black pepper
- ½ teaspoon turmeric
- ¼ teaspoon garlic powder
- ¼ teaspoon paprika

**Directions:**
1. Soak 3 to 4 skewers until ready to use. Peel the veggies and cut them into bite-sized chunks. Place the chunks in a bowl along with the remaining Ingredients Mix until fully coated. Thread the veggies in this order: potato, pepper, beetroot.
2. Place in the Ninja Foodi, close the crisping lid and cook for 15 minutes on Air Crisp mode at 350 F; flip skewers halfway through.

# Tomato and Poblano Stuffed Squash

**(Ready in about:** 50 min | **Servings:** 3)

**Ingredients:**
- ½ butternut squash
- 6 grape tomatoes, halved
- ¼ cup grated mozzarella, optional
- 1 poblano pepper, cut into strips
- 2 teaspoon olive oil divided
- Salt and pepper, to taste

**Directions:**
1. Meanwhile, cut trim the ends and cut the squash lengthwise. You will only need one half for this recipe. Scoop the flash out, so you make room for the filling. Brush 1 teaspoon oil over the squash. Place in the Ninja Foodi and roast for 30 minutes.
2. Combine the other teaspoon of olive oil with the tomatoes and poblanos. Season with salt and pepper, to taste. Place the peppers and tomatoes into the squash. Close the crisping lid and cook for 15 more minutes on Air Crisp mode at 350 F. If using mozzarella, add it on top of the squash, two minutes before the end.

# Rosemary Sweet Potato Medallions

**(Ready in about:** 25 min | **Servings:** 4)

**Ingredients:**

- 4 sweet potatoes, scrubbed clean and dried
- 1 cup water
- 2 tablespoon butter
- 1 tablespoon fresh rosemary
- 1 teaspoon garlic powder
- salt to taste

**Directions:**

1. Into the pot, add water and place the reversible rack over the water. Use a fork to prick sweet potatoes all over and set onto the reversible rack.
2. Seal the pressure lid, choose Pressure, set to High, and set the timer to 12 minutes. Press Start. When ready, release the pressure quickly. Transfer sweet potatoes to a cutting board and slice into 1/2-inch medallions and ensure they are peeled.
3. Melt butter in the pressure cooker on Sear/Sauté. Add in the medallions and cook each side for 2 to 3 minutes until browned. Apply salt and garlic powder to season. Serve topped with fresh rosemary.

# Vegetable Tortilla Pizza

**(Ready in about:** 15 min | **Servings:** 1)

**Ingredients:**

- 4 zucchini slices
- 4 eggplant slices
- 4 red onion Rings
- ½ green bell pepper; chopped
- 3 cherry tomatoes, quartered
- 1 tortilla
- ¼ cup grated mozzarella cheese
- ¼ cup grated cheddar cheese
- 1 ½ tablespoon tomato paste
- 1 tablespoon cooked sweet corn
- ¼ teaspoon basil
- ¼ teaspoon oregano

**Directions:**

1. Spread the tomato paste on the tortilla. Arrange the zucchini and eggplant slices first, then green peppers, and onion rings.
2. Lay the cherry tomatoes and sprinkle the sweet corn over. Sprinkle with oregano and basil. Top with cheddar and mozzarella. Place in the Ninja Foodi close the crisping lid and cook for 10 minutes on Air Crisp mode at 350 F.

# Pineapple Appetizer Ribs

**(Ready in about:** 30 min | **Servings:** 4)

**Ingredients:**

- 2 lb. cut spareribs
- 2 cups water
- 5 oz. canned pineapple juice
- 7 oz. salad dressing
- Garlic salt
- Salt and black pepper

**Directions:**

1. Sprinkle the ribs with salt and pepper and place them in a saucepan. Pour water and cook the ribs for around 12 minutes on high heat. Drain the ribs and arrange them in the Ninja Foodi.
2. Sprinkle with garlic salt. Close the crisping lid and cook for 15 minutes at 390 F on Air Crisp mode.
3. Meanwhile, prepare the sauce by combining the salad dressing and the pineapple juice. Serve the ribs with this delicious dressing sauce!

## Mashed Parsnips and Cauliflower

**(Ready in about:** 15 min | **Servings:** 8)

**Ingredients:**

- 1 (1½ pounds) head cauliflower, cut into small florets
- 1 ½ pounds parsnips, peeled and cubed
- 2 cups water
- ¼ cup sour cream
- ¼ cup grated Parmesan cheese
- 2 garlic cloves
- 1 tablespoon butter
- 2 tablespoon minced chives
- ¾ teaspoon salt
- ¼ teaspoon pepper

**Directions:**

1. In the pot, mix parsnips, garlic, water, salt, cauliflower, and pepper. Seal the pressure lid, choose Pressure, set to High, and set the timer to 4 minutes. Press Start.
2. When ready, release the pressure quickly. Drain parsnips and cauliflower and return to pot; add Parmesan cheese, butter, and sour cream. Use a potato masher to mash until the desired consistency is attained.
3. Into the mashed parsnip, add 1 tablespoon chives; place to a serving plate and garnish with remaining chives.

## Potato Filled Bread Rolls

**(Ready in about:** 25 min | **Servings:** 4)

**Ingredients:**

- 8 slices of bread
- 2 green chilies, deseeded; chopped
- 5 large potatoes, boiled, mashed
- 2 sprigs curry leaf
- 1 medium onion; chopped
- 1 tablespoon olive oil
- ½ teaspoon mustard seeds
- ½ teaspoon turmeric
- Salt, to taste

**Directions:**

1. Combine the olive oil, onion, curry leaves, and mustard seed, in the Ninja Foodi basket. Cook for 5 minutes. Mix the onion mixture with the mashed potatoes, chilies, turmeric, and some salt. Divide the dough into 8 equal pieces.
2. Trim the sides of the bread, and wet it with some water. Make sure to get rid of the excess water. Take one wet bread slice in your palm and place one of the potato pieces in the center.
3. Roll the bread over the filling, sealing the edges. Place the rolls onto a prepared baking dish, close the crisping lid and cook for 12 minutes on Air Crisp at 350 F.

## Red Beans and Rice

**(Ready in about:** 1 hr | **Servings:** 4)

**Ingredients:**

- 1 cup red beans, rinsed and stones removed
- ½ cup rice, rinsed
- 1 ½ cup vegetable broth
- 1 onion; diced
- 1 red bell pepper; diced
- 1 stalk celery; diced
- 1 tablespoon fresh thyme leaves, or to taste
- 2 tablespoon olive oil
- ½ teaspoon cayenne pepper
- water as needed
- salt and freshly ground black pepper to taste

**Directions:**

1. Into the pot, add beans and water to cover about 1-inch. Seal the pressure lid, choose Pressure, set to High, and set the timer to 1 minute. Press Start. When ready, release the pressure quickly. Drain the beans and set aside. Rinse and pat dry the inner pot.

2. Return inner pot to pressure cooker, add oil to the pot and press Sear/Sauté. Add onion to the oil and cook for 3 minutes until soft. Add celery and pepper and cook for 1 to 2 minutes until fragrant. Add garlic and cook for 30 seconds until soft; add rice.
3. Transfer the beans back into inner pot and top with broth. Stir black pepper, thyme, cayenne pepper, and salt into mixture. Seal the pressure lid, choose Pressure, set to High, and set the timer to 15 minutes. Press Start.
4. When ready, release pressure quickly. Add more thyme, black pepper and salt as desired.

## Artichoke with Mayo

**(Ready in about:** 20 min | **Servings:** 4)

**Ingredients:**
- 2 large artichokes
- 2 garlic cloves, smashed
- ½ cup mayonnaise
- 2 cups water
- Juice of 1 lime
- Salt and black pepper to taste

**Directions:**
1. Using a serrated knife, trim about 1 inch from the artichokes' top. Into the pot, add water and set trivet over. Lay the artichokes on the trivet. Seal lid and cook for 14 minutes. Press Start.
2. When ready, release the pressure quickly. Mix the mayonnaise with garlic and lime juice; season with salt and pepper. Serve artichokes in a platter with garlic mayo on the side.

## Asparagus with Feta

**(Ready in about:** 15 min | **Servings:** 4)

**Ingredients:**
- 1 pound asparagus spears, ends trimmed
- 1 lemon, cut into wedges
- 1 cup feta cheese; cubed
- 1 cup water
- 1 tablespoon olive oil
- salt and freshly ground black pepper to taste

**Directions:**
1. Into the pot, add water and set trivet over the water. Place steamer basket on the trivet. Place the asparagus into the steamer basket. Seal the pressure lid, choose Pressure, set to High, and set the timer to 1 minute. Press Start.
2. When ready, release the pressure quickly. Add olive oil in a bowl and toss in asparagus until well coated; season with pepper and salt. Serve alongside feta cheese and lemon wedges.

## Avocado Rolls

**(Ready in about:** 15 min | **Servings:** 5

**Ingredients:**
- 3 avocados, pitted and peeled
- 1 tomato; diced
- 10 egg roll wrappers
- ¼ teaspoon pepper
- ½ teaspoon salt

**Directions:**
1. Place all filling Ingredients in a bowl. Mash with a fork until somewhat smooth. Divide the feeling between the egg wrappers. Wet your finger and brush along the edges so the wrappers can seal well.
2. Roll and seal the wrappers. Arrange them on the lined Ninja Foodi basket, and place into the Ninja Foodi. Close the crisping lid and cook at 350 degrees F; for 5 minutes on Air Crisp mode. Serve with chili dipping.

**(Ready in about:** 15 min | **Servings:** 1)

**Ingredients:**
- 1 small onion, finely chopped
- 2 cup grated paneer
- 1 cup grated cheese
- ½ teaspoon chai masala
- 1 teaspoon butter
- ½ teaspoon garlic powder
- ½ teaspoon oregano
- ½ teaspoon salt

**Directions:**
1. Preheat the Ninja Foodi to 350 degrees F. Oil the Ninja Foodi basket. Mix all Ingredients in a bowl, until well incorporated.
2. Make cutlets out of the mixture and place them on the greased baking dish. Place the baking dish in the Ninja Foodi and cook the cutlets for 10 minutes.

## Roasted Vegetable Salad

**(Ready in about:** 25 min | **Servings:** 1)

**Ingredients:**
- 1 potato, peeled and chopped
- 1 cup cherry tomatoes
- 1 carrot; sliced diagonally
- ½ small beetroot; sliced
- ¼ onion; sliced
- Juice of 1 lemon
- A handful of rocket salad
- A handful of baby spinach
- 2 tablespoon olive oil
- 3 tablespoon canned chickpeas
- ½ teaspoon cumin
- ½ teaspoon turmeric
- ¼ teaspoon sea salt
- Parmesan shavings

**Directions:**
1. Combine the onion, potato, cherry tomatoes, carrot, beetroot, cumin, seas salt, turmeric, and 1 tablespoon olive oil, in a bowl. Place in the Ninja Foodi, close the crisping lid and cook for 20 minutes on Air Crisp mode at 370 F; let cool for 2 minutes.
2. Place the rocket, salad, spinach, lemon juice, and 1 tablespoon olive oil, into a serving bowl. Mix to combine; stir in the roasted veggies.Top with chickpeas and Parmesan shavings.

# Desserts

## Mixed Berry Cobbler

**(Ready in about:** 40 min | **Servings:** 4)

**Ingredients:**
- 2 bags frozen mixed berries
- 1 cup sugar
- 3 tablespoons arrowroot starch

**For the topping**
- 1 cup self-rising flour
- ⅔ cup crème fraiche, plus more as needed
- 1 tablespoon melted unsalted butter
- 1 tablespoon whipping cream
- 5 tablespoons powdered sugar; divided
- ¼ teaspoon cinnamon powder

**Directions:**
1. To make the base, pour the blackberries into the inner pot along with the arrowroot starch and sugar. Mix to combine. Seal the pressure lid, choose Pressure; adjust the pressure to High and the cook time to 3 minutes; press Start. After cooking, perform a quick pressure release and carefully open the lid.
2. To make the topping, in a small bowl, whisk the flour, cinnamon powder, and 3 tablespoons of sugar. In a separate small bowl, whisk the crème fraiche with the melted butter.
3. Pour the cream mixture on the dry ingredients and combine evenly. If the mixture is too dry, mix in 1 tablespoon of crème fraiche at a time until the mixture is soft.
4. Spoon 2 to 3 tablespoons of dough on top over the peaches and spread out slightly on top. Brush the topping with the whipping cream and sprinkle with the remaining sugar.
5. Close the crisping lid and Choose Bake/Roast; adjust the temperature to 325°F and the cook time to 12 minutes. Press Start. Check after 8 minutes; if the dough isn't cooking evenly, rotate the pot about 90 degrees, and continue cooking.
6. When ready, the topping should be cooked through and lightly browned. Allow cooling before slicing. Serve warm.

## Pineapple Cake

**(Ready in about:** 50 min | **Servings:** 4)

**Ingredients:**
- 2 oz. dark chocolate, grated
- 4 oz. butter
- 7 oz. pineapple chunks
- 8 oz. self-rising flour
- ½ cup sugar
- 1 egg
- ½ cup pineapple juice
- 2 tablespoon milk

**Directions:**
1. Preheat the Foodi to 390 F. Place the butter and flour into a bowl and rub the mixture with your fingers until crumbed. Stir in the pineapple, sugar, chocolate, and juice. Beat the eggs and milk separately, and then add them to the batter.
2. Transfer the batter to a previously prepared (greased or lined) cake pan, and cook for 40 minutes on Roast mode. Let cool for at least 10 minutes before serving.

## Blueberry Muffins

**(Ready in about:** 30 min | **Servings:** 10)

**Ingredients:**
- 1 cup blueberries
- 1 ½ cup flour
- ½ cup sugar
- ¼ cup vegetable oil
- 1 egg
- 2 teaspoon vanilla extract
- 2 teaspoon baking powder
- ½ teaspoon salt
- Yogurt, as needed

**Directions:**
1. Combine all the flour, salt and baking powder in a bowl. In a bowl, place the oil, vanilla extract, and egg. Fill the rest of the bowl with yogurt.
2. Whisk the mixture until fully incorporated. Combine the wet and dry ingredients. Gently fold in the blueberries. Divide the mixture between 10 muffin cups.
3. You may need to cook in batches. Close the crisping lid and cook for 10 minutes on Air Crisp mode at 350 F, until nice and crispy.

## Molten Lava Cake

**(Ready in about:** 20 min | **Servings:** 4)

**Ingredients:**
- 3 ½ oz. butter, melted
- 3 ½ oz. dark chocolate, melted
- 2 eggs
- 3 ½ tablespoon sugar
- 1 ½ tablespoon self-rising flour

**Directions:**
1. Grease 4 ramekins with butter. Beat the eggs and sugar until frothy. Stir in the butter and chocolate.
2. Gently fold in the flour. Divide the mixture between the ramekins and bake in the Foodi for 10 minutes on Air Crisp mode at 370 F. Let cool for 2 minutes before turning the lava cakes upside down onto serving plates.

## Cinnamon Butternut Squash Pie

**(Ready in about:** 30 min | **Servings:** 4)

**Ingredients:**
- 1 pound Butternut Squash; diced
- ¼ cup Honey
- 1 cup Water
- ½ cup Milk
- 1 Egg
- ½ tablespoon Cornstarch
- ½ teaspoon Cinnamon
- A pinch of Sea Salt

**Directions:**
1. Pour the water inside your Foodi and add a reversible rack. Lower the butternut squash onto the reversible rack. Seal the pressure lid, and cook on Pressure for 4 minutes at High pressure.
2. Meanwhile, whisk all remaining ingredients in a bowl. Do a quick pressure. Drain the squash and add it to the milk mixture. Pour the batter into a greased baking dish. Place in the cooker, and seal the pressure lid.
3. Choose Pressure, set to High, and set the time to 10 minutes. Press Start. Do a quick pressure release. Transfer pie to wire rack to cool.

## Dark Chocolate Brownies

**(Ready in about:** 40 min | **Servings:** 6)

**Ingredients:**

- 1 cup water
- 2 eggs
- ¼ cup olive oil
- ⅓ cup flour
- ⅓ cup cocoa powder
- ⅓ cup dark chocolate chips
- ⅓ cup chopped Walnuts
- ⅓ cup granulated sugar
- 1 tablespoon vanilla extract
- 1 tablespoon milk
- ½ teaspoon baking powder
- A pinch salt

**Directions:**

1. In the Foodi, add water and set in the reversible rack. Line a parchment paper on. a springform pan. In a bowl, beat eggs and sugar to mix until smooth; stir in olive oil, cocoa powder, milk, salt baking powder, chocolate chips, flour, walnuts, vanilla, and sea salt.
2. Transfer the batter to the prepared springform pan and place the pan in the pot on the rack. Close the crisping lid and select Bake/Roast; adjust the temperature to 250°F and the cook time to 20 minutes. Press Start.
3. When the time is up, open the lid and. and allow the brownie to cool for 10 minutes before cutting. Use powdered sugar to dust the brownies before serving lightly.

## Lemon Cheesecake with Strawberries

**(Ready in about:** 3 hr | **Servings:** 8)

**Ingredients:**
**Crust:**

- 4 ounces graham crackers
- 3 tablespoon butter, melted
- 1 teaspoon ground cinnamon

**Filling:**

- 1 pound mascarpone cheese, at room temperature
- 2 cups water
- 1 cup strawberries, halved
- ¾ cup sugar
- ¼ cup sour cream, at room temperature
- 2 eggs, at room temperature
- 1 tablespoon lemon juice
- 1 teaspoon vanilla extract
- 1 teaspoon lemon zest
- 1 pinch salt

**Directions:**

1. In a food processor, beat cinnamon and graham crackers to attain a texture almost same as sand; mix in melted butter. Press the crumbs into the bottom of a 7-inch springform pan in an even layer.
2. In a stand mixer, beat sugar, mascarpone cheese, and sour cream for 3 minutes to combine well and have a fluffy and smooth mixture. Scrape the bowl's sides and add eggs, lemon zest, salt, lemon juice, and vanilla extract. Carry on to beat the mixture until you obtain a consistent color and all ingredients are completely combined. Pour filling over crust.
3. Into the inner pot of your Foodi, add water and set in the reversible rack. Insert the springform pan on the rack. Close the crisping lid and select Bake/Roast; adjust the temperature to 250°F and the cook time to 40 minutes. Press Start.
4. Remove cheesecake and let cool for 1 hour. Refrigerate for 2 hours. Transfer to a serving plate and garnish with strawberry halves on top. Use a paring knife to run along the edges between the pan and cheesecake to remove the cheesecake and set to the plate.

# Cranberry Cheesecake

**(Ready in about:** 1 hr | **Servings:** 8)

**Ingredients:**

- 1/3 cup dried cranberries
- 1 cup water
- ½ cup sugar
- 1 cup coarsely crumbled cookies
- 1 cup mascarpone cheese, room temperature
- 2 eggs, room temperature
- 2 tablespoon sour cream
- 2 tablespoon butter, melted
- ½ teaspoon vanilla extract

**Directions:**

1. Fold a 20-inch piece of aluminum foil in half lengthwise twice and set on the pressure cooker. In a bowl, combine melted butter and crushed cookies; press firmly to the bottom and about 1/3 of the way up the sides of a 7-inch springform pan. Freeze the crust while the filling is being prepared.
2. In a separate bowl, beat together mascarpone cheese and sugar to obtain a smooth consistency; stir in vanilla extract and sour cream. Beat one egg and add into the cheese mixture to combine well; do the same with the second egg.
3. Stir cranberries into the filling. Transfer the filling into the crust. Into the pot, add water and set the reversible rack at the bottom. Center the springform pan onto the prepared foil sling. Use the sling to lower the pan onto the reversible rack.
4. Fold foil strips out of the way of the lid. Close the crisping lid and select Bake/Roast; adjust the temperature to 250°F and the cook time to 40 minutes. Press Start.
5. When the time is up, open the lid and let to cool the cheesecake. When, transfer the cheesecake to a refrigerator for 2 hours or overnight.
6. Use a paring knife to run along the edges between the pan and cheesecake to remove the cheesecake and set to the plate.

# Raspberry Cream Tart

**(Ready in about:** 55 min+ Chilling time | **Servings:** 4)

**Ingredients:**

- 1 refrigerated piecrust, for the raspberries
- 2½ cups fresh raspberries; divided
- ¼ cup sugar
- 2 tablespoons water
- 1 tablespoon arrowroot starch
- 1 teaspoon lemon juice
- ¼ teaspoon grated lemon zest
- Pinch salt

**For The Filling**

- 8 ounces cream cheese, at room temperature
- ¼ cup heavy cream
- ½ cup confectioners' sugar
- 1 teaspoon vanilla extract

**Directions:**

1. Roll out the pie crust and fit into a tart pan. Do not stretch the dough to prevent shrinking when cooking. Use a fork to prick all over the bottom of the dough. Place the reversible rack in the pot in the lower position of the pot and put the tart pan on top.
2. Close the crisping lid, choose Bake/Roast; adjust the temperature to 250°F, and the cook time to 15 minutes. Press Start. When done baking, open the lid and check the crust. It should be set and lightly brown around the edges.
3. Close the crisping lid again. Adjust the temperature to 375°F and the cook time to 4 minutes. Press Start to begin baking.
4. After 3 minutes, check the crust, which should be a deep golden brown color by now. If not, cook for the remaining 1 minute. Remove the rack and set the crust aside to cool.
5. Fetch out 1 cup of berries into the inner pot. In a small bowl, whisk the arrowroot starch and water until smoothly mixed. Pour the slurry on the raspberries along with the sugar, lemon zest, lemon juice, and salt. Mix to distribute the slurry among the raspberries.

6. Seal the pressure lid, choose Pressure; adjust the pressure to High and the cook time to 2 minutes. Press Start.
7. Once done cooking, perform a quick pressure release and carefully open the lid. The raspberries will have softened. Add the remaining 1½ cups of raspberries, stirring to coat with the cooked mixture. Then, allow cooling.
8. To make the cream filling, in a bowl and with a hand mixer, whisk the vanilla extract and cream cheese until evenly combined and smooth. Mix in the confectioners' sugar and whisk again until the sugar has fully incorporated and the mixture is light and smooth.
9. With clean whisks and in another bowl, beat the heavy cream until soft peaks form. Fold the heavy cream into the vanilla mixture until both are evenly combined. To assemble, spoon the cream filling into the piecrust and scatter the remaining raspberries on the cream. Chill for 30 minutes before cutting and serving.

## Vanilla Cheesecake

(**Ready in about:** 60 min | **Servings:** 6)

**Ingredients:**

- 16 ounces cream cheese, at room temperature
- 2 eggs
- ¼ cup sour cream
- 1½ cups finely crushed graham crackers
- 1 cup water
- ½ cup brown sugar
- 2 tablespoons sugar
- 1 tablespoon all-purpose flour
- 4 tablespoons unsalted butter, melted
- 1½ teaspoons vanilla extract
- ½ teaspoon salt
- Cooking spray

**Directions:**

1. Grease a spring form pan with cooking spray, then line the pan with parchment paper, grease with cooking spray again, and line with aluminium foil. This is to ensure that there are no air gaps in the pan. In a medium mixing bowl, mix the graham cracker crumbs, sugar, and butter. Spoon the mixture into the pan and press firmly into with a spoon.
2. In a deep bowl and with a hand mixer, beat the beat the cream cheese and brown sugar until well-mixed. Whisk in the sour cream to be smooth and stir in the flour, vanilla, and salt.
3. Crack the eggs in and beat but not to be overly smooth. Pour the mixture into the pan over the crumbs. Next, pour the water into the pot. Put the spring form pan on the reversible rack and put the rack in the lower positon of the pot.
4. Seal the pressure lid, choose Pressure, set to High, and set the time to 35 minutes. Choose Start/Stop to begin. Once done baking, perform a natural pressure release for 10 minutes, then a quick pressure release to let out any remaining pressure. Carefully open the lid.
5. Remove the pan from the rack and allow the cheesecake to cool for 1 hour. Cover the cheesecake with foil and chill in the refrigerator for 4 hours.

## Apple Vanilla Hand Pies

(**Ready in about:** 40 min | **Servings:** 8)

**Ingredients:**

- 2 apples, peeled, cored, and diced
- 1 (2-crust) package refrigerated piecrusts, at room temperature
- 1 lemon, juiced
- 3 tablespoons sugar
- ¼ teaspoon salt
- 1 teaspoon vanilla extract
- 1 teaspoon corn-starch
- Cooking spray

**Directions:**

1. In a large mixing bowl, combine the apples, sugar, lemon juice, salt, and vanilla. Allow the mixture to stand for 10 minutes, then drain, and reserve 1 tablespoon of the liquid. In a small bowl, whisk the corn-starch into the reserved liquid and then, mix with the apple mixture. Put the crisping basket in the

pot and close the crisping lid. Choose Air Crisp, set the temperature to 350°F, and the time to 5 minutes. Press Start/Stop to preheat.

2. Put the piecrusts on a lightly floured surface and cut into 8 (4-inch- diameter) circles. Spoon a tablespoon of apple mixture in the center of the circle, with ½ an inch's border around the dough. Brush the edges with water and fold the dough over the filling. Press the edges with a fork to seal.

3. Cut 3 small slits on top of each pie and oil with cooking spray. Arrange the pies in a single layer in the preheated basket. Close the crisping lid. Choose Air Crisp, set the temperature to 350°F, and set the time to 12 minutes. Press Start/Stop to begin baking. Once done baking, remove, and place the pies on a wire rack to cool. Repeat with the remaining hand pies.

## Pumpkin Cake

### (Ready in about: 1 hr 30 min | Servings: 8)

**Ingredients:**

- 1 cup packed shredded pumpkin, plus more for topping
- ½ cup chopped walnuts
- 2 cups water
- 1 cup flour
- ⅔ cup sugar
- ½ cup half-and-half

- ¼ cup olive oil
- 3 eggs
- 1 teaspoon baking powder
- 1 teaspoon vanilla extract
- 1 teaspoon ground cinnamon
- ½ teaspoon ground nutmeg

**Frosting:**

- 4 ounces cream cheese, room temperature
- ½ cup confectioners sugar
- 8 tablespoon butter

- ½ teaspoon vanilla extract
- ⅛ teaspoon salt

**Directions:**

1. In a bowl, beat eggs and sugar to get a smooth mixture; mix in oil, flour, vanilla extract, cinnamon, half-and-half, baking powder, and nutmeg. Stir well to obtain a fluffy batter; fold walnuts and pumpkin through the batter. Add batter into a 6-inch cake pan and cover with aluminum foil.

2. Into the pot, add water and set the reversible rack over the water. Lay cake pan gently onto the trivet. Close the crisping lid and select Bake/Roast; adjust the temperature to 250°F and the cook time to 40 minutes. Press Start.

3. Beat cream cheese, confectioners' sugar, salt, vanilla extract, and butter in a mixing bowl until smooth; place in the refrigerator until needed for use.

4. Remove cake from the pan and transfer to the cooking wire rack to cool. Over the cake, spread frosting and apply a topping of shredded carrots, as desired.

## Cinnamon Apple Crisp

### (Ready in about: 30 min | Servings: 5)

**Ingredients:**
**Topping:**

- ½ cup old-fashioned rolled oats
- ½ cup granulated sugar

- ½ cup oat flour
- ¼ cup olive oil

**Filling:**

- 5 apples, peeled, cored, and halved
- ½ cup water
- 2 tablespoon arrowroot powder

- ¼ teaspoon ground nutmeg
- ½ teaspoon vanilla paste
- 1 teaspoon ground cinnamon

**Directions:**

1. In a bowl, combine sugar, oat flour, rolled oats, and olive oil to form coarse crumbs. Ladle the apples into the pressure cooker. Mix water with arrowroot powder in a small bowl; stir in salt, nutmeg, cinnamon, and vanilla and toss in the apples to coat.

2. Apply oat topping to the apples. Seal the pressure lid, choose Pressure, set to High, and set the timer to 10 minutes. Press Start. Release pressure naturally for 5 minutes, then release the remaining pressure quickly.

## Fruity Sauce

(**Ready in about:** 15 min | **Servings:** 2)

**Ingredients:**
- 1 cup Pineapple Chunks
- ¼ cup Almonds; chopped
- ¼ cup Fresh Orange Juice
- 1 cup Berry Mix
- 2 Apples, peeled and diced
- 1 tablespoon Olive Oil

**Directions:**
1. Pour ½ cup of water, orange juice, and fruits, in the Foodi. Give it a good stir and seal the pressure lid. Press Pressure and set the timer to 5 minutes at High. Press Start.
2. When it goes off, release the pressure quickly. Blend the mixture with a hand blender and immediately stir in the coconut oil. Serve sprinkled with chopped almonds. Enjoy!

## Chocolaty Fudge

(**Ready in about:** 55 min | **Servings:** 8)

**Ingredients:**
- 1 oz. cocoa powder
- 4 oz. butter
- 7 oz. flour, sifted
- 1 cup sugar
- ¼ cup milk
- 2 eggs
- 1 tablespoon honey
- 1 teaspoon vanilla extract
- 1 orange, juice and zest

**Icing:**
- 4 oz. powdered sugar
- 1 oz. butter, melted
- 1 tablespoon milk
- 1 tablespoon brown sugar
- 2 teaspoon honey

**Directions:**
1. In a bowl, mix the dry ingredients for the fudge. Mix the wet ingredients separately. Combine the two mixtures gently. Transfer the batter to a prepared Foodi basket. Close the crisping lid and cook for about 35 minutes on Roast mode at 350 F.
2. Once the timer beeps, check to ensure the cake is cooked. For the Topping: whisk together all of the icing ingredients. When the cake is cooled, coat it with the icing. Let set before slicing the fudge.

## Filling Coconut and Oat Cookies

(**Ready in about:** 30 min | **Servings:** 4)

**Ingredients:**
- 5 ½ oz. flour
- 3 oz. sugar
- 1 small egg, beaten
- ¼ cup coconut flakes
- ½ cup oats
- 1 teaspoon vanilla extract

**Filling:**
- 4 oz. powdered sugar
- 1 oz. white chocolate, melted
- 2 oz. butter
- 1 teaspoon vanilla extract

**Directions:**
1. Beat all cookie ingredients, with an electric mixer, except the flour. When smooth, fold in the flour. Drop spoonfuls of the batter onto a prepared cookie sheet. Close the crisping lid and cook in the Foodi at 350 F for about 18 minutes on Air Crisp mode; let cool.
2. Prepare the filling by beating all ingredients together. Spread the mixture on half of the cookies. Top with the other halves to make cookie sandwiches.

## Egg Custard

(**Ready in about:** 20 min | **Servings:** 4)

**Ingredients:**
- 1 Egg plus 2 Egg yolks
- ½ cups Milk
- 2 cups Heavy Cream
- 2 cups Water
- ½ cup Sugar
- ½ teaspoon pure rum extract

**Directions:**
1. Beat the egg and the egg yolks in a bowl. Gently add pure rum extract. Mix in the milk and heavy cream. Give it a good, and add the sugar. Pour this mixture into 4 ramekins.
2. Add 2 cups of water, insert the reversible rack, and lay the ramekins on the reversible rack. Choose Pressure, set to High, and set the time to 10 minutes. Press Start. Do a quick pressure release. Wait a bit before removing from ramekins.

## Lime Muffins

(**Ready in about:** 30 min | **Servings:** 6)

**Ingredients:**
- 2 eggs plus 1 yolk
- 1 cup yogurt
- ¼ cup superfine sugar
- Juice and zest of 2 limes
- 8 oz. cream cheese
- 1 teaspoon vanilla extract

**Directions:**
1. With a spatula, gently combine the yogurt and cheese. In another bowl, beat together the rest of the ingredients.
2. Gently fold the lime with the cheese mixture. Divide the batter between 6 lined muffin tins. Close the crisping lid and cook in the Foodi for 10 minutes on Air Crisp mode at 330 F.

## Lemon and Blueberries Compote

(**Ready in about:** 10 min + chilling time | **Servings:** 4 |)

**Ingredients:**
- 2 cups Blueberries
- ½ cup Water + 2 tbsp.
- ¾ cups Coconut Sugar
- 2 tablespoon Cornstarch
- Juice of ½ Lemon

**Directions:**
1. Place blueberries, lemon juice, ½ cup water, and coconut sugar in your cooker. Seal the pressure lid, choose Steam and set the timer to 3 minutes at High pressure. Press Start. Once done, do a quick pressure.
2. Meanwhile, combine the cornstarch and water, in a bowl. Stir in the mixture into the blueberries and cook until the mixture thickens, pressure lid off, on Sear/Sauté. Transfer the compote to a bowl and let cool completely before refrigerating for 2 hours.

## Fried Snickerdoodle Poppers

(**Ready in about:** 30 min | **Servings:** 6)

**Ingredients:**
- 1 box instant vanilla Jell-O
- 1 ½ cups cinnamon sugar
- 1 can of Pillsbury Grands Flaky Layers Biscuits
- Melted butter, for brushing

**Directions:**
1. Unroll the flaky biscuits and cut them into fourths. Roll each ¼ into a ball. Arrange the balls on a lined baking sheet, and cook in the Foodi for 7 minutes, or until golden, on Air Crisp mode at 350 F.
2. Prepare the Jell-O following the package's instructions. Using an injector, inject some of the vanilla pudding into each ball. Brush the balls with melted butter and then coat them with cinnamon sugar.

## Apple Cider

**(Ready in about:** 45 min | **Servings:** 6)

**Ingredients:**
- 6 green apples, cored and chopped
- 1/4 cup orange juice
- 3 cups water
- 2 cinnamon sticks

**Directions:**
1. In a blender, add orange juice, apples, and water and blend until smooth; use a fine-mesh strainer to strain and press using a spoon. Get rid of the pulp. In the cooker, mix the strained apple puree, and cinnamon sticks.
2. Seal the pressure lid, choose Pressure, set to High, and set the timer to 10 minutes. Press Start. Release the pressure naturally for 15 minutes, then quick release the remaining pressure. Strain again and do away with the solids.

## Berry Vanilla Pudding

**(Ready in about:** 35 min + 6h for refrigeration | **Servings:** 4)

**Ingredients:**
- 4 raspberries
- 4 blueberries
- 4 egg yolks
- ½ cup sugar
- ½ cup milk
- 1 cup heavy cream
- 1 teaspoon vanilla extract
- 4 tablespoon water + 1 ½ cups water

**Directions:**
1. Turn on your Foodi and select Sear/Sauté mode on Medium. Add four tablespoons for water and the sugar. Stir it constantly until it dissolves. Press Stop. Add milk, heavy cream, and vanilla. Stir it with a whisk until evenly combined.
2. Crack the eggs into a bowl and add a tablespoon of the cream mixture. Whisk it and then very slowly add the remaining cream mixture while whisking. Fit the reversible rack at the bottom of the pot, and pour one and a half cup of water in it. Pour the mixture into four ramekins and place them on the rack.
3. Close the lid of the pot, secure the pressure valve, and select Pressure mode on High Pressure for 4 minutes. Press Start/Stop. Once the timer has gone off, do a quick pressure release, and open the lid.
4. With a napkin in hand, carefully remove the ramekins onto a flat surface. Let cool for about 15 minutes and then refrigerate them for 6 hours.
5. After 6 hours, remove them from the refrigerator and garnish them with the raspberries and blueberries. Enjoy immediately or refrigerate further until dessert time is ready.

## Créme Brulee

**(Ready in about:** 30 min + 6 hours of cooling | **Servings:** 4)

**Ingredients:**
- 3 cups heavy whipping cream
- 7 large egg yolks
- 2 cups water
- 6 tablespoon sugar
- 2 tablespoon vanilla extract

**Directions:**
1. In a mixing bowl, add the yolks, vanilla, whipping cream, and half of the swerve sugar. Use a whisk to mix them until they are well combined. Pour the mixture into the ramekins and cover them with aluminium foil.
2. Open the Foodi, fit the reversible rack into the pot, and pour in the water.
3. Place 3 ramekins on the rack and place the remaining ramekins to sit on the edges of the ramekins below.
4. Close the lid, secure the pressure valve, and select Pressure mode on High for 8 minutes. Press Start/Stop.
5. Once the timer has stopped, do a natural pressure release for 10 minutes, then a quick pressure release to let out the remaining pressure.

6. With a napkin in hand, remove the ramekins onto a flat surface and then into a refrigerator to chill for at least 6 hours. After refrigeration, remove the ramekins and remove the aluminium foil.
7. Equally, sprinkle the remaining sugar on it and return to the pot. Close the crisping lid, select Bake/Roast mode, set the timer to 4 minutes on 380 degrees F. Serve the crème brulee chilled with whipped cream.

## Poached Peaches

### (**Ready in about:** 15 min | Serves: 4)

**Ingredients:**
- 4 Peaches, peeled, pits removed
- 1 cup Freshly Squeezed Orange Juice
- ½ cup Black Currants
- 1 Cinnamon Stick

**Directions:**
1. Place black currants and orange juice in a blender. Blend until the mixture becomes smooth. Pour the mixture in your Foodi, and add the cinnamon stick.
2. Add the peaches to the steamer basket and then insert the basket into the pot. Seal the pressure lid, select Pressure, and set to 5 minutes at High pressure. When done, do a quick pressure release. Serve the peaches drizzled with sauce, to enjoy!

## Cheat Apple Pie

### (**Ready in about:** 30 min | **Servings:** 9)

**Ingredients:**
- 4 apples; diced
- 1 egg, beaten
- 3 large puff pastry sheets
- 2 oz. sugar
- 1 oz. brown sugar
- 2 oz. butter, melted
- 2 teaspoon cinnamon
- ¼ teaspoon salt

**Directions:**
1. Whisk the white sugar, brown sugar, cinnamon, salt, and butter together. Place the apples in a baking dish and coat them with the mixture.
2. Slide the dish into the Foodi and cook for 10 minutes on Roast at 350 F.
3. Meanwhile, roll out the pastry on a floured flat surface, and cut each sheet into 6 equal pieces. Divide the apple filling between the parts.
4. Brush the edges of the pastry squares with the egg. Fold and seal the edges with a fork. Place on a lined baking sheet and cook in the fryer at 350 F for 8 minutes on Roast. Flip over, increase the temperature to 390 F, and cook for 2 more minutes.

## Valencian Horchata

### (**Ready in about:** 20 min | **Servings:** 6)

**Ingredients:**
- 1 cup chufa seed, overnight soak
- ¼ stick cinnamon
- Zest from 1 lemon
- 2 cups water
- 4 cups cold water
- 2 tablespoon sugar

**Directions:**
1. In the pot, combine cinnamon, chufa seed and 4 cups water. Seal the pressure lid, choose Pressure, set to High, and set the timer to 1 minute. Press Start. Release pressure naturally for 10 minutes, then release the remaining pressure quickly. In a blender, add chufa seed mixture, lemon zest and sugar. Blend well to form a paste.
2. Add 2 cups cold water into a large container. Strain the blended chufa mixture into the water. Mix well and place in the refrigerator until ready for serving. Add cinnamon stick for garnishing.

## Strawberry and Lemon Ricotta Cheesecake

**(Ready in about:** 35 min | **Servings:** 6)

**Ingredients:**

- 10 strawberries, halved to decorate
- 10 oz. cream cheese
- 1 ½ cups water
- ¼ cup sugar
- ½ cup Ricotta cheese
- One lemon, zested and juiced
- 2 eggs, cracked into a bowl
- 3 tablespoon sour cream
- 1 teaspoon lemon extract

**Directions:**

1. In the electric mixer, add the cream cheese, quarter cup of sugar, ricotta cheese, lemon zest, lemon juice, and lemon extract. Turn on the mixer and mix the ingredients until a smooth consistency is formed. Adjust the sweet taste to liking with more sugar.
2. Reduce the speed of the mixer and add the eggs. Fold it in at low speed until it is fully incorporated. Make sure not to fold the eggs in high speed to prevent a cracker crust. Grease the spring form pan with cooking spray and use a spatula to spoon the mixture into the pan. Level the top with the spatula and cover it with foil.
3. Open the Foodi, fit in the reversible rack, and pour in the water. Place the cake pan on the rack. Close the lid, secure the pressure valve, and select Pressure mode on High pressure for 15 minutes. Press Start/Stop.
4. Meanwhile, mix the sour cream and one tablespoon of sugar. Set aside. Once the timer has gone off, do a natural pressure release for 10 minutes, then a quick pressure release to let out any extra steam, and open the lid.
5. Remove the rack with pan, place the spring form pan on a flat surface, and open it. Use a spatula to spread the sour cream mixture on the warm cake. Refrigerate the cake for 8 hours. Top with strawberries; slice it into 6 pieces and serve while firming.

## Chocolate Soufflé

**(Ready in about:** 25 min | **Servings:** 2)

**Ingredients:**

- 2 eggs, whites and yolks separated
- 3 oz. chocolate, melted
- ¼ cup butter, melted
- 2 tablespoon flour
- 3 tablespoon sugar
- ½ teaspoon vanilla extract

**Directions:**

1. Beat the yolks along with the sugar and vanilla extract. Stir in butter, chocolate, and flour. Whisk the whites until a stiff peak forms.
2. Working in batches, gently combine the egg whites with the chocolate mixture. Divide the batter between two greased ramekins. Close the crisping lid and cook for 14 minutes on Roast at 330 F.

## Raspberry Crumble

**(Ready in about:** 40 min | **Servings:** 6)

**Ingredients:**

- 1 (16-ounce) package frozen raspberries
- ½ cup rolled oats
- ⅓ cup cold unsalted butter; cut into pieces
- ½ cup all-purpose flour
- ⅔ cup brown sugar
- ½ cup water, plus 1 tablespoon
- 2 tablespoons arrowroot starch
- 5 tablespoons sugar; divided
- 1 teaspoon freshly squeezed lemon juice
- 1 teaspoon cinnamon powder

**Directions:**

1. Place the raspberries in the baking pan. In a small mixing bowl, combine the arrowroot starch, 1 tablespoon of water, lemon juice, and 3 tablespoons of sugar. Pour the mixture all over the raspberries.

2. Put the reversible rack in the lower position of the pot. Cover the pan with foil and pour the remaining water into the pot. Put the pan on the rack in the pot. Put the pressure lid together, and lock in the Seal position. Choose Pressure, set to High, and set the time to 10 minutes, then Choose Start/Stop to begin.
3. In a bowl, mix the flour, brown sugar, oats, butter, cinnamon, and remaining sugar until crumble forms. When done pressure-cooking, do a quick release and carefully open the lid.
4. Remove the foil and stir the fruit mixture. After, spread the crumble evenly on the berries. Close the crisping lid; choose Air Crisp, set the temperature to 400°F, and the time to 10 minutes. Choose Start/Stop to begin crisping. Cook until the top has browned and the fruit is bubbling. When done baking, remove the rack with the pan from the pot, and serve.

## Caramel Walnut Brownies

**(Ready in about:** 60 min+ cooling time | **Servings:** 4)

**Ingredients:**

- 2 large eggs, at room temperature
- 8 ounces white chocolate
- 1 cup sugar
- ½ cup caramel sauce
- ½ cup toasted walnuts
- ¾ cup all-purpose flour
- 8 tablespoons unsalted butter
- 2 teaspoons almond extract
- A pinch of salt
- Cooking spray

**Directions:**

1. Put the white chocolate and butter in a small bowl and pour 1 cup of water into the inner pot. Place the reversible rack in the lower position of the pot and put the bowl on top.
2. Close the crisping lid. Choose Bake/Roast; adjust the temperature to 375°F and the cook time to 10 minutes to melt the white chocolate and butter. Press Start. Check after 5 minutes and stir. As soon as the chocolate has melted, remove the bowl from the pot.
3. Use a small spatula to transfer the chocolate mixture into a medium and stir in the almond extract, sugar, and salt. One after another, crack each egg into the bowl and whisk after each addition. Mix in the flour until smooth, about 1 minute.
4. Grease a round cake pan with cooking spray or line the pan with parchment paper. Pour the batter into the prepared pan and place on the rack.
5. Close the crisping lid and Choose Bake/Roast; adjust the temperature to 250°F and the cook time to 25 minutes. Press Start. Once the time is up, open the lid and check the brownies. The top should be just set. Blot out the butter that may pool to the top using a paper towel.
6. Close the crisping lid again and adjust the temperature to 300°F and the cook time to 15 minutes. Press Start. Once the time is up, open the lid and check the brownies. A toothpick inserted into the center should come out with crumbs sticking to it but no raw batter.
7. Generously drizzle the caramel sauce on top of the brownies and scatter the walnuts on top. Close the crisping lid again and adjust the temperature to 325°F and the cook time to 8 minutes; press Start.
8. When the nuts are brown and the caramel is bubbling, take out the brownies, and allow cooling for at least 30 minutes and cut into squares.

## Coconut Cake

**(Ready in about:** 55 min | **Servings:** 4)

**Ingredients:**

- 3 Eggs, Yolks and Whites separated
- ½ cup Coconut Sugar
- ¾ cup Coconut Flour
- 1 ½ cups warm Coconut Milk
- 1 cup Water
- 2 tablespoon Coconut Oil, melted
- ½ teaspoon Coconut Extract

**Directions:**

1. In a bowl, beat in the egg yolks along with the coconut sugar. In a separate bowl, beat the whites until soft form peaks.
2. Stir in coconut extract and coconut oil. Gently fold in the coconut flour. Line a baking dish and pour the batter inside. Cover with aluminum foil.

3. Pour the water in your Foodi and add a reversible rack. Lower the dish onto the rack.
4. Seal the pressure lid, choose Pressure, set to High, and set the time to 35 minutes. Press Start. Do a quick pressure release, and serve.

## Savory Peaches with Chocolate Biscuits

**(Ready in about:** 20 min | **Servings:** 4)

**Ingredients:**

- 4 small Peaches, halved lengthwise and pitted
- 8 dried Dates; chopped
- 1 cup Coarsely Crumbled Cookies
- 4 tablespoon Walnuts; chopped
- ¼ teaspoon grated nutmeg
- ¼ teaspoon ground Cloves
- 1 teaspoon Cinnamon Powder

**Directions:**

1. Pour 2 cups of water into the Foodi and add a reversible rack. Arrange the peaches on a greased baking dish cut-side-up. To prepare the filling, mix all of the remaining ingredients.
2. Stuff the peaches with the mixture. Cover with aluminium foil and lower it onto the reversible rack. Seal the lid, choose Pressure, set to High, and set the time to 15 minutes. Press Start. Do a quick pressure release.

## Pecan Stuffed Apples

**(Ready in about:** 20 min | **Servings:** 6)

**Ingredients:**

- 3 ½ pounds Apples, cored
- 1 ¼ cups Red Wine
- ¼ cup Pecans; chopped
- ¼ cup Graham Cracker Crumbs
- ½ cup dried Apricots; chopped
- ¼ cup Sugar
- ½ teaspoon grated Nutmeg
- ½ teaspoon ground Cinnamon
- ¼ teaspoon Cardamom

**Directions:**

1. Lay the apples at the bottom of your cooker, and pour in the red wine. Combine the other ingredients, except the crumbs.
2. Seal the pressure lid, and cook at High pressure for 15 minutes. Once ready, do a quick pressure release. Top with graham cracker crumbs and serve!

## Moon Milk

**(Ready in about:** 10 min | **Servings:** 2)

**Ingredients:**

- 1/4 cup hemp hearts
- 1 cup milk
- 1 pinch ground nutmeg
- 1 pinch ground ginger
- 1 pinch freshly ground black pepper
- ½ teaspoon maca powder
- 1/8 teaspoon ground cardamom
- ½ teaspoon ground cinnamon, plus more for garnish
- 1 teaspoon coconut oil
- ½ teaspoon ground turmeric
- 1 teaspoon honey

**Directions:**

1. To the Foodi, add milk. Press Sear/Sauté and heat the milk for 3-4 minutes until the point of starting to bubble; stir in coconut oil, turmeric, nutmeg, pepper, ginger, hemp hearts, maca powder, cinnamon, and cardamom.
2. Press Start/Stop and allow mixture to cool for about a minute; whisk in honey. Transfer the mixture into a mug. Add more cinnamon for garnishing!

## Brown Sugar and Butter Bars

(**Ready in about:** 55 min | **Servings:** 6)

**Ingredients:**
- 1 ½ cups Water
- 1 cup Oats
- ½ cup Brown Sugar
- ½ cup Sugar
- 1 cup Flour
- ½ cup Peanut Butter, softened
- ½ cup Butter, softened
- 1 Egg
- ½ teaspoon Baking Soda
- ½ teaspoon Salt

**Directions:**
1. Grease a springform pan and line it with parchment paper. Set aside. Beat together the eggs, peanut butter, butter, salt, white sugar, and brown sugar. Fold in the oats, flour, and baking soda.
2. Press the batter into the pan. Cover the pan with a paper towel and with a piece of foil. Pour the water into the Foodi and add a reversible rack. Lower the springform pan onto the rack.
3. Seal the pressure lid, choose Pressure, set to High, and set the time to 35 minutes. Press Start. When ready, do a quick release. Wait for 15 minutes before inverting onto a plate and cutting into bars.

## Tiramisu Cheesecake

(**Ready in about:** 1 hour + chilling time | **Servings:** 12)

**Ingredients:**
- 16 ounces Cream Cheese, softened
- 8 ounces Mascarpone Cheese, softened
- 2 Eggs
- ½ cup White Sugar
- 1 ½ cups Ladyfingers, crushed
- 1 tablespoon Cocoa Powder
- 2 tablespoon Powdered Sugar
- 1 tablespoon Kahlua Liquor
- 1 tablespoon Granulated Espresso
- 1 tablespoon Butter, melted
- 1 teaspoon Vanilla Extract

**Directions:**
1. In a bowl beat the cream cheese, mascarpone, and white sugar. Gradually beat in the eggs, the powdered sugar and vanilla. Combine the first 4 ingredients, in another bowl. Spray a springform pan with cooking spray. Press the ladyfinger crust at the bottom. Pour the filling over. Cover the pan with a paper towel and then close it with aluminum foil.
2. Pour 1 cup of water in your Foodi and lower the reversible rack. Place the pan inside and seal the pressure lid. Select Pressure and set time to 35 minutes at High pressure. Press Start. Press Start.
3. Wait for about 10 minutes before releasing the pressure quickly. Allow to cool completely before refrigerating the cheesecake for 4 hours.

## New York Cheese cake

(**Ready in about:** 1 hr | **Servings:** 12)

**Ingredients:**
**For the Crust:**
- 1 cup graham crackers crumbs
- 2 tablespoon butter, melted
- 1/8 teaspoon salt
- 1 teaspoon sugar

**For the Filling:**
- ½ cup sugar
- 2 cups cream cheese, at room temperature
- 2 eggs, at room temperature
- 1 pinch salt
- 1 teaspoon vanilla extract
- Zest from 1 orange

**Directions:**
1. Fold a 20-inch piece of aluminum foil in half lengthwise twice and set on the pressure cooker. Spray a parchment paper with cooking spray and line to the base of a 7-inch springform pan.
2. In a bowl, combine melted butter, salt, sugar and graham crackers crumbs; press into the bottom and about ⅓ up the sides of the pan. Transfer the pan to the freezer as you prepare the filling.

3. In a separate bowl, beat sugar, cream cheese, salt, orange zest, and vanilla until smooth. Beat eggs into the filling, one at a time. Stir until combined. Add the filling over the chilled crust in the pan.
4. To the Foodi, add 1 cup water and set the reversible rack into the pot. Carefully center the springform pan on the prepared foil sling. Lower pan into the inner pot using sling and place on steam reversible rack.
5. Close the crisping lid and select Bake/Roast; adjust the temperature to 250°F and the cook time to 40 minutes. Press Start.
6. Let cool the cheesecake before transferring to a refrigerator for 2 hours or overnight. Use a paring knife to run along the edges between the pan and cheesecake to remove the cheesecake and set to the plate.

## Coconut Milk Crème Caramel

**(Ready in about:** 20 min | **Servings:** 4)

**Ingredients:**
- 7 ounces Condensed Coconut Milk
- 1 ½ cups Water
- ½ cup Coconut Milk
- 2 Eggs
- ½ teaspoon Vanilla
- 4 tablespoon Caramel Syrup

**Directions:**
1. Divide the caramel syrup between 4 small ramekins. Pour water in the Foodi and add the reversible rack. In a bowl, beat the rest of the ingredients. Divide them between the ramekins. Cover them with aluminum foil and lower onto the reversible rack.
2. Seal the pressure lid, and choose Pressure, set to High, and set the time to 15 minutes. Press Start. Once cooking is completed, do a quick pressure release. Let cool completely. To unmold the flan, insert a spatula along the ramekin' sides and flip onto a dish.

## Cinnamon Mulled Red Wine

**(Ready in about:** 30 min | **Servings:** 6)

**Ingredients:**
- 2 cardamom pods
- 8 cinnamon sticks
- 3 cups red wine
- 1/4 cup honey
- 6 whole cloves
- 6 whole black peppercorns
- 6 tangerine wedges
- 2 tangerines; sliced
- 1 teaspoon fresh ginger; sliced
- 1 teaspoon ground cinnamon

**Directions:**
1. In the Foodi, combine red wine, honey, cardamom pods, 2 cinnamon sticks, cloves, tangerines slices, ginger, and peppercorns. Seal the pressure lid, choose Pressure, set to High, and set the timer to 5 minutes. Press Start.
2. Release pressure naturally for 20 minutes. Press Start. Using a fine mesh strainer, strain your wine. Discard spices.
3. Divide the warm wine into glasses and add tangerine wedges and a cinnamon stick for garnishing before serving.

## Milk Dumplings in Sweet Sauce

**(Ready in about:** 30 min | **Servings:** 20) |

**Ingredients:**
- 2 ½ cups Sugar
- 6 cups Milk
- 6 cups Water
- 3 tablespoon Lime Juice
- 1 teaspoon ground Cardamom

**Directions:**
1. Bring to a boil the milk, on Sear/Sauté, and stir in the lime juice. The solids should start to separate. Pour milk through a cheesecloth-lined colander. Drain as much liquid as you can. Place the paneer on a smooth surface. Form a ball and divide into 20 equal pieces.

2. Pour water in the Foofi and bring to a boil on Sear/Sauté. Add in sugar and cardamom and cook until dissolved. Shape the dumplings into balls, and place them in the syrup.
3. Seal the pressure lid and choose Pressure, set to High, and set the time to 5 minutes. Press Start. Once done, do a quick pressure release. Let cool and refrigerate for at least 2 hours.

## Vanilla Hot Lava Cake

(**Ready in about:** 40 min | **Servings:** 8)

**Ingredients:**
- 1 ½ cups chocolate chips
- 1 ½ cups sugar
- 1 cup butter
- 1 cup water
- 5 eggs
- 7 tablespoon flour
- 4 tablespoon milk
- 4 teaspoon vanilla extract
- Powdered sugar to garnish

**Directions:**
1. Grease the cake pan with cooking spray and set aside. Open the Foodi, fit the reversible rack at the bottom of it, and pour in the water. In a medium heatproof bowl, add the butter and chocolate and melt them in the microwave for about 2 minutes. Remove it from the microwave.
2. Add sugar and use a spatula to stir it well. Add the eggs, milk, and vanilla extract and stir again. Finally, add the flour and stir it until even and smooth.
3. Pour the batter into the greased cake pan and use the spatula to level it. Place the pan on the trivet in the pot, close the lid, secure the pressure valve, and select Pressure on High for 15 minutes. Press Start/Stop.
4. Once the timer has gone off, do a natural pressure release for 10 minutes, then a quick pressure release, and open the lid.
5. Remove the rack with the pan on it and place the pan on a flat surface. Put a plate over the pan and flip the cake over into the plate. Pour the powdered sugar in a fine sieve and sift it over the cake. Use a knife to cut the cake into 8 slices and serve immediately (while warm).

## Chocolate Fondue

(**Ready in about:** 5 min | **Servings:** 12)

**Ingredients:**
- 10 ounces Milk Chocolate; chopped into small pieces
- 1 ½ cups Lukewarm Water
- 8 ounces Heavy Whipping Cream
- 2 teaspoon Coconut Liqueur
- ¼ teaspoon Cinnamon Powder
- A pinch of Salt

**Directions:**
1. Melt the chocolate in a heat-proof recipient. Add the remaining ingredients, except for the liqueur. Transfer this recipient to the metal reversible rack. Pour 1 ½ cups of water into the cooker, and place a reversible rack inside.
2. Seal the pressure lid, choose Pressure, set to High, and set the time to 5 minutes. Press Start. Once the cooking is complete, do a quick pressure release. Pull out the container with tongs. Mix in the coconut liqueur and serve right now with fresh fruits. Enjoy!

# Cherry Pie

**(Ready in about:** 45 min **| Servings:** 6)

**Ingredients:**

- 1 9-inch double Pie Crust
- 4 cups Cherries, pitted
- 1 cup Sugar
- 2 cups Water
- 4 tablespoon Quick Tapioca
- ½ teaspoon Vanilla Extract
- ¼ teaspoon Almond Extract
- A pinch of Salt

**Directions:**

1. Pour water inside your cooker and add the reversible rack. Combine the cherries with tapioca, sugar, extracts, and salt, in a bowl. Place one pie crust at the bottom of a lined springform pan.
2. Spread the cherries mixture and top with the other crust. Lower the pan onto the reversible rack.
3. Seal the pressure lid, choose Pressure, set to High, and set the time to 18 minutes. Press Start. Once cooking is completed, do a quick pressure release. Let cool the pie on a cooling rack. Slice to serve.

# Almond Banana Dessert

**(Ready in about:** 8 min **| Servings:** 1)

**Ingredients:**

- 1 Banana; sliced
- 2 tablespoon Almond Butter
- 1 tablespoon Coconut oil
- ½ teaspoon Cinnamon

**Directions:**

1. Melt oil on Sear/Sauté mode. Add banana slices and fry them for a couple of minutes, or until golden on both sides. Top the fried bananas with almond butter and sprinkle with cinnamon.

# Ninja Pear Wedges

**(Ready in about:** 15 min **| Servings:** 3)

**Ingredients:**

- 2 Large Pears, peeled and cut into wedges
- 3 tablespoon Almond Butter
- 2 tablespoon Olive Oil

**Directions:**

1. Pour 1 cup of water in the Foodi. Place the pear wedges in a steamer basket and then lower the basket at the bottom. Seal the pressure lid, and cook for 2 minutes on High pressure.
2. When the timer goes off, do a quick pressure release. Remove the basket, discard the water and wipe clean the cooker. Press the Sear/Sauté and heat the oil. Add the pears and cook until browned. Top them with almond butter, to serve.

# Orange Banana Bread

**(Ready in about:** 45 min **| Servings:** 12)

**Ingredients:**

- 3 ripe Bananas, mashed
- 1 cup Milk
- 1 ¼ cups Sugar
- 2 cups all-purpose Flour
- 1 stick Butter, room temperature
- 1 tablespoon Orange Juice
- 1 teaspoon Baking Soda
- 1 teaspoon Baking Powder
- ¼ teaspoon Cinnamon
- ½ teaspoon Pure Vanilla Extract
- A pinch of Salt

**Directions:**

1. In a bowl, mix together the flour, baking powder, baking soda, sugar, vanilla, and salt. Add in the bananas, cinnamon, and orange juice. Slowly stir in the butter and milk. Give it a good stir until everything is well combined. Pour the batter into a medium-sized round pan.

2. Place the reversible rack at the bottom of the Foodi and fill with 2 cups of water. Place the pan on the reversible rack. Seal the pressure lid, select Pressure and and set the time to 40 minutes at High. Press Start. Do a quick pressure release.

## Almond Milk

**(Ready in about:** 20 min | **Servings:** 4)

**Ingredients:**
- 1 cup raw almonds; soaked overnight, rinsed and peeled
- 2 dried apricots; chopped
- 1 cup cold water
- 4 cups water
- 1 vanilla bean
- 2 tablespoon honey

**Directions:**
1. In the pot, mix a cup of cold water with almonds and apricots. Seal the pressure lid, choose Pressure, set to High, and set the timer to 1 minute.
2. When ready, release the pressure quickly. Open the lid. The almonds should be soft and plump, and the water should be brown and murky. Use a strainer to drain almonds; rinse with cold water for 1 minute.
3. To a high-speed blender, add the rinsed almonds, vanilla bean, honey, and 4 cups water. Blend for 2 minutes until well combined and frothy. Line a cheesecloth to the strainer.
4. Place the strainer over a bowl and strain the milk. Use a wooden spoon to press milk through the cheesecloth and get rid of solids. Place almond milk in an airtight container and refrigerate.

## Chocolate and Banana Squares

**(Ready in about:** 25 min | **Servings:** 6)

**Ingredients:**
- 3 Bananas
- 1 ½ cups Water
- ½ cup Butter
- 2 tablespoon Cocoa Powder
- Cooking spray, to grease

**Directions:**
1. Place the bananas and butter in a bowl and mash finely with a fork. Add the cocoa powder and stir until well combined. Grease a baking dish that fits into the Foodi.
2. Pour the banana and almond batter into the dish. Pour the water in the Foodi and lower the reversible rack. Place the baking dish on top of the reversible rack and seal the pressure lid.
3. Select Pressure, set the timer to 15 minutes at High pressure. Press Start. Press Start. When it goes off, do a quick release. Let cool for a few minutes before cutting into squares

## Vanilla Chocolate Spread

**(Ready in about:** 25 min | **Servings:** 16)

**Ingredients:**
- 1 ¼ pounds Hazelnuts, halved
- ½ cups icing Sugar, sifted
- ½ cup Cocoa Powder
- 10 ounces Water
- 1 teaspoon Vanilla Extract
- ¼ teaspoon Cardamom, grated
- ¼ teaspoon Cinnamon powder
- ½ teaspoon grated Nutmeg

**Directions:**
1. Place the hazelnut in a blender and blend until you obtain a paste. Place in the cooker along with the remaining ingredients.
2. Seal the pressure lid, choose Pressure, set to High, and set the time to 15 minutes. Press Start. Once the cooking is over, allow for a natural pressure release, for 10 minutes.

## Delicious Almond and Apple

**(Ready in about:** 14 min | **Servings:** 4)

**Ingredients:**
- 3 Apples, peeled and diced
- ½ cup Milk
- ½ cup Almonds; chopped or slivered
- ¼ teaspoon Cinnamon

**Directions:**
1. Place all ingredients in the Foodi. Stir well to combine and seal the pressure lid. Cook on Pressure for 4 minutes at High. Release the pressure quickly. Divide the mixture among 4 serving bowls.

## Raspberry Cheesecake

**(Ready in about:** 30 min | **Servings:** 6)

**Ingredients:**
- 1 ½ cups Graham Cracker Crust
- ¾ cup Sugar
- 1 cup Raspberries
- 1 ½ cups Water
- 3 cups Cream Cheese
- 3 Eggs
- ½ stick Butter, melted
- 1 tablespoon fresh Orange Juice
- 1 teaspoon Vanilla Paste
- 1 teaspoon finely grated Orange Zest

**Directions:**
1. Insert the reversible rack into the Foodi, and add 1 ½ cups of water. Grease a spring form. Mix in graham cracker crust with sugar and butter, in a bowl. Press the mixture to form a crust at the bottom.
2. Blend the raspberries and cream cheese with an electric mixer. Crack in the eggs and keep mixing until well combined. Mix in the remaining ingredients, and give it a good stir.
3. Pour this mixture into the pan, and cover the pan with aluminium foil. Lay the spring form on the tray. Select Pressure and set the time to 20 minutes at High pressure. Press Start. Once the cooking is complete, do a quick pressure release. Refrigerate the cheesecake for at least 2 hours.

## Apricots with Honey Sauce

**(Ready in about:** 15 min | **Servings:** 4)

**Ingredients:**
- 8 Apricots, pitted and halved
- ¼ cup Honey
- 2 cups Blueberries
- ½ Cinnamon stick
- 1 ¼ cups Water
- ½ Vanilla Bean; sliced lengthwise
- 1 ½ tablespoon Cornstarch
- ¼ teaspoon ground Cardamom

**Directions:**
1. Add all ingredients, except for the honey and the cornstarch, to your Foodi. Seal the pressure lid, choose Pressure, set to High, and set the time to s 8 minutes. Press Start. Do a quick pressure release and open the pressure lid.
2. Remove the apricots with a slotted spoon. Choose Sear/Sauté, add the honey and cornstarch, then let simmer until the sauce thickens, for about 5 minutes. Split up the apricots among serving plates and top with the blueberry sauce, to serve.

# Fried Doughnuts

**(Ready in about:** 25 min | **Servings:** 4)

**Ingredients:**
- 8 oz. self-rising flour
- 2 oz. brown sugar
- 1 egg
- ½ cup milk
- 2 ½ tablespoon butter
- 1 teaspoon baking powder

**Directions:**
1. Beat the butter with the sugar, until smooth; beat in eggs, and milk. In a bowl, combine the flour with the baking powder. Gently fold the flour into the butter mixture. Form donut shapes and cut off the center with cookie cutters.
2. Arrange on a lined baking sheet and cook in the Foodi for 15 minutes on Air Crisp mode at 350 F. Serve with whipped cream.

# Gingery Chocolate Pudding

**(Ready in about:** 20 min | **Servings:** 4)

**Ingredients:**
- 2 oz. chocolate, coarsely chopped
- 1 ½ cups of Water
- ¼ cup Cornstarch
- 1 cup Almond Milk
- ¼ cup Sugar
- 3 Eggs, separated into whites and yolks
- Zest and Juice from ½ Lime
- 2 tablespoon Butter, softened
- ½ teaspoon Ginger, caramelized
- A pinch of Salt

**Directions:**
1. Combine together the sugar, cornstarch, salt, and softened butter, in a bowl. Mix in lime juice and grated lime zest. Add in the egg yolks, ginger, almond milk, and whisk to mix well.
2. Mix in egg whites. Pour this mixture into custard cups and cover with aluminium foil. Add 1 ½ cups of water to the Foodi. Place a reversible rack into the Foodi, and lower the cups onto the rack.
3. Seal the pressure lid, choose Pressure, set to High, and set the time to 25 minutes. Press Start. Once the cooking is complete, do a quick pressure release. Carefully open the pressure lid, and stir in the chocolate. Serve chilled.

# White Chocolate Chip Cookies

**(Ready in about:** 30 min | **Servings:** 8)

**Ingredients:**
- 2 oz. white chocolate chips
- 6 oz. self-rising flour
- 3 oz. brown sugar
- 4 oz. butter
- 1 tablespoon honey
- 1 ½ tablespoon milk

**Directions:**
1. Beat the butter and sugar until fluffy. Then, beat in the honey, milk, and flour. Gently fold in the chocolate chips. Drop spoonfuls of the mixture onto a prepared cookie sheet.
2. Close the crisping lid and cook for 18 minutes on Air Crisp mode at 350 F. Once the timer beeps, make sure the cookies are just set.

## Coconut Pear Delight

**(Ready in about:** 15 min | **Servings:** 2)

**Ingredients:**

- 2 Large Pears, peeled and diced
- ¼ cup Shredded Coconut, unsweetened
- ¼ cup Flour
- 1 cup Coconut Milk

**Directions:**

1. Combine all ingredients in your Foodi. Seal the pressure lid, select Pressureand set the timer to 5 minutes at High pressure. Press Start. When ready, do a quick pressure release. Divide the mixture between two bowls.

Made in the USA
Monee, IL
05 November 2019